Fandom

Fandom

Identities and Communities in a Mediated World

EDITED BY

*Jonathan Gray, Cornel Sandvoss,
and C. Lee Harrington*

WITH AN AFTERWORD BY

Henry Jenkins

New York University Press
NEW YORK AND LONDON

NEW YORK UNIVERSITY PRESS
New York and London
www.nyupress.org

LIBRARY OF CONGRESS CATALOGING-IN-PUBLICATION DATA

Fandom : identities and communities in a mediated world / edited by
Jonathan Gray, Cornel Sandvoss, and C. Lee Harrington ; with an
afterword by Henry Jenkins.
p. cm.
Includes bibliographical references and index.
ISBN-13: 978-0-8147-3181-9 (cloth : alk. paper)
ISBN-10: 0-8147-3181-3 (cloth : alk. paper)
ISBN-13: 978-0-8147-3182-6 (pbk. : alk. paper)
ISBN-10: 0-8147-3182-1 (pbk. : alk. paper)
1. Fans (Persons) 2. Subculture. 3. Popular culture—Psychological aspects. I. Gray,
Jonathan (Jonathan Alan) II. Sandvoss, Cornel. III. Harrington, C. Lee, 1964–
HM646.F36   2007
306.4'87—dc22
2006101774

New York University Press books are printed on acid-free paper,
and their binding materials are chosen for strength and durability.

Manufactured in the United States of America
c 10 9 8 7 6 5 4 3 2 1
p 10 9 8 7 6 5 4 3 2 1

Contents

Acknowledgments

The editors would like to thank all the contributors; Emily Park at NYU Press; Matt Hills for invaluable help and ideas in the book's early stages; our families, friends, Monica Grant, and Kim Schimmel.

Introduction

Why Study Fans?

Jonathan Gray, Cornel Sandvoss, and C. Lee Harrington

Most people are fans of something. If not, they are bound to know some-one who is. As much as we all have a sense of who fans are and what they do, the question arises as to why we need to further study a phenomenon we seem so familiar with. Why do the questions of which television program, music, or artist we follow make an important contribution to our understanding of modern life? How can a focus on pleasure and enter-tainment be justified at the end of what will enter history books as a cen-tury of violence, driven by rapid social, cultural, economic, and technological change, and with the twenty-first century set to follow the same trajectory? What contribution can the study of fans make to a world faced with war, ethnic conflicts, widening inequality, political and reli-gious violence, and irreversible climate change, among other disasters?

The laconic answer to these questions is that fandom matters because it matters to those who are fans. However, beyond this, the contributions fan studies have made have varied in the course of what we, in retrospect, can summarize as three generations of fan scholarship over the past two decades.

"Fandom Is Beautiful"

For the first wave of scholars who took their particular inspiration from de Certeau's (1984) distinction between the strategies of the powerful and the tactics of the disempowered, the consumption of popular mass media was a site of power struggles and fandom the guerilla-style tactics of those with lesser resources to win this battle. The study of fandom was thus automatically considered a worthy cause, one that represented and championed those disadvantaged within society, as fans, in John Fiske's words, are "associated with the cultural tastes of subordinated formations of the people, particularly those disempowered by any combination of gender, age, class and race" (1992: 30).

Within this tradition, which spanned from Fiske to Henry Jenkins's (1992) canonical *Textual Poachers*, fandom was automatically more than the mere act of being a fan of something: it was a collective strategy, a communal effort to form interpretive communities that in their subcultural cohesion evaded the preferred and intended meanings of the "power bloc" (Fiske 1989) represented by popular media. Fan studies therefore constituted a purposeful political intervention that sided with the tactics of fan audiences in their evasion of dominant ideologies, and that set out to rigorously defend fan communities against their ridicule in the mass media and by non-fans. Joli Jensen (1992), for instance, highlighted the similarities in the portrayal of fans as part of an undifferentiated, easily manipulated mass in media representations and early mass communication scholarship. Instances of such stereotypical treatment, which always involve a deliberate distancing from fan audiences, still persist today. When in November 2005 the fourth installment of the *Harry Potter* films opened in theaters across North America, much of the media coverage exhibited inordinate fascination with the fan cultures that surround this multimedia blockbuster. The *New York Post* offered a two-page spread on "Potterheads: Wizards of Odd," in which writer Maureen Callahan described, as her subtitle reads, how "adult fans go hogwart's [sic] wild as new Trekkies" (2005: 46–47). Seemingly an earnest attempt to enter into the mind of the fan, the article in its frequently snide tone and vocabulary and its belittling of fans as "otherwise functioning adults" "in the weird house" (2005: 46) reveals a firm desire to understand fandom solely as Other. While more thoughtful commentary is provided courtesy of Syracuse University's Robert Thompson later in the article, his lead quote asks, "Who better than the socially awkward to be engaged by a story about a kid with no friends, abused by his guardians, who becomes a savior with stigmata on his forehead?" The point of reference to which the *Post* resorts in its effort to illustrate the social inadequacy of Potterheads is familiar to anyone who has ever given a thought to the stereotypical media coverage of fans: the embedded infographic compares Potterheads to Trekkies, listing, for instance, the future employment of a Potterhead as "Extrovert IT help desk worker," while the Trekkie is deemed an "Introvert IT help desk worker" in waiting (2005: 47). The invocation of "Trekkies" (particularly as "Trekkies" rather than their preferred "Trekkers") once lent particular vigor to the defenses of *Star Trek* fans in the first wave of fan studies by playing a key role in the work of five of its earliest champions: Camille Bacon-Smith, Henry Jenkins, Roberta Pearson, Constance Penley, and John Tulloch.

The assumption of an underlying duality of power that marked the first wave of fan studies has, however, attracted increasing critical scrutiny for two key reasons: first, the *Post* article reveals how it is all too common for fans to be dismissed as Others. As the wealth of literature on Othering makes clear, the Other is always a reflection and a projection of ourselves (see Said 1979). Moreover, as Stallybrass and White (1986) have illustrated, frequently our gaze at the Other is imbued with significant desire and longing. This, however, still applied and applies to media as well as scholarly representations of fandom. For all their sympathy, early fan scholars who were outsiders to the fan communities they studied ultimately pulled back from their observations, concluding, "right, now we can arrive at the truth that the fans don't yet recognize about their own political activity" (Jenkins 2001: n.p) (see Hills 2002 on Penley). While subsequent work, including most notably Bacon-Smith (1992), Harrington and Bielby (1995), Jenkins (1992), and Tulloch and Jenkins (1995) allowed fans to speak of and for themselves and was often written by those inside respective fan cultures, the rhetorical defense of fans by some first-generation fan scholars left media and cultural studies with considerable baggage.

We could perhaps refer to this stage of fan studies as the "Fandom Is Beautiful" phase. As is common in the early stages of identity politics for groups heretofore Othered by mainstream society, early fan studies did not so much deconstruct the binary structure in which the fan had been placed as they tried to differently value the fan's place in said binary. As such, early fan studies (and much of the work it inspired) often turned to the very activities and practices—convention attendance, fan fiction writing, fanzine editing and collection, letter-writing campaigns—that had been coded as pathological, and attempted to redeem them as creative, thoughtful, and productive. Rhetorically, this work aimed to render normative the very end point of caricature that popular and academic accounts of fandom often presented. However, as a result, rarely in such accounts do we encounter fans who merely love a show, watch it religiously, talk about it, and yet engage in no other fan practices or activities. As such, fandom in one of its most common forms was excluded from systematic academic study, and thus to all but those with engagement in fan practices, "fandom" in its academic definition risked being continually reified as Other, hence keeping many of the terms of the non-fan/fan binary alive, albeit differently valued.

Fans in the Mainstream

This leads us to the second reason for the various departures from the established canon of early fan studies since the mid-1990s, which in contrast to the first point is not conceptual but historical: the public recognition and evaluation of the practice of being a fan has itself profoundly changed over the past several decades. As we have moved from an era of broadcasting to one of narrowcasting, a process fueled by the deregulation of media markets and reflected in the rise of new media technologies, the fan as a specialized yet dedicated consumer has become a centerpiece of media industries' marketing strategies (see McCourt & Burkart in this volume). Rather than ridiculed, fan audiences are now wooed and championed by cultural industries, at least as long as their activities do not divert from principles of capitalist exchange and recognize industries' legal ownership of the object of fandom.

Moreover, if representations of fandom in the media are still an indicator of its social and cultural recognition, there can be no doubt that the stereotypical coverage exemplified in the *New York Post* article on Potterheads has given way to mainstreamed appreciation of being a fan. In fact, what is under attack in the *Post* article is not the state of being a fan as such but particular texts as objects of fandom. While Harry Potter fandom, according to Callahan and *The New York Post,* is infinitely geeky and fans the quintessential losers (albeit "extrovert" ones!), we can rest assured that the editors of the *Post* would not like to see this description extended to their loyal, pinstripe-wearing readership of New York Yankees fans who are extensively catered to in its back pages. Hence, what is at stake in the changing representation of fans in the mass media is more than the obvious difference between sports fandom and fan audiences in other areas of popular culture, which Fiske highlighted more than a decade ago (1992) and which until recently led to the widespread disregard of sport fans in audience studies, not least because sport fans—in light of the violence and racism that marked much of their representation in particular in the 1980s—were a much less likely and indeed likable subject of study, who evaded the paradigm of a bipolar power struggle between hegemonic culture industries and fans. Today, the evocation of Trekkies by the *Post* reveals how far we need to stroll into the past—at least in the relative terms of the fast-lived entertainment universe—to salvage rudiments of such stereotypical portrayals of fans: none of the high-profile fan cultures in recent years—from X-Philes via Eminem fans to *Sex in the City* enthusiasts—had to endure the derogative treatment of *Star Trek* fans.

The changing cultural status of fans is probably best illustrated by the efforts of those in the public gaze, such as celebrities and politicians seeking to connect with consumers and voters by publicly emphasizing their fan credentials, from Ben Affleck's highly visible visits to Fenway Park to British Prime Minister Tony Blair's surprise appearance on a football chat show after his government plunged into new depths of crisis in November 2005 (Sandvoss forthcoming). However, in both cases, it is the choice of the object of fandom that matters most (note that no machismo-conscious actor or politician has yet outed himself as a soap opera fan). Let's compare the representation of Potterheads in the *Post* with an article published by the BBC online news service seven months earlier, which under the headline "Bush's iPod reveals music tastes" portrayed the U.S. president "as a fan of country music and classical rock" who "also likes 'a little bit of hard core and honky tonk'" (BBC News 2005: n.p). The story, based on testimony from Bush's cycling partner Mark McKinnon, highlights the way we communicate through our fandoms. Bush's choice of country music and classical rock further contributes to his public perception as a "straight-shooting" guy, which his team has long sought to perpetuate, although, as everywhere in mediated communication, the semiotic power of readers will allow them to emphasize either "straight" or "shooting." It illustrates how, as cultural judgment has become increasingly detached from the state of being a fan, our attention shifts to the choice of fan object and its surrounding practices, and what they tell us about the fan him- or herself.

Fan Cultures and Social Hierarchy

It is, of course, not only public figures that communicate through their fandom and choice of fan objects, nor are fans' tastes and consumption choices coincidental. The fact that they tell us something about fans' selves, and possibly more than one might like to reveal, must also have dawned on McKinnon when he warned readers not to "psychoanalyze" the president's playlist (BBC News 2005: n.p). Yet, it was not psychoanalysis as feared by McKinnon that scholars turned to in the second wave of fan studies. Rather, they moved beyond the "incorporation/resistance paradigm" (Abercrombie & Longhurst 1998), which saw fans pinned into perennial battle against the power bloc, by finding a new conceptual leitmotif in the sociology of consumption developed by the French sociologist Pierre Bourdieu (1984). This second wave of work on fan audiences (see, for example, Dell 1998; Harris 1998; Jancovich 2002) highlighted the replication of social and cultural hierarchies within fan- and subcultures, as the choice of fan objects and practices of fan consumption are structured through our habitus as a reflection and further manifestation of our social, cultural, and economic capital. In these studies, the answer to the question of why fandom and its academic analysis matter is thus a very different one. Scholars are still concerned with questions of power, inequality, and discrimination, but rather than seeing fandom as a tool of empowerment they suggest that the interpretive communities of fandom (as well as individual acts of fan consumption) are embedded in the existing economic, social, and cultural status quo. These studies are still concerned, for instance, with questions of gender, but they no longer portray fandom as an extraordinary space of emancipation and reformulation of gender relations. Instead, the taste hierarchies among fans themselves are described as the continuation of wider social inequalities (Thornton 1995). Herein lies a significant conceptual shift that profoundly shapes our answer to the question of why we study fans: fans are seen not as a counterforce to existing social hierarchies and structures but, in sharp contrast, as agents of maintaining social and cultural systems of classification and thus existing hierarchies. These Bourdieuian perspectives thus aimed to unmask the false notion of popular culture as a realm of emancipation. In doing so, they also raised the stakes for subsequent research, for if fandom did not constitute a form of resistance and subversion, then uncovering this mistaken belief formed a worthy academic course in itself. Yet, once this task had been completed, there no longer seemed a valid rationale for subsequent studies of fan audiences.

However, while the second wave of fan studies proved effective in demonstrating what fandom is not—an a priori space of cultural autonomy and resistance—it had little to say about the individual motivations, enjoyment, and pleasures of fans. If Fiske's (1989, 1992) explanation of fandom as subversive pleasure was overtly functionalist, so would be attempts to explain fans' interests and motivations through the notion of the habitus alone. As much as popular media representations of fans have failed to ask why audiences become fans and why "fans act as they do" (Harrington & Bielby 1995: 3), the academic analysis of fandom was now in danger of commiting the same omissions.

Fandom and Modernity

The subsequent set of work, which we here describe as fan studies' third wave, departed from but also built on the conceptual heritage of its first two generations. The first and most obvious departure in much contemporary work on fan audiences has been an empirical rather than a conceptual one. Reflecting their ostensibly sociological concerns, the first two generations of fan scholars had focused on particular audience groups, such as fan communities and subcultures, and the interaction between the members of such groups either as interpretive community and support networks, or in terms of cultural hierarchization and discrimination through distinction. However, as being a fan has become an ever more common mode of cultural consumption, these approaches based on a model of fans as tightly organized participants in fan- and subcultures did not match the self-description and experience of many audience members who describe themselves as fans (see Sandvoss 2005a). When Jenkins wrote *Textual Poachers* (1992), fan communities were often relegated to conventions and fanzines. Today, with many such communities' migration to the Internet, the thousands of fan discussion groups, web sites, and mailing lists populating the Web are only eclipsed in presence by pornography (which, of course, has its own thriving fan base). And far from solely occupying their own segregated realms of cyberspace for each fan object, many fans also congregate at sites for genre fandom or at hubs such as *Television without Pity* and *Ain't It Cool News*. Off the Web, too, magazine stands buckle under the weight of pages dedicated to celebrities, sports, cinephilia, music, and multiple other fan objects; the 7:00–8:00 P.M. slot on American television has virtually been colonized by entertainment news programs catering to fan interests; many cable, radio, and satellite channels address a specific genre's fans; and entire neighborhoods can become awash with the colors of local or national sports teams on certain holy days of competition.

Similarly, the Internet has been joined by a host of other technologies that extend both fandom and the prospects for engaging in fan activities into multiple pockets of everyday life. Blackberries, iPods, PSPs, laptops, PDAs, and cell phones all bring fan objects out with their users to the subway, the street, and even the classroom. In turn, these changing communication technologies and media texts contribute to and reflect the increasing entrenchment of fan consumption in the structure of our everyday life.

From a contemporary perspective, the first and the second wave of fan studies therefore focused primarily on what we now recognize (in line with Abercrombie and Longhurst's [1998] typology of fan audiences) to be only one, and possibly the smallest subset of fan groups on a wide spectrum spanning from regular, emotionally uninvolved audience members to petty producers. The immediate, if sometimes implicit intervention of recent work on fan audiences (Aden 1999; Harrington & Bielby 2005b; Barker & Brooks 1998; Brooker 2002; Brown 2001; Cavicchi 1998; Hills 2002; Sandvoss 2003; Scodari 2004; Thomas 2002) has thus been to change the goalposts of inquiry and to broaden our analytic scope to a wide range of different audiences reflecting fandom's growing cultural currency. With this empirical shift, the field of fan studies has become increasingly diverse in conceptual, theoretical, and methodological terms, and has broadened the scope of its inquiry on both ends of the spectrum between self and society. We should add that this diversity has been endorsed by those who have contributed to fan studies throughout its different phases, most notably Henry Jenkins.

On the micro level of fan consumption, recent studies have explored the *intra*personal pleasures and motivations among fans, thus refocusing on the relationship between fans' selves and their fan objects (see Thompson 1995). This has resulted in a range of psychoanalytic or psychoanalytically inspired approaches (Elliott 1999; Harrington & Bielby 1995a; Hills 2002, 2005a; Sandvoss 2005a; Stacey 1994). On the macro level, contemporary research on fans (like its predecessors) acknowledges that fans' readings, tastes, and practices are tied to wider social structures, yet extends the conceptual focus beyond questions of hegemony and class to the overarching social, cultural, and economic transformations of our time, including the dialectic between the global and the local (e.g. Harrington & Bielby 2005; Juluri 2003a, 2003b; Sandvoss 2003; Tufte 2000) and the rise of spectacle and performance in fan consumption (Abercrombie & Longhurst 1998).

However, while we remain conscious of the need to avoid the teleological trap of constructing a single master narrative of fan research, there is one theme that allows us to set many recent studies of fan audiences in meaningful relation to each other and to span a conceptual arch across them. As the particular mode of reading that marks the way in which fans approach (media) texts, the particular and conspicuous patterns of fan consumption and the specific forms of social interaction that take place between fans have become an ever more integral part of everyday life in modern societies; and as fandom has grown into a truly global phenomenon drawing on popular texts ranging from the global media spectacles of American exports like Hollywood blockbuster films or the Super Bowl to local appropriations such as Afghanistan's very own adaptation of the popular casting show *Afghan Idol,* fandom has emerged as an ever more integral aspect of lifeworlds in global capitalism, and an important interface between the dominant micro and macro forces of our time. In illustrating the degree to which the various semiotic, enunciative, and textual activities of fans have become part of our everyday lives, audience research has revealed the deep-seated symbiosis between the cultural practice and perspective of being a fan and industrial modernity at large. Rather than being a transhistorical phenomenon, fandom emerges in historical studies as a cultural practice tied to specific forms of social and economic organization. For example, see Cavicchi's study of nineteenth-century music lovers in this volume, or explorations of the historical foundations of the rise of modern (spectator) sports in figurational sociology (Elias & Dunning 1986) and beyond (Guttman 1994).

The third wave of fan studies thus offers new answers to the question of what they are for. Here fandom is no longer only an object of study in and for itself. Instead, through the investigation of fandom as part of the fabric of our everyday lives, third wave work aims to capture fundamental insights into modern life. In answer to our initial questions, then, it is precisely *because* fan consumption has grown into a taken-for-granted aspect of modern communication and consumption that it warrants critical analysis and investigation more than ever. As Zygmunt Bauman, in reference to Cornelius Castoriadis, once put it, "the trouble with the contemporary condition of our modern civilization is that it stopped questioning itself[. . . .] Questioning the ostensibly unquestionable premises of our way of life is arguably the most urgent of services we owe our fellow humans and ourselves" (1998b: 4). The contribution of fan studies in providing answers to the pressing issues of global modernity is thus far less remote than it may have appeared at first sight. The answer to the questions formulated in the opening paragraph, then, is that studies of fan audiences help us to understand and meet challenges far beyond the realm of popular culture because they tell us something about the way in which we relate to those around us, as well as the way we read the mediated texts that constitute an ever larger part of our horizon of experience. Fans, for better or for worse, tend to engage with these texts not in a rationally detached but in an emotionally involved and invested way. Yet this particular form of engagement with media and our fellow audiences is, as this volume sets out to demonstrate, not limited to commonly acknowledged fan objects such as *Star Trek,* soap operas, or sports teams. Instead, it also shapes the way in which many of us read the news (Gray), choose which plays we see at the theater (Tulloch), listen to Bach (Pearson), or make sense of social theory (McKee).

Moreover, as much as fan objects are experienced in and through mediated texts, so are the very challenges to life in the twenty-first century that we set out at the beginning of this chapter: war, ethnic conflicts, widening inequality, political and religious violence, and ecological disasters are to most of us, most of the time, experienced through the same patterns of mass mediation, and, crucially, often related to by the same mechanisms of emotionally involved reading as fan objects. The often cited "battles over hearts and minds" by which elections are won, and by which individuals' behavior towards their health or the environment is changed, or millions decide to turn to the streets in protest against war, racism, or poverty—all do not solely depend on rational discourses but on the ability to present a cause or public figure in which we, as readers, can find ourselves and to which we emotionally relate. Hence, studying fan audiences allows us to explore some of the key mechanisms through which we interact with the mediated world at the heart of our social, political, and cultural realities and identities. Perhaps the most important contribution of contemporary research into fan audiences thus lies in furthering our understanding of how we form emotional bonds with ourselves and others in a modern, mediated world.

Six Directions of Fan Studies

It is no surprise that, being both reflective and constitutive of contemporary life, the empirical and conceptual themes that have formed much of the third wave of fan studies would equally serve as useful headings for the further exploration of our contemporary social and cultural order, described variously as "postmodernity" (Harvey 1990), "late modernity" (Giddens 1991), or "supermodernity" (Augé 1995). These themes are the emphasis on the symbolic and representations that mark contemporary mediated worlds (part 1); the dissolution of boundaries between different textual and cultural forms leading to the erosion of binary oppositions between popular and high culture (part 2); the changing relationship between physical place and virtual space and the social interactions and performances taking place within them in an increasing deterritorialized world (part 3); the interplay between the global and the local in processes of cultural globalization (part 4); new identities and practices arising out of the transformation of production and consumption in light of social and technological change (part 5); and the formation of conflict, distinction, and discrimination in mediated discourses (part 6). It is through these themes that we hope this collection will further our understanding of both fans and the mediated world around them.

The first section, "Fan Texts: From Aesthetic to Legal Judgments," returns to the concerns over cultural judgment at the heart of the second wave of fan studies. However, it does so in reference to one of the most underdeveloped aspects of Bourdieu's work (see Frow 1987)—the object of consumption—exploring the texts that fans so cherish, yet that due to our emphasis on audience activity have hitherto remained largely neglected as an object of study. Its first two chapters go in search of the categories through which we can evaluate and appreciate different fan texts aesthetically, culturally, and socially in a post-Bourdieuian era and thereby critique the neglect of aesthetics in contemporary cultural studies. Sandvoss, in juxtaposing traditions of textual criticism in literary theory and media studies, proposes a model of aesthetic judgment rooted in reception aesthetics that reemphasize the act of reading as a form of communication and dialogue with a textual other. Matt Hills, following similar initial concerns, yet rejecting a notion of aesthetics that serves as functional political judgments, questions the role of fan scholars as both academics and part of media audiences and suggests, on the basis of a critical reading of Barthes's lectures on the neutral, a reflexive understanding of fan scholars' aesthetic judgments as hermeneutic constructions of self-identity. Christine Scodari's chapter, based on an investigation of fans' reading of John Lennon's former wife Yoko Ono, addresses two important themes concerning fan texts: the impact of computer mediation on fan cultures and

the formation of popular myth surrounding increasingly open and decentered texts. Scodari argues that the continuation of hegemonic gender
relations in web-based discourses illustrates cyberspace's entrapment in
wider social and cultural relations, and that these difficulties of fan audiences in mounting ideological challenges are underscored by the neutrosemic condition of fan texts and popular artifacts in which they no
longer "govern signification." The questions over the role of cultural producers in processes of meaning production that find their primary reference in fans themselves and that follow from Scodari's and Sandvoss's
chapters, also underscore the legal issues concerning textual ownership
and copyright that Rebecca Tushnet then explores. In tracing recent judgments and controversies concerning fans' alleged infringement of copyright laws, Tushnet suggests that fan fiction sheds further light on the
meaning and implications of copyright, as copyright's fair use doctrine
grants fans' textual productivity both moral and legal legitimacy.

Questions of judgment also form the starting point of the second section, "Beyond Pop Culture: Fandom from News to High Culture," which
attacks the myth that fans are peculiar to popular culture by examining
fans of reputable and "high" culture. Jonathan Gray examines news fans,
studying the intersection of a mode of audience reception—fandom—
that has long been derided as trivial, overly emotional, and peripheral to
the political sphere, and the news. Gray sees these viewers' fannish proclivities as potentially contributing to, not detracting from, the serious functioning of politics and citizenship formation. Alan McKee then turns his
attention, with tongue firmly in cheek, to the active audience of theory
fans, those who love Karl Marx, Michel Foucault, and other social theorists. McKee criticizes academic double standards that see fan practices as
neutered within a capitalist society, yet that code academic practices as
bold and revolutionary, and his chapter asks us to reevaluate our preferred
tropes for discussing fans, at the same time as it shows a mode of study
now old and developed enough to warrant parody. Echoing McKee's call
for greater attention to varied fandoms, Roberta Pearson argues for an
analysis of high-culture and middlebrow fandoms. Drawing from her own
experience with Bach and Sherlock Holmes fan cultures, she places high
culture on the plate for future fan studies, and denies high-culture fans
their long-held place in the shadows of fan studies. Following suit, John
Tulloch examines fans of Chekhov, engaging in ethnographic study of various fans of the playwright and of the stars of Chekhov productions. Part
2, then, writes back to fan studies' usual focus on popular or "mass" cul-

ture, and proposes studies that examine fans across class and cultural boundaries.

As much as the demarcations between different cultural spheres have been eroded, the increasing entanglement of territorial place and virtual space has shaped fans' experiences, performances, and identities. Opening the third section, "Spaces of Fandom: From Place to Performance," Brian Longhurst, Gaynor Bagnall, and Mike Savage explore the relationship among place, locality, and different forms of audience consumption, from home-based media such as television and music to in situ media such as cinema and theater. Based on their study of four contrasting locations near the northern English city of Manchester, they develop a concept of "elective belonging" that is underscored by media consumption. From Manchester, the location of his past research (Couldry 2000), we travel with Nick Couldry to the set of *The Sopranos* in New Jersey. Couldry highlights the importance of territorial place in fans' experiences and pilgrimages, but also emphasizes questions of power as well as the social and cultural contradictions that continue and emerge during fans' journeys through place (not least when visitors arrive at the real strip joint where the Bada Bing is filmed), and that supersede a priori individual psychological investments in a given narrative: "There is," as Couldry notes, "no way of standing ironically." The theme of fan pilgrimages is pursued further in Will Brooker's chapter, which in reference to Roger C. Aden's (1999) work juxtaposes physical pilgrimages with the virtual travels of *X-Files* fans who immerse themselves in their favorite texts. Like Couldry and Longhurst, Bagnall, and Savage, Brooker documents a dual process in which our experience of place is shaped through media consumption and vice versa. Lawrence B. McBride and S. Elizabeth Bird move the discussion from physical places to the performances that are manifested within them. On the basis of an (auto-)ethnographic study of backyard wrestling, they argue that wrestling as local, backyard activity emerged not as a mere act of imitation of televised wrestling but as a result of the uniform availability and particular structure of material culture, drawing on different mass media as well as recording devices such as video cameras and the promise of an "unparalleled" realness of experience, as fans cross the boundaries between consumption and (bodily) participation.

From the complex interplay of fans' identities and performances with territorial and physical place follows the need to further reflect on the local, regional, and global dimensions of fans' experiences. In this spirit, part 4, "Fan Audiences Worldwide: From the Global to the Local," moves toward de-"Westernizing" fan studies by focusing on fans and fandoms in contexts *other* than the English-speaking Western world. In the opening chapter, C. Lee Harrington and Denise D. Bielby explore the possibilities for global fandom and global fan studies through email interviews with sixty-five scholars. Situating their analysis in a number of ongoing debates in global media studies and (Western) fan studies, they examine areas of both consensus and debate over where fan studies is at present, and where it is headed. The section next turns to three case studies of Asian film fandom. First, Aswin Punathambekar explores fans of Indian cinema and questions of public culture and citizenship in contemporary India. Through an analysis of fans' engagement with Indian film music, Punathambekar challenges global media studies to treat seriously the implications of fan practices for the development of culture industries worldwide. In her discussion of East Asian cinema fandom, Bertha Chin explores the meaning(s) of "cult cinema" in different cultural contexts, ultimately questioning the extent to which Western fan theory assumes a homogeneous fan culture, and the implications of this assumption. While Punathambekar argues that global media studies should "go fannish," then, Chin argues that fan studies should "go global," engaging explicitly with the cultural contexts that shape what we know (or think we know) about fans and fandoms. Finally, Anne Ciecko and Hunju Lee raise key questions of gender and the construction of stardom in their discussion of South Korean film star Han Suk-kyu. Through an investigation of Han Suk-kyu's film characters and career choices in the context of changing norms of masculinity and evolving priorities within the South Korean film industry, Ciecko and Lee question the "timeliness" of fandom. Part 4 thus moves beyond familiar borders—disciplinary, cultural, and geographic—to propose new ways of thinking about fans, fan practices, and the global development of fan studies.

Part 5, "Shifting Contexts, Changing Fan Cultures: From Concert Halls to Console Games," examines the ways in which fans' attachments to particular icons and texts are informed not only by the geographical and cultural but also the historical, social, and technological contexts of their consumption practices. Through an analysis of material artifacts from nineteenth-century American "music lovers," Daniel Cavicchi explores how the commodification of music generated a new form of fandom engaged with music's own singular effects and the personal qualities of music performers, and investigates early models for cultural consumption predating the development of mass communication technologies, thereby highlighting the inherent symbiosis between fandom and modernity even preceding the formation of the term "fan" in late nineteenth-century sports coverage. Moving the discussion to this possibly oldest recognized fan culture, Victoria K. Gosling explores the marginalization of women in sport fan communities and in academic writings on sport fans, arguing that the emphasis on a social-class framework within sport fan studies obscures key questions surrounding gender. Her discussion sheds new light on the role of gendered power relations in shaping fans' social practices. As much as by gender relations, though, fan cultures have also been shaped by technological innovation. In their analysis of the online music industry, Tom McCourt and Patrick Burkart examine the implications of personalization systems (such as collaborative filtering or genre/mood "matching" systems) for our understandings of fans and fan communities. They ultimately argue that these technologies attempt the impossible by trying to reduce the immense plasticity of fan preferences to something knowable and predictable. Finally, Garry Crawford and Jason Rutter draw together the literatures on digital gaming and media audiences to move beyond the idea of gamers as individual players to a broader understanding of gamers as a socially situated audience. Focusing on gamers' performativity, Crawford and Rutter explore the wider social implications of gaming practices. Part 5, then, focuses on the myriad shifting contexts that shape fan practices and pleasures.

While pleasure and love of the fan object are often seen as quintessential qualities of fan consumption, our final section, "Fans and Anti-Fans: From Love to Hate," returns to the fundamental polarities of human emotions by examining a spectrum of dislike, distaste, and hate both within fan cultures and in closely related anti-fan cultures. First, focusing on *Buffy the Vampire Slayer*'s much debated sixth season, Derek Johnson examines conflict and "fan-tagonisms" between rival fan factions, and between fans and the institutional producers of fan objects, each battling for control of the diegetic universe. Melissa Click then examines Martha Stewart fans; their varying levels of ambivalence towards, distaste for, and admiration of "Martha"; and the ways in which such fan and anti-fan discourse constructs the ever changing text/public figure. Vivi Theodoropoulou studies the fan within the anti-fan, and the anti-fan within the fan, focusing on sports rivalries and the development therein of "*antipalon deos*," or awe of the enemy. In doing so, she paints a vivid picture of how fan objects and discursive strategies clash and interact. Next, Jeffrey Sconce analyzes the fan/anti-fan object that is Paris Hilton. Hilton attracts both endless public attention and ignominy with such seeming lack of effort, and Sconce analyzes this lack of effort, and Hilton's skillful display of skillessness, in Baudrillardian terms as a contemporary manifestation of hyperreal celebrity. Finally, Diane Alters's close study of two families' televisual tastes illustrates how such (post)modernity is regulated at the micro level of the home. She argues that anti-fandom and textual dislike can be mobilized—much as previous studies have suggested of fandom—to manage the lived environment and to avoid the "hurts of history" (Lipsitz 1990). In traveling through dual spectra of media love and hate, fandom and anti-fandom, Part 6 completes our journey, visiting fans' readings, performances, identities, and communities in a mediated world.

Undoubtedly, readers of this collection will find their own pathways and trajectories through the material. They will also find omissions—there is, for instance, no chapter examining race and fandom specifically, nor are there chapters on comic book fans, telenovela fans, or teen fandom, to name only a few of the many inevitably missing genres out of the vast universe of popular culture. More than merely bring together extant work on fandom, though, we hope that this collection will inspire and encourage new research on these and all other sorts of fandom, from a healthy variety of disciplinary perspectives. As Henry Jenkins's provocative afterword poses, fandom is ever expanding into "regular" consumption, and as we have argued above, to study fans is to study many of the key structuring mechanisms by which contemporary culture and society work; thus, the future of reception and audience studies requires thoughtful and innovative study of fans in all their forms, identities, media, and spaces.

Part I

Fan Texts

From Aesthetic to Legal Judgments

The Death of the Reader?
*Literary Theory and the Study of
Texts in Popular Culture*

Cornel Sandvoss

Concerns over meaning and aesthetic value have continually haunted media and cultural studies. In many ways the field of fan studies epitomizes these concerns. The relative neglect of the question of aesthetic value (see also Hills, this volume) has made the field of media and cultural studies (hereafter cultural studies) a popular target as a "Mickey Mouse" subject. On the one hand, this is, quite literally, true: fan studies have focused on popular texts from horror films via sports events to, indeed, comics. Beyond this, however, the notion of a "Mickey Mouse" subject implies a lack of depth and theoretical rigor. It is on this level that it remains most hurtful, especially when such criticism is reiterated by those in neighboring disciplines such as literary theory. Echoing such themes and pointing to structuralism paving the way for the rise of cultural studies, Eagleton accuses the new discipline of taking advantage of the fact that,

> methodologically speaking, nobody quite knew where *Coriolanus* ended and *Coronation Street* began and constructed an entirely fresh field of enquiry which would gratify the anti-elitist iconoclasm of the sixty-eighters[. . . .] It was, in its academicist way, the latest version of the traditional avant-garde project of leaping barriers between art and society, and was bound to make its appeal to those who found, rather like an apprentice chef cooking his evening meal, that it linked classroom and leisure time with wonderful economy. (Eagleton 1996: 192)

If Eagleton's words were addressed to the discipline as a whole, nowhere do they reverberate more loudly than in fan studies. Fan studies have indeed eroded the boundaries between audiences and scholars, between fan and academic more than any other field (see Hills 2002; Tulloch 2000). To Eagleton, the blurring of these formerly distinct categories has led to a decline in analytic depth and an ideological stagnation: "what happened in the event was not a defeat for this project, which has indeed been gaining institutional strength ever since, but a defeat for the political forces which originally underpinned the new evolutions in literary theory" (1996: 192). Eagleton's critique raises a number of important questions: have fan studies unduly neglected aesthetic value and thus become complicit in the decline of literary quality and theory alike? Have sociological studies of fan audiences in their emphasis on the micro over the macro, on fans in their subcultural context over wider social relations, undermined progressive traditions and forms of radical enquiry, as Bryan Turner (2005) has recently suggested? Are fan studies unwittingly part of a revisionist wave that has suffocated the final sparks of 1960s radicalism? Or is Eagleton's critique just the bitter *réplique* of a scholar who in the shifting sands of history sees the scholarly foundations of his discipline running through his hands, witnessing the dunes of social, cultural, economic, and technological relations upon which all intellectual projects are built shifting from his field of inquiry to another?

In order to answer these questions by comparing the traditions and aims of literary theory with those of fan studies, we need to find a point of—if not compatibility—convertibility between these two fields. This point is found in the shared essence of both disciplines: the analysis and interpretation of meaning in the study of texts and their readings.

Texts and Textuality

While both disciplines share a focus on texts and the meanings that evolve around them, they already diverge in their definition of what actually constitutes a "text." Our common understanding of texts is rooted in the idealization and imagination of closed forms of textuality that have shaped the study of written texts from the rise of modern aesthetics in Enlightenment philosophy via the Romantics, who "denied any influence from previous writers and asserted the text's utter uniqueness" (Gray 2006: 20), to Edmund Husserl's phenomenological search for the author's pure intent in literary texts. "Textual studies" have thus, as Gray notes, "a long history of fetishizing the text as a solitary, pristinely autonomous object, and this notion of textuality has exerted considerable pressure, particularly on literary and film studies" (2006: 19–20). In fan studies, however, the task of defining the text has been rather more complex. To understand the origin of this difficulty, we need to briefly draw the admittedly crude distinction between form and content. Take the following textual fragment or statement: "My name is Dr. Serenus Zeitblom, Ph.D." To those who share English as a common language, the content of this brief sentence appears clear, but it is quite impossible for anyone, myself included, to describe its content in any form other than its meaning or, even if I could, to communicate this content to others. When I summarize the content of this statement as "someone is called Serenus Zeitblom, and he has a doctorate in philosophy," I am already describing the *meaning* I have generated in the act of the reading. All encounters with textual structures thus require ideational activity that inherently ties the text to its reader. No text (and content) exists independently (see Fish 1981; Holub 1992; Iser 1978).

This is, of course, hardly news. Yet, while we cannot separate content from meaning, we can observe how meaning changes in different forms of communication. If we set the same utterance or textual fragment into different contexts, its meaning, or at least its possible meanings, change. In the case of face-to-face interaction—let's say we meet someone on the street who introduces himself with the above words—the *someone* who is or claims to be Serenus Zeitblom is effectively limited to the person who has been seen or heard to make this statement. Here, the reciprocity of the text limits its possible meanings. The reader of this chapter in contrast will have found it more difficult to identify who the name points to when reading the above statement. The utterer of these words does not correspond with the author, leaving you with countless possibilities as to who the possessive pronoun in "my name" refers to. It is this fundamental difference in form between written and spoken texts that Paul Ricœur accredits with what he labels as "difficulties of interpretation": "in face-to-face interaction problems [of interpretation] are solved through a form of exchange we call conversation. In written texts discourse has to speak for itself" (1996: 56). Our observation that texts change meaning through their form, in conjunction with Ricœur's assessment of the changing role of authorial intent in written texts, points to two important differences between fan texts and literary texts. First, in studying media audiences, we are confronted with a variety of different textual forms around which fandom evolves: alongside written texts, these include audio and sound, visual texts, audiovisual texts, and hypertexts.

The second difference concerns the way fan texts are formed across these media. Here, I owe the reader three belated definitions of "fans," "texts," and "fan texts." In my earlier work, I defined "fandom as the regular, emotionally involved consumption of a given popular narrative or text" (Sandvoss 2005a: 8). In its inclusion of both texts and narratives, this definition mirrored a level of uncertainty. While we all have a sense of who fans are, conceptualizing the textual basis of their fandom seems far more difficult. Hills (1999) distinguishes between popular texts (fictional) and popular icons (factual) as possible fan objects. On the level of the author, this distinction is of course correct. In the cases of literary fandom (see Brooker 2005b) or fandom based on television shows, texts are written or controlled by copyright and license holders; they are in one form or another authored. In contrast, we do not describe popular icons such as musicians, actors, or athletes, or other fan objects such as sport teams, as deliberately authored texts. Even where those in the center of the public gaze aim to maintain a public and hence staged persona, fans' interests often focus on what lies behind the public façade, as is exemplified in the title of celebrity biographies from *The Real David Beckham* (Morgan 2004) to Albert Goldman's (2001) notorious *The Lives of John Lennon*. However, the popularity of such biographies already signals that we cannot rely on authorship as a defining element of textuality; indeed, the success of these books is often not based on their actual author, who may be unknown to readers, but on the subject—the object of fandom. Whether a given fan object is found in a novel, a television program, or a popular icon, fan objects are read as texts on the level of the fan/reader. They all constitute a set of signs and symbols that fans encounter in their frames of representation and mediation, and from which they create meaning in the process of reading. Consequently, what is needed is a broad definition of texts that is not based on authorship, but on texts as frames of realizable meanings that span across single or multiple communicative acts, including visual, sound-based, and written communication. Yet, what the example of celebrity biographies shows is that we need to reflect on textual boundaries too. As we remove authorship as the essence of textuality, the notion of the single text that can be distinguished from other texts becomes impossible to maintain, as it is now not by the producer but by the reader that the boundaries of texts are set (Sandvoss 2005a; 2005b).

The capability of media audiences to define textual boundaries is inextricably linked with their media of delivery. The home-based and mobile media through which most fan texts are consumed—television, radio, magazines, walkmen and iPods, the Internet—are firmly entrenched in the structure of everyday life in late industrialism, embedding the act of reading in a social and technological context that is not only nonreciprocal (Thompson 1995), but in which textual boundaries at the point of production are evaded through the technological essence of such media as spaces of flow (see Williams 1974; see also Corner 1999). Television finds its true narrative form in seriality (Eco 1994), while the hypertextuality of the Internet forces the reader/user into the active construction of the text's boundaries. Moreover, through notions of genre and the capitalist imperative of market enlargements that drives them, textual motives from narratives to fictional characters and popular icons are constituted and reconstituted across different media. A sports fan will read and watch texts in reference to his or her favorite team on television, on the radio, in newspapers, in sport magazines, and, increasingly, on the Internet; soap fans (Baym 2000) turn to the World Wide Web and entertainment magazines as part of their fandom; the fan of a given actress will watch her in different films but also follow further coverage in newspapers or read the abovementioned celebrity biographies. Fan objects thus form a *field of gravity,* which may or may not have an *urtext* in its epicenter, but which in any case corresponds with the fundamental meaning structure through which all these texts are read. The fan text is thus constituted through a multiplicity of textual elements; it is by definition intertextual and formed between and across texts as defined at the point of production.

The single "episodes" that fans patch together to form a fan text are usefully described by Gray, drawing on Genette, as "paratext" that "infringes upon the text, and invades its meaning-making process" (2006: 36). As the fan text takes different forms among different fan groups—namely, the audience sections "fans," "cultists," and "enthusiasts," with their different use of mass media, which Abercrombie and Longhurst (1998) describe—the balance between urtext and paratexts changes. In Gray's words, to the degree that "we actually consume some texts through paratexts and supportive intertexts, the text itself becoming expendable" (2006: 37). What follows is a radically different conceptualization of "texts" than in literary theory. Individual texts at the point of production are part of a wider web of textual occurrences and the meanings derived from them. These textual elements are read in the context of other texts. Intertextuality is thus the essence of all texts. While many contemporary fan texts such as *The Simpsons,* on which Gray focuses, or *South Park* are based on parody and thus more ostensibly intertextual than others, meaning construction through text *and* context does not by itself allow us to distinguish between literary and mediated texts. The field of comparative literature, for instance, draws on the long-standing tradition of motive and theme research. Yet in each and every case, the textual field in which the individual text is positioned will allow the reader to construct different meanings.

On a most obvious level, this relates to existing knowledge. Those readers with an interest in twentieth-century German literature will not have been quite as clueless about who the abovementioned Serenus Zeitblom was. They will have recognized the sentence "My name is Dr. Serenus Zeitblom, Ph.D.," as the opening sentence of the second chapter of Thomas Mann's *Doktor Faustus,* in which the narrator, Serenus Zeitblom, apologizes for his belated introduction. It is then a form of preexisting interest or what we might call an object of fandom (the work of Thomas Mann) that allows us to create meaning through contextualization that will have remained hidden to other readers—just as if the sentence in question had been "My name is Slim Shady," different paratexts would have come into play for different fan groups. Beyond this, Mann's *Doktor Faustus* serves as a lucid example of intertextuality in literary works in their literary and multimediated context: "the life of the German composer Adrian Leverkühn as told by a friend," as the subtitle of its English translations goes, is an adaptation of the Faust motive—the selling of one's soul to the devil for earthly talents, powers, or knowledge—that spans through all forms of textuality in European literature and storytelling, beginning with the late medieval German myth via Goethe's *Urfaust* to Bulgakov's *Мастер и Маргарита,* poetry (Heine's *Der Doktor Faust*), theater such as Paul Valéry's fragment *Mon Faust,* music by Berlioz, Wagner, Liszt, and the *Einstürzenden Neubauten,* filmic adaptations, including Murnau's *Faust: Eine Deutsche Volkssage,* to comic supervillains such as DC Comics's *Felix Faust,* to name only a few.[1] Beyond such direct adaptations, the Faust motive resurfaces in a plethora of popular texts including George Lucas's *Star Wars.* Yet, Mann's *Doktor Faustus* is not only part of an intertextual web; it also, like Mann's preceding work, is based on an ironic gesture of the narrator, the by now familiar Serenus Zeitblom, which takes back the narrative and the pretense of representing the real; a gesture in Mann's work that according to Adorno (1991) reflects the crisis of the narrator in the modern novel as a direct consequence of the proliferation of new modes and media of representation, namely, film (see also Benjamin 1983). The difference between intertextuality in mediated and literary texts is thus one of degree rather than kind. For both sets of textuality, the crisis of the text (in its boundaries at the point of production) is thus the crisis of the narrator as literary and actual figure: the author him- or herself.

The fan scholar, coincidentally, is thus no more or less an "apprentice chef" than the philologist. Both rely on intertextual knowledge to interpret text and context. To the degree that the fan text is constituted on the level of consumption, the reading position of the fan is actually the premise for identifying the text and its boundaries—rather than to an apprentice chef, the fan scholar compares to a restaurant critic, who to do his job also needs to know how to cook.

On a wider point, our reflections of what constitutes a text coincide with the critical reflections on authorship and textuality in structuralism and poststructuralism. The study of fans further underlines a process of growing intertextuality, multimediated narrative figures, and multiple authorship that has eroded the concept of the author that, as Barthes (1977) notes, reached its zenith in the formation of high modernity as the culmination of a rationalist, positivist capitalist system. It is indeed Barthes's analysis of Balzac's *Sarrasine* that accurately prefigures the condition of textuality as decentered and refocused on the level of the fan/reader I have sought to describe here:

> A text is not a line of words releasing a single "theological" meaning [. . .] but a multi-dimensional space in which a variety of writings, none of them original, blend and clash[. . . .] A text is made of multiple writings, drawn from many cultures and entering into mutual relations of dialogue, parody, contestation, but there is one place where this multiplicity is focused and that place is the reader, not, as was hitherto said, the author. The reader is the space on which all the quotations that make up a writing are inscribed without any of them being lost; a text's unity lies not in its origin but in its destination. (Barthes 1977: 146–48)

If the poststructuralist turn in Barthes's work furnishes us with a conceptual basis for the study and analysis of fandom, it is his earlier work and structuralism in general that allowed cultural studies to extend the study of interpretation and meaning beyond literary texts. As Eagleton notes resentfully (1996: 192), "structuralism had apparently revealed that the same codes and conventions traversed both 'high' and 'low' cultures, with scant regard for the classical distinction of value." When Eagleton laments the disappearing boundaries between *Coriolanus* and *Coronation Street*, he has thus already identified the guilty party. Eagleton's critique of course fails to acknowledge that the formation of structuralism was itself a reaction to changing forms of textuality that much of literary theory had been unable to address, continuing the study of literary texts as if they existed in splendid isolation. This, however, is not to dismiss Eagleton's concern over value out of hand. Many studies illustrate how fans themselves— from Tulloch and Jenkins's (1995) and McKee's (2001b) *Dr. Who* to Cavicchi's (1998) Springsteen and Thomas's (2002) *The Archers* fans—are concerned with value. Yet, if Eagleton's comparison between cultural studies and literary theory is ill judged for lacking recognition of the multiple methodological grounds for the rise of the former and the inability to address new forms of textuality of the latter, his warning that in its heightened emphasis on structuralist and poststructuralist approaches cultural studies has lost the vocabulary to evaluate texts is less easily dismissed.

The Death of the Author and Audience Activity

The notion of intertextuality has been pivotal to fan studies from their very beginning. Jenkins (1992: 67), in the context of new technological developments such as VCRs, explored the notion of "rereading." Jenkins differed from Barthes's description of the irregularity of rereadings, noting that they are commercially attractive to the television industry. This distinction between reading and rereading belongs to the less widely recognized aspects of Jenkins's work, not least because he admits that it is difficult to maintain, since in an intertextual-structuralist approach, reading and rereading are the same phenomenon. However, terminology aside, Jenkins finds himself in fundamental agreement with Barthes's model of reading. In his canonical work of the first wave of fan studies, a basic model of fan textuality thus emerges that has come to prevail until today. As fan studies found new conceptual grounds throughout the 1990s describing fandom as a form of spectacle and performance (Abercrombie & Longhurst 1998; see also Lancaster 2001), as a manifestation of subcultural hierarchies (Jancovich 2002; Thornton 1995), or as a transitional space (Harrington & Bielby 1995; Hills 2002), the implicit assumption remained a model of textuality that distinguished between "exceptional texts" and "exceptional readings" and that allocated the specificities of fandom on the side of the fan/reader rather than the text. With few exceptions, studies of fan audiences have challenged the idea of "correct" or even dominant readings. Hence, fan studies with their critical attention to the power of meaning construction not only underline Barthes's pronouncement of the terminal state of the modern author but also inherit its inherent ideological stance:

> Once the author is removed, the claim to decipher a text becomes quite futile. To give a text an Author is to impose a limit on the text [. . . .], literature by refusing to assign a "secret," an ultimate meaning to the text (and to the world as text), liberates what may be called an anti-theological activity that is truly revolutionary since to refuse to fix meaning is in the end, to refuse God and his hypostases—reason, science, law. [. . .] [T]he birth of the reader must be at the cost of the death of the author. (Barthes 1977: 147–48)

This self-proclaimed radicalism, which has marked poststructuralism and fan studies alike, fostering relativism in aesthetic judgment as radical rejection of positivism and science, is, according to Eagleton (1996), based on "straw targets." Eagleton sees poststructuralism as rooted in the specific historic moment of disillusionment, as 1960s oppositional movements were uncovered as complicit in the very structures they set out to overthrow, hence leading to a total rejection of all structures and thus the concept of truth: "an invulnerable position, and the fact it is also purely empty is simply the price one has to pay for this" (Eagleton 1996: 125).

Here, Eagleton has a point, not least because if all that fan studies can do is to highlight the relative value of all texts and the inherent supremacy of the reader over the text, the field has reached its conceptual and empirical frontiers. What, however, are the alternatives? Fan studies drawing on the work of Pierre Bourdieu (1984) have too convincingly unmasked forms of judgment based on authenticity and originality—which persist among fans as well as scholars—as means of social and cultural distinction (and domination) for a return to textual critique on such grounds to be considered a possibility. If it is only in these terms that we can maintain a distinction between *Coriolanus* and *Coronation Street,* it is a distinction not worth making.

The Death of the Reader

If we cannot locate aesthetic value of texts in themselves—and Eagleton's (1996) discussion of hermeneutics admits as much—yet do not want to abolish questions of value altogether, it needs to be located elsewhere. The author, pronounced dead in post-structuralism, and in any case conspicuously absent in most mass-mediated forms of textuality, has proven an unsuitable basis for textual interpretation and evaluation. However, if we can distinguish texts and meaning creation as radically as Jenkins's (1992) distinction between exceptional texts and exceptional readings suggests, the reader appears to be a no-better indicator of the aesthetic value of texts, since exceptional readings would thus appear to be based upon forms of audience activity quite independent of texts themselves. If we cannot locate aesthetic value in the author, text, or reader alone, it is in the process of interaction between these that aesthetic value is manifested. Hence, we need to define the act of reading in a manner that may appear obvious but has profound normative consequences. By defining the act of reading as a form of dialogue between text and reader (see Sandvoss 2005b), in fandom and elsewhere, we enter into a wider social and cultural commitment as to what texts are for and what we believe the uses of reading to be.

In doing so, I want to turn to Wolfgang Iser (1971, 1978), who, like other reception theorists (see Jauss 1982; Vodička 1975), moves the focus of literary theory from the text to the processes of reading. The premise of Iser's argument is that texts only acquire meaning when they are being read. The process of reading, however, is no simple realization of prepacked meanings controlled by the author, but rather an interaction in which the structures and figures of the text collide with the reader's (subjective) knowledge, experiences, and expectations, all in turn formed, we may add, in an intertextual field. In this process of dialogue between text and reader, meaning is created as the reader "concretizes" the text. Hence Iser focuses on textual elements of indeterminacy that only come to life through the interaction with the reader: textual gaps and blanks. In contrast to hermeneutical approaches, including the work of Ingarden (1973), who similarly speaks of "spots of indeterminacy," textual gaps have no theological, metaphysical function but are constituted and filled in each individual act of reading. In their recognition of the absence of inherent meanings and universal aesthetic value, Iser and fellow reception theorists thus actually share fundamental assumptions with Barthes's work. Yet, in contrast to the poststructuralist approaches to textuality that have given birth to fan studies, Iser establishes a firm basis on which the aesthetic value of a given text can be assessed. According to Iser, the act of concretization is underscored by readers' inherent striving to "normalize" texts. The notion of normalization is in turn linked to textual gaps: in their attempt to concretize textual gaps, readers are required to draw on their own knowledge and experience—on what Jauss (1982) has described as "horizon of expectation." It is therefore an inherent aspect of all ideational activity to align the Otherness encountered in the text, its alien elements, as closely with our past experience as possible. If we are successful, the text is fully normalized and "appears to be nothing more than a mirror-reflection" of the reader and his or her schemes of perception (Iser 1971: 9).

We must not, as Eagleton does, confuse Iser's observations with normative claims. Eagleton denounces normalization as a "revealingly authoritarian term," suggesting that a text should be "tamed and subdued to some firm sense of structure" as readers struggle to pin down "its anarchic 'polysemantic' potential" (1996: 71). Eagleton's adventurous reading itself tests the boundaries of polysemy, as in fact, Iser argues the opposite: normalization is an inherent aspect of cognition and all ideational activity, but one that the text can evade. It is precisely the ability of a text to avoid normalization in which its aesthetic value lies. While readers strive to normalize texts, the question is to what extent texts will let them do so. If a text is readily normalized, it "seems trivial, because it merely echoes our own" experience (Iser 1978: 109). Conversely, those texts that profoundly contradict readers' experiences and thus challenge our expectations require a reflexive engagement that reveals "aspects (e.g. of social norms) which had remained hidden as long as the frame of reference remained intact" (Iser 1978: 109).

In this formulation of aesthetic value as defamiliarization lies a profound challenge to mediated textuality and fan texts in particular. The obstacles to normalization in literary texts, such as *Doktor Faustus,* are rooted in a range of narrative and metaphorical techniques that depend on defined boundaries at the point of production—and hence the persistence of, if not the author, then at least his or her chosen narrative form. In mediated texts, as I have argued above, these boundaries are eroded. As the object of fandom corresponds with a textual field of gravity, rather than a text in its classical sense, readers gain new tools to normalize texts and to reconcile their object of fandom with their expectations, beliefs, and sense of self. As the fan's semiotic power extends beyond the bridging of textual gaps to the inclusion and exclusion of textual episodes, fan readers exclude those textual elements that impede the normalization of the text and fail to correspond with their horizon of expectation (see Scodari, Johnson in this volume). It is thus that Elvis can be claimed as an object of fandom by white supremacists and black soul singers alike (see Rodman 1996), that sport teams serve as spaces of self-projection to fans with varying habitus, beliefs, and convictions (Sandvoss 2003), and that Springsteen fans find themselves in his lyrics (Cavicchi 1998). These fan texts are void of inherent meaning and thus no longer polysemic, but what I have described elsewhere as "neutrosemic" (Sandvoss 2005a)—in other words, they are polysemic to the degree that the endless multiplicity of meaning has collapsed into complete absence of intersubjective meaning.

In all conceptualizations of fandom spanning from the early work of Fiske to the present day, fandom as a form of audienceship has been defined by its use: as a tool of pleasurable subversion, as the rallying point of communities, as focus of audiences' own textual activities or performances, serving a range of psychological functions or as semiotic space of narcissistic self-reflection. Yet, in this emphasis on audience activity, fan studies have neglected the act of reading as the interface between micro (reader) and macro (the text and its systems of production).

If aesthetic value is based on transgression and estrangement, the reading of fan texts strives for the opposite: familiarity and the fulfillment of expectations. Iser's work translates thus into a fundamental question in the study of fan texts: can the reader survive the death of the author? The fate of the author and reader are rather more intertwined than Barthes suggests; the process of reading as an act of communication spans like a line between two poles—one depends on the other. When the author is eradicated from the text, when all gaps disappear, the meaning that fans create is no longer based on reading but on audience activity. However, the disappearance of the author and fundamental redrawing of textual boundaries at the point of consumption are rarely complete, as is evident in fans' frequent sense of disappointment with their fan texts. Most texts—mediated or literary—can neither be fully normalized and thus emptied of all alien elements, nor truly fantastic, evading all forms of concretization. The extent to which (fan) texts thus reflexively challenge our perception is a matter of degree and one that requires a different answer in each and every case of text-reader interaction.

Two conclusions follow. First, fandom as a mode of reading sits uneasily with the aesthetic principles of reception theory. It constitutes a particular form of engagement with the text that presupposes familiarity and in which our expectations are more rigid, our determination to construct meaning in reference to the function of fandom greater than in other processes of reading. However, it does so in relation to no specific texts, but applies across the spectrum of textuality from romantic poetry to television cartoon programs. We can judge a text's aesthetic value thus only in relation to its reader.

In turn, this means that manifested in the act or reading, aesthetic value nevertheless persists and remains a category worthy of exploration in all forms of textuality from literary to fan texts. It is admittedly a functionalist definition of value and one that Eagleton (1996) dismisses with the same vigor as he attacks poststructuralism. While the latter is disregarded for its hollow political gesture, the functionalism of Iser faces the opposite charge: according to Eagleton (1996: 71), the value of estrangement is rooted in a "definite attitude to the social and cultural systems [. . .] which amounts to suspecting thought-systems as such" and is thus embedded in liberalism. This much is true—and it is equally true that those who do not share such a broad vision of emancipation through communication, those who do not share a belief in the necessity of reflexive engagement with our social, economic, and cultural norms and conditions may quickly dismiss such aesthetics, however curious a position this may be for anyone with the loosest affiliation to the Enlightenment project, not least those drawing their conceptual and ethical inspiration from Marxism—cultural studies and Eagleton included.

Yet this is precisely the lesson that emerges from the study of fan texts and my attempted synthesis between cultural studies and literary theory: the empirical study of fan audiences over the past two decades has indisputably documented the absence of universal and inherent aesthetic values of texts. However, to remain true to its own roots, our discipline needs to find new vocabulary and concepts to analyze aesthetic value in its function: the process of reading. Here, studies of fan audiences can learn as much from literary theory as vice versa: in a state of constant audienceship in which we consume mediated and fragmented texts and reconstitute textual boundaries in the act of reading in an intertextual field, we need to formulate aesthetic categories that avoid the absolutism of traditional textual interpretation as much as the relativism of poststructuralism and deconstructionism. Aesthetic value can thus neither be an objective category with what have been unmasked to be subjective criteria; nor can we afford the aesthetic (and ultimately social and cultural) indifference of conveniently abolishing aesthetics by relegating them to a subjective category with subjective criteria. Instead, the synthesis of fan studies and reception aesthetics enables us to explore aesthetics as a *subjective* category with *objective* criteria. In doing so, fan studies will not avoid ridicule for analyzing texts and their audiences that to some appear trivial; but it will move further towards exploring why fan texts mean so much to so many people and the meaning of this affective bond between text and reader in a mediated world.

Note

1. For a critique of intertextuality, and Kristeva's work in particular, see Stierle (1996).

2

Media Academics *as* Media Audiences
Aesthetic Judgments in Media and Cultural Studies

Matt Hills

In this chapter I want to argue that the dismissal of aesthetic considerations from much work in media/cultural studies—a foundational gesture aimed at distinguishing academics from both "naïve" consumers and "imposed" ideologies—does not, in fact, work to install critical rationality or desired neutrality (Barthes 2005). I will suggest that via its anti-aesthetics (see also Sandvoss, this volume) much cultural studies work has constructed cultural distinction for itself by implying that its scholars are exempt from the domains of fan culture and/or popular culture (Hills 2002, 2005b). However, such a fantasized exemption has not at all produced an escape from "popular aesthetics" (Bird 2003) but has instead recoded aesthetic judgments within the supposedly pristine spaces of academia.

If attempts to displace aesthetics produce only distorted shadows of the very problematic they seek to short-circuit, then might aesthetics not be returned more positively to circulation in cultural studies? As Hunter and Kaye have pointed out, scholars are usually "urged [. . .] not to take aesthetic judgements for granted. We should understand them instead as [. . .] exertions of social power" (1997: 3). But what would aesthetics look like if it were not treated merely as an ideological imposition?

By way of exploring this possibility, I will suggest that a rehabilitated aesthetics might emerge from the fact that media academics are themselves members of media audiences (Osborne 2000; Wright Wexman 1999), quite apart from the issue of whether or not they are also media fans. Curiously, debates in media/cultural studies have frequently returned to the question of whether the media academic who is also a media fan represents some kind of problematic or scandalous figure (Hills 2002; Michael 2000; White 2005). My concern is that this apparent destabilizing of scholar versus fan identity may have worked as a kind of academic-ideological feint. That is, for some it may operate to restore the illusion that academics who can announce their non-fandom are in the clear, as it were, their modernist, rational, scholarly selves safely set apart from their simultaneous identities as "ordinary" media consumers. However, going beyond fan audiences—but still learning from work in fan studies—we should perhaps really be asking not "what does it mean if an academic studying fans is also a fan?" but rather "what does it mean when an academic studying the media audience is also part of a media audience?" This latter question also includes those who may not directly or obviously be part of a media audience, since contemporary media are dispersed into everyday life and culture rather than being isolated to specific screens at specific times (Abercrombie & Longhurst 1998; Bird 2003).

Oddly, only scholar-fans have been interpreted as carrying some hybridized or logically regressive identity in relation to their academic status—i.e., they have been viewed in some quarters as "not proper academics"—whereas I want to argue here that this is in fact a special case of a more general problem. Academics, far more generally, are "not proper academics" either, if by this we mean that their scholarly selves cannot be cleanly separated out from their media-audience-based identities. Criticisms of specific scholar-fans, or even specific scholar-fan conferences, may arguably carry more weight (see Burr 2005), but all too often attacks on scholar-fandom have sought to attack this hybrid category per se for its supposed transgression of scholarly detachment, while exempting academia in general from any related critique or censure.

I will set out my argument here in three sections: (1) how the exclusion of aesthetics produces academic distinction; (2) how academic distinction recodes aesthetic judgment; and finally (3) how a general theory of hybridized academia—going beyond fandom—can restore the aesthetic.

How the Exclusion of Aesthetics Produces Academic Distinction

There can be little doubt that aesthetics has been powerfully detached from the academic study of popular culture. Analyzing this, Geraghty suggests "a number of reasons why making judgments about aesthetics has proved to be a difficult task in [. . .] the broader areas of media and cultural studies" (2003: 27). These include

> the impact of semiotics [. . .] with its pseudo-scientific claims about objectivity; the impact of postmodernism with its emphasis on diversity, decentring and play; the need to establish popular culture [. . .] as worthy of study that involved refusing the traditional modes of judgement; the impact of feminist work, with its demand that certain kinds of denigrated fictions should be taken seriously; the notion, coming rather differently from Foucault and Bourdieu, that to make aesthetic judgements was to impose the cultural norms of the powerful. (2003: 27–28)

Geraghty's list takes in the role of different academic schools of thought such as feminism, structuralism (figured as "semiotics"), and poststructuralism (represented as postmodern "play"). And yet, some of Geraghty's stated reasons have not been restricted to the operation of specific intellectual movements, or wider philosophies, and have instead formed parts of *the general legitimation of academic study of the popular.* Among these accounts of why aesthetics has found no place in media/cultural studies we might number "claims to objectivity"; the refusal of "traditional modes of judgment"; and the argument that making aesthetic judgments means imposing "cultural norms of the powerful." These rationales for abandoning aesthetics can all be said to work in one way. They each discursively construct media/cultural studies academics as "set apart" from popular culture, and as "set above" its consumers and fans (Hills 2005b, chapters 6 & 7).

By laying claim to the nonaestheticized study of popular culture, scholars have sought to discursively distance themselves from what are viewed as normative practices of media consumerism. Consumers routinely assess what they like and dislike, fans passionately favor certain texts (Sandvoss 2005a), and anti-fans equally passionately detest others (Gray 2003), but almost magically set outside these domains of taste, academia is positioned as carrying its own distinctive "imagined subjectivity" (Hills 2002: 3). That is, the academic's self-legitimating and claimed identity—split off from his or her identity as a media consumer—has typically been imaged and imagined as one of critical rationality, objectivity, and neutrality. As Barthes has written,

> I define the Neutral as that which outplays [. . .] the paradigm, or rather . . . everything that baffles the paradigm[. . . .] The paradigm, what is that? It's

the opposition of two virtual terms from which [. . .] I actualize one to produce meaning[. . . .] Whence the idea of a structural creation that would defeat, annul, or contradict the implacable binarism of the paradigm by means of a third term. (2005: 6–7)

And media/cultural studies scholarship has, I am suggesting, adopted this kind of desired and desiring role as "tertium" (Barthes 2005: 7). Here, scholarly identity has formed a kind of third term that assumes an ability to "outplay the paradigm" of media consumer/producer, with the theorist adopting a performed role supposedly outside the identity of the "naïve" media consumer who proclaims their pop-cultural tastes, while also going beyond the identity of the ideology-imposing or ideology-circulating media producer. Neither imposing ideological strictures, nor being subjected to them, there stands the properly disciplined media/cultural studies exegete.

Aesthetic judgments are treated as something belonging outside media/cultural studies. They are enacted and carried out by others, often fans of pop-cultural texts. Though writers such as Bird (2003) and Miller (2003) have reached very different conclusions over the value and elitism, or lack thereof, of fans' aesthetic judgments, they have nevertheless both advanced the notion that aesthetic criteria only exist properly and firmly outside media scholarship (Hills 2005a). Miller is especially scathing about fan practices of aesthetic judgment, which he depicts as an anathema to the anticanonical and anti-elitist ethics of cultural studies:

These forms of fandom are straight-forwardly dedicated to replicating a college of *aficionadi,* who by their knowledge of elevating texts are somehow superior to the rest of us. This [. . .] replicates the very forms of quality discourse that were supposedly toppled by anti-canonical cultural studies. Instead, the best readers of the best texts are back, armed with their best interpretations. No thank you[. . . .] Leave spotting trainspotters to trainspotters. (Miller 2003: 22)

However, such a rejection of aesthetics does not constitute the only possible academic strategy of distinction. For example, in "film studies, the decisions about which texts deserve a place in the canon have often been achieved through aesthetic judgements" (McKee 2001a: 4). In this context, *the legitimation of academic study proceeds by appropriating rather than opposing aesthetic discourses,* with film being positioned as worthy of study precisely because it can be viewed as "a particular sort of aesthetic experience" (Kuhn 2005: 401).

Outside of film studies, however, aesthetics has remained something of a dark art in media/cultural studies. Aesthetics can be studied, but aesthetic judgments must not corrupt the media/cultural scholar's disciplinary reason and situated neutrality. Thomas J. Roberts carefully negotiates this terrain in *An Aesthetics of Junk Fiction:*

> What shall we say is the difference [. . .] between a *discipline* and a *fan club,* however learned? This difference, at least, is worth noticing: a *fan club* says, "What we love, you should love too," but a *discipline* says, "What we are discovering about what we love will be useful to you in your investigations of what you love." (1990: 5–6)

At the very moment when Roberts entertains the possibility that studying culture may involve "loving" some cultural texts, he nevertheless converts this into a curious kind of impassioned neutrality. For Roberts, work in an academic discipline should never seek to convert or critique the tastes of others but should seek only to generalize from its understanding of how (beloved) cultural texts operate on their readers. Again, the "imagined subjectivity" of the scholar is rendered distinct from that of the fan club member, who supposedly believes his or her aesthetic judgments are the only right ones. By marked contrast, even where aesthetic judgments seem to move dangerously close to academic work, Roberts suggests that they can be sublimated and transformed into a more generalizable or objectively useful knowledge.

Although it is fandom that has repeatedly borne the brunt of cultural studies scholars' need to bracket themselves off from the aesthetic judgments of media audiences, I want to go beyond the issue of fandom here, arguing that the anti-aesthetics of media/cultural studies simply cannot achieve its aim of securing academic distinction from media consumers and industries. This is so, because regardless of whether or not any given academic is a "fan" of what he or she is studying, the "cultural analyst is at once 1) a reader/interpreter and member of a community of recipients [of media messages . . .]; and 2) an analyst of the messages at another level, via a different theoretical problematic" (Osborne 2000: 116).

Purging aesthetics as a marker of what Osborne terms this "level 2" difference does not, unfortunately, do away with the fact that media/cultural studies academics remain "level 1" media and cultural consumers, with all that this might imply about their tastes, distastes, identities, and affective engagements with media culture. "Making a reading" at level 2— e.g., a disciplined structuralist/poststructuralist reading—is not ever fully coterminous with the analyst's embodied "reading experience" of that same text (Pearce 1997: 215 & 220).

However, a focus on the intersections of fandom and academia in the wake of Jenkins's (1992) seminal work has, I would say, succeeded in rendering relatively invisible the issue of academia's far more wide-reaching complicities with popular and media culture. The general question of whether or not academic identities can be distanced from consumer identities has not been convincingly tackled, since this logical regression—the academic studying media consumers and industries who is placed within the object of study as a media consumer of such industries—has been neglected in favor of picking over the special rather than the general case, that of the scholar who is also a fan of the type she or he is analyzing. If this special case is marked as a category violation demanding attention, the general case whereby "scholars, like others, have [. . .] interests at stake: we are not only critics but also consumers" (Wright Wexman 1999: 89) is left unmarked. As Wright Wexman has argued, "Critics customarily consider themselves disinterested observers [. . . although their activities lead . . .] to practical valuations of [. . .] texts, [and] one can view current scholarly practices in the light of these valuations. Why are certain [. . .] texts chosen for special attention?" (Wright Wexman 1999: 77).

This is the question I will now consider, arguing that the supposed removal of aesthetics from media/cultural studies has not, in fact, fully secured academics' cultural distinctions from "ordinary" media consumers, but has instead worked to recode aesthetic judgments in a variety of ways. Focusing only on the situation of academics who are also fans has been a highly effective way of sustaining the academic-ideological illusion that, for everybody else studying media culture, it's just "disinterested" and symbolically "set apart" business as usual.

How Academic Distinction Recodes Aesthetic Judgment

S. Elizabeth Bird has pointed out that the suspension of explicitly aesthetic judgments in media/cultural studies has been strongly linked to "the replacement of aesthetic standards by political and social ones" (2003: 118).

The evaluation of texts has not, by any means, been taken off the scholarly agenda: far from it. Instead, alternative evaluative criteria have been set out, operating largely within what I've termed a "decisionist" approach to the cultural politics of media texts (Hills 2002: 182). Here, texts are routinely judged for their reactionary/progressive representations and meanings.

As if Derridean thought had never existed, this exercising of scholarly judgment assumes that clear lines can be drawn between the politically good and the politically bad text. Such an approach also assumes, of course, that Osborne's "level 1" aesthetic responses to media texts can be wholly divorced from distinctively "level 2" theoretical problematics—i.e., that the political evaluation of texts can proceed without any reference to academics' "ordinary" consumer tastes or distastes for certain media texts. "Decisionist" analyses of popular media may also attempt to invert Osborne's "level 1" and "level 2" responses to texts, implying that a rigorous and rational political evaluation can actually underlie, at all times, scholars' more personal "level 1" tastes and distastes.

In film studies, which I've already noted has been historically less fearful of aesthetic judgment, some *Screen* theory scholars went as far as explicitly collapsing together aesthetic and political evaluations. However, this generalizing compression of politics and aesthetics was soon subjected to critique for its reductiveness (see MacCabe 1981a, 1981b; McArthur 1981). Adornian and Frankfurt School approaches to aesthetics, which again construe the aesthetic primarily as a category of the political, would appear to be similarly problematic, since they too assume that aesthetics can be reduced to stable, fixed, and functional political codifications or judgments.

Seeking either to ground the aesthetic in the political or wholly to divorce the two modes of evaluation, "decisionist" approaches have hence sought to identify texts, and audiences, that "resist" dominant ideologies. Despite the fact that many media/cultural studies writers have long recognized the problems inherent in isolating out resistance (Abercrombie & Longhurst 1998; Jenkins 1992), the lure of being able to decisively sift out resistant or politically good texts has not passed away. In a review of my book *Fan Cultures* (2002) that claims that my own attack on decisionist narratives is decisionist itself, Christine Scodari argues that "resistance (or not) with respect to particular operations of power (including commodification) . . . might well [still] be determinable" (2003b: 182). In other words, scholarly machineries of political evaluation can continue onward, even if specific assumptions of active resistance and passive incorporation are inverted (Scodari 2003a: 125).

What I want to suggest here is that the foundational gesture of decisionist media/cultural studies—that aesthetic judgments can supposedly be grounded in, or displaced by, political evaluation—does not, in fact, evade the properly aesthetic: that which intersubjectively exceeds a priori pure reduction to, or pure separation from, the plane of political effectivity. Rather, aesthetic judgments are frequently *recoded* by media/cultural studies as strictly political ones. The aesthetic and the political are never as cleanly separable, nor as clearly interrelated, as decisionist strategies prefer to assert. Aesthetic judgments therefore remain surreptitiously and excessively in place, being masked behind or carried within supposedly purely political evaluations.

The recoding of aesthetic judgments results in a number of problems for media/cultural studies. The primary one can be described succinctly as *the canon problem*. By this, I mean that a severely limited range of media texts (and audiences) has been subjected to detailed academic study. Both scholar-fans and scholar-anti-fans or scholar-non-fans have contributed to this state of affairs.

Scholar-fans are those scholars who are also self-identified fans of what they study (Hills 2002: 11–15). By contrast, what we could call scholar-non-fans or scholar-anti-fans (following Gray 2003) are those who parade their disinterest in, or distaste for, specific media texts. Each faction of media/cultural studies academics has played a part in the "canon problem." Scholar-fans have tended to study texts that they profess to love, and this has resulted in specific taste cultures being overrepresented academically, with certain texts being far more likely to be canonized in academic study: "there is a tendency to favour programs and genres that may be considered edgy, avant-garde, or attracting a 'cult' audience[. . . .] I have rarely heard a [conference] presentation about successful 'middle-of-the-road' offerings—and never from scholars who identified as fans" (Bird 2003: 121).

Texts aimed at upscale audiences, favoring reflexive sophistication or postmodern playfulness with genre, or enacting a "cult" anticommercial and antimainstream ideology, are all thus more likely to meet with academic fervor and canonization. However, this limiting of academic attention is far from only being a result of celebratory scholar-fandom. It is also attributable to the critical work of scholar-anti-fans, who enact their distaste for certain forms of popular culture by dismissing, ignoring, or stereotyping them. As Jonathan Gray has said of anti-fans: "[they] construct an image of the text [...] sufficiently enough that they can react [...] against it[. . . . They routinely] engage in distant reading, responding to texts that have not been viewed" (2003: 71).

This would appear to be an accurate description of a range of critical theorists in media studies, who don't actually seem to closely read the texts they are so quick to condemn. Alan McKee has written of this type of scholar,

> I have noticed that many [...] teaching Media Studies, strongly organize their viewing schedules around public service broadcasting at the expense of commercial programming. Of course, this is not in itself problematic—unless the academics in question then begin to speak as experts about all television. At this point, a refusal to actually watch the medium being discussed seems [...] to be a little odd. (2003: 181)

There is indeed a kind of scholarly "distant reading" going on here, as academics write in a cursory, nondetailed, and dismissive manner about highly commercial or middle-brow TV shows (and other media) they feel an aesthetic distaste for. Bird argues that, as a result, academics' aesthetic judgments are replayed not only through scholar-fan celebrations of favored texts but also through neo-Marxist, anti-fan, or non-fan critiques of disfavored texts:

> [Critical] scholars do not care to define what is "wrong" with the middle-brow [and the commercial] in terms of taste or aesthetic judgement; they just ignore it. Yet inherent in that ignoring is a clear aesthetic judgement; these cultural forms indeed [are assumed to] constitute a vast wasteland, and people who consume them are probably not that capable of refined aesthetic judgement. (2003: 121–22)

The "canon problem" thus emerges out of two seemingly opposed currents of thought that, in actuality, work in concert to restrict which texts are studied in detail and canonized. Celebratory scholar-fans and critical scholar-anti-fans both demonstrate tendencies to marginalize the middle-brow and the commercial, favoring "cult" forms that symbolically enact a certain distance from "the mainstream," as well as favoring public service TV, which enacts a not-unrelated anticommercial ideology. Though the binary of "cult" versus "mainstream" can clearly be deconstructed—and an increasing number of texts are both cultish and very much main-streamed (Brooker 2002; Gray 2006; Hills 2003, 2004)—I would argue that these cultural categories continue to be used within the sense-making practices of scholar-fans and scholar-anti-fans. In each case, "level 1" aesthetic judgments are recoded as "level 2" theoretical problematics, in a way that thus goes firmly beyond the issue of whether academics are also fans, to encompass the more general issue of how media academics are always-already media audiences. Moreover, they are audiences with specifiable aesthetic tastes that cannot simply be read off from their scholarly cultural politics.

The problem of restricted canonization (Hills 2004, 2005d) therefore devolves into two related forms of aesthetic judgment underpinning academic work: celebratory scholar-fandom and critical scholar-anti-fandom. In extreme instances of the latter, any attention to media fictions is wholly devalued in favor of "real" engagements with political issues (Philo and Miller 2001). Replaying a powerful cultural system of value that favors the factual over the fictional, and the supposedly real object over the aesthetic creation (Harrington & Bielby 1995: 135–36), such approaches install fatal blind spots within their analyses by neglecting to address how media fictions, as well as media reportage, can work to construct and circulate a variety of (de)politicized meanings about the world. Again, a type of aesthetic judgment is recoded in the somewhat infantilized and autoheroic writing of Philo and Miller (2001), albeit a judgment that refutes the aesthetic as being worthy of study *tout court.*

Meanwhile, the celebratory tones of certain scholar-fans have been picked apart in relation to a very much canonical object of study, the TV series *Buffy the Vampire Slayer.* Levine and Schneider have argued that many *Buffy* "scholars are [. . .] projecting, and 'acting out' their fantasies in relation to the program. They love *BtVS*" (2003: 299). These writers go on to imply that scholar-fans have prioritized their fandom—their "level 1" aesthetic responses—over their scholarly identities:

> *BtVS* is often entertaining, amusing, gripping—even exciting and titillating. But it is little more. Primarily, *BtVS* scholars are the ones who attempt to make the show out to be [. . .] something more than this[. . . .] If Joss Whedon is in fact a "genius," this is not because he manages to do any of those things that *BtVS* scholars bizarrely claim he does by erecting their

own fictions and fantasies about what is going on in various episodes. (2003: 297–98 & 299)

Scholar-fans such as David Lavery and Rhonda Wilcox stand accused of "emotivism" (Friedman & Squire 1998: 14), where moral judgments over the goodness or not of an object proceed on the basis of one's feelings in relation to that thing. In other words, these scholars allegedly let their enthusiasm for *Buffy* run away with them.

Buffy scholarship has provided rich pickings for those wanting to assess the impact of taste cultures on academia. In a study of the *Slayage* academic conference on *Buffy the Vampire the Slayer*—held in Nashville, May 2004, and affiliated with the online journal *Slayage* (McKee 2002: 69)— Vivien Burr gathered written responses from thirteen attendees, and supplemented these with her own participant observations. Burr's findings resonate with the concerns of Levine and Schneider, suggesting that "level 1" fannish aesthetics may have potentially usurped academic "level 2" theoretical problematics:

> Many delegates felt that fandom interfered with academic rigour on occasion. For example, Holly said, "I believe there was significant resistance in the audience to a reading of *Buffy* that was not laudatory"[. . . .] Alan remarked that [. . .] "the tone of [some questions . . .] and the ensuing discussion was more on a level of people's personal opinions and tastes about this character or another." (Burr 2005: 377–78)

To reiterate: these are *not* problems restricted to the intrusion of fannish aesthetics into academic work. They are more wide-ranging than this, moving far outside the matter of scholar-fan hybridity to take in the "anti-fandom" (Gray 2003) of critical media theorists who prefer to attack or ignore "commercial" forms of television/film, or even ignore media fictions altogether. Neither impassioned scholar-fans nor "disinterested" political-economy critics disclaiming their objectivity automatically have any monopoly on virtue. Aligning the academic self with one side of the reason/passion binary (Burr 2005: 380–81) does not ward off the problem of aesthetics in media/cultural studies. Instead, some (not all) scholar-fans and some (not all) scholar-anti-fans or scholar-non-fans have been structurally implicated in the recoding of aesthetic judgments, and hence in the "canon problem."

But how can media academics' status as media audiences be properly tackled, acknowledged, even utilized, without audience-based identities and tastes being seen as a "threat to academic identity?" (Burr 2005: 378). To consider this question means going beyond fandom, and conceding that the distinctive expulsion of aesthetics—resulting in its various scholar-fan and anti-fan recodings—is a general rather than a special problem in media/cultural studies.

How a General Theory of Hybridized Academia— Going Beyond Fandom—Can Restore the Aesthetic

As Geraghty has argued, media/cultural studies may benefit "from academics being more explicit about the evaluative judgements we inevitably make" (2003: 40). However, it is hardly the case that aesthetic judgments have been properly expelled from these areas of study. It is, perhaps, fairer to say that they have continued, either in the name of political evaluation or via the impassioned critical/celebratory analyses of scholar-anti-fans and scholar-fans. Despite this recoded continuation, aesthetic judgments have also partly been nominally ruled out of media/cultural studies as a result of the work of Pierre Bourdieu (1984, 1993). Bourdieu argues that aesthetic judgments are inseparable from the exercising of "cultural capital" and are thus linked to the cultural reproduction of systematic power inequalities (see Hills 2002; Williamson 2005). Debates concerned with more fully restoring aesthetic judgments to media and cultural studies have tended to revolve around whether it is necessary or desirable for scholars to uphold specific notions of quality media (Jacobs 2001; Thomas 2002), and in this ongoing discussion, the work of Bourdieu—and his argument that aesthetics are linked to macro-level cultural reproduction—has been somewhat suspended in favour of more micro-level textual analysis. Aesthetic judgments, it seems, steadfastly refuse to go away (see Bérubé 2005; Hills 2005b: 142–44).

One way to move forward would be to argue that film studies can provide a model for media/cultural studies. Opposition to aesthetics could be replaced by an appropriation of art discourses, with "television art" finally taking its place alongside long-established disciplinary discussions of film art. This is Turnbull's (2005: 368–69) argument, as she ponders whether media studies might make a place for "ekphrasis," the linguistic re-expression of a text's aesthetic impact on the self. Though this seems promising, the question that remains is how ekphrasis would connect up with media/cultural studies' theorizing. Is it the place of such theory to re-express subjective and aesthetic experiences, or should these experiences be remediated, worked over, or even modified through the reflexivity of theory? Turnbull seems to take media/cultural studies back to the collapsing together of politics and aesthetics that marred the *Screen* theory of MacCabe (1981a, 1981b), or to the prioritizing of subjective aesthetics over politics.

Another way forward would be not to ape film theory, but rather to pay attention to a path not taken in Barthes's lectures on the neutral. Challenged as to whether his desire for the neutral is in some sense itself merely an ideological restatement of the "petit-bourgeois [. . .] ideology of the balanced account" (2005: 79), Barthes responds,

> I could, and it is, by the way, what I am doing, recognize that in me there are "petit-bourgeois" elements in my tastes, in my discourse are petit-bourgeois features (without going into the discussion of this cursed denomination here)[. . . .] These features are not clandestine[. . . .] However, that's not the direction I will take to answer. I will say: the Neutral is connected with [petit-bourgeois-ideological] neither-norism and nevertheless is absolutely different from it. (2005: 79–80)

Barthes's argument is that petit-bourgeois ideology is "social" and grants a "subject-position," whereas his discourse is "existential" and suspends any subject-position (2005: 80). We could hardly wish for a more condensed statement of the ideology of the nonplaced, free-floating academic who is assumed to stand outside social affiliations and contexts, thereby representing a near mystical tertium.

And yet Barthes's preceding and refuted acknowledgment is, I would say, actually a more promising answer to the question posed, even though it undermines the autoheroics of the allegedly acontextual academic always symbolically distanced from ideology. Barthes comes close to conceding that his discourse, even while it seeks to demystify and politically evaluate, is also permeated by the very ideology it opposes and unveils. This, I think, offers a better way forward for media/cultural studies: not a rise in aesthetic subjectivism, but instead a reflexive approach to scholars' aesthetic judgments as hermeneutic constructions of self-identity (Bailey 2005; Sandvoss 2005a), and a recognition of how these may be *both* ideological *and* opposed to specific ideologies. The problem addressed by

Barthes also captures a far wider difficulty, since all those working in the humanities and social sciences are, in a range of ways, caught up in versions of this binary: disciplinary knowledge versus cultural identity and experience. The literary scholar is an "ordinary" reader as well as a scholar; the political scientist is both a citizen and an academic; the sociologist is always part of a society, and so on. Disciplined scholarship may always require a series of Others from which it can disentangle its own supposed purity and specificity. However, such processes of Othering and their cultural exclusions can also be highlighted and challenged (Hills 2005b), and thus should not be assumed to be monolithically fixed, inevitable, or essential in their specifiable forms and contents.

Work in media/cultural studies may, then, benefit from shifting its legitimating discourses away from the anti-aesthetic, moving towards an acknowledgment that present-day scholarship can no longer be "set apart" from the culture and ideology it studies, but is rather "set in relation" with these contexts (Hills 2005b: 172–73). Though critical scholars have been happy to redescribe the worlds of media audiences, e.g., shifting audience "leisure" into the register of "labor" (Meehan 2000; Shimpach 2005), the possibility of redescribing scholarship's own foundational self-descriptions has rarely been pursued. Recognizing that media academics are always-already media audiences, whether or not they are fans, would mean giving up the notion that media and cultural studies are enterprises outside the paradigm of consumer/producer, and outside the realms of aesthetic taste as well as ideology.

Will the entire edifice of media/cultural studies crumble away if we surrender the legitimating prop that academic work is essentially and purely different to the tastes/ideologies of everyday consumer and media-industry culture? I would say not: indeed, it may be easier for both critical scholar-anti-fans and celebratory scholar-fans to articulate exactly which cultural texts and media systems they are "for," without the need to cloak and recode aesthetic judgments. It may also allow the "canon problem" to be openly addressed and creatively opened out, with a wider range of cultural tastes and identities—a wider range of "projects of self"—then being archived and canonized by scholarship.

For some, the cost will undoubtedly be too high. Ideology will only ever be elsewhere in their worldview. But this splitting of the cultural world into highly legible heroes and victims is really a very simple story, however many lengthy words it loves to use. Recognizing the *generalized hybridity* of contemporary media academics—academics who are also audiences and consumers of the type they write about—surely means letting go of an infantile fantasy of omnipotence in which scholars are imagined as the bearers of pure, anti-ideological thought. At the same time, it means going beyond viewing fan audiences as *the* problematic site of aesthetic judgments—hence concomitantly depicting scholar-fandom as a threatening hybridity—in order to safely reconjure notions of academic authenticity.

3

Yoko in Cyberspace with Beatles Fans
Gender and the Re-Creation of Popular Mythology

Christine Scodari

In 2003, a discussant on the Usenet newsgroup devoted to the Beatles contributed the following:

> I had a nightmare last night. I woke up screaming. I dreamed that: Paul, with the help of the BBC, produce[d] a movie that claimed to be the "real" story of the Beatles. We all learned how [. . .] Paul was the real talent behind the Beatles[. . . .] Paul was the force that turned John Lennon's half-baked scribble of songs into the classics they are today[. . . .] In response, Yoko release[d] a statement of outrage and announced plans for her own movie about the Beatles. She states in her press release: "John always said that I was the fifth Beatle, and if anyone knows the truth to this story, it is me"[. . . .] The movie will show how Yoko was the force that turned John Lennon's half-baked scribble of songs into the classics they are today.[1]

This message illustrates the propensities of those John Lennon fans who display gender-inflected subjectivities in relation to their idol and antagonize other Beatles fans by rendering his closest real-life partnerships as inauthentic. As popular texts, genres, personalities, and their original enthusiasts age, the prospect of waning significance and the influx of younger cohorts of followers amplify and multiply such tensions. Computer-mediated communication accentuates this effect and, as the millennium approached, began to broaden and diversify creative and interactive modes and opportunities for preexisting fan cultures, allowing meanings and mythologies to be recycled, contested, and/or re-created via such activities as the archival of fan art and fiction, Web site creation, and discussion board and chat participation.

Fan practices entail the maintenance, adoption, negotiation, and/or refusal of hegemonic methods and messages. A fan community's dense, distant history escalates such struggles for meaning. Beatles cyberfans, as a prime example, labor to shape the canon and mythology of this group, its music, and its cast of personae so as to privilege their favored subjectivities, thereby implicating, among others, gendered power relations of sexuality, sociality, and romance.

This essay contextualizes key issues before discerning the prevailing, gender-related subjectivities of Beatles fans as exemplified among a decade's worth of postings on rec.music beatles (RMB), one of Usenet's myriad, asynchronous discussion groups. Postings were unearthed via the Google Usenet search engine (groups.google.com). Contestations of meaning and subjective preferences are tracked and theorized, the influence of computer-mediated communication upon such practices is pondered, and gender is examined as a focal point around which fan investments and, by extension, social and political bearings, continue to be negotiated.

The "Yoko Factor," Cyberfandom, and Neutrosemy

Most gender-related analyses of Beatles culture and fandom address shifting constructions of masculinity and femininity represented or roused by this group, its music, and/or its style (Ehrenreich, Hess, & Jacobs 1992; Stark 2003). While nominally a topic in such research, Yoko Ono, artist-musician and widow of Beatle John Lennon, is perhaps the most pivotal female subject in Beatles lore. Ono can be generically regarded as a "public widow" who, upon her husband's murder in 1980, attained an enhanced position from which to step in and ensure his legacy. However, unlike the previously uncelebrated women who went on to replace their deceased husbands in Congress, what Solowiej and Brunell (2003) referred to as the "Widow Effect," Ono had a dual purpose—that of "rehabilitating her own image, then assuring through her songs, actions, and memorials" that Lennon be remembered through the screens she erected (Pinsdorf 2002: n. p.). Such rehabilitation is crucial in light of the enmity brandished by some of her critics. In reviewing a musical composed by Ono, the *New York Times* (Witchell 1994: AE1) observed that among her greatest achievements were "destroying the most popular music group of the century" and "brainwashing her third husband [Lennon] into marrying her."

Many gender issues associated with Ono's controversial status in Beatles culture and fandom crystallize in terms of the "Yoko Factor," which is the "inevitable moment when you're dating a guy in a band and he lectures you about Yoko Ono, the message being that women are a suck on male creativity" (Marcotte 2005: n. p.). However, some insist that Ono was ahead of her time, both positively influencing Lennon's work and paving a way for alternative music and women's involvement in it (Gottlieb & Wald 1994; Marcotte 2005; Prose 2002; Wiener 1998). If, as Stark (2003: 3–5) insisted, much of the Beatles' initial popularity was based on female fans' resistive appreciation of their "feminine" group dynamic or "collective synergy," it is nonetheless questionable whether it is also resistive for these fans, even decades later, to fixate on one woman as the primary obstacle to continuing, positive reminiscence of this dynamic.

For adherents of the "Yoko Factor," the particular cast of personae do not seem to matter. Some fans of Kurt Cobain, the Nirvana frontman whose 1994 death was ruled a suicide, play off and perpetuate this discourse in conspiratorial chatter and even a book (Wallace & Halperin 2004) postulating that his wife, actor-musician Courtney Love, solicited his murder.

I unpacked analogous phenomena by investigating fans of science fiction television as they engage online (Scodari 2003a; Scodari & Felder 2000). FOX's hit series *The X-Files* (1993–2002) was groundbreaking for its genre and target audience in rendering the professional but potentially romantic partnership of a man and woman in roughly egalitarian terms. However, perhaps because the genre predisposes its audience to patriarchal avenues of interpellation, many fans of both sexes preferred the male hero, Agent Mulder, to the female hero, Agent Scully. Mulder devotees posting on either of two *X-Files* newsgroups (alt.tv.x-files; alt.tv.x-files.analysis) regarded Scully's professional challenge of her partner as "obstinate, insensitive, and lacking in appropriate deference" (Scodari & Felder 2000: 243). One male "Mulderist" bemoaned Scully's very presence as inhibiting "Mulder eyeing [. . .] someone else" (241), another remarked that Scully would make "such an awful significant other to any but the wussiest of men" (243), while a female fan declared, "I have a problem with Scully [. . .] and the last thing I want is to see Mulder kissing her, or telling her that she's his everything. [. . .] She doesn't deserve him" (243). Many such fans also reacted to a decision by creators to continue the series after David Duchovny (Mulder) resigned by heaping venom on the character that replaced his and the actor who portrayed him. This is yet another gendered, hegemonic subjectivity—that of positioning one masculine persona as competing with and superior to another.

Countless fans of the Sci Fi Channel's *Farscape* (1999–2004) and *Stargate SG-1* (1997–) also impugned these series' female heroes, particularly in response to actual or potential romances between them and esteemed male heroes (Scodari 2003a). I described a female cyberfan of *Farscape* who complained that her idol, hero John Crichton, displayed a "god complex" in investing hope and love in the soldier Aeryn Sun, his shipmate and romantic interest, whom she considered to be too headstrong and therefore unworthy (121). Female fans of *Stargate SG-1*'s male heroes, Jack O'Neill and Daniel Jackson, resented the admirable traits and screen time given to the female hero, military officer and physicist Samantha Carter, as well as perceived attempts by creators to inject "sexual tension" into the otherwise professional and platonic relationship between her and O'Neill, her unit commander (123–24).

Many of the female fans who revere male heroes and devalue their female counterparts also tend to write and/or read slash fan fiction featuring male characters. Slash is homoerotic fiction that can be composed by gay, bisexual, or lesbian fans about characters of their own sex, thereby challenging heteronormativity. However, my inquiry (Scodari 2003a) shows that the more typical slash authored by women about male personae can often be motivated by patriarchal, hegemonic stereotypes of competition among women over men that lead to regarding even fictional female characters as rivals to be marginalized and disparaged. Female fans adopting such a subjectivity, that of fantasy lover or confidante to a male hero, consequently clash with those in the audience eager to identify with female heroes in ways that resist tendencies of popular culture texts and creators to reproduce male dominance.

This same body of research (Scodari 2003a; Scodari & Felder 2000) disputed claims by some scholars (see Brown 1994; Fiske 1987; Jenkins 1992) that the practices of "active" fans are oppositional by virtue of generating pleasure and resistance to producerly authority. Kellner (1997: n.p.) warned that "resistance and pleasure cannot [. . .] be valorized *per se* as progressive elements of the appropriation of cultural texts" and that "difficult discriminations must be made as to whether resistance, oppositional reading, or pleasure in a given experience is progressive or reactionary, emancipatory or destructive." So, it is vital to acknowledge when some

fans' devotions and/or practices undermine the equally or more oppositional meanings and desires of others. Additional study (Scodari 2004,
2005) seconded this perspective and the notion that while "cyberfandom
makes private meanings a bit more public," it also "forces marginal fans to
confront the denigration of their tastes by authors and other fans" (Scodari & Felder 2000: 254). As Interrogate the Internet (1995: 127) predicted,
"the structure of the technology and the content" would coincide with values predominant in the "broader cultural context."

The following analysis of Beatles fandom as it has circulated on the
Internet reveals parallels to the gendered subjectivities demonstrated or
implied above, even if much to which Beatles fans are committed has its
roots in "real life" rather than fiction, and entails a multiplicity of texts
and paratexts emerging over more than four decades. Indeed, Sandvoss
(2005b: 832) has theorized "neutrosemy," a state most readily achieved by
texts that defy the neatly defined boundaries typical of a book, film, or
television series, and that are of a "mediated and distanciated nature."
Neutrosemy exists when there is so much textual openness that "actual
signification value" is neutralized and overtaken by "fans' existing schemes
of perception and horizons of expectations" (832, 835). Thus, texts, paratexts, and fan discourses coalesce to reveal more about the identities,
desires, and histories of readers than about particular texts, contexts, creators, or mechanics of production.

"The Beatles" as Text, Cyberfan Negotiations, and Gendered Subjectivities

Neutrosemic potential invites consideration of what constitutes "The Beatles" as text. On a primary level, there are the television and radio performances, movies, songs, recordings, and other creative offerings with which
the group or its members as solo agents were involved. On a secondary
level, there are the immediate, paratextual elements such as packaging and
other promotional materials, articles, news stories, reviews, and interviews
relating to the primary-level texts. Third are paratexts and metatexts of a
more remote sort, such as other interviews, news stories, and articles, as
well as retrospectives, biographies, docudramas, documentaries, and theatrical productions based on the professional and/or personal history of
the group and/or its members. Fourth are fan discourses that deliberate
the other, various levels of text. Within this array are appreciations of

"fact" concerning the Beatles, with some less constructed and contested, such as release dates of albums, that the Beatles first visited the United States in 1964, that John Lennon was murdered by Mark David Chapman, and so on. Deliberations of less straightforward questions such as who broke up the Beatles or who was the creative force behind the Beatles are more telling with regard to gender, other issues of power relations, and the "existing schemes of perception and horizons of expectations" of fans (Sandvoss 2005b: 835).

Fan discourses themselves attest to the multiplicity and types of relevant texts and the elasticity of meaning regarding the Beatles. Here, one RMB poster attempted, in 1998, to differentiate between primary levels of text and others in determining matters of "truth":

> How are we going to prove whether Yoko is a bitch or not a bitch? How are we going to prove whether or not Paul was a clod for his comments about John's murder? [. . .] As far as caring who had blisters on their fingers [. . .] that's a different thing altogether cause it was the lyrics of a Beatles song.

Moreover, fans can recognize and debate many of the perceptions, conditions, and motivations that lead to tangential talk as well as rake over some of the more controversial, Beatles-related matters. As an apparently male RMB poster argued in 1998, "There's a much simpler explanation for why things such as Yoko and Bill Clinton come up. There's nothing new under the sun in Pepperland. When the bones have been thoroughly picked over, the carrion birds have to feed on something." In rebuttal, another fan sought to justify such conversation while simultaneously making a flattering comparison: "In fact, we've not even scratched the surface. Two hundred years later in Freuderland [Germany] [and] we're just starting to make some headway with understanding how Beethoven work[e]d." Amid a discussion thread in the year 2000, another user raised a more depressing prospect for Beatles fans, and one that could also amplify contentiousness about highly debatable issues: "[A]s far as lasting, measurable impact on music today, you and I, both Beatles fans, have to admit that the [B]eatles' influence on music is steadily dwindling, esp. with the rise of hip-hop/rap music, which has practically no heritage in [B]eatles and traces its roots back to James [B]rown, Parliament, and Grandmaster [F]lash."

Scholarly accounts also have difficulty pinning down the ideological meanings of "The Beatles." Ehrenreich, Hess, and Jacobs (1992) lauded the freedom, sexual and otherwise, that the early Beatles inspired in young female fans, but dramatically limited the time frame and "text" of the Beatles in doing so. Similarly, Wolfe and Haefner (1996) conceived of Beatles fans as forging what Grossberg (1984a) termed an "affective alliance" that enables them to endure within dominant culture, but restricted their study to analyzing college students' interpretations of a single, relatively innocuous song and recording. Frontani (2002) chronicled struggles among the editorial staff of *Rolling Stone* magazine in the late 1960s and early 1970s concerning whether the Beatles truly epitomized countercultural values.

The existence of such textual and ideological slipperiness shifts critical focus to the subjectivities from which Beatles fans negotiate meanings. The standpoint from which fans regard textual personae as romantic fantasy objects, for example, intensifies when the idolized persona(e) and any perceived competitors are not fictional characters but have real-life referents.

One such faction of Beatles fans tends to romanticize and/or homoeroticize relationships among the Beatles, especially between songwriting partners John Lennon and Paul McCartney. A few of these fans compose slash stories envisioning such dalliances, often set in the red light district of Hamburg, Germany, where the prefame Beatles honed their craft. Selection from a potpourri of texts and a desire to safeguard and celebrate masculine homosociality can be seen in the following 2002 RMB post:

> Of the four Beatles, Paul is my favorite. But I really love John too. Actually, I love and respect all of them—and would love to think they all loved each other. [. . .] Paul has said many wonderful things about John. [. . .] So we have one side of the story and not the other. [. . .] Other evidence of the strength of their relationship is seen in photographs. There seems to be quite a few pictures where John actually looks quite affectionately at Paul. [. . .] [R]eading [McCartney's] *Many Years from Now* and *Get Back* and Hunter Davies' books actually provided me with a better understanding of their relationship.

In response, an apparently female discussant wrote,

> I think John and Paul loved each other like brothers. You can fight so viciously with someone you care enough about to get that mad at in the first place. [. . .] When it came to songwriting and making the music happen, they were like one entity. That kind of synergy has deep roots. [. . .]

But I don't doubt that it went way beyond music. They were soulmates (*not* in a sexual way!).

Cognizant of but careful not to lend credence to other fans' eroticization of John and Paul's collaboration, this poster echoes the first in valuing the feminine bond between male personae, thereby conceiving them as one unit and implicitly placing others outside this parasocial (or parasexual) relationship, and the relationship between fan and idols, as interlopers.

For many such fans, one of these others is surely Yoko Ono. Aficionados of Beatles homosociality are positioned to perceive her as a threat, as are those Paul McCartney fans who interpret her actions in boosting Lennon's legacy (and her own) as a vendetta against their idol and as are Lennon admirers such as the one whose words began this essay, whose parasocial or parasexual attachment to the departed icon situates them to regard both Ono and McCartney as trespassers and usurpers. These stances reflect legendary squabbles among factions, particularly since the Internet added worldwide immediacy to the mix, in the sense that each bloc projects its disputes with other fans onto these fans' favored personae. Thus, a Lennon fan might associate a "snarky" remark about Lennon made by a McCartney fan with McCartney himself, a sign of neutrosemy in which the distinction between a "text" and reader-audience proclivities is blurred.

To the extent that they exist among Beatles fans, defenders of Ono are often those Lennon devotees who are unwilling to divorce his apparent allegiances from their own, and who support her out of respect for him even if they cannot commend her artistry. Also, for some fans who seek to promote Lennon as the most creative, most cutting-edge Beatle, Ono's connection to the avant-garde art world emerges as a point of argument. Wiener (1998) has added scholarly weight to such a thesis, lauding Ono's influence on Lennon in favorably distinguishing his post-Beatles work from that of McCartney, Harrison, and Starr. The assertions of several fans participating in a 2000 RMB discussion thread reflect such stances:

> I think it's pretty easy to dump on Yoko here. [. . .] However, her idea [of advancing the medium] is a MAJOR force in modern or post-modern art.

> I see her as John's widow, one that inspired some of John's BEST work. [. . .] I've heard it said that there is no greater insult to John than to hate his wife. [. . .] As far as Yoko's music [. . .] well, I agree with what Mozart wrote in a letter to his father, "Music must first be pleasing to the ear."

What's always been more obvious to me, is what Yoko meant to John. Amazing people can't accept that, when he made it abundantly clear in his songs, interviews (the few I've read, that is), and photographs. I assume her point of view showed him a new & different way of looking at the world. Why anyone would disparage & belittle that is beyond me.

Dissenting opinions emanating from other Lennon and/or Beatles followers included,

Well, if not for the Beatles [. . .] Yoko would not have furthered the medium as far as she did. [. . .] right? People [. . .] didn't know who the hell she was until she was with John Lennon.

Yoko claimed, however, that the Beatles were pedestrian, and that SHE was the revolutionary one!

I think her art is questionable as far as talent is concerned and borders on offensive at times. [. . .] I know that the croissant crowd is going to say otherwise.

Efforts to fix the Beatles' canon and lore so as to establish a single group member as leader and primary creative force have gender-related implications. Strong idolization of a Beatle can engender avowals of his exalted role in hierarchically masculine terms that, in turn, reflect parasocial and/or parasexual subjectivities. Such debate generally centers on Lennon vs. McCartney, with Lennon fans seemingly more proactive in their claims and McCartney enthusiasts adopting a more defensive posture. First, as suggested earlier, Yoko Ono's role in Beatles history can be employed to advance a pro-Lennon case. A 1998 exchange between a Lennon advocate and a McCartney fan illustrates this first perspective and its rejoinder:

Yoko knows more about being married to John Lennon than anyone here will ever know. [. . .] To assume, or even believe, that we know better than she in many of these areas, is too bizarre to comment upon.

Here's the thing. It's not that we think WE know better, but that we think Paul does. . . . Are you saying that since Yoko "is" an expert Paul WAS merely a sideman for John? Because essentially this is what Yoko meant: "[John]

used the Beatles to change the world, with help from the other three, of course."

Second, as with the sarcasm that launched this article, both Ono and McCartney can be regarded as pretenders to the throne, with the significance of either or both disputed in any given discussion. This mirrors the perspective of those fans of *The X-Files'* Agent Mulder who impugned both the program's female hero and Mulder's male replacement (Scodari & Felder 2000). Such a position can be appreciated in the following 2003 debate among several posters in which McCartney's merit as an authentic, nonderivative musician is challenged without specific mention of Ono but, nevertheless, by echoing sentiments often attributed to her:

Paul had more generic, formal music training as a kid. This was because his father was a part-time jazz musician.

Ya know [name of first poster], you really *don't* HAVE to diminish Paul to exalt John every single time.

He [the first poster] must have leadership issues in his childhood [. . .] because being a "leader" is so important to him. [. . .] Maybe [name of first poster] will someday be able to resolve his personal issues and then see John in a more realistic light.

"Formal training?" He [Paul] couldn't read music. What "formal training" did he have?

At the end of the day, I am far more impressed with things like John's: "Happy Christmas—War is Over" classic, "Girl," "Because," "Strawberry Fields Forever" [. . .] on a musical level than I am with [Paul's] "The Long and [W]inding song," "Sgt. Pepper," "Hello Goodbye" [. . .] or "Ebony and Ivory."

That's called "cherry picking" and I can do it too.

Before Lennon's death, McCartney defended his "pop" turf with complete pride. [. . .] Only after Lennon's death, he decided to reinvent his image as the Beatles avant garde guy [. . .] by pirating Lennon's material.

The feminine collectivity said by analysts (Ehrenreich, Hess, & Jacobs 1992; Stark 2003) to appeal to female fans and hegemonically masculine values of hierarchy and competition are evident in the above expression and rebuke of an urge to proclaim the subject of one's devotion to be the most esteemed and skillful male in a company of men. The exchange also illustrates that some fans, in pointing to other fans' apparent need to determine a leader, its roots in childhood experience, and a tendency to "cherry pick" evidence, recognize not only hierarchical thinking but attributes of neutrosemy—namely, "select[ing] given parts while disregarding others" according to one's "existing schemes of perception" (Sandvoss 2005b: 828, 835).

Conclusion

In analyzing the fans of Bruce Springsteen, Cavicchi (1998: 135) remarked, "Indeed, by studying fandom, I have, in many ways, been studying people and who they think they are." Yet, it is easier to recognize overarching themes in Springsteen's oeuvre on which his fans can and often do focus than in the very eclectic back catalogues of the Beatles as group and solo artists. Neutrosemy appears, consequently, even likelier to situate the deliberations of Beatles fans.

This investigation of Beatles cyberfans and their struggles to create and re-create popular mythology unpacks a neutrosemic condition in which a popular artifact framed by dense, distant history, enmeshing a multiplicity of texts, ceases to effectively govern signification. Instead, the predilections of fans are projected onto said artifact.

This is not to say, however, that ideology plays no role in the negotiation of meaning surrounding a neutrosemic cultural object. In this case, we observe gender-related subjectivities that, for the most part, reproduce hegemonic, patriarchal power relations. Female fans' celebration of the Beatles' alleged feminine collectivity, advanced as emancipatory by some commentators (Ehrenreich, Hess, & Jacobs 1992; Stark 2003), here presents as feminine but not feminist. Disillusionment with the fact and perceived manner of the group's breakup is projected onto a single female persona—Yoko Ono. The resulting "Yoko Factor" assumes a misanthropic role for any woman purported to be pivotal in the life of one or more members of a venerated male collective. Parasexual fantasies are also implicated, in that a segment of these fans, as with their counterparts in fandoms devoted to narrative texts, envision homoerotic relationships among male idols so as to preclude and devalue female "rivals." Either way, hegemonic stereotypes of women are invigorated, and the preferences of other fans counterhegemonically interpellated by influential female subjects are dismissed. On the other hand, those whose wont is to distinguish a single male as most accomplished and crucial to the success of a group and/or artifact expose a hierarchical, competitive subjectivity based in hegemonic masculinity.

The significance of this study reaches beyond the specific case, as the parallel tendencies evident in my previous research on science fiction television and its fans indicate (Scodari 2004, 2005; Scodari & Felder 2000). Moreover, there are implications for determining methodology in critical media studies, in that a state of neutrosemy with respect to many a popular artifact can obviate close textual analysis and recommends empirical scrutiny not only of fans' readings but also of their everyday lives, from which subjectivities emerge via myriad variables, play out in social relations, and potentially reveal larger hegemonic operations. Considering the heuristic trajectory of this analysis and my prior work, it would follow to perform an ethnography of fans who migrate from fandom to fandom, adopting a similar, ideological subjectivity within each, as occurs with female enthusiasts of homoerotic, "slash" tales featuring male icons.

As for the computer-mediation of fan culture, this investigation also corroborates others I have performed, in that such mediation magnifies frustration and conflict among fans, thus mitigating potentially liberating rewards. As Interrogate the Internet (1995: 127) warned, cyberspace is not immune to, and is hard-pressed to challenge, the "broader cultural context."

Note

1. IRB regulations for this chapter restrict provision of identifying information for all fan quotation.

4

Copyright Law, Fan Practices, and the Rights of the Author

Rebecca Tushnet

Fans of popular media who write stories about their favorite characters, draw pictures of them, and edit music videos reworking the original sources occasionally stop to think about whether what they are doing is legal under copyright law. Many fans assume that these creations are technically illegal—in copyright-specific terms, infringing—but not harmful to copyright owners and therefore not truly wrong, at least as long as fans keep relatively quiet about their creative practices (e.g., Brook n.d.). Others think that fan creations count as "fair use," and thus as noninfringing, at least as long as no one is making any money from selling them (e.g., Gran 1999). Either way, fans tend to see their legal status as similar to their social status: marginal and, at best, tolerated rather than accepted as a legitimate part of the universe of creators.

Shortly after I found online fandom, I wrote an article on the subject, which is now often cited in fan discussions, and occasionally in discussions with skeptics who find fan fiction immoral and infringing (Tushnet 1997). I concluded that most fan fiction, particularly that disseminated on the Internet, would be classified as fair use under U.S. copyright law.[1] Since then, fan fiction has attracted more attention from "free culture" advocates who are concerned about copyright owners' attempts to channel and control popular culture. Some copyright owners have also taken an aggressive stance against fan creativity, sending enough cease-and-desist letters threatening lawsuits to fan websites that the Electronic Frontier Foundation's anticensorship website, chillingeffects.org, has a section dedicated to fan fiction.

The formal legal landscape is more favorable to fans than it was nine years ago, as courts have been more willing to protect "transformative" unauthorized uses against copyright owners' allegations of infringement. Transformative uses are uses that add new insights or meaning to the original work, often in ways that copyright owners don't like. For instance, a book review that quotes a work in order to criticize it, or a retelling of a story that offers the villain's point of view sympathetically or adds explicit sexual content, can be a transformative fair use. Recent cases emphasize that copyright owners can't suppress unwanted interpretations of their works by asserting copyright. The most notable litigation involved a book by Alice Randall, *The Wind Done Gone*, which retold the story of Margaret Mitchell's *Gone With the Wind* from the perspective of a new character, the mixed-race daughter of a slave and a master. A federal court of appeals held that Randall's book was likely to be a fair use, largely because of the ways in which it criticized the racism of the original (*SunTrust Bank v. Houghton Mifflin Co.*, 268 F.3d 1257 [11th Cir. 2001]).

Legal doctrine is not all that matters, however. When copyright owners aggressively allege infringement, threatening fans with massive civil penalties, fans may naturally choose to shut down or hide their activities rather than stand their ground. The *Wind Done Gone* case involved a publisher-defendant whose monetary interests justified a full-scale defense. No similar cases from the fan community have been litigated.

Despite the absence of cases, fan practices do offer lessons for copyright law. In particular, fan practices provide insights into moral rights, a category of author's rights that is well recognized in Europe but has been far less successful in the United States. Various types of moral rights allow an author (or an author's heirs) to control the attribution of a work, to withdraw it from circulation, or to protect it from mutilation or distortion by unwanted adaptations or alterations. Moral-rights theory posits a deep and unique connection between author and text such that an insult to the text is an assault on the author. Moral rights thus seem inherently in conflict with fans' willingness to take liberties with source texts. Yet not all moral-rights claims are inconsistent with fan interpretive practices. Although protection against *distortion* conflicts with much fan creative activity, moral claims to *attribution* are widely recognized in fandom, and attribution rights are far less disruptive to ordinary interpretive practices than other kinds of moral rights. At the same time, fan practices demonstrate that attribution can come from context, while the law has tended to assume that only explicit credit suffices to give authors proper acknowledgement.

A second, related point illustrated by fan practices of alteration and attribution is that the fair use concept of transformation needs to be better theorized. Courts are more likely to find a use fair when it comments on the underlying work—when it brings out in the open what was present in the subtext or context—and common fan understandings of good characterization are consistent with that idea. If that is so, however, then the original author is partly responsible for later interpretations. Thus, a determination of transformative fair use is often a judgment that the original author did not have full control over the original text—that the text was not received in just the way she wanted it to be received. While this is a perfectly standard result from the perspective of literary theory, the law has yet to make explicit what fans have always known, that meaning cannot be imposed by authors or owners but rather is negotiated among texts, authors, and audiences.

Fan Creativity and Its Dissemination in the Internet Era

Because search engines have made it simple for anyone to find stories and art featuring copyrighted characters behaving in unauthorized ways, fan creations are now easily found by copyright owners, as well as by non-fans. The popular *Television without Pity* website (www.televisionwithoutpity.com), for instance, has many user forums that include discussions of fan creations, and TV producers regularly read the fan forums (though they may not read the fan fiction threads in those forums) (Sella 2002). Someone who enjoys watching a show may thus slide easily into the world of fan-generated content, without any prior screening and without much effort. This accessibility means that a reader's view of Harry Potter may be altered by an unexpected encounter with a sexually explicit or graphically violent story about him, increasing copyright owners' anxieties about losing control of their characters' images.

The Internet, and the widespread deployment of broadband access, have increased accessibility to fan creations in several ways. First, the number of fandoms represented has exploded. When I wrote about fan fiction in 1997, it was possible for a diligent person to attempt a comprehensive listing of fan fiction sites, from *The A-Team* to *Zorro* (Nicholas n.d.). I was amazed by the scope of online fandom—there were hundreds of sites listed. Today, Google lists over 1.2 million results for a search of the phrase "fan fiction." If you're one in a million, you can find a 250-person mailing list of people just like you. Even if your fandom is smaller, there's the yearly Rare Fandoms Challenge to connect the one person who wants to read a story with the one person who wants to write it (*Yuletide FAQ* 2005). Second, the quality of what is available varies wildly. In the bad old days, when fans distributed work via mimeographed or photocopied zines, editors usually reviewed content. Now, anyone can post a story minutes after writing it, before even using a spellchecker. To put it more positively, today anyone can post a story on her own web page even if its content is not popular enough to support a zine. Third and relatedly, the people who participate and their reasons for doing so vary widely—there are twelve-year-olds just having fun sharing stories with their friends and there are published writers practicing their craft for a guaranteed audience. Fourth, now that text-only browsers are a fading memory, the *types* of fan productions are more varied: fan fiction is the phenomenon to which scholars have paid most attention, but fan drawings, photomanipulations, and music videos are also widely available.[2]

This visibility is important. Fans who find fan fiction, art, and videos often feel a sense of validation, and they may feel that their own interests are more normal. Whether this reassurance is a good thing or not depends on what we think of the value of fan creativity. Online support groups for young gays and lesbians in conservative small towns are a lot more appealing than online support groups for girls who are anorexic and want to stay that way. Countervailingly, the fact that these creations are no longer mimeographed and circulated among a circle of friends who already knew one another can create a greater sense of exposure, and a certain fear that the powers that be might crack down if the fans aren't careful. Visibility invites study, and sometimes legal threats, as shown by the section of chillingeffects.org that hosts copies of cease and desist letters received by various fan sites.

Who Gets the Credit?

When I first wrote about fan fiction, disclaimer statements by fan authors were common and prominent: the author would state that she did not own the copyright in the characters and situations, name the entity that did (or the original creator, who is usually not the copyright owner), and sometimes add a request that the copyright owner not sue her. While I have not conducted a scientific survey, my strong impression is that disclaimers are less common today. When they are present, they may not seem all that much like pleas for forbearance. For example, the tone of a disclaimer discussed in Esther Saxey's essay on *Buffy the Vampire Slayer* fan fiction (2002: 208) is casual enough that it is difficult to tell what is being disclaimed: "Joss moves in mysterious ways. But, damn his eyes, he owns the two lovlies [*sic*] and their auras. He created them, made them what they are, and I bow to you."

I think this informality in disclaiming ownership is tied to a sense of greater normalcy. Fewer fan creators are worried that they are somehow doing something wrong, and they are more likely to expect that their readers will understand their basic premises. After four hundred disclaimers, the four hundred and first is likely to seem a lot less important. Another likely related factor is that with the increasing variety and visibility of fan creativity, new fans are not always initiated by more experienced ones. They may not learn the norms of the preexisting community when they start sharing their own stories and art, including norms of explicitly disclaiming ownership.

One question about this normalization of creating and disseminating unauthorized derivative works is whether it is related to "Napsterization" of intellectual property—is it part of a breakdown of respect for intellectual property and authors' interests? I think the answer is generally no. In fact, fans who create derivative works tend to be sensitive to the interests of copyright owners in getting attribution for the original, canonical versions of their characters, offering "subversive respect" (Saxey 2002: 208). Fans acknowledge copyright owners' legitimate economic interests, but maintain that their activities do not hurt and even help revenues from authorized works, by increasing loyalty to and interest in the official versions (Tushnet 1997: 669). A Lockean theory of adding value through labor plays a role in fan concepts of artists' rights, where it does not for music downloaders; few downloaders would claim to have invested labor in any relevant sense when they search for and select music to copy. Fan authors and artists, by contrast, seek recognition from their peers for adding new perspectives and twists to the official texts.

An absence of disclaimers might be thought to show unconcern for proper attribution. But that interpretation would ignore the importance of context: if I say that life is "A tale / Told by an idiot, full of sound and fury / Signifying nothing" without attribution, I don't expect you to think

I made up those words myself. No more do fans expect other fans—their intended audience—to think that they created Superman or Captain Kirk. Indeed, fan creators are usually highly concerned with proper attribution. Plagiarism, that is, verbatim copying without attribution where the copier apparently expects to receive credit for the words or images as if they were her own, is one of the most serious offenses against the fan community, and when discovered the plagiarist is generally publicly excoriated (e.g., Lady Macbeth 2004; *The Lois & Clark Fanfic Archive FAQ* n.d.).

Disclaimers were never intended to inform other fans; it was always fairly easy to tell an authorized *Star Trek* novel from an unauthorized fan creation. Rather, disclaimers were directed at an imagined audience, the copyright owners/original creators—disclaimers often included the request "Please don't sue." At the same time, most fans never thought that the copyright owner would actually read fan fiction in the first place.[3] The ebbing of the disclaimer may indicate that fan creators feel less of a need to justify themselves, but it does not signal a sea change in fans' attitudes towards authors' rights.

Fan practices surrounding attribution may have several lessons for the law. Trademark law is centrally concerned with attribution: its goal is to help consumers easily find the products they want, ensuring that a can of Coke is really made in a Coca-Cola bottling plant. Trademark can also protect against false claims of credit, for example, if a new soda company put Coke in its bottles in order to deceive people into thinking that the new soda was just as good. In the past, authors have used trademark law to assert their rights to get proper credit and to keep their names off unwanted projects, as when Stephen King stopped a movie studio from calling its film *Stephen King's The Lawnmower Man* (*King v. Innovation Books*, 976 F.2d 824 [2d Cir. 1992]).

Recently, the Supreme Court decided *Dastar Corp. v. Twentieth-Century Fox Film Corp.*, 539 U.S. 23 (2003), which involved a videotape series about World War II that was mostly composed of footage from an earlier series; the earlier series was no longer protected by copyright. A lower court had ruled that Dastar, the series producer, had violated federal trademark law by failing to attribute the footage to the (former) copyright owner, Fox, which had purchased the rights from Time-Life. The Supreme Court disagreed with the lower court, holding that using trademark law as a means to enforce attribution rights would threaten infinite battles over the true source of a work's ideas or expressions—some of the footage in the Time-Life series, for example, came from films made by servicemen for the U.S.

government. Justice Antonin Scalia, engaging in unattributed borrowing from Dastar's briefs (Band & Schruers 2005: 15), refused to require later creators to engage in a "search for the source of the Nile and all its tributaries" (*Dastar* 2003: 36).

As fan practices reveal, however, there can be a social consensus within a relevant community about how far to trace and when, providing the limiting principle that Justice Scalia felt was absent.[4] Trademark law often takes account of what consumers think is true about the connection between a trademark owner and a product, such as whether a T-shirt maker needs a trademark owner's permission to put the trademark on a shirt. The law could also look to consumer beliefs in determining whether the absence of credit to a more or less distant creator of a film was misleading. Often, missing credits aren't deceptive. Justice Scalia's uncredited borrowing from a party's legal brief escapes condemnation because the social context of his copying makes him a jurist, not a plagiarist. Similarly, fan creations, even without disclaimers, usually announce their unauthorized status so clearly through context that no deception is likely.

Nonetheless, traditional trademark law presumes that the presence or absence of a name is important. False advertising law is a better model for issues about attribution of texts, because that body of law takes into account whether a particular claim or omission makes a difference to consumers' decisions. An advertisement that does not mention an item's price is not therefore misleading; consumers know that goods have prices. Analogously, in the fan context, lack of explicit attribution may not be a material omission because the audience already knows that the fan is not the original creator. Moreover, fans are unlikely to know or care about the complex web of contracts and law that regulates relations between individual creators and the large corporations that usually own the rights to popular works. Though fans sometimes offer explicit disclaimers that refer to a specific creator or copyright owner, the relevant information is that the fan makes no ownership or authorship claims to the characters and situations.

Fan practices are not unique in their contextualization of the idea of proper credit. Jonathan Band and Matt Schruers point out that historical scholarship has similar norms that distinguish between the attribution required in publications for the in-group and that required in publications for the out-group (2005: 16–17). That is, historians expect that scholarly monographs will credit the work of other historians much more often and more specifically than popular historical works such as textbooks and encyclopedia entries (American Historical Association 2005). Historians, who generally rely on reputation more than money as compensation for their contributions to the sum of knowledge, care more about proper attribution within the profession than outside it.

More generally, audiences value attribution in a different way than they value trademarks for ordinary goods like soda. Authorization, which is what trademark law protects, is different from authorship. Consider a copy of Tom Clancy's *The Hunt for Red October* published by a pirate publisher in India versus an authorized "Tom Clancy's Op Center" novel written by a ghostwriter. Even if the pirate introduced a number of typographical errors into *The Hunt for Red October,* many of us would feel that the pirated book had a stronger claim to being a real Tom Clancy novel than the authorized book.

Fan texts are a third type of creation, neither pure copies of another author's work nor authorized additions to the original. Fan authors are often explicit about their relationship to the real, canonical texts: the fan creations lack the authority of official texts. Because they are not canonical, fan stories can offer a thousand different ways that Mulder and Scully first slept together, none of which contradict the others, or one author can write "Five Things That Never Happened"—five alternate histories for a favorite character, all of which are, as the title states, repudiated by the author (*Because AUs Make Us Happy* n.d.). Lack of authority, which stems from lack of authorization, allows a freedom unavailable to an official canon striving for internal consistency.

Who Gets the Blame?

Related to attribution and to moral rights against distortion is the question of who is *responsible* for the interpretations of the original text provided by fan creators. Texts invite interpretation, and making a text available to the public necessarily cedes some control over it, though copyright law has struggled to deal with this truism. The rhetoric used by courts in transformative use cases suggests that, to be fair, a transformative use must add new material that reflects critically on the original. According to the Supreme Court, a parody, by distorting elements of the original, causes readers to rethink the messages of the original, while a satire merely uses the original to "avoid the drudgery in working up something fresh" and does not challenge readers to reassess the original (*Campbell v. Acuff-*

Rose Music, Inc., 510 U.S. 569, 580 [1994]). Under the definitions used by fair use doctrine, a parody mocks the original specifically, like Weird Al Yankovic's "This Song Is Just Six Words Long," which is set to the tune of "I Got My Mind Set on You." A satire borrows a familiar work to get its audience's attention and to make fun of something other than the original, like a satirical song using a popular tune to lambaste a politician. Although both parody and satire require the addition of creative labor to change a work into a caricature of itself, a parody is more likely to succeed on a fair use defense than a satire is, because the parody has a better reason to copy from the original.

Using the parody/satire division as a guide, courts find that a legitimate transformation exists when the new work makes overt that which was present in the original text covertly (at least as some readers saw it): transformative fair uses make subtext text. In two important parody cases involving the Barbie doll, for example, Mattel's attempts to protect its doll's image by using copyright law were thwarted by courts that found that overtly sexualizing Barbie constituted commentary on Barbie *because Barbie already had sexual connotations* (*Mattel, Inc. v. Walking Mountain Productions*, 353 F.3d 792 [9th Cir. 2003]; *Mattel, Inc. v. Pitt*, 229 F. Supp. 2d 315 [S.D.N.Y. 2002]). Another court used similar reasoning to reject Mattel's trademark claims against Aqua's popular novelty song "Barbie Girl" (*Mattel, Inc. v. MCA Records, Inc.*, 296 F.3d 894 [9th Cir. 2002]).

Even more fascinating is the discussion in the *Wind Done Gone* case about the relevance of homosexuality and miscegenation to fair use. The Mitchell estate didn't want *Gone with the Wind* to be associated with such controversial topics. The Eleventh Circuit Court of Appeals held that Alice Randall's insertion of homosexuality, in the form of a gay Ashley Wilkes, into the world of *Gone with the Wind* was an important part of what made her book transformative. The court quoted *Gone with the Wind*'s description of the Wilkes family as artistic and "queer" (*SunTrust* 2001: 1270 n. 26), a term already widely used to describe homosexuals when Mitchell wrote the novel (*Dictionary of American Slang* 1967: 415). (The similarities to slash fan fiction, which picks up on homoerotic elements in the original texts, are evident.)

In other words, the court held that transformation consists of making clear or exaggerated what was opaque or limited in the original text.[5] As a result, the legal defense of parodies and other literary transformations protects critics as creators in their own right only when they draw deeply from a preexisting well. Because courts require a second-comer to criticize an element in the text rather than use the text to criticize something else—the parody/satire distinction—the fair use test asks whether the critic has found something in the original or has simply added unrelated content to it. As applied to fan creations, then, the test would find transformation if the new work was far enough from the original, but not too far.

A court's determination that a work is critically transformative is therefore also a ruling that the original author is partly responsible for the content of the critical work, often content the author finds extremely objectionable. There is, however, tension between courts' requirement that a tranformative fair user must bring some subtext to light and their simultaneous celebration of the transformative fair user as an original creator in her own right. If adding new material were all that was required for transformative fair use, as many legal theorists believe it should be, then the parody/satire distinction would be unnecessary. The persistence of the parody/satire divide indicates that courts are concerned with giving proper credit—or proper blame—to authors whose works inspire others to react by altering the original: if there is no real connection between an original and an unauthorized transformation, then it isn't fair, and isn't fair use, to connect the author with the new work. But if there is a connection, then the author's disagreement with or distaste for an interpretation isn't a justification for suppressing it.

Within fandom, the question of proper attribution often comes up as a question of characterization. Most fan creators are concerned to some extent with making the characters they use recognizable as related to the official versions. If they show Captain Kirk and Mister Spock having a sexual relationship, they want readers to see them as extensions of the canonical characters, not as two random men who happen to have the names "Kirk" and "Spock." Different readers may disagree about whether proper characterization has been achieved, but the goal itself is common, if not universal. Fans, like courts analyzing transformative fair uses, see their work as inextricably related to the source texts, bringing meaning out as much as they are putting meaning in.

Attribution and Moral Rights

Lawyers have begun to warn copyright owners that fans make texts and that these texts must be taken account of in any strategy for managing relationships with fans. Reciprocally, fans often have at least vague ideas about how copyright law would apply to their activities. Concepts of proper attribution and credit play a major role in fan creators' theories of intellectual property (Tushnet 1997: 678–80). The practices of a community may provide attribution where it is not apparent on the face of the text, and the connections between original and fan creations are complex, with credit properly going in part to the original author and in part to the fan.

The doctrine of transformative fair use has difficulty with attribution when it ascribes creative labor to critics of a work who are restating what they see in the original. The more successfully a work is transformed in the technical legal sense, the more we are likely to be able to see that the evidence supporting the transformation was present all along in the original. The legal concept of transformative use denies the author the authority to control all interpretations of his text, not just practically but conceptually. This is in obvious tension with moral rights against distortion, and many legal scholars thus conclude that moral rights don't fit into the American copyright system. But, as fan practices demonstrate, not all moral rights are the same: attribution, though it may not be explicit, can and should be given to creators even if total control is denied them.

By contrast, moral rights against distortion appear even more ill suited to the realities of creativity once we accept that criticism, mockery, and other uncomfortable transformations draw on material present in the original works. What an author intends to produce and what others understand her to have produced often diverge. Fan practices that emphasize the indelible connections between originals and unauthorized creative responses can thus help illuminate the meaning and implications of copyright, just as copyright's fair use doctrine gives fans reasons why their unauthorized creations are neither unlawful nor immoral.

Notes

1. My focus has been on U.S. law, even though media fandom is a global phenomenon, because U.S. law is unusually open-ended, whereas many other countries have limited exceptions to copyright for which fan creations are less likely to qualify, and also because U.S. copyright owners, like many other U.S. entities, are relatively swift to threaten lawsuits when they perceive an interference with their rights.

2. While I concluded in my article on the topic that fan fiction was generally fair use, I am not as confident about all fan creativity. In particular, the use of

music in fan music videos is often hard to defend as transformative. Though editing footage to music often works as insightful commentary on the original movie or TV show, the music usually serves its ordinary function and doesn't gain new meaning, at least not in the way that a court is likely to accept as transformative for purposes of the fair use test.

3. Disclaimers in fan fiction are something like the "mouseprint" in ads, which is not really for consumers, who tend to skim over it, but works as a signal to regulators and competitors that the advertiser is aware of various legal requirements.

4. As Francesca Coppa pointed out to me, the social consensus about credit might be morally questionable, as when white performers take credit for popularizing African-American forms of music, and a consensus might also change over time as political and social trends lead to different origin stories. This is another reason why using law to enforce credit-tracing norms might not be a good idea.

5. Miscegenation, the other taboo topic, is even more deeply buried in *Gone with the Wind*. One might say that, in a slave society, miscegenation is inevitably part of the context.

Part II

Beyond Pop Culture
Fandom from News to High Culture

5

The News

You Gotta Love It

Jonathan Gray

This chapter began while I was conducting interviews with *Simpsons* viewers about parody and satire (see Gray 2006). While discussing *The Simpons'* news parody, one of my interviewees talked at length about her love for politics and the news. She watched, by her estimate, three to four hours each day of Canadian parliamentary access television, and was a voracious news consumer. Yet quite impassionedly, and with more than just Canadian humility, she insisted that a great deal of this was entertainment for her:

> Don't get me wrong: I do know every MP in Canada, and when it's an election, I'll tell you their opponents too. I can tell you what they believe, how well they debate, and how ugly or handsome they are. But I don't just watch "to be a good citizen" and do my "Canadian duty" [laughs]. Really, I, it's entertainment. I love it. I really *love* it. It's my soap opera. There are, are villains, and good guys, you can cheer some on, and get involved. If I did all this just to vote, that would be excessive. I watch because it amuses me.

At the time, her comments were off-topic, so I rushed her along. But I remained fascinated by what was clearly a news *fan,* and by someone so impressively involved in Canadian polity, yet who talked of it in very un-Habermasian ways. This chapter marks a return to the site of news fandom, as I explore the love and passion for a genre that is given plenty of academic consideration, but rarely if ever as a fan object. "Serious" news and fandom are typically described with wholly different theoretical tool kits, but here I examine their points of contact to suggest a more profound marriage among news, politics, and fandom than many would deem either existent or appropriate.

To perform such a marriage between the news and an idea of fandom may seem either unholy or odd to some readers. Certainly, there is much established work to suggest that they are fundamentally different. Thomas Patterson defines what in America is frequently called "hard news" (or what others might call "real" or "political" news) as "coverage of breaking events involving top leaders, major issues, or significant disruptions in the routines of daily life, such as earthquakes or airline disasters. Information about these events is presumably important to citizens' ability to understand and respond to the world of public affairs" (2000: 3). Amid the many concerns regarding contemporary infotainment and dumbed-down, "soft" journalism (e.g., Kerbel 2000; Patterson 2000; Postman & Powers 1992), and amid endless accusations of news bias, a very clear notion of news appears. News should, so goes the rationale, offer objective facts and reporting on current events, and other information relevant to the practice of citizenship, hailing its viewers as intelligent, cerebral individuals in search of rational debate and thought. Ingrained in the First Amendment of the United States Constitution and in its protection of the press is the reflection that the free flow of information and opinions is vital to democratic citizenship and participation in civic society, and hence that the news acts as the very doorway to the public sphere, or agora. Indeed, Habermas's notion of the public sphere (1989)[1] is perhaps the most academically invoked ideal for news and media practice. Particularly important to this ideal is Habermas's call for *rational* discourse: borrowing from a long line of post-Enlightenment thinking (see Marcus 2002), Habermas believed in the emotional as irrational, and thus in the need to separate heart from mind in this public sphere. Especially in the wake of Lippman (1922) and others' fear of propaganda and emotional appeals polluting the news and, through it, democratic society, entertainment and the emotional have been seen as incommensurate with hard news, and as poisonous to its realm.

In contrast to the news as a supposedly somber, rational, informational genre would seem to lie the very concept of fans. By definition, fans have an avid like or love for something. Hills (2002) plumbs psychological depths to offer the elaborated idea that fans are those who have made of their beloved text a transitional object, in Winnicott's terms (1974), imbuing it with special personal and/or communal symbolic value, and Hills, along with many others (e.g., Brooker 2002; Harrington & Bielby 1995; Jenkins 1992; Lewis 1992), has shown how fandom is a site of intense pleasure and often of play. In other words, fans have a remarkably emotional relationship to their beloved text. But Habermas (1989) documented the degree to which emotion, and particularly emotive forms of political communication, refeudalizes the public sphere, acting as an obstacle to a meaningful and active deliberative democracy in which all citizens are open to engage with all contributions to the public sphere. Hard news and fandom, then, would seem to be at loggerheads, as any ideal news program (ideally and supposedly the preeminent genre of political communication) would act as a paragon of (masculine) rationality, while the play, emotions, and entertainment of fandom mark it and the objects of fandom definitively as the (supposedly) emotional, feminine, bodily, and less civilizing.

But what about news fans? By news fans, I do not mean merely those who consume a lot of news, but those who construct fan-like relationships to certain news programs or texts, characters, and journalists, and those who speak of and relate to the news in fan-like ways. Furthermore, where infotainment detractors may well *expect* to see fan cultures surround soft news, here I am interested only in fans of hard news—congress or parliamentary access channels, and reports on stories of obvious and direct civic importance.[2] In other words, what happens with and what can we learn from instances when the rational, uplifting, cerebral content of hard news encounters the emotion, enthusiasm, and excitement of fans?

As should be clear by now, I ultimately intend to suggest a confusion and a thorough mixing of rationality and emotion. But before we see this blurring in action, it is important to set the stage by beginning a deconstruction of the binaries between news and fandom, between elite ideals for news consumption and elite ideas of how the (fan) masses consume, and between rationality and emotion.

The Emotional News Consumer

The notion that the news does or should serve primarily an informational purpose has been easier to sustain when many studies of the news have focused either on its production or on idealized discussion of what the news *should* do. When we turn to audience theorists and researchers, though, we encounter many different uses for the news. In particular,

Roger Silverstone discusses television's, and especially television news', role as a transitional object that creates for its viewers a sense of ontological security. The news, he notes, "holds pride of place as the genre in which it is possible to see most clearly the dialectical articulation of anxiety and security—and the criterion of trust—which overdetermines television as a transitional object, particularly for adult viewers" (1994: 16). The news tells us of how horrific the world is, but then controls this chaos with its perky newscasters, highly polished look, human interest stories, and the relaxed banter with weather and sports reporters; after suggesting that the world might fall apart, it rocks us to sleep at night, assuring us that everything will be okay, dear. In this way, Silverstone suggests, the news has become one of the primary coping mechanisms for living in a world replete with risk and fear.

Meanwhile, both Silverstone (1994) and Morley (2000) examine the news' role in managing our sense of home and belonging. As a prime instance of what Hartley calls television as "cross-demographic communication" (1999), television news brings all sorts of ideas, people, and places across the threshold of our front doorstep, telling us of the world "out there." By doing so, the news, and our use of it, becomes a key site for the negotiation not only of the idea of the family home but also of neighborhood and national home (Morley 2000). Hence, television news acts as a command center for many projects of identity and personal security that are deeply emotional, and not at all coldly "rational," and yet that allow us to place ourselves in our house, neighborhood, nation, and world. Indeed, it is particularly noteworthy that both Silverstone and Hills draw from the same theoretical well—that of Winnicott's object-relations theory (1974)—to explain, respectively, the news and fandom.

The likelihood that news reception and fan reception come from and draw on similar mental faculties is given further support by the recent neuro-political science of George Marcus (Marcus 2002; Marcus, Neuman, & MacKuen 2000). Marcus takes aim at the age-old belief in the separation of mind and heart, and at political and media theorists' concern that the heart, passions, and emotion might invade the rational deliberative zone that is the mind. Drawing from Lakoff and Johnson's work on the power of metaphors (1980), he shows the dangers of conceiving of heart and mind as distinct, independent, and antagonistic, and instead he consults neuroscience to paint a very different picture. Rational thought, he proves scientifically, *requires* emotions; indeed, neuroscience shows that much of our rational decision making is performed by our brain's emotional center, or is at the very least made wholly possible by our brain's emotional faculties. Thus, Marcus rebukes the common assertion that democracy is in danger, with entertainment and emotional appeal solely trivializing serious issues; rather, he argues, "rationality is a special set of abilities that are recruited by the emotion systems in the brain to enable us to adapt to the challenges that daily confront us" (2002: 7), and, therefore, "emotion is required to invoke reason and to enable reason's conclusions to be enacted" (2002: 31). Emotion, after all, is what makes us care to think rationally in the first place, and it is emotion that drives us to work for change or for conservation. Emotion lets us deliberate, and then encourages us to act on that deliberation. Consequently, Marcus calls for "a sentimental citizen" (2002), gifted with "affective intelligence" (Marcus, Neuman, & MacKuen 2000), and he flips common assumptions to suggest that a wholly "rational," "cerebral" electorate is one unfit to govern.

Drawing on the ideas of Marcus and others, Liesbet Van Zoonen (2005) examines how fan cultures display numerous traits of an ideal citizenship. Van Zoonen realizes the boldness of this idea, given many critics' belief that, "Supposedly, entertainment brings audiences consisting of fans into being, whereas politics produces publics composed of citizens. Audiences and publics, fans and citizens, are thus constructed as involving radically different social formations and identities" (2005: 56). But she then observes numerous close parallels between fans and the ideal citizens of a deliberative democracy. First, she notes that "fan groups are social formations that are structurally equivalent to political constituencies" (2005: 58), groups united by a shared sense of values and a proclivity and willingness to act upon those values to some degree. Therefore, she observes an "equivalence of fan practices and political practices" (2005: 63), which leads her to ask provocatively, "Maybe, then, the only difference between fans and citizens is located in the different subjectivities on which they seem based; affective relations in the case of fans, cognitive processes in the case of citizens. Is this difference bona fide, though?" (2005: 63).

Van Zoonen is careful not to suggest a complete equivalence between fans and (ideal) citizens, but nevertheless denies the tenuous distinction as being based on affectivity rather than cognitive, rational thinking. She is also careful not to suggest that fan engagement could in any way be seen as a desirable *alternative* to political involvement; certainly, while some fan cultures are driven by deeply political motives, we must avoid seeing, for instance, a campaign to reinstate a favorite love interest on a television show as on a par with a presidential campaign. However, Van Zoonen sees

[margin annotation: More to this association]

great potential in fan cultures and their structuring logic for modeling meaningful citizenship. (Fandom, she notes, "is built on psychological mechanisms that are relevant to political involvement: these are concerned with the realm of fantasy and imagination on the one hand, and with emotional processes on the other") (2005: 64). Fantasy, and a *desire* for change, along with the emotional investment required to work towards it, is a prerequisite to any and all political movements. Van Zoonen points to political rallies and conventions as some of the more obviously fan-like events in civic life, and realizes the need for such fan-like elements to motor both politics and citizens.

Clearly, then, we can see how politics and the news overlap with fan behavior and practice in many ways. Van Zoonen, Marcus, Morley, and Silverstone all show not only how the political is deeply affective and how it succeeds in part by offering emotional appeal but also how it must matter to the individual and must be consumed emotively to some degree if it is to become meaningful to its viewers. Hence, these writers suggest that fandom and political citizenship and an ideal consumption of the news are by no means foreign to each other. Meanwhile, we could also consult the wealth of fan studies literature to point out how highly literate, rational, and cerebral many fans are. If, though, as Van Zoonen argues, fandom offers models for political citizenship, this would seem to suggest that fans of the news itself might prove a particularly rich example of fandom and the political uniting to improve citizenship.

News Fandom: Ever the Twain Shall Meet

The beginning of November 2005 brought plenty of serious news to American readers and viewers. Vice President Dick Cheney's chief of staff, "Scooter" Libby, had been charged with leaking classified information; Hurricane Wilma had hit Florida; an earthquake in Pakistan had killed thousands; Harriet Miers had withdrawn her nomination for the U.S. Supreme Court, quickly followed by President Bush's nomination of Samuel Alito; Asian bird flu fears were arising; and civil rights hero Rosa Parks had died. Thus, multiple issues ripe for discussion were on the table, ranging from the state of civil rights today to governmental response to natural disasters to the future balance of power in the Supreme Court. During a two-week span at the end of October and beginning of November, I explored several sites for the discussion of this news and the reporting of it. I consulted all of the news threads on *Television without Pity* (www.televisionwithoutpity.com), a site known for fan discussion of all things televisual, and I monitored three of the most popular news and politics blogs that allow room for discussion, one typically liberal—*Daily Kos* (www.dailykos.com)—and two typically conservative—*Right Wing News* (www.rightwingnews.com) and *Little Green Footballs* (www.littlegreenfootballs.com). I read through pages upon pages of commentary to see how this news was discussed both by people who identified themselves as fans of a particular news program and by posters whose frequency of visits and posts to a particular news thread, combined with the ways in which they discussed the news, coded them as either fans or at least fan-like.

This methodology was not intended to be wholly scientific; rather, it, like this chapter, is rudimentary and exploratory. In a cyberspace and blogosphere as vast as the Internet provides, accurate sampling is impossible, as can be the act of ascertaining accurate poster demographics upon which such sampling could be based. Ultimately, my methods represent an attempt to take a brief peek at how professed or obvious fans of the news talk about the news; deeper ethnography could undoubtedly reveal more, and I hope others take me up on this challenge for future work. Meanwhile, here I conflate individuals with different objects of fandom, ranging from a certain presenter to a party to a news program itself. Important differences exist among these subgroups, but, with very few exceptions, these posters only have access to these political "realities" through the textualized form of the news. Hence, just as, for instance, two fans, one of a character on a reality show and one of the show itself, both experience their object of fandom through reality television, and thus could be described as reality television fans, so too can these various subgroups be talked of here generically as news fans.

Perhaps most immediately surprising was the remarkable level of *play* with the news and its newscasters exhibited by these posters, even while they made serious points. For instance, a poster on *Daily Kos* (hereafter *DK*) dubbed prime-time cable-news debate-program host Chris Matthews "Tweety" in his/her post about press reaction to the alleged Libby leak, entitled "Tweety is schizophrenic":

> One day he's all over the story, the next day Bush reacts with "nobility" to Libby's resignation. Yeah, it's so noble to let a perjurious, leaking aide resign instead of firing him, while keeping another perjurious leaking aide stay on the job. Maybe Tweety takes his meds for some shows and not others?

Or, on *Television without Pity* (hereafter *TwoP*), after opening a post by asking, "Does [prime-time cable-news-journal host] Keith Olbermann have no friends? Does his assistant secretly hate him? Is his producer blind? Because the man's clothes? They BLIND me," and continuing with fashion advice, a poster concludes by adding, "Also? I expected everyone else to report the standard Rosa Parks the tired seamstress story, but I expected more of Olbermann, to report the fact that Parks was a wonderful activist and organizer way before she even got on the bus." Another poster, on *Little Green Footballs* (hereafter *LGF*), discussing the Democrats' call for a closed Senate to debate intelligence that led to the invasion of Iraq, states, "Yes, our intelligence stunk at the start of the war, I'm entirely in favor of investigating it until the cows come home. And it may just force a more open and honest accounting by Dubya of why we went in and why we now see additional justifications," before adding, "But geesh, the grandstanding ignorant sluts of the Democratic rump, unbefreakinglievable."

What we see in all three above-quoted remarks is an interesting mix of deliberative, "rational" opinion, and emotive, playful elements far more fan-like (or, in the last case, anti-fan-like) by nature. At one moment, for instance, Olbermann's fashion sense is being discussed, then his coverage of Rosa Park's death, with a point that addresses both the content and form of the news article in a smart, "rational" manner. Certainly, quotations like these abounded, to the point of being standard. Another poster at *DK*, for instance, addresses other posters' comments that Bush has effectively ended the marriage between liberalism and Catholicism in America:

> My spouse and I attend regularly, we teach catechism, and Bush can kiss my rosy, red butt. Go see Pax Christi and National Catholic Reporter, then read Fr. Andrew Greeley and Sr. Joan Chittister, and you'll find reports of the death of liberals in the Catholic church are greatly exaggerated.

Significant evidence is marshaled to support the poster's view, and he shares this with others, contributing to the wealth of this public sphere, but his summation of his regard for President Bush and his conservatism takes the emotive form of "Bush can kiss my rosy, red butt." Or, one final example of this overlapping of emotionalism and rationality comes from a highly detailed attack on irascible right-wing ideologue and debate show host Bill O'Reilly's reporting of illegal aliens. The *TwoP* poster engages in close analysis of O'Reilly's words to note that he denies ever describing illegal aliens as "biological weapons." He swears to his audience that he "never said anything like that," and claims to be the victim of "smear merchants." And, yes, technically, he never said the words "biological weapons." However, a caller on his show did use those words. The charming caller described illegal aliens as biological weapons because of the alleged diseases they carry, and likened them to the 9/11 terrorist attacks. And Bill responded by agreeing with the caller, saying, "I think you could probably make an absolutely airtight case that more than 3,000 Americans have been either killed or injured, based upon the 11 million illegals who are here." And yet he cries that he is the victim of malicious lies.

However, in opening the post, the writer responds to an ongoing discussion about O'Reilly's views on spanking children as a punishment by opining, "O'Reilly's spanking fetish confirms my suspicion that he's secretly an ass freak."

Name calling such as this is rampant, as, for instance, liberal discussion on DK often reverts to describing conservatives as "wingnuts" and painting crude caricatures of uneducated rednecks, while conservative discussion on *LGF* and *Right Wing News* (hereafter *RWN*) lashes out at the "moonbats" who, as one poster at *RWN* states, "hate America" and "have no ideas for the future [and] no ideas for the nation." Particularly in such crude, childish forms, it would be easy to point to such statements as prime examples of where emotions destroy rationality, and indeed if one standard is to mix rational discussion with emotional play, sadly another is to merely curse and rage. Some such posts should hardly be looked to as helping deliberative democracy. When this same poster at *RWN*, for instance, chides liberals for possessing ideas that have already "failed in the Soviet Union," the laughable equation of Soviet communism to the Democratic Party platform is worrying. This therefore illustrates a dire risk of fannish involvement with the news, for fans can at times adopt preformulated reading positions that only seek to find reaffirmation of already held beliefs (see Johnson in this volume; Sandvoss 2005a), which when applied to news consumption and political debate stands to harm the vitality of the public sphere. Certainly, the bulk of one-line posts that read, as does one at *DK*, "dumb-ass Republican hicks" in response to breaking news could hardly be seen as contributing greatly to public political discourse.

However, in the many instances when such emotional outburst and/or play *is* mixed with rational, thoughtful discussion, we should not be so quick to write off the emotional. One could, perhaps, see the emotional here as the assumed pass-key to community discussion—a display of "hip factor" to show that one belongs. But in many other ways, these sites are not fan communities in a traditional sense—there is little friendly banter, off-topic asides about struggles in life, supportive advice (see Bird 2003), or, as *TwoP* calls them, "meet markets." The dictates of a political discussion board, as is shown, do not preclude emotionalism, but they clearly limit it. Thus, it seems unlikely that posters would feel the need to offer elaborated emotional pass-keys. Or, alternatively, we could see the emotional as variously motivating the commentary, or adding a human element to an otherwise cold, uninviting discussion. After all, it is in these emotive moments that the poster's feelings are most evident, and hence they are the moments when we are invited to connect to the comment as something human, something more than disembodied typeface on our computer screen. They are moments that color and code the commentary as felt and as lived, and hence that call to us as readers. As much fan theory shows, the fan's emotional play with texts frequently gives life and meaning to those texts—the Velveteen Rabbit principle that Jenkins discusses (1992: 50). While we must avoid thinking that *only* fans turn texts into rich symbolic products (see Gray 2003), fandom and fan-like feelings are a key mode by which many viewers can approach the world's saturation with texts, and assign personal or communal meaning and value to any given text. In reading these news fans' discussion of topics, I was watching a similar process at work, whereby the emotional investment with the story or newscaster framed and made possible the ensuing rational debate.

Above, I have quoted numerous examples of motivation to post out of anger or disappointment (themselves both key emotions in the fan's repertoire), but, amusingly, many newscasters attracted love and adoration too. CNN reporter Anderson Cooper proved particularly popular with *TwoP* posters, as amid thoughtful discussion regarding his previous on-the-spot reporting on Hurricane Katrina's aftermath, some posters worried about why he was currently off the air, with one joking, "He's at my house getting hot baths and massages. No more hurricanes for my man!" Keith Olbermann also had his share of fans, with the previously quoted discussion of his clothes coming in the middle of numerous *TwoP* posts expressing significant admiration for the man, yet playful concern for his wardrobe, hair, and even his "womanly hips." NBC reporter Brian Williams, Tim Russert (host of CBS's famed political interview program, *Meet the Press*), and Bill O'Reilly all had vocal fans too. However, while I am left with only their postings to judge from, the expressed basis of fandom was not merely looks or sense of humor, but reporting vigilance. Cooper's fans talked glowingly of how informative and challenging his reports from New Orleans had been, as did Williams's fans. O'Reilly's felt his combative style broke through many guests' rehearsed veneer, thus offering more of the story. Olbermann's fans praised his sly wit and ability to see other, less-remarked-upon sides of various issues. And Russert's fans felt his economy of reporting gave them, as one poster observed, "more news and more ideas per minute than many of the other schleps out there." Therefore, rather than fantasies of hot baths with Cooper or of making over Olbermann being on the opposite end of a scale from attending carefully to what the newsmen were reporting, in many cases, the news fans showed the ability for fan-like engagement and civic duty to work together.

Furthermore, while these fans were hardly writing Russert fanfic or arranging O'Reilly cons, their fandom proved productive in its own ways. To begin with, in a deliberative democracy, to post one's political beliefs and reactions to news stories and the perceived quality or reporting (or lack thereof), and to enter into political dialogue with others, is already productive, and contributive to civic discourse. Thus, their mere presence online is often automatically productive, and a key reason behind many excited appraisals of the blogosphere's potential to re-energize politics (e.g., Gillmor 2003). But beyond posting, several posters share their letters either to news stations, newscasters, or politicians. Also, one *DK* poster, whose posts frequently appeared on the site, suggesting an active news viewership, included the transcript of a phone call he made to conservative pundit Sean Hannity's talk radio program. Other entries at the blogs, too, showed remarkable footwork, as, for example, one *DK* poster compiled a list of all one hundred senators' reactions to Harriet Miers, and another *RWN* poster offered a painstaking line-by-line refutation of an excerpted article from *DK*. Finally, many posters write of off-line political activity, making it clear that these websites had by no means become virtual agoras far removed from flesh-and-bone reality.[3]

Taking the News to Heart

While I hesitate to offer any grand conclusions based on a limited study, the activities of these news fans are nevertheless revealing. First of all, we (and political communication scholars in particular) must acknowledge that news fans exist, and in significant numbers; thus, clearly, entertainment, fiction, and supposedly "low" culture are not alone in inspiring such audiences. Beyond mere existence, though, remains the issue of the nature and meaning of their activity. Most democratic political theorists dream of an electorate who continually update themselves with news and opinions, who discuss this news and these opinions with others, and who take politics and policy seriously. Here, I found many such individuals. And yet far from being somber, rational conversationalists, these individuals were emotionally involved, exhibiting many of the emotive, playful qualities of fandom in the ways in which they consumed, processed, and discussed the news. Many were savvy viewers, keen to critically evaluate, and yet they also cared, ranted, had fun, and got angry. Ultimately, though, rather than read this as an indictment of these viewers, I pose that we instead indict the unrealistic and unhelpful desire for a politics without emotion. Habermas is still right to point us towards some of the dangers of emotive citizenship, but opening the door to emotion does not necessitate *giving up* on rationality. *Of course* we still require some balance, and so we would be foolish to believe that either all emotions or all political fandoms are necessarily a good to be cherished. As Sandvoss (2005a) points out, fans can at times overload a text with meaning, rendering it "neutrosemic"—a potentially worrying development if the fan object is a political party or the nightly news. Similarly, a fan polity could restrict the free flow of ideas if fans became as rigidly sure of their facts and politics as, say, a Yankees fan is sure of his team's divine superiority. Finally, too, the excesses of Fox News's emotive and heavily biased format illustrate the dangers of incorporating too much emotion on the *production* end. Skeptics of emotion in politics, in other words, still have much to justifiably concern them. But at the same time, an absolute rationality would leave no room for caring, for personal or communal drive, nor for belief, engagement, or enjoyment, all of which are basic requirements for an active electorate.

Such emotions risk overlooking important realities, but this is where, why, and how fandom can help the news. With so many texts out there, fandom allows us to chart paths of value and meaning through this semiotic wilderness, and becomes a way of coping, a way of being able to move forward. While this is true of fandom and entertainment and/or fiction, it is also true of fandom, politics, and the news, for we also need paths through the wilderness of facts, policies, movements, issues, and spin before us. Some such paths are unhealthy, but perhaps it is by examining them in light of fan engagement that analysts will find better ways to account for them, and, ultimately, to challenge them. However, while both fears of the emotional and reverence for the rational are age-old, and at times justified, it is often emotions—and fandom, as a particular nexus of emotions—that point us forward, not just backward. This long-standing distrust of emotions and enjoyment is partially behind the pathologization and disapproval of fandom, but perhaps then by seeing fandom at times in, behind, allowing, and *driving* rationality, we might learn better to value not only emotions in politics but also fandom more generally, not as a magic tonic for citizenship—for that it is not—but as a constitutive element of it, for worse and for better. ⌐

Notes

1. Dahlgren neatly defines the public sphere as "a space—a discursive, institutional, topographical space—where people in their roles as citizens have access to what can be metaphorically called societal dialogues, which deal with questions of common concern: in other words, with politics in the broad sense" (1995: 9).

2. I do not wish to brand other news as unimportant, however, for as Glynn (2000) and Hartley (1999) have argued, "soft" or tabloid news also offers its viewers political, meaningful commentary.

3. More deviously, leading on from both McKee's and Hills's arguments in this volume regarding fan-academic practice, we might even pose that our own universities' media and journalism departments contain some of the most active news fans of all.

6

The Fans of Cultural Theory

Alan McKee

The Fans of Theory

In common usage, the word "theory" refers to a "scheme or system of ideas or statements held as an explanation or account of a group of facts or phenomena" (OED). But in the humanities, the word "theory" (sometimes capitalized to "Theory") has a particular usage. For humanities academics (particularly in cultural studies, philosophy, and literary studies), "Theory" is the term used to describe a subset of philosophical writings—those that pay attention to questions of representation and culture, and particularly those written by the philosophers of continental Europe. Among the most influential "Theorists" are Karl Marx, Sigmund Freud, Gayatri Spivak, Edward Said, Homi Bhabha, Julia Kristeva, Judith Butler, Jacques Lacan, Theodor Adorno, Antonio Gramsci, Louis Althusser, Michel Foucault, Jacques Derrida, Gilles Deleuze, Felix Guattari, Slavoj Žižek, Jean Baudrillard, Paul Virilio, Jürgen Habermas, Michael Hardt, and Antonio Negri.

Many academics in the humanities—as well as other intellectuals and artists—use Theory in their work. Some go further, and enjoy reading Theory for the pleasure it gives them. And others go further still—not only using Theory and reading it for pleasure, but even integrating it into their everyday lives and identities (calling themselves by titles such as "Foucauldians" or "Marxists"), spending large amounts of time and money on collecting the books and publications of Theorists, and traveling around the world to attend meetings with other people who feel the same way. It is these "Theory fans" who are the focus of this chapter.

The Activity of Theory Fans

In some ways, Theory fans are typical cultural consumers: they buy books and journals (or borrow copies bought by libraries), and read these for pleasure. But in other ways, Theory fans—like other groups of fans—are an atypical audience. They do not just consume Theory passively. Indeed, in some ways they are remarkably active. I would distinguish three key ways in which we can describe the consumption practices of Theory fans as being "active." First, Theory fans have a passion for Theory that goes beyond a passive acceptance of whatever they are given by publishers and conference organizers. They actively seek out more work by their favorite authors and build strong emotional relationships with it. While some consumers read Theory for purely utilitarian, work-related purposes (for example, to complete a Ph.D., prepare a lecture, or write an article that will be useful on their c.v.), Theory fans will also read it for pleasure. In order to illustrate this point, let me quote some fan comments.

I surveyed a group of Theory fans on the email list of the Cultural Studies Association of Australasia in 2003 and 2005.[1] One of the questions I asked was whether they read Theory for pleasure as well as for work. Of the fourteen respondents, all stated that this is indeed the case. As one fan put it, "Yes. It can feel wickedly unproductive." Another says, "Yes, it is *always* a pleasure," while a third reads Theory "even at bedtime." One described his fandom of Walter Benjamin as "a private passion and I can also make a living teaching and writing about his ideas."

The fans describe a heady mix of emotional pleasures from consuming Theory. One Theory fan describes her emotional involvement with the work of Adorno: "Determination in the face of the weight of the text, like climbing. Pain at the lyric beauty of some lines. Shame that I will never be so clever"; for another, his consumption of the work of Australian philosopher Muecke "fill[s] me" with "both exhilaration and sadness." A Foucault fan notes that his work gives her "an emotional feeling [. . .] of challenge, satisfaction but, best of all, excitement." Another notes that "Foucault always cheers me up [. . .] I get very happy and stimulated, sometimes with a pleasurably manic edge." A Barthes fan claims that "fundamentally it [reading Barthes's writing] makes me happy. Without fail." Some fans even go so far as to claim the ultimate emotional relationship with Theory, writing "I love Foucault," or "I love [Benjamin]." Trinh Minh Ha inspires "love and anger" from her fans; and another Theory fan talks in similar terms as she notes of her fanship of Kristeva that "I certainly hold a special place in my heart for her." These are all powerful emotional responses. Indeed, a Judith Butler fan writes, "When I finally understood Butler's work, I stood up and screamed YEAH! and started laughing"—a very active response to a text!

Second, Theory fans meet together—often traveling large distances to do so—at conventions (or "conferences," "seminars," or "workshops"). Sometimes these events replicate the largely passive structure of mass media consumption—Theory fans will attend an event simply to listen to a favored Theorist talk to them, for example. As one Spivak fan notes, "she is brand-like, meaning that if I see a product with her name I will be attracted to it. If I saw [an] event she would be speaking at, I would want to go." Theory fans like to feel the thrill of physical presence with their heroes—although several pointed out that they would not actually want to speak to them ("I'd have nothing to say and would instantly lose my voice and any cognitive capacity I might at times possess"). It should be noted that at these events there is little space for active engagement by Theory fans. Organizers may allow a short period at the end of the talk in which questions can be asked in a formulaic way, but while this is obviously "active" in some sense, it is not truly creative in that attendees have no opportunity to challenge the structure of the event, but remain within a circumscribed structure set up by organizers.

An example of such an event would be "Giving an Account of Oneself: A Public Lecture by Judith Butler." This talk, given by the popular American Theorist, took place in Sydney, Australia, in June 2005. Theory fans attended from around Australia—and were charged Aus$25 for the privilege. Butler's reason for attending this event was not that she is genuinely interested in forming real relationships with the attendees. The power relationship between the Theorist and the fan, and the intervening levels of institutional structures, remained firmly in place.

An alternative mode of meeting is the Theory convention (or "conference") where Theory fans will perform their own pieces of writing for fellow attendees. For example, "The Political Futures of Jacques Derrida" was a one-day symposium held in Sydney in February 2005, where Theory fans gathered not to meet a Theorist but to share their own enthusiasm for the Theorist Derrida. As the convention flyer put it, "The Political Futures of Jacques Derrida will celebrate the enduring and urgent political significance and relevance of his work" (note the uncritical tenor of that "celebrate"). The fans gathered in order to share their enthusiasm about this

Theorist, to listen to other fans offer celebratory accounts of why they like his work so much, to argue about interpretations of favored texts, and primarily—as the convention flyer suggests—to produce and circulate secondary texts—what we might call "Fan Theory"—that develop and build on the authorized canon of texts by the Theorist. This convention offered Fan Theory talks with titles such as "Derrida and the Future of Critical Theory," "On Derrida and Feeling," and "Derrida, Decision, and Absolute Risk."

This leads us on to my third and final point about the activity of Theory fans: they are clearly, in some way, cultural *producers* as well as *consumers*. They do not simply read the work of Theorists—they also produce, as mentioned above "fan Theory" (much like other fan groups produce "fan fiction"). Fans will write short pieces of Theory in which they examine the work of favored Theorists in detail, explaining their favorite bits of the work (key ideas, concepts that they think are useful), and arguing with other fans over interpretations of texts. Sometimes they will produce work that is more creative and will actually propose their own Theories—although always within the structural framework laid down by the Theorists of whom they are fans. And this work will sometimes even be published. As with all fan cultures, some of this is simple cottage-industry publishing—email lists, photocopied newsletters, or websites. But some Theory fans go even further. There does actually exist a whole—extremely profitable—transnational publishing industry that publishes this Fan Theory. These fans are productive, then, even to the extent of contributing to the distribution of Theory by global capitalism.

The Nature of Activity

As I have outlined above, Theory fans are clearly, in some sense, active audiences. In the 1980s and early 1990s, there was a tendency in fan studies to argue that the fact that fans are active consumers automatically implied that they were resisting capitalism. As John Fiske argued in 1987 in relation to Madonna fans, "If her fans are not 'cultural dupes' but actively choose to watch, listen to and imitate her rather than anyone else, there must be some gaps or spaces in her image that escape ideological control" (quoted in Gripsrud 1995: 121).

However, many writers have now pointed out that we cannot assume that this is in fact the case. Just because Theory fans are active in the sense of choosing their favored texts, building intense relationships with them, putting effort into constructing interpretations, building communities, and even producing their own texts about their favorite Theorists, this does not mean that they are genuinely resisting capitalist ideologies in doing so. As Toby Miller has recently pointed out, even as fans build communities, there is no evidence that they are using the collectivities that develop around their shared interest (such as Theory) for "some larger political purpose" that goes "beyond that interest" (Richard Butsch, quoted in Miller 2004: 193). The fact that fans are "active" consumers does not automatically mean that their practices are subversive or progressive. Theory fans do indeed put a lot of effort into producing interpretations—often quite radical and surprising—of their favored texts. But as Jostein Gripsrud has argued, this does not necessarily mean that they are resisting capitalist ideologies. In fact, as he argues, this is precisely what the transnational publishers want them to do. It is in their best interests for the Theory texts to be open to multiple readings, for two reasons. First, this maximizes their possible audience; and second, it allows for the possibility of a continuing industry of interpretation to be sold to Theory fans—books of exegesis and commentary, collections of critical essays, and "Readers" of Theorists' writings. Gripsrud points out that the multiple readings of texts that Theory fans produce are in fact the result of "culture industry strategies" and are not "oppositional": "If the 'multitude' of 'selective' readings are already intended or calculated by the industry, 'the individual's manipulation of commodity [e.g., Theory books] discourses may not testify to his/her autonomy [. . .] but to the achieved strategies of these discourses'" (Griprsud 1995: 143, quoting Klinger).

And in fact, when we begin to investigate the structures of publishing and distribution of Theory, it seems clear that Theory fans are in fact *supporting* the publishing industries of global capitalism as they buy and write books of Theory. They are consumers of commodified culture. Their primary engagement with their favorite Theorists comes through reading books and journals that publish works of Theory. Some of this material is published by small-scale "cottage publishers," some by university presses, and an increasing amount by transnational publishers such as Routledge (a subsidiary of Taylor & Francis) and Penguin (a subsidiary of the Pearson group). Even the material that is published by cottage publishers and university presses is produced within a capitalist framework, and increasingly follows market models of production and distribution (see Moran

1998: 70). And there is no doubt that the circulation of Theory published by transnational publishers supports global capitalism. Fans of Karl Marx, for example, might read a book such as *Capital*. They may buy a copy published by Penguin—which is owned by the transnational corporation Pearson. So when a Theory fan buys this book—or even borrows it from a library that has bought a copy—he or she (or the library) will have contributed US$12 to the earnings of a publisher that in 2004 had sales of over US$1,509 million and profits of over US$104 million (Penguin 2005). If the fan buys Marx's text from a bookshop like Borders or online at Amazon, then again he or she will be contributing to the profits of a transnational corporation.

It could be argued that the ideas in Theory fandom can sometimes be surprisingly anticapitalist—as indeed is the case with Marx's *Capital*. However, this represents a form of assimilation. Capitalism allows such Theorists to write and publish simply because Theory fans are a good market that creates profits for international corporations. It is true that the ideas circulated are not always procapitalist in any simple sense (although it is certainly possible to demonstrate capitalist ideologies at work in a text such as *Capital*—for example in the individualist ideology of publishing a book with the name of a single author on it): but Theory fans cannot escape the international system of commodification that they—literally—buy into every time they purchase a book. As Gripsrud points out, superficially resistant, anticapitalist products (such as pop stars with rebel images—and, we might add, critical Theorists) circulated within the mainstream do not lead to genuine resistance, but act more as a form of inoculation (Gripsrud 1995: 121).

Theory fans' own productive fan activity becomes part of the same system when their articles and books are published by a company such as Routledge or Sage. Their labor, often given freely, is then commodified and sold back to them by the capitalist system. Theory fans are kept acquiescent to capitalism's project by the feeling that they have some agency or control. But what they are actually doing is publishing their fan writing in cultural sites that are either rigidly circumscribed (within the publishing realms of global capitalism, or already-existing institutions such as universities that are funded by right-wing states or liberal capitalist endowments) or largely powerless (new forms of Internet "publishing" that are easily accessible but have little political purchase). And when they do publish in the mainstream, they give their labor for free in order to produce profits for transnational corporations.

Of course, I'm not saying that Theory fans are simply cultural dupes who passively consume whatever they are given. But at the same time, I am wary of romanticizing them, of assuming that just because they are in some way "active," this should be understood as rebellion against the system of capitalism. It is simply not the case. Active Theory fans are just as much consumers of commodified culture as are those everyday readers of Theory who don't become part of this productive fan culture. They are a key part of the international system of commodified culture that sells their favored Theorists to them, and makes money from their freely given labor.

Game over.
OK.

So. Hopefully it's obvious by now that this chapter isn't entirely serious. It takes the form, if you'll forgive me, of a scherzo—a cheerful and light piece of work. It aims to make a single, straightforward point.

I would like to thank everyone who took part in the survey—their input was invaluable, and I hope they feel that the underlying point here is serious, even if the mode of argument is light-hearted. (And I must apologize to John Fiske. On every important point about cultural theory, I think that Fiske was right. Indeed, my own position as a Theory fan is Fiskean. I am a Populist.) Lest I be misunderstood, let me make my point with a leaden lack of irony. I am not seriously suggesting that we should in fact treat Theory fans as I have treated them in this chapter. My point is the opposite. I am arguing that we should not treat any fans in this way. To do so is, quite simply, disrespectful of their status as thinking, self-aware beings.

There exists a history of debate in fan studies as to whether fans really resist capitalism as a system. We can find in the self-image of some fans a claim to be resisting mainstream commodification (Jancovich & Hunt 2004: 28). And it has been charged that some early fan theorists claimed that by making unexpected uses of texts, fans were escaping the ideological control of the culture industries (as with Gripsrud, above)—although I suspect this point is overstated by critics (Fiske, for example, is usually careful to distinguish between different kinds of "productivity"). The latest stage in this argument has been for writers to point out that fans occupy a subject position that is actually constructed within, and taken account of by, capitalist media production. This fact is sometimes presented with a rhetorical flourish—fans' media uses and fan products are made and circulated within capitalism; therefore they are not really resisting that system. The end.

I'm not convinced by this chain of reasoning. Hence the scherzo. Yes, I think it is clearly the case that fans make use of, and create, new, media texts within the system of capitalism. Just as academics do. But even if we want to retain the issue of challenging capitalism as our primary focus—and I would say that I don't think this exhausts the potential of cultural politics—simply demonstrating an imbrication within commodified culture doesn't exhaust the potential interest of fan culture.

Academics conduct their work of consumption and production just as much within capitalist culture as do other kinds of fans. Of course there are some elements of the academic exchange of ideas that are outside of, or at least exist tangentially to, capitalist practices (our teaching, conferences, seminars); just as is the case for other kinds of fans (fanzines, conventions, fan websites). And, more importantly, we are willing to allow that academic ideas can be of interest for the purposes of exegesis and discussion, even given the fact that significant elements of them are produced within the capitalist system. We acknowledge that it is possible for a commodified product—such as a copy of *Capital*, for example—to lead to the generation and distribution of ideas that are genuinely challenging. And this despite its status as a commodity. Joe Moran, in the article cited above, goes on to point out that even though academic publishing is indeed a part of commodified culture, "It is […] important not to jettison the questioning of the significance of intellectual work within cultural studies, simply because it may be implicated with academic stardom […] there is a danger of dismissing interesting and valuable academic work by automatically accusing critics of bad faith" (Moran 1998: 78). As Theory fans we believe that when a transnational publisher commodifies our ideas about "gender politics on TV, or postcolonialism, or the fashion industry and tie-ins," those ideas can still, somehow, function as a genuine, political act—a "critique of capitalism" (Miller 2004: 194). And so I am suggesting that we extend the same courtesy to fan production: that we judge ideas on their merit, rather than on the conditions of their production.

There are a couple of arguments against this position. One could argue that academic writing, like "serious art" (Horkheimer & Adorno 1972 [1944]: 135), can escape the conditions of its production and express "a negative truth" (130), whereas popular culture can never do this because its apparent transgressions are in fact "calculated mutations which serve all the more strongly to confirm the validity of the system" (129). Whether or not one believes this to be the case is a matter of faith, turning on one's perception of what counts as genuine critique. One cannot make rational arguments for or against believing critique to be "genuine"; it is a not a matter of empirical or historical testing (let us see what effects these critiques have) but of moral judgment (this critique is necessarily flawed because it is produced within the system capitalism) (see McKee 2005: 18). My own personal faith is not to believe that there is such a difference in essence between art and mass culture. There's not much further we can go with that debate.

Similarly, one could argue that an interest in academic writing is rational for it speaks the Truth about the world, whereas an interest in the entertainment of fan writing is irrational and emotional. But as the quotes from the Theory fans above make clear, this is not the case (see Hills 2002: 3–7). Indeed, we already know that Theory fandom is not distinct from other forms of intense cultural consumption. Stanley Cavell made the point clearly in 1981 when he noted that "I have spoken as if, for example, Wittgenstein and Heidegger [. . .] were clear candidates for a university curriculum, yet I know that each of them is mainly the object of a cult" (1981, quoted in Hills 2002: 4). Academics are fans, by any workable definition. We know very well that a passion for Theory is just as much a form of fandom as is loving *Star Trek*. We know very well, but all the same . . . in a classic instance of disavowal we sometimes choose to forget this, and proceed as though it weren't the case—as though, despite all the evidence to the contrary, *our* cultural pleasures are rational and our ideas are genuinely challenging to capitalism, while the cultural pleasures of *others* are emotional and their ideas don't genuinely challenge the system.

In this, I am arguing for opening up the methodologies of analysis—not closing them down. I don't think we should stop examining the material conditions of production for fan texts. We need to continue doing political economy (what are the structures and institutions that enable the production and circulation of these ideas?); ideological critique (how can we interpret these texts in order to relate them back to the conditions of their production?); and audience work (what do the fans of these texts say about them?). But rather than using these approaches only to study popular culture, let's apply them to the texts of Theory fans as well—that is, academic writing. We rarely ask about the conditions of production, distribution, and consumption of Theory. So let's analyze not just the Truth of what Theorists say, writing exegeses of the ideas in their published works. Let's also examine who gets to speak, which books get written, which books get published, who gets to evaluate the worth of Theory, what criteria are used to do that, and where those criteria come from; let's find out what are the ideological underpinnings in Theory, and what effects books of Theory have on readers and on the culture more widely. Of course there already exists some work in this area (see Moran 1998: 78). Let's have more.

And we should expand the methodologies for studying fan texts to include the exegetical modes that we currently apply to academic writing. Let's look at fan production and judge it on the criteria of being informed, intelligent, interesting, or convincing. Ask what intellectual work it does. Indeed, much of it may be dull and nitpicking ("trainspotting" as Toby Miller recently put it—2004: 187). But so is much academic writing (is there any other way to describe yet another detailed exegesis of the writings of an individual Theorist, proclaiming the Truth of his or her insights, for example?). Much of it may not challenge capitalism directly; but the same is true of much academic work that is still regarded as worthwhile. And there may indeed be some fan production that does indeed produce and circulate interesting ideas that challenge the ideological foundations of capitalist social systems (perhaps the *Star Trek* fan novel *The Weight,* for example—see Jenkins 1992: 152–84).

We Theory fans work with passion, uncomfortably situated within commodified capitalist systems. Just as other fans do. In such a situation we occasionally manage to produce work that is interesting, intelligent, or challenging. And it is possible that other fans manage to pull off the same trick. At the moment, I suspect that the way we distribute our analytical methodologies makes it that much more difficult to acknowledge the fact that this is the case.

NOTE

1. All quotations come from fourteen surveys completed by Theory fans accessed through the Cultural Studies Association of Australasia email list, in response to questions posted on the list on 25 July 2003 and then again on 17 February 2005.

7

Bachies, Bardies, Trekkies, and Sherlockians

Roberta Pearson

Let's begin with a quiz.¹ Which of the appellations in this chapter's title would fans/buffs/enthusiasts/devotees/aficionados/cognoscenti/connoisseurs of J. S. Bach, William Shakespeare, Sherlock Holmes, and *Star Trek* accept, and which not? Adherents of the popular and the middle-brow have nicknames. North American devotees of the great detective call themselves "Sherlockians"; the British prefer the more formal but less euphonious "Holmesians." Some *Star Trek* fans accept the "Trekkie" nomenclature; others see it as derogatory and opt for the more serious "Trekkers." Adherents of high culture don't have nicknames.² "Bachies" is my coinage and "Bardies" Henry Jenkins's (for which I thank him); they are not in common currency but perhaps should be. My (entirely unproven) assumption is that Bach and Shakespeare fans would reject the semi-derisory nicknames; I suspect (again with no evidence, but that's the nature of this chapter) that most would also reject the term "fan" and opt for another of the labels under offer. Both the specific playful diminutives and the general label of "fan" extend popular culture practices to the rarefied realms of baroque music and Elizabethan drama, a leveling that those with allegiances to the supposedly higher realms of "serious" music and literature might resent. The absence of a single agreed-upon name signals the invisibility in which power often cloaks itself. Those involved in popular or middle-brow culture are generally seen as fans or, more specifically, Trekkies, Whovians, Sherlockians, or Wodehousians and the like; their firm categorization is a social judgment, sometimes a negative one. The adherents of high culture are similarly categorized, but the multiplication of labels avoids negative connotation. The terms "buffs"/"enthusiasts"/ "devotees" are at worst neutral, while "aficionados"/"cognoscenti"/

"connoisseurs," with their implications of specialized, and more importantly, worthwhile knowledge, positively value those to whom they are applied.

The differences in labels and their associated valuations gives rise to several questions. Which labels would people choose to apply to themselves and why? Do the words "fans"/"enthusiasts"/"devotees"/"aficionados"/"cognoscenti"/"connoisseurs" signal different degrees and kinds of engagements with the beloved object? What's the difference between those who engage with "serious" music and those who engage with "serious" literature? What's the difference between adherents of Shakespeare, a writer acclaimed as the greatest playwright of all time and serving as a bastion of British national identity, and those of Conan Doyle, a second-rank writer who did what he did very well and whose output some might classify as fiction rather than literature? How different are the high-culture Bachies and Bardies from the middle-brow Sherlockians from the vast popular culture fandoms (e.g. Trekkies) in their appropriations/pleasures and their social organizations? Or should we perhaps be seeking similarity rather than difference? As John Frow argues, "There is no longer a stable hierarchy of value running from 'low' to 'high' culture, and 'high' and 'low' culture can no longer be neatly correlated with a hierarchy of social classes" (1995: 1). Frow's cautionary quotation marks signal contemporary scholars' uneasiness not only with correlating a hierarchy of value with social class but also with having to designate the steps of that hierarchy by distinct terms such as "high-", "low-", and "middle-brow." The relationship among cultural values bears greater resemblance to an Escher print than a real stairway, but in an article of this length, I can do no more than acknowledge the problem, admitting that my personal aesthetic judgments drive the distinctions. The reader should insert her own scare quotes or reflect upon her own aesthetic criteria as necessary.

The larger point here is that while fan studies has extensively engaged with the popular and even occasionally with the middle-brow (see Brooker 2005a), it has almost entirely refused to engage with the high. The study of high culture still undeniably thrives in the academy; Shakespeare is far from taking up residence on the dust heap of history. But within the strain of cultural studies that traces its lineage to Birmingham, high culture figures only as a repressive other against which to celebrate the virtues of the popular. When challenged, the implicit preference among cultural studies scholars for popular culture can become aggressively explicit. Some of my (mostly younger) colleagues are suspicious of my wanting to study Shakespeare as well as *Star Trek,* viewing this as a dangerous apostasy that threatens to reinstate ideologically invidious cultural hierarchies. Studying high culture and high-culture fans is seen as a back-door method of reintroducing debates around cultural value long abandoned in favor of orthodox adherence to cultural relativism and textual instability. While such study might sometimes be an attempt to reestablish high-culture hegemony, fears of such ulterior motives should not preclude questions of cultural value being at the center of the cultural studies project. These questions must inevitably involve the high as well as the low. For example, does the value of high-cultural forms such as Shakespeare stem purely from ideological and institutional mechanisms or, as some might argue, does the fact that Shakespeare's texts have survived for over four centuries in and of itself connote some kind of inherent value? Has popular cultural studies valued its objects purely for ideological reasons— the resistance it supposedly attests to among its receivers? And now that the resistance paradigm is somewhat discredited, does popular cultural studies value its objects on the basis of popularity alone? Is it possible to say that one popular culture text is better than another and if so, why? Should popular cultural forms be judged by the same criteria as high culture or should different modes of evaluation be evolved?

But this article is not the place to discuss why cultural studies should return to questions of cultural value; for the moment the focus is on the exclusion of high culture within fan studies. Why have Trekkies et al. been studied ad infinitum and the Bachies, Bardies, and their ilk hardly at all? The stifling orthodoxy of the cultural relativist credo accounts for much, but there's also a generational explanation for the embrace of popular culture fandoms and the exclusion of everything else. I know other cultural studies scholars of roughly my generation who, like myself, are both passionate about and understand the need to study the more restricted realms of music, literature, or art. And I know of at least one younger scholar, a contributor to this very volume (although I shall refrain from outing him/her) with a detailed knowledge of and love for classical music. And it turns out that one of the editors is a devoted Mozart fan, so we must beware of generational generalizations. But we do undeniably inhabit a historical moment in which the distribution of high-cultural capital has declined due to the very leveling of cultural hierarchies celebrated by cultural studies. Younger scholars may know a great deal about the latest pop idol phenomenon and hit television series but not much at all about baroque music or Elizabethan drama. There's also a more discipline-specific reason for younger scholars' lack of high-cultural capital. My and earlier generations came to the then relatively new fields of film/television/cultural studies from a variety of other disciplines, bringing with us knowledge of many subjects. The subsequent success and growth of those disciplines means that younger scholars may have studied nothing except popular culture for a significant proportion of their academic lives. In the United Kingdom, students can begin film or media studies at sixteen, continue at university, and then go on to postgraduate study. No wonder most of our postgrads feel more comfortable with rock fans than baroque fans.

These remarks may sound like a typical older generational jeremiad, but we should acknowledge the structural determinants of scholarly inquiry in the history of a discipline, even if in slightly grumpy fashion. But the rant's now at an end. The remainder of this article interrogates my own fandoms (what fellow contributor Matt Hills would call an auto-ethnography—and no, he's not the classical music fan mentioned above) to sketch some of the issues that scholars studying high-culture fandom might wish to address. My former colleague, frequent coauthor, and dear friend Professor William Uricchio of MIT tells me that I have a fannish disposition while he, despite sharing my love of early (roughly pre-nineteenth-century) music and other high-cultural forms, admits to no fandoms as such. He's right about me; at various times I'm a sports fan (in the past Duke University basketball, New York Mets baseball, and now occasionally England football and most recently England cricket), a music fan (Bach and Mozart above all, but others as well), a literature fan (Shakespeare above all, but also Dickens, Conan Doyle, and many others), a television fan (*Star Trek* above all, but others include *The Prisoner* and *The Avengers*), a film fan (Keaton, Hitchcock, and Welles rather predictably ranking first among my favorite directors), in addition to less classifiable fandoms (?) such as Horatio Nelson and the eighteenth-century Royal Navy. I'm also what another former colleague, frequent coauthor, and dear friend, Professor Maire Messenger Davies of the University of Ulster, calls a serial enthusiast; in Italy I become temporarily enthralled by Renaissance art, and in the Netherlands, the seventeenth century Golden Age; when a favorite actor appears in an Ibsen, Miller, or Pinter play, I become temporarily fascinated by the rest of the playwright's oeuvre.

When first thinking about this article, I rang Uricchio and asked him, rather unfairly on the spur of the moment, to elaborate in scholarly fashion upon the fannish and non-fannish disposition idea that had previously figured in casual conversation and friendly banter. He speculated that non-fans like himself engage in aesthetic reflection or are temporarily moved by cultural texts but that fans like me incorporate the cultural texts as part of their self-identity, often going on to build social networks on the basis of shared fandoms. Centrality to identity and social networks handily distinguish my fandoms from my enthusiasms. Many of my fandoms were acquired in early to midadolescence, a crucial period for the formation of self-identity; a good psychologist could probably determine my fandoms' origins in my early life circumstances. Many of these fandoms later led to social relationships; I am a proud, if somewhat lapsed, member of the Adventuresses of Sherlock Holmes (ASH), although I can still tell you the number of steps up to Holmes's flat (seventeen) and the number of varieties of cigarette ash he could distinguish (140). There have also been less formal social relationships; many of my friends have tended to share one or the other of my fandoms. My enthusiasms are more ephemeral, resulting from proximate and identifiable factors such as travel or following the work of a favorite actor. The issue of terminology arises again; I accept the word "fan," where others would reject it, but apply it to those cultural texts most central to my identity, relegating others to the category of enthusiasms. My personal experiences point to many questions that are to my knowledge as yet unanswered by fan studies. How do people acquire their fandoms or their enthusiasms? Which of these lead to social networks? Do other people make the kinds of distinctions I do with regard to their leisure activities and interests, with some more central to identity than others? And how do the differences among popular, middlebrow, and high culture play out across all these questions?

Central to these questions is the idea of overlapping fandoms. Fandoms have tended to be studied in isolation, or at best as amalgams of interests within the same field of cultural production—the fans of English television discussed by Henry Jenkins in *Textual Poachers*. But if there truly is such a thing as a fannish disposition, then there should be many whose multiple fandoms range widely across fields of cultural production and up and down cultural hierarchies; I've certainly met many *Star Trek* and *Avengers* fans at Sherlockian gatherings, and my closest Sherlockian friends number among them Detroit Tigers, New York Mets, Melissa Etheridge, and P. G. Wodehouse fans, as well as a woman who turned her enjoyment of wine into a living and became a professional oenologist. These Sherlockians are, like myself, solidly middle-class, and the ability to range across fields of cultural production and up and down cultural hierarchies is certainly correlated with class. As Jostein Gripsrud puts it,

"While the audiences in the opera almost certainly go to movies and even watch television, the majority of movie and television audiences will never go to the opera; or visit places like museums of contemporary art, certain theatres. The reception of high and low culture is still clearly linked to the social formations we call classes" (1999: 199). Peterson and Kern provide empirical support for Gripsrud's assertion, arguing that in the United States, there is an historical shift among the higher social categories from highbrow snob (one who does not participate in any lowbrow or middle-brow activity) to "omnivore" (capable of appreciating them all) (1996). Of course, as I've pointed out above, traditional high-cultural capital seems to be declining among younger age cohorts, which might mean that the phenomenon of the omnivore, or as I have put it, the person capable of ranging across fields of cultural production and up and down cultural hierarchies, is a historically restricted one.

The issue of class also comes into play with the list of terms that began this article: "fans"/"buffs"/"enthusiasts"/"devotees"/"aficionados"/"cognoscenti"/"connoisseurs." The worthwhile and specialized knowledge accredited to the aficionados/cognoscenti/connoisseurs implies a higher class position than that of the fans/buffs/enthusiasts and devotees. Fans of high-culture forms may consciously seek to distinguish themselves from fans of popular culture forms through consumption patterns seen as appropriate to their class formations. While high culture is as fully imbricated in the commodity circulation of late capitalism as popular culture, it may be so in interestingly different ways; one of the great strengths of capitalism lies in its ever more refined appeals to ever smaller and more distinct niche markets. Again I turn to my own experience. An action figure of *Star Trek*'s Data sits on top of a bookshelf in my study, one of the few visible manifestations of a fandom that has extended neither to collecting nor to active association with other fans (on-line chat groups, conventions, or clubs). Data was bought in a second-hand shop for five pounds and is displayed in semi-ironic fashion next to a small aboriginal sculpture, which he's using his tricorder to analyze. No ironic bust of Shakespeare or Bach sits in my study since these artifacts bear class associations (nouveau riche, trying too hard to acquire cultural capital, pretentious) difficult to ironize. But I do have ironic Shakespeare tchatkes, one of my favorites being a really kitschy, made-in-China, bought-in-Stratford pencil sharpener. It's a bit like a flattened snowdome, a tiny cut-out Bard's head floating above a black and white picture of Anne Hathaway's cottage. Just the thing for a postmodern academic Bardie who wants to declare an allegiance without committing a class faux pas. I have also bought the occasional Shakespeare t-shirt and fridge magnet, but there's a limited range of items I feel comfortable acquiring. Once again, however, I am generalizing from my own aesthetic preferences, and this is a dangerous enterprise. Another of my dear friends, this time a fellow contributor to this volume, John Tulloch, rebuked me upon reading my first draft. He has a friend who "is a great lover of opera and Handel, *and* has a small bust of Beethoven on her mantelpiece. So does that make her 'nouveau riche'? She thinks you 'a bit snobby' for saying so."[3] It's a fair cop, guv!

I may have an aversion to busts, but had I the income and the leisure I would happily embark on one of the cultural tours to artistic, musical, or literary sites constantly advertised in up-market print venues such as *The Guardian, The Gramophone,* and *The New Yorker.* In this 250th anniversary of Mozart's birth, for example, a spare one thousand six hundred to two thousand five hundred quid will launch you on a "Mozart on the romantic Danube" cruise, visiting "many of the places that played a prominent role in his all too short life." The governments of the cities that played that prominent role, e.g., Vienna, Salzburg, and Prague, are meanwhile concentrating on extracting every Euro from the anticipated tourist trade of the anniversary year. Readers of this volume might well characterize a Mozart-inspired cruise or city-break as a fan pilgrimage, but I would point out that high culture got there first. After all, what was the grand tour of Europe expected of every elite young American male in the nineteenth century but a high-culture fan pilgrimage? And Bardies have been flocking to Stratford since the eighteenth century (see Pearson 2002). These are precisely the interesting antecedents, parallels, and connections we miss by excluding high culture from cultural studies (although geographers and economists recognize the key role played by high culture in urban regeneration).

Since my economic capital lags considerably behind my cultural capital, my high-culture fandoms must be sated primarily through consumption of the works (going to the theater, cinema, and concerts, purchasing DVDs and CDs, listening to the radio, and engaging in occasional discussions with the similarly high-minded). Trekkies and Sherlockians, however, can acquire an endless array of artifacts in addition to the core television shows and Conan Doyle works, some made for them and some made by them. Truly dedicated fans can even recreate the settings of the beloved texts, turning their flats into the Enterprise or their living rooms into the 221-B sitting room. Consumption in the form of collecting is a key element of the popular stereotype of the nerdy, needs-to-get-a-life fan

(*The Simpsons*' Comic Book Guy being a high-profile example). How do different fandoms relate differently to commodification? Do certain cultural forms lend themselves more easily to commodification than others? Fully kitted-out, narrativized virtual worlds such as *Star Trek, The Lord of the Rings,* and Sherlock Holmes seem to produce the widest range of commodities, but there's a distinction even here between copyrights vested in a single media franchise and those not; as a result, the first two examples give rise to more centralized production of commodities than the third. Might associations with certain kinds of consumption (attending "serious" theater versus purchasing action figures) contribute to the social valuations made of high and popular culture fans?

The remainder of this article consists of some brief observations about two of my four titular fandoms, Sherlockians and Bachies (Trekkies have had more than enough press and the word count prohibits giving the Bardies any). Sherlockians have so far (with the exception of a previous article of mine: see Pearson 1997) escaped academic scrutiny, despite being probably the oldest established fandom. The first official Sherlockians, those readers who successfully responded to a quiz in Christopher Morley's column in *The Saturday Review,* gathered at a New York City drinking establishment in 1934. There they formed the Baker Street Irregulars (BSI), the first and most famous of Sherlockian societies, named after the street urchins whom Holmes occasionally employed to assist him. Holmes fandom remains primarily an Anglo-American phenomenon, with more than a hundred of the so-called scion societies in the United States and several in Britain, including the premier English organization, the Sherlock Holmes Society of London. Sherlockians engage in similar activities to other fans. Members of scion societies meet on a regular basis to eat, drink, take quizzes, listen to talks, engage in theatrical presentations, sing, play games, and, most importantly, escape into a world where all the inhabitants share a similar passion. Individual Sherlockians produce Sherlockian "art"—ranging from paintings to hand-painted sweat-shirts—for their own pleasure or for sale. Sherlockians write what others would call fan fiction, pastiches of the original stories and novels, and what they themselves call Sherlockian scholarship, nonfiction that employs the techniques of textual hermeneutics and historical contextualization to clarify the contradictions and lacunae that stemmed from Conan Doyle's writing in the serial format.

Sherlockians talk like fans and walk like fans but would they consider themselves fans? When I wrote my article about Sherlockians in cyberspace, I said in a footnote, "I should note that many of my friends within the Sherlockian world would contest the appellations of 'fan' and 'fandom,' their resistance to these labels stemming from an implicit hierarchization of the print media over the moving image media" (1997: 160). I made this smug judgment about motivation without consulting those concerned, and this time, partly by way of apology, I decided actually to ask some Sherlockians what they thought of the word "fan." The word's associations with the most prominent of popular culture fandoms made my admittedly small sample (three respondents) reluctant to adopt it themselves. Anne Cotton, a 72-year-old retiree, said, "When I think of real fans, I think more of the Trekkers (Star Trek folks) who show up at conventions dressed as favorite characters, or miscellaneous Klingons, or whatever." Susan Rice, a 63-year-old travel agent, said, "To me it's redolent of sports fandom and painting one's face, or rock/movie idols who have idolatrous fans." Katherine Karlson, a 53-year-old freelance writer and part-time legal secretary, agreed. "I usually associate being a 'Fan' with mainly support of sports teams, and by extension, some highly egregious behavior. When dealing with hobby interests, 'fan' also has a slightly loony association: vide Trekkies." It's the perceived "loony" or irrational nature of the fannish response that puts these Sherlockians off. "I guess I think of a fan response as visceral, not reasoned," says Susan. Anne, referring to those who dress up as favorite characters, thinks that "the real definition of 'fan' just might have to do with the degree to which this alter ego is confused with, or even becomes, one's own real identity." For Sherlockians, however, "the dividing line between the literary world and the real one is quite clear." Rationality is a key distinction between the Sherlockians and those whom they think of as fans. Says Katherine, "Fans don't necessarily do 'scholarship' as we do, and this was the original impetus behind the earliest SH societies. Even with the BSI and their antecedents, it may have been tongue-in-cheek, but a certain amount of knowledge combined with mental dexterity and wit was required for full membership/acceptance." If not "fans," what would these Sherlockians call themselves (other than "Sherlockian," of course, which all would prefer)? Susan sums it up nicely. "If called a fan, I wouldn't correct the speaker, but it's not the word I would choose. I would choose devotee or aficionado which both sound snootier than fan, but I would prefer to separate myself from teenagers and testosterone-charged boys of all ages."

My knowledge of the Sherlockian worlds leads me to believe that most Sherlockians, like my three respondents, would reject the label of "fan," even if, like Susan, they are fully aware of the cultural hierarchies at play. The terms they prefer—"admirer," "enthusiast," "devotee," "aficionado"— disassociate them from the excessive affect and hormone-induced behavior connoted by fan. Common sense leads me to believe that Bachies and Bardies would similarly want to distinguish themselves from the loonies who dress up as Klingons and can't tell fantasy from reality. The first and second generations of fan researchers insisted on attributing rationality to fans precisely to counter the popular image of the irrational fan so prevalent in the media (and still, it would seem, prevalent among Sherlockians). The third generation of researchers has insisted on the importance of fannish affect. Of course, given the reluctance to investigate high culture, no researcher that I know of wonders about the relationship between affect and high-culture fandom. Pierre Bourdieu, whose work fan studies so often invokes, tells us that the perceived engagement of the intellect rather than the emotions often serves to distinguish high from popular culture, and his opinion seems to be generally accepted. But I often find that high-culture texts tap more directly and profoundly into my emotions than popular culture texts.

As I sit at my desk writing this chapter, I'm listening to a live performance of one of the late Mozart quartets broadcast by Radio 3 (the BBC's classical music station) in honor of the composer's 250th birthday. The music moves me to the very core of my being, my emotions fully engaged by what I can only characterize verbally as the transcendent, the sublime, the divinely inspired. Affect is central to my experience of Mozart, as it is of Bach. That I'm not unique in this regard can be seen in the seven thousand-plus responses posted on Radio 3's message board to the Bach Christmas, ten days, twenty-four hours a day, of Bach's music—every note he wrote, as the promos put it.[4] One of the more prolific posters, Annebach, responded to the thread "what would life be without JSB," "My life would be much impoverished. His music affects me profoundly and joyfully and enriches every second I hear it and afterwards because it changes me. The music is also so profoundly beautiful and sublime. It calms me, it soothes me, it uplifts me, it energizes me, it makes me think better, it makes me so very happy." If Annebach admitted emotional dependency on Bach, the language of another thread, "withdrawal from Bach," playfully but revealingly intimated physical dependency. Said GBGlin, "I suspected I was slightly addicted to Bach's music. Now I know, and I'm dreading the impending withdrawal phase." MistyJeanette responded, "The sense of loss when this is over will be great. I have always been addicted to Bach and this is beyond my wildest dreams." Then there was the chap, in a post which I've unfortunately misplaced, who admitted to hearing "phantom Bach," even when the radio was turned off. This post has stuck in my memory if not in my files because I too suffered from the same complaint, not a particular composition but constant Bach-like sounds, counterpoint and all, in my mind's ear whenever I wasn't listening to the real thing. The Bachies on the message board confessed to the total immersion in the text, the merging of fantasy with reality, the delusional behavior that the elitist critics of popular culture have so often deplored. If Theodor Adorno himself had experienced the Bach Christmas, he too might have complained of phantom Bach.

This outpouring of emotion is a far cry from the cool contemplation supposedly characteristic of the consumption of high culture, but this seething affect didn't prohibit rational discussion or, rather, debate. The Bachies happily engaged in the distinction making so crucial to most fandoms, arguing the toss over period (on original instruments with great attention to original performance practices) versus modern (on contemporary instruments with no great concern about historically informed performance practices) style or Bach versus Beethoven or Mozart. 26jacqueline26 angrily declared that "it needs to be yelled from the rooftops that radio 3 has been abducted by the 'period people,'" while an email read on air begged the presenters not to play anything recorded before 1985 (when the period performance style came into the ascendancy re: Bach). Mumblesford, a Bachie par excellence, deprecated the competition. "The choice is between Beethoven's music which is bombastic junk 80% of the time. Or then there's Mozart's frivolous bluffing" whereas in Bach "all the parts are worked out properly . . . as opposed to the frivolous twiddly clichés we hear in so much of Mozart's music." Auntie_Joan contributed the following assessment of Bach v. Beethoven: "It does seem a little unfair to compare one of the key figures of Western art with Beethoven—a composer who never really got a handle on how to finish a piece. Or bridge passages. Or subtlety of any form."

Expecting dissonances between Bachies and popular culture fandoms, I instead found harmony. Bachies are every bit as emotional as their popular culture counterparts and every bit as bloody minded about their own particular preferences (Mozart twiddly! I can barely bring myself to quote the vicious canard, but the slagging off of Beethoven bothers me not at all). So might high-culture fans look a lot more like popular culture fans than we might expect? Sherlockians, by contrast, play down affect in favor of rationality, perhaps made more insecure by their positioning in the middle of the cultural hierarchy rather than at the top. Or might the favoring of affect over rationality be related to the difference between music fandom and literature fandom? Perhaps, but I suspect that the absent Bardies are every bit as passionate about their icon's work as the Bachies. The ancient Greeks knew all about drama as catharsis and a great performance of one of the four great Shakespearean tragedies certainly leaves me emotionally wracked. Interrogating my own fandoms in this manner has raised many questions and given few answers. But I do hope that this chapter has at least given some indication of the fascinating research questions and insights into cultural production and consumption that would result from cultural studies embracing the study of high culture and high-culture fandom.

Notes

1. I'd like to thank the editors, Karen Backstein, and John Tulloch for their helpful suggestions for revision of a hastily written first draft.

2. With the single exception that I can think of, the Jane-ites or Jane Austen fans.

3. Personal email communication.

4. The seven thousand figure is derived from Higgins (2006). According to the article, the station also received nearly two thousand emails, nearly 90 percent of them in favor of the "Bachathon" as it was dubbed.

8

Fans of Chekhov
Re-Approaching "High Culture"

John Tulloch

The academic literature on fandom is both extensive and central within popular cultural studies. Yet there is little comparable analysis of fans of high-culture entertainment forms like theater. Superficially, this may be due to an old-fashioned cultural studies rejection of high culture, even though some of the founding fathers of the field, like Raymond Williams, worked comfortably in both television and theater studies (see Roberta Pearson's polemic—with which I agree—on behalf of the return to discussion of cultural value in the previous chapter). But nor has there been much help from within theater studies. Despite a powerful theorization of performance in recent years, audience studies within theater/performance analysis have tended to remain a marginal activity, and where these have existed (as in Susan Bennett's work, 1997), they have not engaged with theories of fandom.

However, a sociological version of performative analysis, in Abercrombie and Longhurst's *Audiences* (1998), has focused on fandom as part of a consumer-to-enthusiast spectrum. Their specification of differentiated identities (of consumption and production) among consumers, fans, cultists, and enthusiasts is part of a broader "audiencing" move beyond the "resistant reading" tradition in audience research (see also Alasuutari 1999b).

In turn, though, Abercrombie and Longhurst's underpinning postmodernist emphasis on "the play and the pleasure that is involved in fandom" (1998: 155) is itself being superseded after 9/11 and the 7/7 London bombings by an extension of "risk society," "risk culture," and "risk governmentality" debates. These re-emphasize the interplay of reflexive individualization linked to Foucauldian surveillance that Abercrombie and Longhurst seek to downplay. Symptomatically, Abercrombie and Longhurst draw significantly on Beck's and Giddens's "risk society" thinking about the reflexive project of the self, but only by lifting the notion of the individualized ordering of self-narratives without any reference to the "risk society" and "risk governmentality" debate it depends on.

Risk theorists argue that audiences, wherever they are in the spectrum from consumers to enthusiasts, are living in a darker context than Abercrombie and Longhurst's more ludic preference for performativity and pleasure. Rather, in a world hegemonically defined as part of the "war against terror," risk thinking—from leading international power brokers and globalizing sections of the media, as well as in parts of academia—has increasing discursive salience among publics, and has political outcomes in mounting governmental threats to civil liberties. Further, de Zengotita refers to the profound tension between, on one hand, Abercrombie and Longhurst's Western world of postmodern, reflexive performativity, in which the possibilities of choice seem endless and, on the other hand, the world of millions of others "dominated by our interests" (2005: 291). This, even in Western societies, is "part of the unrepresentable mood that eludes mediation at the dawn of the age of terror" (2005: 287).

This is the broader framework within which my piece on Chekhov fans needs to be positioned. But it has not yet been fully worked through. I was myself seriously injured by a suicide bomber three feet from me in a London underground train on July 7, 2005, an event that terminated my writing for an extended period. However, preliminary work (Tulloch 2004: 29–36) had been done in bringing together performance, risk, and audience theory in theater production and reception, and my brief excursion into Chekhov fandom in this chapter should be seen in this context. It remains part of my own "reflexive project of the self" (Tulloch 2006), to which I'll return at the end.

Chekhov Fans: A Local Study

As part of an Australian Research Council funded project, "Chekhov: In Performance, Criticism, and Reading," I designed one study to focus more closely on theater fandom, while also opening up the possibility of risk analysis. I chose one particular theater, the Theatre Royal, Bath (TRB), one country (England), in one season, playing one particular author (Chekhov) in three different productions. Chekhov is the second most popular "classic" playwright (after Shakespeare) on the British stage—and probably first among actors. So popularity and fandom were central to my choice of research subject. The three productions studied at the TRB were the English Touring Theatre's *Cherry Orchard*, starring Prunella Scales and Frank Middlemas; the Royal Shakespeare Company's *Seagull*, starring Richard Pasco and Penelope Wilson; and Janet Suzman's *Free State*, a contemporary South African adaptation of *The Cherry Orchard*. So all were popular classics of Chekhov, with highly visible and popular stars; while one, Suzman's adaptation, allowed analysis of audiences' rethinking of Chekhov's fin-de-siècle social transition in *The Cherry Orchard* in a different context, of risk and racism, in late twentieth-century Britain and South Africa.

Rather than follow the empiricist demographic approach of much theater audience research, both my quantitative and qualitative questions began by emphasizing what going to this particular theater event *meant* to particular audience members in the context of their everyday life. "Why did you come to this particular production of *The Cherry Orchard* today?" was, for example, the opening question of my theater audience survey, which also examined in detail respondents' liking/disliking of two key features of live theater: its multimediality (Eversmann 2003) across acting, costume, lighting, set design, sound, etc.; and its live interaction between performances and audiences. Readings of both the semiotic density of theatrical performance and its live performer/performer/audience interaction could then be correlated with audience members' everyday choices as to why they were at the theater that day.

The open-ended first question ("Why did you come . . . today?") was postcoded according to the respondents' *own* categories, and revealed a relatively small number of generic leisure-time categories. It was quite easy to spot the various fan and non-fan responses. For example, the following questionnaire responses were classified as "Chekhov fans": "Whenever possible I see—whether on the stage, film or TV—Chekhov's plays," and "Love a Chekhov 'fix.'"

A different kind of fan response was from audience members who went to a particular production because they loved seeing a particular star actor. One respondent, for example, talked about Janet Suzman in *The Free State* as "almost as good" in her "live aura" as her "all-time love," Vanessa Redgrave. Another was disappointed that Prunella Scales, the star she had especially gone to see in the TRB's *Cherry Orchard*, was "not as good" as she had been in an Ibsen play the respondent had seen. Again, these different fans' responses to the multimediality and live interaction of a particular production could be compared with those who are not fans of anything, but are studying the play for school exams, are looking for a night out (with dinner afterwards at a restaurant), were "told to go" by a husband or schoolteacher, or were given a ticket "blind" as a birthday treat.

There are all kinds of practical difficulties in getting this kind of complex data from theater audiences (Tulloch 2004). But it can be very rich research, and offers the opportunity to compare the *readings* of both the semiotic variations of production and the live interaction of performance between fans and non-fans, as well as between different kinds of fan and non-fan. In the space I have here, I will begin to explore some variations in response between two of my fan classification groups: Chekhov fans and star fans.

I choose these two classifications for my focus because, according to *both audience-led* and *researcher-led* quantitative survey questions, these particular motivations—being fans of Chekhov and being fans of a particular star—came first and second as reasons for coming to a particular production at the TRB. My methodology also contained a number of different qualitative approaches to the audiences of the three Chekhov productions, but this chapter will focus mainly on part of the questionnaires handed out and returned after two evening and one matinee performance of the third production in the TRB Chekhov sequence: *The Cherry Orchard*, produced by the English Touring Theatre (ETT). This survey also contained questions about the two earlier Chekhov productions, *The Free State* and *The Seagull* (including a question as to whether and why audiences members *didn't* go to these productions).

The TRB was, in the words of its marketing manager, a "star-driven, not playwright-driven" theater, which meant a long-term encouragement of audiences as star fans. In fact, both the Chekhov fans and the star fans have a clear marketing institutional basis in British theater. According to an individual theater's perceived market profile, they are produced because this playwright or this star is thought likely to put bums-on-seats in this regional town on a pre- or post-London run by major touring companies like the RSC, the National, or the ETT. In contrast, a third type of theater fandom has a different economic-institutional base: the need among poorly subsidized theaters for out-of-house productions. Touring companies can thus build up their own fan base, who follow their productions around. As I discovered from various theater surveys I conducted at regional theaters, theater fans go to the theater very frequently (many visit as much as 40-plus times a year), and often drive significant distances by car to a number of theaters in their region or to follow a production company while on holiday. Thus, some tourists from Dorset said, "We saw the English Touring Theatre's production of *The Master Builder,* which we enjoyed very much—so thought we'd try a Chekhov. (Also we are on holiday this week, so were able to spend a day in Bath!)"

My first approach to examining the mix of quantitative and open-ended qualitative data I have in my theater-fan research has been to consider similarities and differences within and between each of the generic leisure-time ("why I came?") categories. I also looked at the responses across any one questionnaire as an individual mini-narrative that tells us quite a lot about the profile of each audience respondent, his/her horizon of expectations, and the meanings he or she generated in watching the multimediality and the interactivity of this particular production of the play.

For example, across one questionnaire I could trace whether a particular Chekhov fan really "loves Chekhov" to the extent of having such a cultural competence in terms of conventionally sedimented notions of "Chekhov" (e.g. ensemble acting, tragicomedy, balance between change and inevitability, etc.) that he/she knows "how Chekhov *should* be performed" in terms of acting, set design, lighting, and so on, and responds in evaluating the current performance accordingly. Fans of popular cultural performances quite systematically draw on their cultural competences to construct "all-time best" and "all-time worst" productions of their favorite show (Tulloch & Jenkins 1995). Might this same fan effect not operate in relation to high-cultural texts and performances?

A first significant finding was that, examined quantitatively, the Chekhov fans rated the ETT production of *The Cherry Orchard* less pleasurable than the star fans did: 81 percent of the star fans but only 56 percent of the Chekhov fans liked it. But was this the result of the particular cultural competences associated with different forms of fandom? Three survey-narratives from Chekhov fans who disliked the ETT *Cherry Orchard* are symptomatic of what I found more generally in this category of theater fan.

Margaret (who went to the play because of her "love of Chekhov," having enjoyed *The Cherry Orchard* in the past) disliked the ETT production because it was a "very 'flat' production. There was little atmosphere, and the characters generally did not evoke the audience's empathy. It did not 'feel' Russian." "Conflicts of the period [are] in the text, but easily missed." She also disliked the set because the "cherry orchard was not evident, [so you were] not aware of its importance as the central theme (It was like a cheap American hotel)." In contrast, *The Seagull* was a "wonderful production. Beautifully acted—felt really involved—a very believable production. You felt the resonance of the period." Margaret came all the way to Bath from Weymouth to see this production, and her disappointment was all the keener for it: "Two gentlemen near me snored their way through sections of the play[. . . .] Only the final moments of the play moved me in any way. In fact, the leading lady seemed to be as bored as some of the audience."

Cassy, another Chekhov lover, disliked the production, the acting ("technically competent but they failed to communicate that complicated detail beneath the text"), the interpretation ("it seemed just a performance of the plot like a competent amateur show"), the sets ("clumsy, badly changed"), and the costumes ("didn't look as if they belonged to the characters"). In contrast, *The Seagull* was "brilliant . . . I was completely drawn into this production. There wasn't a moment in the play when you weren't aware of what was going on in their minds. The set made you feel there was no one really looking after it. It was impermanent, which added to the discordant element. The costumes looked like the characters had lived in them for the last 20 years."

John (who loves Chekhov and needs his "annual fix") disliked this production. "The actors appeared bored, poor diction, over-acting." The interpretation "failed to convey the changing times in society, the 'fin de siècle' theme within the play." He also disliked the set with its "dominant doorway dividing the stage, while one side to the right seemed bare." *The Seagull* was "much better—good directing, well acted; an enjoyable performance."

Chekhov fans at the TRB talked a lot about the "subtlety" of Chekhov's text, and his "balance" between pathos and humor, which they felt was lost in the "shouting" and "OTT" acting of the English Touring Theatre's *Cherry Orchard.* They spoke of the loss of "Russian feel" or of "fin-de-siècle atmosphere" or of the "resonance" of "changing times" conveyed by set design, costuming, and performative mood. They regretted the production's loss of the "complicated detail" and the "conflicts of the period in the text." They knew about Chekhov's "ensemble" acting and complained about the "insufficient attention to the relationship *between* characters" because actors looked "bored," walking through their parts in a "flat" production.

Chekhov fans also tend to have a particular notion of Chekhov's "history," which is to do with end-of-nineteenth-century social change in Russia, prior to the 1905, then 1917, revolutions. This does not necessarily preclude the enjoyment of contemporary adaptations of Chekhov. Thus, Anne (who liked Chekhov and saw *The Free State* with her husband because she wanted to compare the two versions) disliked the ETT *Cherry Orchard* because of "too exaggerated" acting, making "silly" characters (thus depriving the play of subtlety), and the "silly bookcase." In contrast, she found *The Free State* to be "a much stronger production—less overacted and more powerful for it." Here, Chekhov was "translated very well to South Africa" at the time of Nelson Mandela's 1993 election victory. Similarly, Jim (who very much likes *The Cherry Orchard* and enjoys the TRB's pre-London season touring policy) disliked the unsubtle performances of the ETT production of *The Cherry Orchard* ("just speaking their lines"), the lack of ensemble integration, Lopakhin's "raving after buying the orchard," and Ranyevskaya "weeping too long" in overpassive response. He liked *The Seagull* for the Russian atmosphere it created through acting, lighting, scenery, and subtle character development. And he very much liked *The Free State* for its convincing performances and characterization ("an excellent transfer to South African modernity").

In contrast, other Chekhov fans did not like the "politicization" of Chekhov in Suzman's *Free State*. Thus, David (who has a particular interest in *The Cherry Orchard*) disliked the ETT production because of "too many anachronisms and too frantic acting [. . .] some performances were *unbelievably* 'over the top.'" But he didn't go to *The Free State* because he saw it as "too political (in a modern sense)." And Ellen (who "loves Chekhov" and hoped *The Cherry Orchard* "would be as good as *The Seagull*") didn't like much of the ETT production. "It did not seem very Russian. I was a little disappointed by Prunella Scales' interpretation." But Ellen chose not to see *The Free State*. "I thought that Chekhov knew what he was at, so why change him?"—though after reading good reviews, she thought she might have made a mistake not going.

There were, then, some variations between Chekhov fans over the *historical/ideological* interpretation of Chekhov—which matches, of course, different theater critical positions over a century of Chekhov production, circulation, and reception (Tulloch 1985). But the "truths" about Chekhov performance that seem to cross almost all critical traditions—subtlety of mood, ensemble playing, fin-de-siècle feeling (Chekhov, unlike Shakespeare, is almost always played in period dress), social change, tragicomic "balance"—form a core of agreement among Chekhov fans as they watch and interpret set design, costumes, lighting atmosphere, and actors' interactions with each other and with the audience. These audience members were usually patiently aware of the minimalist tendencies in stage design imposed on theater companies that tour from town to town. So their impatience with a "silly bookcase," or an invisible cherry orchard, or a "dominant doorway unattached to walls on either side" is not normally the result of a demand for complete nineteenth-century naturalism. Rather, as one can tell by reading responses across individual questionnaires, it relates to fans' dismay over a "missing" Chekhovian mood or sense of historical moment.

It is important to note that among the ETT *Cherry Orchard* audience who were Chekhov fans and *liked* the production, there were similar expectations about "Chekhov," though in this case usually rated positively rather than negatively. Thus, Sean (who went "because I am a big Chekhov fan") liked an "excellent Ranevskaya and Michael Feast [as] a brilliant Lopakhin—both the best I've seen for many productions. Excellent smaller parts too." The play was "rightly set in its period," and the interpretation was "faithful to Chekhov's intentions." He chose not to see *The Free State* "because I was afraid it would be a violation of Chekhov." And Vicky (who went to see a favorite play that she had acted in) liked this "superb production. It is easy to exaggerate the characters to lighten the text, but this was done to perfection and was very moving." As to interpretation, the "eternal conflict/difference between young hope and the desire of the older characters to hold the past was well drawn—particularly in Ranevskaya's speech to Trofimov where she says he was too young to understand." While quite a number of the respondents said they disliked the set, Vicky felt the "minimal set suited the play well, as does the period costume, and the lighting was not noticeable, as it should be."

Notably, the positive Chekhov fans drew on the same sets of expectations of "Chekhov" as the more negative ones. Thus, they looked for (1) Russianness ("never better than when in Russia," the "symbolism" of the passage of time, the conflict between old and new orders—so that sets, costumes, music, and lighting were appraised in relation to this particular sense of "atmosphere"); (2) ensemble—with particular performances pronounced strong or weak according to their ability to portray a particular character's contribution to this ensemble: thus Ranyevskaya's need to be "mercurial," "generous," "feckless," and Lopakhin's "mixture of humility and pride and passion and arrogance which makes him destroy those he loves"; (3) Chekhov's "balances"—between "humour and inevitability," and the "eternal conflict between young hope and desire to hold to the past."

Star Fans

In marked contrast to the Chekhov fans were the respondents who said they went to this *Cherry Orchard* production because they "adore Prunella Scales," or "to see Prunella" together with an "outstanding cast." For them, the "star" was the major feature of the theatrical event that drew them from their homes that day.

As we saw quantitatively, this category of respondent was *far* more positive than the Chekhov fan about the ETT *Cherry Orchard*. Andrew (who went "primarily because Prunella Scales was playing a leading role") liked it, "although I would say the production was diverting rather than gripping." The "lighting was excellent—real sense of the orchard representing some perfect ideal, just out of sight, out of reach, but bathed in golden light." Pat (who went particularly "to see Prunella Scales") liked *The Cherry Orchard*. "Everybody did well" and it was "easy to follow." This respondent even liked what many others disliked intensely: "It was unusual to see the set being changed in between acts when lights went up." Like Andrew, she had not been to see *The Seagull* or *The Free State* because neither "appealed to me" in terms of stars. R. J. B. (who went to see "Prunella Scales/Hopefully No SWEARING!") liked every aspect of the production, except one thing. "Excellent atmosphere—except the very LOUD SHOUTING!" The light, music, set, and costumes were all enjoyed, as was the interpretation, "except shouting!" This respondent was attracted to the Bath Theatre Royal by "classical/traditional plays with 'star leads.'" Jonathan (who had always wanted to see *The Cherry Orchard,* and was particularly attracted to this version, having seen "P. Scales in *The Birthday Party*") liked the production. The "leads were very strong, nice to see experienced hands working their craft." Though he had "no knowledge of Chekhov or the story prior to that night," he found the interpretation interesting; and liked the sets. "Simple but effective, uncluttered and gave the actors freedom to move." K. S. (who was drawn by "the reputations of

Prunella Scales and Frank Middlemas") liked the production. Not know-ing the play or dramatist, this respondent says that he or she cannot com-ment on the interpretation, but "Prunella Scales was excellent [. . .] I thought the lighting and the music were effective and unobtrusive." June (who went because a "great fan of Prunella Scales and Frank Middlemas") liked all aspects of the production: "Impressed by all the performances. I was sitting in the rear of Royal Circle and able to hear all." She also "partic-ularly enjoyed the music and the costumes were good."

Unlike the Chekhov fans, the star fans were almost unanimous in their pleasure in *The Cherry Orchard.* But there was a tendency to rather differ-ent measures for excellence. Star actors tend to be contrasted with their performances in other theater parts or on TV, rather than critiqued or praised intratextually in terms of a prior expectation of the character within the ensemble (the star fans tend to have much less knowledge of "Chekhov"). Like Janet, who enjoys "a good straight play," star fans tended to be happy if the production was "uncomplicated," "direct," and "easy to follow" (an effect, probably, of expecting Chekhov to be "difficult"). Sets were seen more functionally—giving actors "space to move." Lighting and music for these respondents should be "expressive," perhaps evoking an "ideal, just out of sight, out of reach," but otherwise "unobtrusive" in order to be "effective." Similarly functional were some of the (very few) criticisms of the acting: not being able to hear Prunella Scales's voice in the back of the theater—or, conversely, hearing everything "beautifully" from the Royal Circle. "Diction" was important—and this became an increasing feature with older people who were hard of hearing.

A Typology of Fandom: Postscript

One of the valuable aspects of Abercrombie and Longhurst's study of audiences is their fan typology in terms of textual production. Thus the average consumer is involved in little textual production, other than "fleet-ing and not written down" texts (1998: 149) through casual talk about the potential actions of characters. Fans, in contrast, "produce something 'material' which can be passed on to others. Therefore when young chil-dren act as fans, characters from films and television series will be incor-porated into the general playground games but will also be included in their drawings" (1998: 149). Cultists (which is where they place *Star Trek* fans) generate and circulate across the cult community "new texts of a variety of types on the basis of the characters and situations depicted in the television programmes and films" (1998: 149). The "enthusiast tends to revolve around the production of things, from railway models to plays to second-hand dresses" (1998: 150).

Schematically this is useful, so that we can begin to position some of the different "fan" positions described by Pearson and myself in our chapters. Thus, according to their typology, my "star fans" might be classified as "those people who become particularly attached to certain programmes or stars within the context of relatively high mass media use. They are individuals who are not yet in contact with other people who share their attachments" (1998: 138). In contrast, the not inconsiderable number of amateur actors among my Chekhov fans would be enthusiasts whose pleasure "tends to revolve around the production of things" (1998: 150). Further, it would be valuable to explore the interaction of consumers, fans, cultists, and enthusiasts with the theatrical event itself, via its multimediality and actor/audience interaction.

However, schematic analyses are only a start, and Abercrombie and Longhurst are right to emphasize "in the context of the postmodernist debate" the "fluidity of identity formulation and reformulation" (1998: 154). Thus, by way of notions of reflexive individualization, I was able to explore the pleasures in Suzman's *Free State* sets and acting style of an "enthusiast" audience member who had recently acted in the Trevor Griffiths version of *The Cherry Orchard* according to his different identities as "Trevor Griffiths' actor," "actor insider," Chekhov-lover, and senior teacher of Russian at a prestigious English school. In contrast, some other actors in the audience also had experience of the African continent, and so played through their own reflexive ordering of (white) self-narratives via the performative context of racist social gaffes among Suzman's white characters in her explicit "risk society" of apartheid, life destruction, scientific surveillance, and torture. Further, members of *The Free State* audience who were clearly Suzman fans engaged not only with her "aura" through other TV or theater performances but also with her political status in South Africa.

Abercrombie and Longhurst, following Debord (1994) and Featherstone (1991), also talk valuably of the "aestheticization of everyday life" as style and design pervade the selling of all commodities, and the culture industries themselves become commodified. Thus everyday life "can be turned into a work of art" and "the boundary between high and popular culture may be undermined by de-emphasizing the auratic quality of art" (1998: 86).

This is familiar postmodernist analysis, and yet it fails to account for the strength of feeling among my star fans for the relationship among star, aura, and risk politics in Suzman's *Free State*. Nor does it go far in exploring the different *kinds* of audience aestheticizing. Here I found "risk culture" analysis valuable, for example, Scott Lash's (2000) distinction between two different kinds of aesthetic reflexivity: on the one hand "judgments of the beautiful" within the conventionalized aesthetics of high culture (for instance, the "authentic Chekhov" of "Russianness," "ensemble," and "balance" among Chekhov fans) and the "terrible sublime," which many audience members experienced at the shattering finale of Suzman's *Free State,* where the Firs character, transformed into a faithful black retainer to white masters, spat out at the end of apartheid, affected audience members "paralysed by the silence of it—the ending of an era, which didn't mean the next one would be O.K." (Tulloch 2004: 240).

The next time I encountered this "paralysis" affect among audiences in the theatre was at the end of a performance of *Hecuba* in London in 2004, where many of the audience sat silent and motionless for many minutes after an Iraq War–inflected production, where the Trojan War–humiliated queen extends her horror over the killing of her children by cutting into pieces—into a see-through bag of body parts—the young children of one of her betrayers. Less than one year later, I was myself surrounded by human body parts in a Tube carriage near Edgware Road station, London, on July 7, 2005; and certainly I—and I suspect many "audiences" for 7/7—felt the sense of contingency and lack that Lash describes: "Aesthetic judgments of the sublime expose bodies with lack, expose open bodies to the ravages of contingency, to darkness and 'fear and trembling'[. . . .] Risks and threats, thus re-experienced and subsumed under neither determinate judgment of the understanding nor the judgments and syntheses of the imagination therefore bring us in touch with our finitude" (2000: 57).

Writing about postmodernity and terrorism, the actor-academic Thomas de Zengotita speaks of a profound tension between our Western world of postmodern virtuality, where the possibilities of choice and self-aware performance seem endless, and the world of millions of others dominated by our interests—not least those parts of the world that generate the ideas and ideologies of terrorism. If the world of postmodernism is performative and ludic, that "Other" world counters with the sureality of an everyday life in which the "mighty bridges, the highways and tunnels, the mountainous buildings" are reduced to ground zero—and "[o]nce apparent only to artists and metaphysicians, the contingency of all things became apparent to everyone" (2005: 283–84).

In the months before 7/7, I had begun to explore the way audiences were responding to the astonishing wave of live theater plays in Britain in 2004–2005 that revisited Greek tragedy in the context of the Iraq invasion and the "war on terror" (Tulloch 2006). How do lovers of Greek tragedy and star fans respond to what is in essence a form of "resistance" within British theater to post-9/11 and post-7/7 surveillance and neoliberal governmentality? And how does the array of discursive rationalities (and of image assemblages, like newspaper cartoons and photographs) across different media outlets, including the wide spectrum of political positions adopted by British newspapers in relation to "new wars" like the Iraq invasion and the "war against terror," interact with the multimediality and actor/audience interaction of theater, and with the aestheticization of everyday life among consumers, fans, cultists, and enthusiasts inside and outside the theater auditorium? That bigger picture of high (and popular) cultural fandom has only just begun to be explored, and for me it was ruthlessly cut off. But there's a lot still to be done!

Part III

Spaces of Fandom
From Place to Performance

9

Place, Elective Belonging, and the Diffused Audience

Brian Longhurst, Gaynor Bagnall, and Mike Savage

The changing nature of social and cultural life requires a new understanding of interconnections among types of audience experience, simple, mass, and diffused.[1] In turn, this necessitates attention to relationships among narcissism, spectacle, performance, and imagination in the flow of everyday life in a media-saturated world. This is encapsulated in the idea of a spectacle/performance paradigm (SPP).

This is not the place to outline in detail the argument for this approach.[2] However, to contextualize, we introduce key points, which provide our starting ground in this paper. Audience research should begin from the localities where people live. Such "roots" are important despite the ways people travel for various reasons. Further, many media-based experiences are still dependent on place, despite new worlds opened by broadcast, cable, and satellite television. Research could develop ideas of scene (see Bennett & Peterson 2004) to examine the interaction around a range of media conditioned by the experience of particular localities. Furthermore, this focus entails attention to the role of media in the constitution and reconstitution of identity in everyday life. This point has been made in the study of media, but often in generalist and generalizing terms. More attention to ordinary identity processes, as parents, neighbors, workers, and so on, should benefit the understanding of social life and audience processes (see also Lembo 2000). Debates on trust and social capital are important to those writing on the media in the context of globalizing social change. Again, somewhat paradoxically, large claims for the significance of media are often made by such writers (e.g. Putnam 2000) without attention to the specific points made by those who research the media (Savage, Bagnall, &

Longhurst 2005: 153–57). Finally, a fuller understanding of contemporary sociation is therefore needed. While, for example, the "uses and gratifications" approach sought a more social understanding of audience processes, it has many limitations (see Barker & Brooks 1998).

Work on audiences should consider the detail of audience responses to a range of media (not just TV, which has been by far the dominant form studied) in the context of attention to processes of everyday life that takes cognizance of new forms of cultural theory that emphasize the conditionality of identity, community, and performativity, while not losing sight of the ordinariness of everyday life as involving shopping, going on holiday, looking after children, keeping in touch with parents by telephone, and so on. In recent work, we deploy the concept of "elective belonging" to examine attachment of people to places where they have decided to live (Savage, Bagnall, & Longhurst 2005). Such attachment to place should move debate around issues of globalization and attachment away from dichotomies like locals/incomers to consider how people locate themselves in places though parenting, shopping, working, and engaging with media and so on. This chapter considers audience experiences against the backdrop of "elective belonging" to show how media processes contribute to subtle processes of ordinary living in places, with due attention to identity, imagination, and performance.[3] Specifically, we show how attention to cinema facilitates consideration of the relation between the mass and diffused audience processes and how discussion of theater permits examination of that between simple and diffused processes. We comment on the implications of this discussion for the idea of an audience continuum. We also explore imagination, spectacle, identity, and performance.

First, we briefly introduce the project from which the data discussed arise (for more detail, see Savage, Bagnall, & Longhurst et al. 2005). This is followed by consideration of findings with respect to attachment to cinema and theater. These more descriptive sections lead to consideration of implications of these data for the approach and concepts summarized in this paper.

The Project

In accord with the strategy of the SPP, we took four contrasting locations near Manchester, in the Northwest of England, as the site for between forty and fifty in-depth interviews.[4] In each location we took the electoral register as our sampling frame, took a one-in-three sample of particular streets, and arranged interviews. Our research was based in particular locales but not predicated on the existence of bounded living. Rather, the places were sites to investigate people's connectivity and its relationship to everyday life and experience.

Central to our interest in understanding the significance of social and cultural practices in their contexts was the need to be able to relate people's narratives to work, residence, and leisure. Our interview schedule asked people about their daily routines around work, household, kin, friends, and leisure so that we could ascertain both the kinds of spatial ranges of such practices and the extent to which people's narratives spontaneously invoked other kinds of issue as they talked.

The four areas were as follows:

Wilmslow—a town twelve miles south of Manchester, which is in a desirable suburban belt. We expected to find high-status, affluent, middle-class residents and interviewed in areas of detached housing, where properties were valued in 1997 at between £250,000 ($415,000) and £750,000 ($1,245,000) (see Savage, Bagnall, & Longhurst 2004). We chose Wilmslow as a location where those with relatively large amounts of economic capital were located.

Ramsbottom—an old Lancashire mill town twelve miles north of Manchester, which had been subject to considerable new building and had become a popular commuter belt location. We interviewed in large older terraced and newer semidetached housing, which sold for between £50,000 ($83,000) and £150,000 ($249,000). We expected to find residents with reasonable amounts of economic and cultural capital.

Chorlton—an area of urban gentrification close to the center of Manchester, with new cafes, wine bars, restaurants, and specialist shops. We expected to find large numbers of academically well-qualified public-sector workers, and interviewed in "desirable" streets where properties ranged in price from £50,000 ($83,000) for small terraces to £200,000 ($332,000) for the largest terraced houses. We expected to find respondents with high levels of cultural capital.

Cheadle—an interwar suburban estate of three-bedroom semidetached housing. In 1997–1998 houses were valued at between £50,000 ($83,000) and £65,000 ($107,900), and we expected to find large numbers of intermediate-class white-collar workers.

TABLE 9.1.
Key Features of Achieved Sample

Dimensions	Cheadle	Chorlton	Ramsbottom	Wilmslow
Av Household income	£23K	£30K	£36K	£68K
	($38K)	($50K)	($60K)	($113K)
% Graduates	14	60	19	45
% Upper service class	3	18	26	42
% Service class	24	60	62	63
Interviews	43	47	47	45
Response rates	29%	39%	30%	41%

TABLE 9.2.
Number of References to Attendance at Cinema and Theatre

	Cheadle	Chorlton	Ramsbottom	Wilmslow
Cinema	20	36	25	24
Theatre	9	33	16	28
Total asked	40	46	41	41
Missing	3	1	6	4
Total Sample	43	47	47	45

Patterns of Involvement with Cinema and Theater

Patterns of cinema and theater attendance were differentially spread over the areas (see table 9.2).

Table 9.2 shows whether the respondent had attended cinema or the theater within a two-year period. Cinema is a popular form of media consumption. Fifty percent or more of the sample in each area attend. Chorltonians were much more likely to be heavy cinemagoers than those resident in the other areas. In all areas, most cinema going is to nearby multiplexes, located in suburban or out-of-town shopping complexes (though the multiplex in nearby Salford Quays—a dockside area of gentrification—was also popular with Chorltonians). For Ramsbottom residents, the only multiplex that was ever mentioned was on the motorway, approximately five miles away. Respondents in the other areas had some choice, and this was normally made in terms of the convenience of a particular site or complex. Chorltonians were the only group likely to visit a "mainstream" cinema in the center of Manchester, where for some this added to the "event" as it felt more like a night out than a visit to the suburbs. Chorltonians were the only people (with one or two exceptions of those from other areas) likely to visit the Corner House, Manchester's Art

Cinema complex, located in the city center, close to Manchester and Manchester Metropolitan Universities. It is also close to the bars and clubs that form Manchester's night-time economy.

There were some people (again overwhelmingly in Chorlton) who are enthusiastic about cinema and who go regularly. For the others, it is something done irregularly, mainly to see the latest Hollywood "blockbuster" (at the time of our research, especially *Titanic*) or a popular British film of particular contemporary relevance (again, at the time of our research, *The Full Monty*). These films were "water-cooler" cinema, as people would often mention them, even if they had not seen them, or indeed expressly did not want to see them—which might be something that required explanation, as it was perceived that one should be seeing this film. However, even with these films, the question about cinema virtually never produced anything that might count as even the most rudimentary textual analysis.

Theater attendance was more skewed than cinema going. Few Cheadle residents ever attend, and when they do their attendance tends to be very irregular and involve a musical or "show" (see below on such fluidity of meaning). This pattern is pretty much repeated in Ramsbottom, though there were some who attended more regularly. In these cases, attendance was to a theater in Manchester and to the Octagon in nearby Bolton. There were also a small number of people who would attend local amateur theater. Wilmslow residents were the only group to attend the theater more than the cinema. They attended in Manchester in the main, but also visited a number of other regional theaters. There were a number of people who visited Stratford-upon-Avon for Shakespeare on a regular basis, perhaps for a weekend. Wilmslow is distinctive in this sense. There are also a significant number of people who attend the theater as part of an organized group. Again, this is something that is most talked about in Wilmslow. Chorltonians also tend to visit the theater, mostly in Manchester at the Royal Exchange Theatre in the center of town.

The Meanings of Cinema and Theater: Simple, Mass, and Diffused Audiences

Having considered the broad patterns of engagement with cinema and theater, we examine the meanings of these patterns in the context of the SPP. Due to space limitations, we have not included quotations from our respondents in this paper. *Globalization and Belonging* and our other papers may be consulted for the voices of our respondents on a range of issues. Four contextual points require brief consideration. First, research on audiences for cinema and theater has been thin compared to that on television. There is some excellent work on cinema. However, the best of it has tended to take a historical perspective (for example, Kuhn 2002; Stacey 1994; Staiger 1992) and to be concerned with the memories of fans. More contemporary analysis has also offered a range of insights. For example, Barker and Brooks (1998) comprehensively consider *Judge Dredd* and responses to the movie, but focus on this film and offer little analysis of what they term "low investors" in the film and cinema in general (1998: 232–33). Attention here is precisely one of our intentions and a strength of the SPP. Audience studies of the theater are rarer and have tended not to make great use of the current trends in audience analysis and, again, not to address the differential impact of the theater (Bennett 1997, Hayes 2002 and her ongoing Ph.D. work at Salford University).

Second, there are definitional issues with both cinema and the theater. While it may appear that these are bounded forms and experiences, respondents offered a range of interpretations of them. Thus, a question about cinema might quickly lead to consideration of films on TV, or how a video would substitute for seeing the film at the cinema. Likewise, a question about theater might provoke a discussion of the enjoyment of "shows" of the "mega musical" type, attendance at musical gigs, or attendance at comedy clubs. In this sense "theater" has a fluid meaning.

Third, the key characteristics of the simple, mass, and diffused audiences should be noted (see figure 9.1).

FIGURE 9.1.
Modes of Audience Experience

	Simple	Mass	Diffused
Communication	Direct	Mediated	Fused
Local/Global	Local	Global	Universal
Ceremony	High	Medium	Low
Public/Private	Public	Private	Public and Private
Distance	High	Very High	Low
Attention	High	Variable	Civil inattention

Source: Abercrombie and Longhurst (1998: 44)

Here we concentrate on consideration of these modes of audience experience in the context of the data on cinema and theater.

Finally, a contrast can be drawn between respondents' initial responses to questions about television and music and those to questions about cinema and theater. As discussed by Savage, Bagnall, & Longhurst (see especially 2005: 157–70), responses to questions about television produced in the main extreme defensiveness. Despite its centrality to their lives, respondents played down the amount of TV that they watched. Responses to inquiries about music were different. People often emphasized the broad range of their musical tastes in what we termed an "omnivoric refrain," derived from the omnivore thesis (e.g. Peterson & Kern 1996; Peterson & Anand 2004). They tended not to exhibit defensiveness. Cinema and theater provoked neither of these initial responses to any degree. While a number of people expressed a desire to go to the cinema and theater more often (see further below), they did not invest as strongly in either form—that is, the denial of TV or the desire to foreground varied musical taste. People were initially more indifferent to both cinema and theater, though as will be suggested below, traces of the desire to foreground taste can be found. Having addressed these contextualizing points, we consider the main domains of the response to the questions about cinema and theater: place, space, sociation (in particular the family), and enthusiasm.

Place figured strongly in different ways in responses to the cinema and theater. While prompted at times by the way the questions about these forms and experiences were asked, in general the discussion went in this direction rapidly. Place occurred in different ways. First, it figured with respect to the characterization of the actual locality of residence itself. Thus, a question about cinema could lead to a lament about the area in question no longer having a local cinema. While this was mentioned at least once in each area, it was very strong in Wilmslow. The loss of the Rex (the name itself is emblematic of a particular era of the cinema in Britain) was commented upon without prompt in no less than eight of the discussions of cinema with the Wilmslow residents, so that it informed their general perception of the place. Some of the more established residents of Wilmslow lament the loss of the village nature of the place as it has changed to a suburb like many others with out-of-town shopping. The decline of Wilmslow as a "village" can be seen in the loss of the high street cinema as much as in the transformation of the varied shops of the high street as café bars and bistros have moved in (see further Savage, Bagnall, & Longhurst 2004). The absence of a cinema is thus a way to capture the nature of a locale, as is the presence of some kind of local theater activity.

While again, this was a minority response, some of the Ramsbottom residents discussed the local theater group and the local theater in the town positively, suggesting that their narration of elective belonging to the place was reinforced by this local phenomenon. It did not matter that none of the Ramsbottom residents who mentioned the existence of the local theater had actually attended it; rather, it mattered that this imagined possibility was a way of characterizing the nature of the place and their attachment to it.

Place figured in a second and related sense, as the nature and locality of the multiplex was an indication of the suburban or distinctive nature of the place itself and its connections to facilities of different types. Thus a possible story about why a place is a good locale to which to elect to belong mobilizes its convenience for a range of services—or consumer experiences—of which cinema is one like others. The multiplexes that serve this function are increasingly in the same sites as shops and chains of restaurants like Pizza Hut and McDonalds. So while the multiplex sums up a lack of local identity for some of those who have been longer-term residents of a place, for many others it captures the appeal of a place because it is convenient. There is no investment in the multiplex itself—there was relatively little positive comment on them, though they were seen as more comfortable than the Corner House by some Chorlton residents—they are "there" as part of the landscape of consumption. However, this should not suggest that they are unimportant or subjected to a fundamentalist critique; rather, they are one of the "pathways" through which dimensions of elective belonging can be mobilized.

Third, Manchester figured as site of cinema attendance. This was overwhelmingly true for the residents of Chorlton who as well as using multiplexes would also attend the multiscreen Odeon in the center of town, or in one case a multiscreen at one of the two central stations (a cinema since closed). They were also the only people to attend the art cinema complex—the Corner House. In itself this provoked some mixed feelings. While it enabled the viewing of a greater range of films and could offer more "enthusiast" pleasures, it was sometimes criticized as lacking comfort and having an obscured view. Thus, in a pained manner, the possibilities that it offered for a more cosmopolitan experience came up against its lack of consumer comfort—where the multiplexes scored. Lack and expense of parking were also sometimes used to compare the city center cinemas with suburban multiplexes. This is significant as it offers a sense of the contradictions between texts and places. For this group, art cinema texts (and indeed other cinema texts) should best be enjoyed in the art cinema space; however, the actual relatively poor consumer experience of that space overrode such concerns. While there are clear connections between places and texts, in that theaters are known for putting on specific types of plays and mainstream films play in multiplexes, it would be useful to explore how texts shift in meaning and audience response in different environments, especially when they are "out of place." For example, how does it affect audience response and meaning to see the same film in a multiplex as opposed to an art cinema? However, further exploration of these matters for our perspective would require additional data.

Manchester city center was a key site of theater attendance. Nearly all those who attended the theater used the city center theaters (in particular the Royal Exchange). Some of those who attend theater had (or had in the past) season tickets for the Royal Exchange. However, despite this there was little attachment to this theater as a place. This is of significance as other research with theatergoers suggests attachment to a theater because of its local nature and its architecture (Hayes 2002 and ongoing). As mentioned above, some people attend Shakespeare productions in Stratford-upon-Avon and may indeed have season tickets for this. Even among this group, there was little discussion of the plays and pleasures that they had seen in the past or were going to see in the future. Other places that were mentioned as sites of theater attendance include the Octagon in Bolton, just north of Manchester and Mold in North Wales, which is convenient for some Wilmslow residents. Sometimes the theater going in other cities was used as a point of comparison with Manchester. Cities and other places become partly described via media experiences and potential. The place that scored in these terms—though it was not discussed that often—is Edinburgh, which is seen by many to be a significant site of cultural experience that could not be matched by Manchester. London was sometimes mentioned as a place to see theater, but without any sense of investment in it. There was some comment that part of the appeal of Manchester is its cinemas and theaters and aspects of this were something to take some pride in, but this was in no sense dominant.

The final sense of place that emerged concerns "northernness." Mention (discussion would be too strong a term) of *The Full Monty* often occurred in terms of a vague consideration of being northern. While the experiences of many of our respondents were removed from those of the film's male victims of deindustrialization, who turn to stripping, the fact that this was northern (and hence somewhat local) carried much resonance, as offering a reason why this film could be talked about and a desire to see it could be expressed.

Space in a more generalized sense also figured significantly in the meaning of cinema and theater. Cinemas were compared by convenience, as discussed above, but also by comfort. The literature on cinema audiences cited above draws attention to different dimensions of the cinema-going experience in these terms. We found this also to be a key in the orientation to cinema. Thus, some would prefer the multiplexes because of the better view, the more comfortable seats, and so on. Others would criticize the cinematic experience because of the noise made by others and in one memorable case because it is impossible to read a newspaper while watching a film at the cinema.

The experience as an audience member for cinema and theater is bound up concretely with a number of meanings of place and space, such as where a car can be parked, and with respect to the imagination of what places are and can be (Urry 1990)—from the "idea" of Ramsbottom as a site of local theater to the condensations of Edinburgh as a city of culture. As we found with respect to Manchester, cities are compared through the spectacle of the cultural experience and as consumption sites. This fuels some of the dilemmas of elective belonging, in that the place of residence may suffer by comparison with the imagined possibilities of other places.

Before addressing further the conceptual issues involved, we consider the other most significant dimension of the meaning of cinema and theater—its implication in patterns of sociation. While television has been much studied as a domestic form, entailing interactions among household and family members, other media forms have been less discussed in such contexts. Different dimensions of this came through in the meanings of cinema and theater. Often, asking a question about these forms would provoke a comparison with the respondent's partner. Comment was made on the pleasures of engaging with these media with a partner, or that they never went because the partner does not like the form, or that the respondent only went alone as the partner was not interested. In these ways, media are crucially part of a relationship. Moreover, cinema (and less often theater) is attended with children. A significant number of people only attend with children. It is one of the consumption experiences that are part of such aspects of family life. Children also figure in narratives about cinema and theater in other ways. People talked of how their cinema attendance was affected by the problems of securing a babysitter for young children. Pretty obviously, the ability of people to attend forms outside the home is affected by such domestic responsibilities. This seems a fairly mundane (if relatively neglected) point, but it is significant that it connects to the performance of what it is to be a parent, and to the imagination of what other experiences might be possible if children were not there. Some older respondents also talked about cinema/theater and their grandchildren in ways like parents taking their children to these forms— as something to do.

Cinema and theater are aspects of patterns of friendship and organized groups. Many people talked of the forms as things that they do with friends, either in a group or with a close friend (for some of the older respondents). The media forms are part of the ongoing constitution and reconstitution of patterns of sociability and friendship. Cinema is sometimes seen as "something to do" as part of the weekend activity and occurred in this way when we asked our respondents to describe a typical week or weekend. Media are part of the detail and management of the interactions of everyday life.

Finally, there were a small number of enthusiasts or fans of cinema and theater. The sorts of responses that we have detailed so far vastly outnumbered such attachments. However, we did interview someone who talked enthusiastically of Spanish cinema, a *Star Wars* fan, and several people who talked of their love of cinema or theater. Those who expressed most passion for cinema mainly lived in Chorlton. They talked about the way in which attendance at the Corner House allowed them to access a wider range of films and especially foreign films. This is part of the imagined cosmopolitanism of this group (see Savage et al. 2005). In this way cinema attendance fueled a more "globalized" attachment, which was signaled for them in other ways as well. In their minds, Chorlton is liked because it has these characteristics. Significant attachment to theater was most common in Wilmslow. This was rather like residents' tastes in radio (Longhurst, Bagnall, & Savage 2001) and music (Savage, Bagnall, & Longhurst 2005) as they like "mainstream" theater, but not experimental works. The enthusiasm might include trips to Stratford for Shakespeare. In some interviews this led to a longer interchange concerning this form. The places in which they lived facilitated these attachments for Chorltonians and Wilmslovians, but in ways similar to those in which the places worked for those who were not enthusiastic. It is possible to speculate on the paradoxes of how home and mobile media facilitate fandom of particular types through repeat consumption and so on, whereas attendance at cinema and theater is in some sense more consumer-like, while it has often been thought to involve more conscious choice. However, consideration of these issues in detail would again require further research.

This evidence shows the interaction of the different forms of audience experience outlined above. Thus, the audience in a theater, which is a good example of a simple audience, is contextualized or framed by the diffused audience processes of everyday life. Neither of these experiences can be fully understood without reference to the other. Analysis can begin from either the experience of the theater audience member, thereby being very likely to raise wider issues of sociability and so on, or from the wider processes. Overall, one mode of analysis is likely to suffer without the other. Similar points can be made about mass and diffused audiencing of cinema. This is not about classifying the audience, but shows the analytical power of an approach that attempts to deal with issues of audiencing on interconnected levels. We conclude with other implications of our discussion.

Conclusions

Our data provide evidence for the analytic power of the simple, mass, diffused characterizations. We wish to conclude by emphasizing the connections between recent social and cultural theory and our approach and data. We remain concerned that arguments about spectacle, performance, imagination, narrativity, and so on might be more likely to be connected to cultural practices that are themselves exceptional or spectacular in the more extreme sense. In itself this is not to deny the significance of such theoretical innovation or where it has been "applied"; it is to argue that this cannot then be used as a general or wider conclusion. Likewise, as is commonly recognized, points about fans or enthusiasts cannot be made straightforwardly to characterize those with little investment in the practices or attachment to the objects of fandom. There is an audience continuum that is defined across the positions of consumer, fan, cultist, enthusiast, and petty producer. Most of the people discussed in this paper can be seen as consumers (which does not carry pejorative connotations) and some were fans, in that they had attachments to programs (or films and plays) but were not in contact with others who had that interest. It is significant that those who commented on their attachment to a film (e.g. *Star Wars*) usually sought to distance themselves from those who had, in their minds, "pathological" attachments to such media texts.

We seek to connect contemporary cultural theory to the "mundane" practices of everyday life (see also, for television specifically, Lembo 2000). One of the concerns about such a move might be that it undercuts the theoretical (and disciplinary) concerns of media and cultural studies, as it might suggest an inattention to the texts of cinema and theater and so on. We reject such a position. However, it does mean that analyses that begin with texts and audience responses to them need to recognize that such analyses can only have wider application with caution and in specific ways. Fandom is not significant in its generality, but as indicating aspects of everyday performance and imagination that are informing mundane practices. This chapter argues for the social and cultural significance of the media considered (and other media more widely). Thus, performance, imagination, and spectacle are embroiled in practices of attachment and identity in everyday life of media-drenched societies at many levels and any social and cultural analysis that does not pay them detailed attention will be deficient. This is not to rest with generalizations about media power or experience but to show the implication of those processes in the substance of ordinary life. Thus power needs to be theorized in the context of media interaction in different ways. Too many studies of the audience are affected by versions of power and ideology that were critiqued by poststructuralist writers and in books like *The Dominant Ideology Thesis* (Abercrombie, Hill, & Turner 1980). Power, in the Foucauldian sense, is part of ordinary relations and audiencing processes—it is diffused and layered, like modes of audience experience. It resides in the powers of parents and children, as well as with those who decide the news. To foreground this point we seek a shift in understandings and an analysis of the relativities of power, recognizing that power is critical and dispersed and not sovereign.

The place of media power (e.g. Couldry 2000) is important, as is the way in which sociation is fueled and fed by media to become increasingly audienced. Media are critically significant. Our concept of elective belonging captures aspects of this process. People make choices about where they live. Belonging to an area is not simply about being born there, or a matter of conforming to local tradition. We recognize that not all people can afford to live in the places that we researched. Elective belonging (and audiencing) takes place in unequal and divided societies (for class, see for example Devine 2004; Devine et al. 2004; Savage 2000). Such divisions are not only structural, but cultural through and through. It is to exploring the way in which different modes of audience experience and process contribute to modes of belonging that this chapter has been devoted.

NOTES

1. Thanks to Sylvia Hayes for comments on an earlier draft.

2. See Abercrombie and Longhurst 1998; Longhurst, Bagnall, & Savage 2004; and for commentary and development e.g. Couldry 2000; Crawford 2002, 2003; Hills 2002; Jewkes 2002; Laughey 2006; Sandvoss 2003, 2005a.

3. Some discussion of these processes can be found in *Globalization and Belonging*, where chapter 7 considers television, music, and reading in some detail, and much more briefly some aspects of cinema and theater, in pointing out how media are "incorporated into narratives of elective belonging" (179). Radio is discussed in Longhurst, Bagnall, & Savage 2001.

4. We are very pleased to acknowledge the support of the ESRC (Reference No. R000236929).

10

On the Set of *The Sopranos*
"Inside" a Fan's Construction of Nearness

Nick Couldry

Introduction: The Paradox of Fandom Research

When people use up a great deal of time and energy in interpreting a specific text, their subsequent actions oriented to that text pose interesting problems for social scientific interpretation. While the early history of fandom research was dominated by deconstructing fans' subordination in an outdated taste hierarchy, one challenge for current research is to gain a clearer, more inclusive view of the underlying interpretative problem that fan practices pose.

This is a problem in which unwittingly I have found myself entangled. My book *The Place of Media Power: Pilgrims and Witnesses of the Media Age* (Couldry 2000) was not intended as part of fandom research, and its emphasis was on questions of media, power, and space more generally. But it could not avoid the link, because one of its case studies involved making sense of what fans and others did when they visited the set of the UK soap *Coronation Street* in Manchester. However, the anger I felt at the frequent pathologizing of fans' perfectly legitimate interpretative practice was one reason I avoided all trace of individual psychology in my analysis. I was trying to avoid what I saw as a reduction of such practice to the "defects" of individual psyches, and so set off in the opposite direction to see how far one could go in understanding an (admittedly) highly specific fan practice—journeys to the location where a media text is produced—relying only on a sociology that had excised psychology.[1] This was clearly too limited a solution to the interpretative problem of fandom, and in any case the emergence since of sensitive treatments of fan psychology that simultaneously deconstruct and move beyond the old taste hierarchy (Hills 2002; Sandvoss 2005a) removes any justification for my rhetorical exclusion of psychological perspectives.

Another criticism has been made of my earlier treatment of fans that I want to mention as a jumping-off point for some reflections on the wider difficulties inherent in interpreting fan practice, reflections that I hope will be appropriately self-critical. I have been accused in my reading of fan journeys to the set of *Coronation Street* of overemphasizing questions of power—that is, the power relations between those outside media and those within media institutions, and the social power of media generally—or at least of operating with an oversimplified and binary division between media and audiences (Sandvoss 2005a).[2] There is no space here to debate the wider question of media power,[3] but in any case there were other dimensions of my interpretation that were not about power but emphasized memory, pilgrimage, and the paradoxes of getting close to the production site of fiction. So this criticism, while rightly pointing out my earlier (and deliberate) neglect of individual psychology, is in turn a reduction. I am not complaining (far from it), since my point is that the multilayered complexity of fans' actions in relation to texts they love makes *any* account liable to charges of reductionism: there is always more to say, and more perspectives from which to say it. Sandvoss's overall analysis of fandom (2005a) offers a very interesting resolution of the sociology/psychology binary by showing, along the lines of the Frankfurt School, how a sociology of late capitalism that does not pass through the psychological dynamics of individual investments in particular texts and commodities is incomplete. This is clearly right—and a valid criticism of my earlier sociological reduction—but that does not mean an account that corrects for this automatically, in turn, offers a complete interpretative framework of what fans do. There is the separate, and independently difficult, issue of how we take sufficient account of the space of the text, and fans' relatively underdetermined activities as interpreters within that space. There is a great deal to be learned from models drawn primarily from literary theory (Gray 2006); indeed, studying fans' "interpretative communities" (in Stanley Fish's sense) is a route *back* to a sociological interpretation, even if one that considers power in a very different light from my earlier account.

My point then is that reductionism is not a fatal interpretative flaw that distinguishes good from bad accounts of fandom, but something endemic to *all* accounts that aspire to offer a total model of what fans do. Maybe it's that aspiration that has to be abandoned. After a period when various rival models of fan practices have emerged in competition with each other, we may now be on the threshold of a different phase where the interpretative challenge is different: how to find the right mix (from the range of sociological, psychological, sociological/psychological, and literary models available) for interpreting *this particular* fan practice? In which case, fandom research is best seen as an open, cross-disciplinary space for grappling with the highly various consequences of being a more than casual interpreter of a text.

Against that background, I would still want to defend my own emphasis on power and space, but only as one strand that sometimes is more salient than others but cannot yield an overall model. I agree with Sandvoss that "in fandom [. . .] place remains a fundamental point of reference" (2005a: 66), but this, I would add, is difficult to separate from questions of power that do not necessarily pass through individual psychology. Even if these can never provide the whole picture, they should not be ignored either.

I want to develop these thoughts in a spirit that is explicitly self-critical and reflexive, by recalling a visit I made in May 2005 to "The Original Locations for *The Sopranos*" run in New York by On Location Tours, Inc.[4] When writing about the *Coronation Street* set, what I shared with the program's fans was not fandom of the program (beyond a basic level of interest) but an excitement and fascination with places featured in media, and the rich meaning of such places. But here my situation was different: I am a fan of *The Sopranos,* a fandom I share with family and friends. With my wife Louise I have cooked meals from *The Sopranos* cookbook for evenings of *Sopranos* video watching with friends! I was keen to visit *The Sopranos* locations, and knew of the tour well in advance from fellow *Sopranos* fan and film and television scholar Dana Polan. We shared photos of our visits, as would any friends who were also fans. But how would my "internal" account of my visit fit, if at all, with any "external" sociological interpretation (let alone deconstruction) I might imagine myself making of the same experience?

The dialectic of internal/external is inherent, of course, to any attempt at general interpretation of what people do and think; it cannot ever fully be resolved. What I want to argue, however, is that this interpretative tension, far from being artificially imposed on "real life" by the curious and privileged practice of sociology[5] (or psychology or literary theory for that matter) is in fact integral to this particular fan tour in ways that connect interestingly with the text that is its origin.

Getting Close to the Fiction

Media—as a highly centralized mechanism for distributing narratives that are themselves produced in quite specific places—generate many paradoxes of place. There is the paradox of a phenomenological "nearness" (to a news event, a character, a story line, or the excitement of a game show studio) that is inseparable from a practical and material *distance* from its production. Martin Heidegger was one of the first writers to pick up on this contradictory feature of broadcasting (1962: 141): radio, he argued, bring us existentially "near" to places that are distant. In relation to media news, this feature has generated contrasting assessments: some argue that media events remain too distant for moral engagement, while others fear news brings those events trivially close (see, respectively, Robins 1995; Silverstone 2003). Media fictions, of course, raise completely different issues: we know they never happened, even if they encourage us to imagine a not-so-different world where we are told they did (notably with *The X-Files,* for example). Sometimes a narrative relies upon, and allows its readers to develop, a sense of place that is validated by a general belief that a very specific place exists where such things might have happened. In this respect, fictions like *The Sopranos,* that rely on a highly specific sense of situated historical events, differ markedly from soaps such as *Coronation Street* where the associated sense of place is always, from the beginning, based on a generality (life as it once was in the north of England). In the case of *The Sopranos,* visiting New Jersey would *already,* for a fan of the program, mean entering the space of the real events that the fiction models and reworks—and this would be true without us ever discovering locations where particular shots were filmed.

The *Sopranos* tour I did therefore doubled for those on the day (who disclosed themselves as coming from the United States including Alaska, Canada, and Norway, as well as Liverpool and London in the UK) as an introduction to a real region (New Jersey) and a journey to real sites of television production. Neither journey by itself was in the least problematic. Everyone is familiar with the experience of tourism, and most people are fairly familiar also with the experience of media tourism, visiting sites specifically and only because they have featured in a media narrative. It is commonplace now for the second type of journey to be used to market the first (Couldry 2000: 65). We are familiar, also, as part of the second type of tourism, with being taken "inside" the fiction, even if many media tourist sites offer this only minimally, with that experience being limited to a basic moment of recognition ("Oh, *that's* where it was filmed"). The explorations of *X-Files* sites in Vancouver that Matt Hills describes (2002: chapter 7) would appear however to involve more than just noting where something was filmed: the uncertainties of exact location feed into the spatial ambiguities and uncertainties of the *X-Files* narrative itself, generating the possibility of imagining, for a moment, that you are a character exploring the narrative space of the program.

The *Sopranos* tour then combined three spaces that by themselves are unproblematic: (1) the space of general tourism, (2) the space of media tourism, and (3) the imaginary action-space "within" the fictional narrative that (2) sometimes generates. I will return to the contradictions between (3) and (1)/(2) later on, for it is the contradictions that may be problematic. First, however, let's consider the interaction between spaces (1) and (2).

Unlike many tourist guides, the tour guide for the *Sopranos* tour could assume considerable shared knowledge among those paying on the day. Everyone might be dressed pretty much the same with no obvious signs of expertise or interest, but anyone who in a city as packed with tourist opportunities as New York considered this bus tour a good use of his or her time could safely be assumed to have watched with enthusiasm at least one series of *The Sopranos.* The main feature of the witty tour commentary was to acknowledge this knowledge and indeed flatter the participants: quiz questions were opportunities to display special levels of fan knowledge, but a considerable basic level of familiarity with the show, its character and ethos, was generally assumed in any jokes and patter. There was virtually nothing on the tour, after the initial "housekeeping" announcements, that was not reflexive to this extent, right down to the snack of cannoli delivered to us midtour (a recipe for "Carmela's" cannoli recipe was included in the tour booklet). The knowing sophistication of those on the tour was consistently primed—not just sophistication about the quirks of television production (the hidden nepotism and sheer chance that lie behind any complex cultural production) but also sophistication about the meaning of the program, with its story of a mafia culture in steady decline. The guide, acknowledging some people's concerns about the program, asked the party whether the show defamed Italians or was it "just television." "Just television" came the reply. On the tour one learned a lot about the real functions of the buildings used as backdrops, and I won't reveal any secrets here so as not to spoil the fun of future visitors!

The guide was in a strong position to share minor "secrets" of the business, since he had been an actor and extra in many *Sopranos* episodes. From the point of view of the space of media tourism, those of us on the bus could reflect at some distance on the less knowledgeable space of general tourism, even though for most of us I suspect we were in both spaces, since this was our first trip specifically to New Jersey.

Indeed, what we saw of New Jersey—from the famous Turnpike onwards—was shot through with memories, prompted by the guide, of narrative moments from the series. The Turnpike is where the show's opening sequence was filmed. With the theme tune playing, we watched on the video monitors the sequence where Tony Soprano inserts his ticket into the entry barrier, and looks in vain for the view and the light shown on the program sequence. There were many other such moments, not spoiled by the irony sensed by both guide and tourists of the mismatch between the extreme banality of many locations (a one-room diner by a parking lot under a bridge, for example) and the narrative significance of the fictional locations they embodied. Here we were looking back on the space of media tourism, from the space of the narrative. We could laugh at the same relation in reverse, as when we were told that the owner of the tiny "Pizza Land" outlet on Belleville turnpike (shown in the opening credits) gets real orders to send pizzas by Fedex from addresses all over the world (he smiled and waved at us as our bus drove past).

Negative Aura?

"Just think, within two hours we'll be at the Bada Bing," I said to Louise as we entered the lift from a drab hotel landing, to walk down to Thirty-ninth Street where we were to pick up the bus for *The Sopranos* tour.

It's no secret that a *Sopranos* tour culminates at the Bada Bing, a strip joint that provides the "glamorous" end of Tony Soprano's chain of business interests (their core is "waste management" and building site racketeering). Many scenes are set around the Bada Bing dance floor and bar, or in the office where members of Tony's crew relax, playing pool or cards, and Tony takes important business calls and visitors. Along with Satriale's "meat market" and Tony and Carmela's kitchen and pool, the Bada Bing is one of the consistent spatial reference points in the *Sopranos* narrative.

Our bus pulled up behind the building and we were shown the guard rail where in series 3 Ralphie committed a particularly gruesome assault on a stripper who had annoyed him, earning Tony's retribution. We were also given very strict instructions about what we could and could not do once inside, instructions that we were told came from its owner. For "the Bada Bing" is not a set made for television, but a real strip club called Satin Dolls on Route 17, South Lodi, New Jersey.

As we entered the club at 4:30 P.M., after touring the car park to get a good view of its outside, I was still recalling incidents from the plot that had occurred there. I was still thinking, in other words, within the narrative space of the program. By entering the dance space, and like most of the rest of the tour party edging nervously along the wall while looking in towards the raised dance floor beyond the bar counter, I had of course entered a space of media tourism as well. There was no doubt this was the actual place where all those scenes had been filmed: the lighting rig, we had been told, was now permanently installed to save time putting it up and taking it down for each shoot. But in the fifteen or twenty minutes allotted for our tour stop, there was nowhere else to go apart from the dance floor or the club's perfectly ordinary toilets; everywhere leading off from the club area was backstage for its staff, and not part of the set, let alone part of the narrative space of the series. Around the edge of the room, the three tourism spaces (the space of tourism, the space of media tourism, and the space of the narrative) became fused in the club's marketing strategy; the club sold itself as "Satin Dolls aka the Bada Bing Club," with club-type merchandise (tank tops, thongs, g-strings, and the like) that marketed both the real and fictional location. A *Sopranos* pinball machine jokily used the mafia hierarchy (from "Associate" to "Boss") to customize the path of the pinball around the table. But this was the only spot where one could lose oneself in the show's narrative (or at least a commodified reworking of one of its terms). For, as my eyes got used to the light, the sound levels, and the social scene (three or four men sat hunched around the bar, looking up occasionally at the sole dancer on the stage), it became obvious that the only space we were in was the commercial space where this sex club on a bleak transit route marketed itself.

A fascination with the narrative of *The Sopranos* had led me, and thousands of others, by a simple commercial logic into looking on as a tourist in a New Jersey strip joint on a grey Saturday afternoon. For sure, the club is entitled to conduct its business, although I personally am uncomfortable with the sour patriarchy that I sense saturates such places. The morality of all this is less interesting than the meaning. What did my act of standing there by the dance floor communicate? Clearly not ironic distance: there is no way of standing ironically. Clearly not anger or moral distance, since neither I nor any other visitor had, as it were, *locus standi* to complain: we had paid to see *Sopranos* locations, and this was what we were being allowed to do, and the club was carrying on its lawful business. In any case, it was clear from the weary contempt with which the off-floor dancing staff looked at us that we had no moral standing in their eyes: not customers (although a few on the tour bought a drink at the bar), not enforcement authorities with a power to interfere, just tourists who had come to "see" the fiction with which their real working lives were for commercial benefit incidentally associated.

As tourists we were in a "nonplace," but in a sense rather different from Augé's (Augé 1995). For this was not so much a place without "place-like" features, a mere route of passage, like a freeway, although as it happens the club's location was a bleak spot by a freeway (interestingly this is not something the program emphasizes about the fictional location, as far as I recall). It was a real place with many place-like features, yet a nonplace *to us* because it was somewhere we had not wanted to visit as such (under *this* description, as a philosopher might say), a place where we had no ability or right to act.

So we said and did nothing—until we were back on the bus, on the return trip to Manhattan with old *Sopranos* clips for entertainment. This climax to our tour had unexpectedly brought a melancholia at which Adorno might have grimaced. Blithely at play in the space of the series' large and tangled narrative and enjoying the chance to map that narrative space onto the array of New Jersey streets, retail outlets, and parking lots, we had stumbled into the material reality of an all-too-ordinary place of capitalist work from which our narrative engagement had distracted us. While many such media tourist sites have an "aura" in Benjamin's sense (1968), as a place of actual filming (see Couldry 2000: 81), aura depends on a particular type of encounter—touching the place where the actual thing was/happened/happens—and it was just this possibility of encounter with the fiction and its filming that had been occluded by our uneasy realization of where it was we were standing.

Concluding Thoughts

The *Sopranos* tour carried many of the auratic expectations that a media location conventionally has, but it culminated, I have suggested, in a site of negative aura, a site whose different reality effaced any aura associated with the fiction and its process of production.

But this contradiction is, perhaps, not so foreign to the narrative offered by *The Sopranos*. For, from its outset, the series has been distinctive for a double narrative: the "public" story of the outer edges of a New York Italian mafia "family" in terminal decline, and the "private" story of Tony Soprano's health and psychological problems and imperfectly managed family life. This doubleness is more than a narrative conceit, since at various levels *The Sopranos* shows it at work in characters' lives, and the painful contradictions that flow from this. In this sense, and this has always been part of its attraction to me as a fan, *The Sopranos* addresses on a large scale some of the contradictions between "work" and "life" that are central issues in late modernity. That the *Sopranos* tour should have generated its own contradictions between "play" and "life" seemed, on reflection, somehow appropriate, whether or not those contradictions were intended by the tour's organizers. What emerged was at the same time a contradiction, between different levels of narrative absorption, in my own experience as a fan.

Where do these recollections take us in terms of the choice from which this chapter started—the puzzle over the disciplinary space in which we should locate our academic accounts of what fans, ourselves included, do. In one way, they might seem to confirm Sandvoss's argument that our psychological investments in narrative commodities are an essential part of how we are entrenched within capitalism's order. A complication is that one attraction of *The Sopranos*'s narrative is its implicitly *critical* exploration of the linkages among exploitation, violence, and everyday comfort in contemporary society; but a Frankfurt School reading would have us ensnared within capitalism's order, *whether or not* the narratives that are the objects of our passion are critical. A further complication is that, as visitors, our entanglement with the reality of a New Jersey strip joint was not shaped in any way by the specificities of our individual *psychological* investment in *The Sopranos*'s narrative; one might just as well say that it was shaped by the social pleasures afforded by *The Sopranos* as a complex, evolving narrative that provokes discussion based on the deep generic foundations of mafia narratives. On the other hand, I would happily acknowledge that, on this tour at least, issues of symbolic power (while present at some level throughout) were outweighed in terms of analytic interest by the spatial and narrative ambiguities into which the tour drew its participants.

The only safe conclusion, I suggest, is to acknowledge that fandom research needs a theoretical flexibility to match the phenomenological complexity of much fan experience. Instead of a "unified" model that privileges one framework of interpretation (psychological, sociological, economic, textual, spatial), we need perhaps a toolkit from which, when faced with particular fan experiences, we can draw on any or all of these frameworks. Indeed, it is in part just this complexity—this sense at times of moving uncertainly between different levels, and perspectives, of inter-pretation—that gives the practice of fandom its rich fascination.

Notes

1. I realized a little later that some sociologists (but against the grain) have argued that sociology needs to integrate psychology into its regular discourse (Craib 1998), but that remains a minority position. I was also aware of sociological approaches that emphasized different dimensions from my account: Abercrombie and Longhurst (1998), Harrington and Bielby (1995).

2. See Corner (2003).

3. Key here, and relied on in part by Sandvoss at this point, is the argument of Abercrombie and Longhurst (1998); for a discussion of what I see as weaknesses in that latter position, see Couldry (2005).

4. For details see www.screentours.com.

5. See Bourdieu (1998).

11

A Sort of Homecoming
Fan Viewing and Symbolic Pilgrimage

Will Brooker

She says nobody wants to believe
You're the same as everyone.
What makes me unique? My dark life.
. . . And you think you're a guest, you're a tourist at best
Peering into the corners of your dark life
—Elvis Costello, "My Dark Life" from *Songs in the Key of X*

A back alley in Vancouver. A road tunnel in Los Angeles. A gravestone in Guildford. A mock-up of the *Rover's Return* pub. Graceland. The study of fan pilgrimages is sufficiently established for us readily to accept the idea that some dedicated followers of cultural texts or icons—in the above cases, *The X-Files, Blade Runner,* Lewis Carroll, *Coronation Street,* and Elvis Presley—will travel across the world to often mundane places that fandom has made sacred and special (see, respectively, Hills 2002; Brooker 2005b; Brooker 2005a; Couldry 2000; King 1993). But the idea that watching television constitutes a "symbolic pilgrimage" may still prompt a sceptical response. Such is Roger Aden's assertion in his chapter "Transforming the Panopticon into the Funhouse: Negotiating Disorientation in *The X-Files*" (1999: 149).

Aden makes grand claims about fan viewing, presenting the experience of sitting down to watch *The X-Files* as *symbolic pilgrimage*—a trip without drugs, a journey and return without leaving the easy chair. Fans, according to Aden, leave their structured, everyday environment to enter Agents Fox Mulder and Dana Scully's diegesis—a fictional world that echoes the panoptic control of normal working life, yet allows a playful exploration of these structures and always includes, at the end of the episode, the reassurance of an exit. The show's panoptic environment of surveillance and control is a pleasurably threatening but safe simulation; a "funhouse" where viewers test themselves, scare themselves, and equip themselves with coping strategies for the real structures of social life. Aden has no hesitation in describing this psychological immersion and return from the show's fictional world in the same terms as physical, geographical pilgrimage, relating it to the tripartite structure used by Victor and Edith Turner (after Arnold Van Gennep):

> Each trip to the funhouse is a new yet ritualistic experience for both the agents [Mulder and Scully] and their vicarious partners, the fans. In fact, the show's recurring form mirrors the pilgrim's journey as described by Edith Turner: [. . .] "(1) separation (the start of the journey), (2) the liminal stage (the journey itself, the sojourn at the shrine, and the encounter with the sacred) and (3) reaggregation (the homecoming)." (Aden 1999: 152)

My main intention in this chapter is to explore the validity of terms such as "symbolic pilgrimage" to describe the experience of viewing a TV show. I discuss metaphors of interior journey, then examine the testimonies of my own *X-Files* fan sample in terms of the tripartite structure Aden takes from Van Gennep through Turner, and Csikszentmihalyi's concept of "flow." In the third and fourth sections, I explore two further issues raised by this case study: whether a lack of fellow travelers—a lack of physical, spiritual, or virtual connection with other people—impoverishes the pilgrimage, and what difference it makes when the symbolic pilgrimage is not a trip into the unknown but an immersion in a familiar fiction where the protagonists are old friends. Ultimately, I suggest that instead of treating symbolic pilgrimage as a separate category, we should ask whether all geographical pilgrimage in fact involves a degree of conceptual, inner, symbolic travel.

Traveling without Moving

The whole concept of TV viewers as pilgrims, entering a different state that qualifies as a journey, albeit "symbolic," may initially sound far-fetched. When we consider a *Lord of the Rings* fan making the trip from

Britain to the New Zealand film locations, the word "pilgrim" comes more easily, but does a fan sitting in his or her own domestic environment, watching a screen—even though we readily grant the fan the status of an active viewer rather than a passive receiver—really deserve such associations of adventure?

Aden uses the metaphor repeatedly and without qualms: "just what in the series spawns the pilgrimages of X-philes is difficult to pinpoint" (1999: 151), viewers "accompany the agents on their journey" (1999: 153), "fans leave their homes to enter the invisible liminoid aura surrounding *The X-Files*" (1999: 162).

Though this language of physical journey seems unusual when applied to TV viewing, the idea of traveling without moving has various precedents in religion and anthropology. Alan Morinis's study, *Sacred Journeys*, opens with the reminder that it is "questionable to distinguish between terrestrial and 'metaphorical' pilgrimages. This distinction portrays the earthly journey as somehow more real, when, in fact, most cultures subsume physical journeys and other quests into one more inclusive category: the spiritual life is a pilgrimage" (1992: 4). Morinis includes in his discussion of "nongeographical goings-forth" (1992: 2) the "inner pilgrimage" to sacred places within the mind and body, practiced by Hindu mystics (1992: 3), and the celestial "Vrndavana of the mind," the city inhabited by Krishna that devotees can "visit" through perfect prayer.

As already indicated, Aden's notion that fans "travel" while engrossed in the show is tied to Victor Turner's anthropological structure of pilgrimage—yet that structure refers, in both Turner and Van Gennep's work, not specifically to pilgrimage but to a more general "rite of passage." Turner describes *rites de passage*, after Van Gennep, as "rites which accompany every change of place, state, social position and age" (Turner 1969: 94; see Van Gennep 1960: vii). Although the word "passage" of course implies journey, a change of place is only one of the possible transitions connoted by the phrase, and the shifts from one state to another that Turner describes are by no means exclusively physical. When, for instance, he writes in *The Ritual Process* of the ritual subject in Zambian tribal culture as a "passenger," "passing through a cultural realm" (1969: 94), the individual may be going physically no further than to a shelter a mile from his village, though symbolically the ritual may involve a transit from boy to man, man to chief.

This notion of passage as a spiritual and symbolic state rather than a literal movement can be identified in Christianity, as well as African tribal culture. Turner notes that "traces of the *passage* quality of the religious life remain in such formulations as: 'The Christian is a stranger to the world, a pilgrim, a traveller, with no place to rest his head.' Transition has here become a permanent condition" (1969: 107). Indeed, in his later work with Edith Turner, *Image and Pilgrimage in Christian Culture*, Turner describes physical travel to a sacred shrine as a second-best, layman's substitute for the "interior salvific journeys" practiced only by "monastic contemplatives and mystics" (Turner & Turner 1978: 7).

Another promising metaphor of interior travel can be found in Csikszentmihalyi's theory of "flow experience," which shaped Turner's later work and also explicitly informs Aden's study. Flow, in this context, is the pleasurable sensation of losing oneself in an activity—work, a game, a physical or mental challenge—and becoming immersed, with everything perfectly meshing in a harmonious state where goals are set and satisfyingly met. Time contracts or stretches, and the individual merges with the activity, totally absorbed.

This sense of immersion, where the everyday is transcended and the participant enters a different state of being, a form of communion with a text, with a process, and sometimes with other participants, seems to offer a productive approach to the experience of watching television: in particular, the more intense viewing practiced by fans with their favored shows. Aden uses the term in this sense when he describes the "deep sense of involvement" reported by *X-Files* fans as similar to the "'flow experiences reported by pilgrims."

However, in applying Csikszentmihalyi's concept of "flow" to television fandom, Aden ignores the fact that Csikszentmihalyi does not merely fail to mention TV viewing in his discussion of flow activities; he deliberately excludes it, denying it any such potential and only referring to it as a negative example, a contrast to more worthwhile practices. Reading is, to Csikszentmihalyi, "the most often mentioned flow activity around the world," and studying a work of art can transport the viewer symbolically to "a separate reality" (2002: 118–19). Sex and eating can be transformed from biological urges into flow experience with the right kind of discipline and discrimination (2002: 101, 114). Even trench warfare and criminal activity such as vandalism or joyriding are, according to Csikszentmihalyi's respondents, potential sources of flow (2002: 68). Yet Csikszentmihalyi refuses to discuss television viewing as anything but a passive, brainless, numbing act. "Watching TV is far from being a positive experience—people generally report feeling passive, weak, rather irritable, and sad when doing it" (2002: 169). In order to apply Csikszentmihalyi's concept to a fan's immersion in his or her favorite show, we have to negotiate this prejudice and find, as I later suggest, a loophole in his damning ruling against television viewing as flow experience.

I Want to Believe

Aden's study is based primarily on a textual analysis of ten episodes from *X-Files* seasons 1 and 4, and interviews carried out in person and by email with fans. The viewer feedback, however, is not extensively used, and fan voices only emerge occasionally through the discussion of theory, narrative, and character. I want to address that here by giving more space to viewer response. My own data are drawn from a survey (thirty questions, inviting lengthy qualitative replies) submitted to thirteen *X-Files* fans, recruited from the *Xfiles* community of *Livejournal.com*. While the sample is small-scale, the responses were rich, sometimes running to several pages for each question. These data can, of course, only be suggestive of possible trends, but the fan voices are intriguing nonetheless.

First, we can return to Van Gennep's tripartite structure of a rite of passage. In Aden's application of the theory, this involves a separation from the habitus, the "panopticon-like culture" of postindustrial culture with its "constant surveillance," employment and financial insecurities, and controlling social structures (1999: 160). The second stage of pilgrimage involves an in-between, liminal transit, away from home but not yet at the "promised land," the sacred site that marks the pilgrim's goal:

> Once we are immersed in the liminoid flow of watching *The X-Files*, fans such as myself can begin the rhetorical process of constructing a symbolic community that offers an outpost for transcending the habitus. In this case our construction efforts build a community that exists in between the real and unreal, with faith generating the bonds of connection. (1999: 165)

Aden's two references to the blurred boundaries between real and fictional worlds repeat the theme of ambiguity and liminality, while the viewer's involvement in the fictional world is characterized as "immersion" in "flow." This latter term is, of course, a reference to Csikszentmihalyi's theory of "optimal experience," the state of being pleasurably lost in an activity to the extent that the outside world drops away, and the individual meshes per-

154 SPACES OF FANDOM: FROM PLACE TO PERFORMANCE

fectly with his or her goals (1999: 164). It also implies a state of ambiguity and being between, as flow experience, like liminality, seems to contract and expand time, and combines the paradoxes of structure and freedom, work and effortlessness, individual achievement and a sense of community.

Aden's respondents are briefly cited to support his argument that the *X-Files* viewing experience is immersive, which in turn helps indirectly to justify his use of terms like "journey," "trip," and "traveling." Aden's interview subject Sandy emails, "While I'm watching, I'm only involved with the show and don't do anything else" (1999: 164). Other fans tell Aden that they "control their material environments to make the move to the symbolic even easier"—that is, they turn off the lights, "enhancing the distinction between being materially positioned in a living room to being symbolically ensconced in a liminoid flow" (1999: 164). Finally, Aden's subjects shut out interruptions, telling their mothers not to call during the show or ignoring telephones and doorbells so as not to disturb the "flow experience" (1999: 164).

Our initial response to this passage may well be skeptical; a single quotation from Sandy, who doesn't do anything else when the show is on, seems quite a stretch away from providing convincing evidence that watching *The X-Files* qualifies as immersion in liminality. The other half of Sandy's testimony, in fact, suggests that a more half-hearted, absent-minded involvement with the show is equally likely: "I watch *The X-Files* by myself, while my husband works on the computer and listens to it."

However, my own respondents went some way towards justifying Aden's characterization of the viewing experience as absorption in flow, and even as a metaphorical "trip." Eleven of the thirteen fans I asked reported that they felt "anticipation" or "excitement" just prior to an unfamiliar episode, comparable perhaps to the enjoyable nerves a traveler might feel before setting off on a journey. Twenty-three-year-old Schally's response was typical:

> When the show was airing on television I would often get a little nervous before the second or third part of a multipart episode because those had invariably ended at an unpleasant cliffhanger the week before and I was usually worried about the characters. The season four finale "Gethsemane" absolutely killed me. I was very worried about Mulder and extremely anxious about the upcoming season premier. I used to also get very excited about episodes that had had particularly funny or suspenseful teasers the week before.

The fact that most episodes now are familiar to X-philes, and the difference this makes to their viewing experience, will be discussed below; as will be evident, the respondents often made a distinction between watching for the first time and reacquainting themselves with a favorite installment.

"Trip," of course, has a double meaning of drug-induced-trance, and a number of responses suggested that this dual connotation may be appropriate. Only one respondent, 41-year-old Steve, stated explicitly that his preparation for watching *The X-Files* involved getting "hammered (ie. indulge in alcohol and drugs)," but Schally spoke of her "cravings" for the show, and Seoirse, a 29-year-old woman, described it as "like an addiction for me. If I catch an episode on TV [. . .] it starts this cycle of needing to watch at least 6 episodes before I'm satisfied." Maddy Martin, aged twenty-one, talked about becoming "annoyed and fidgety" if she was called away from an episode to work; Katherine, aged seventeen, exclaimed, "I always feel like watching another—they are addictive!"; and Bellefleur, aged twenty-nine, confessed a "withdrawal feeling" during the week while waiting for the next installment. Thirty-year-old Jamie's observation that if the flow of the episode is interrupted, "I tend to lose interest [. . .] it feels as though the 'magic' is lost" also carries overtones of a ritualized trance state.

Some form of preparation ritual is not uncommon among media fans, and this often seems to approach an act of communion, a symbolic activity that removes the participant from the everyday and brings him or her closer to the fiction. To draw two examples from my own research, listening to the soundtrack CD and wearing an authentically "distressed" Capeside t-shirt before an episode of *Dawson's Creek* (Brooker 2004: 572), or dressing up for a *Star Wars* home screening in Queen Amidala lipstick with Leia hair-buns while feasting on "Wookiee Cookies" and "Yoda Soda" (Brooker 2002: 35) are both forms of bonding with the text, taking the fan a little way out of normal structures and arguably into a liminal border zone between the real world and the diegesis, where the viewer eats the same snacks or wears the same outfits as the characters on screen. The *Twin Peaks* cultists who gathered religiously for a new episode with cherry pie and coffee, and the "Dinner & Dynasty" meetings of the 1980s (Fiske 1987: 71) provide a further example of this ritualized viewing; most recently, fans of the BBC time-travel cop show *Life on Mars* (2006) celebrated its season 1 finale by eating 1970s-style Viscount biscuits and spaghetti hoops.

Aden's X-philes described turning out the lights, unplugging the phones, and creating an appropriate environment for undisturbed passage into "flow"; each of my respondents independently testified to a similar routine. Seoirse made this ceremonial aspect explicit: "Before, when there were still new episodes, I would unplug the phone, switch of all the lights and make myself a pot of tea—it's a ritual!" The common practice among these respondents was notable, with six of the thirteen mentioning that they turn off or unplug telephones, and seven preferring to watch *The X-Files* in the dark.

> I usually watch the show right before I go to sleep, Lights off, door shut, so on. (Schally)

> A lot of the people I watch episodes with prefer to watch it in the dark: all lights out and curtains drawn. When the show used to be on TV, I had to ignore my phone, ignore my parents, and I was unable to draw my gaze from the TV screen. (Maddy Martin)

> When it was on the BBC it was a case of turning out the lights [. . .] getting away for the fifty or so minutes of the programme. (Jamie)

In part, this may be an attempt to transform the domestic viewing environment into a kind of home cinema, with the screen as main focus. The preference for dimmed lights or total darkness could also be related to the horror and suspense aspects of *The X-Files;* this creation of a setting particularly conducive to "flow" may be shaped by the genre and the need for an appropriately spooky setting.

Already we can see that the fans' language suggests immersion and journey. Maddy's gaze is fixed on the screen for almost an hour, as if hypnotized, while Jamie speaks of "getting away," clearly conveying the idea of a "trip" and departure from the everyday world. This terminology is particularly appropriate to a show that, in addition to the geographical journeys and emotional quests of its protagonists, frequently returns to the motif of alien abduction.

These experiences of partial to total absorption were typical of the responses I received. "On good episodes," Schally became "completely engrossed in the show." Jamie stated that "the show makes you forget the real world in its opening moments," while Seoirse and Katherine Woodruff were both "completely involved." Kevin, aged fifty-one, entered the story-world through a main character: "I identify with Mulder in particular and so feel totally immersed [. . .] often very moved by it, always thrilled by it."

Those fans who qualified their replies nevertheless felt enough connection with the fiction for it to prompt a dramatic emotional response. Steve reported, "I lose myself, but not to the extent of forgetting the real world," yet added, "I've felt the whole range of emotions, ranging from extreme joy to anger"; and Ceruleanjen, aged twenty-two, stressed that she was always aware of her "real" surroundings as she watched the show, but continued, "if something sad happens I might cry [. . .] nothing out of the ordinary."

Ten respondents echoed Jamie's comment that external distractions broke the spell of the *X-Files;* disruption often riled them to hostility. "I really don't like it" (Schally), "I was never happy about interruption" (Bellefleur), "It has happened—and I'm not pleased when it does!" (Kevin), "It would greatly annoy me" (Chantal), "I hated being interrupted [. . .] I responded with anger" (Steve). Again, these reports tally with Aden's theory of viewers becoming "enmeshed in flow experiences while consuming popular stories."

We should also note the echoes of Csikszentmihalyi's "flow" experience. The sensations described by his research subjects, from mountaineers through chess and basketball players to dancers—"that's all that matters" (2002: 58), "it becomes your total world" (58), "your concentration is very complete" (52), "the concentration is like breathing—you never think of it" (53), "your comrades are there, but you all feel the same way anyway, you're all in it together" (40)—tally closely with the reports from these fans at the moment of closest engagement with their favored show. It seems even more perverse in this context that Csikszentmihalyi takes such an outdated view of television, excluding its potential for active involvement; although he does unwittingly provide a gap where his theory can be levered open to include certain forms of viewing.

Csikszentmihalyi dismissively compares television with a "drug" (2002: 169) that "keeps the mind from having to face depressing thoughts," but then allows that drugs can only produce optimal experience, or flow, when used "in highly skilled ritual contexts, as is practiced in many traditional societies." Unsurprisingly, he declines to consider the possibility that television viewing could bear any similarities to the ceremonial trances of shamans and priests, but this chink in his condemnation offers some space for a reevaluation of ritualistic fan viewing as a source of flow experience.

You're the Same As Everyone—What Makes Me Unique?

So far, the testimonies of my respondents tend to support Aden's characterization of immersive viewing as a transition to a world "between the real and unreal" (1999: 165), "a sacred place where 'real' time and space are excluded" (1999: 164). Another integral aspect of this journey away from the immediate, material surroundings into a liminal state is "connection with a spiritual community of others [. . .] as vicarious participants in the stories" (1999: 166–67). Just as the fans' journey, in Aden's account, does not involve physical movement from the sofa, so the community is also symbolic, and can take place even if the individual is sitting alone. "Despite watching the show by themselves, they feel attached to the community of nonpresent viewers" (1999: 168).

This congregation, an invisible network uniting fellow fans—dependent in part on traditional schedule-based broadcasting, so the viewer can imagine millions of others doing the same thing at the same time—unites individual viewers, according to Aden, in a kind of intellectual elite. My respondents, as members of *Livejournal*'s *Xfiles* community, were part of a virtual, invisible network that enabled them to communicate with other fans instantaneously, across geographical distance. However, few of them mentioned community as a major aspect of their pleasure in the show. Several stated that they kept their *X-Files* enthusiasm mainly to themselves and felt no close connection with like-minded viewers, whether physically (in real life), virtually (through the internet), or, in Aden's sense of communion with nonpresent fellow travelers, spiritually. Some expressed regret that the most vibrant and rewarding period in the show's fandom was now lost in nostalgic memory:

> I think it would have been cool to have been one of the ardent online fans back in the show's early broadcast days in the US. I've never really met anyone who has more than a casual interest in the show, which is a shame. (Nina)

The fact that the show is now complete and finished, having reached its final closure—it ran over nine seasons, from September 1993 to May 2002—may make all the difference; when fans watch their DVDs or videos now, they have the convenience of deciding how long their "journey" is and when it starts and finishes, but have lost the sense that they are undertaking it at the same time as a nationwide community, undergoing the same or similar experiences during the same time scale. Katherine, like Nina, mourned this loss: "I would love to talk about it with other people—I'm desperate for fellow Philes!"

Communitas is discussed by Turner as a significant aspect of the transition from everyday frameworks into liminality, and back again with an enhanced status or understanding. "In *rites de passage,* men are released from structure into communitas only to return to structure revitalised by their experience of communitas" (1969: 129). His quotation from Martin Buber—"community is the being no longer side by side [...] but *with* one another of a multitude of persons. And this multitude, though it moves towards one goal, yet experiences everywhere [...] a flowing from *I* to *Thou*" (Buber 1961: 51, cited in Turner 1969: 127)—reminds us of Csikszentmihalyi's respondents describing the single purpose of a group in "flow": "your comrades are there, but you all feel the same way anyway, you're all in it together" (2002: 40).

However, while the lack of perceived connection with fellow fans, even on a virtual or spiritual level, may impoverish the sense of communion to some extent—Nina expresses regret for the loss of an intense sharing, and Katherine is desperate for a bond with others—a pleasurable immersion in liminality, outside normal space and time, does not seem *dependent* on the company of others. Csikszentmihalyi's testimonies of flow experience include competitive activities like chess, public debate, hurdling, and tennis, where the player is usually pitted against an opponent rather than moving as one with a team, and solitary pursuits like rock climbing, solo ocean cruising, music composing, and orchard tending (2002: 53–59). Community is clearly not a requirement of the total immersion and connection Csikszentmihalyi describes.

In my own work on geographical pilgrimages to the *Blade Runner* locations of Los Angeles, my respondents reflected on the lack of potential for community bonding with fellow fans, partly because of the key sites' multiple coding as everyday utilities (the Second Street road tunnel, Union Station) or architectural landmarks (the Bradbury Building, the Ennis-Brown house) and the lack of any organized *Blade Runner* pilgrimage culture. One fan reported that "the group I toured [the Ennis-Brown house] with were all fans of its architect, Frank Lloyd-Wright"; another complained that "I actually tried to shoot a short film at Union Station, but the Grand Concourse was booked solid with weddings and stuff" (Brooker 2005b: 24).

However, these obstacles failed to prevent even these cynical fans from expressing some sense of wonder and immersion: "If a movie is like a dream, then standing in an actual location is like stepping into the dream. There's a weird kind of energy to it" (Brooker 2005b: 25). The feeling of connection is not with other fans, but with the fiction; with Rick Deckard and Los Angeles 2019. It is a need for connection with the *text,* not with fellow travelers, that motivated my respondents to take photographs and shoot digital video from the precise angles Ridley Scott used, in an attempt to capture the fictional space of the film. This is the same impulse we see in the photographs of *Star Wars* pilgrims who painstakingly seek out the exact dune framed for a shot of Tatooine, and place themselves into the fictional world by striking the pose Mark Hamill adopted in the 1977 movie. This, too, is the impulse behind websites that place precisely composed images of contemporary San Francisco streets alongside screen-grabs from Hitchcock's *Vertigo* (1958), pinpointing the location and direction of Hitchcock's camera, and pilgrims' photographs of Vancouver that echo *The X-Files*'s shots of a hotel, a bridge, a Skytrain overpass. As Sandvoss writes of pilgrims to Graceland and the *Coronation Street* set, "the emotional significance of visiting fan places lies in the ability of fans to put themselves physically into the otherwise textual universe" (2005a: 61).

These pilgrims are not necessarily bonding with others like them; they are bonding with Luke Skywalker, Scottie and Madeleine, Mulder and Scully. Remember in this context how Kevin and Schally described themselves as becoming immersed in the text through an emotional identification with Fox Mulder. Chantal described the characters as "old friends," a term repeated by Nina: "I am sitting down with old friends; I know they are not going to let me down." As already noted, Aden suggests that viewers "accompany the agents on their journeys" (1999: 153); Bellefleur echoes this idea that the characters, rather than other fans, can be a viewer's fellow travelers. "They take the audience on a journey, or Mulder takes Scully on a journey and thus the audience along with her." Fans can achieve a sense of belonging by entering on their own into the familiar world of the text, and a sense of companionship from reuniting with characters they know almost as family.

A Sort of Homecoming

Fan viewing of *The X-Files* has changed since Aden's research. Seven of my thirteen respondents made a distinction between watching new and unfamiliar episodes, which for them was now only a nostalgic memory, and their current practice of re-viewing the show on DVD and video, or catching a repeated episode by chance on TV. In the latter case, the experience was entirely different. Kevin spoke of feeling "just reassured because it's familiar [. . .] I could have a really bad day, and pop in an episode"; Maddy expressed her feelings of "relaxation, assurance, happiness—I am always cheered up." To Chantal, episodes now are "a much more relaxing experience[. . . .] I really miss the excitement of having unfamiliar episodes," and Nina, as already shown, used similar terms: "I feel relaxed and reassured. I am sitting down with old friends; I know they are not going to let me down."

Is "pilgrimage" still the right word for these reassuring, therapeutic, cheering sessions with familiar guides and confidantes? Revisiting one of Mulder and Scully's old journeys evokes a nostalgic trip to the known past, like an evening with old diaries and holiday videos, rather than an expedition into the unknown. Should pilgrimage not involve more sense of effort, struggle, trial, and test, and imply a transit away from the homely towards the sacred? How can an immersion in both physical and emotional comfort, a session with "old friends," be discussed alongside the ordeal of pilgrims at St. Patrick's Purgatory at Lough Derg, where sleep- and food-deprived visitors must repeat night-long circuits along stony paths, repeating scores of Hail Marys and Our Fathers? (Turner 1978: 119).

Alan Morinis, while embracing the concept of inner, or nongeographical, pilgrimage alongside more traditional, physical journeys, suggests that a factor in all pilgrimage must be a passage from one pole (which he lists as familiar, known, human, social) to the other (mysterious, divine, ideal, perfect); a movement between the "all-too-known" and the "unknown" (1992: 25–26). These fan testimonies of watching *The X-Files* in its current form—and the same must be true of every show that has passed from the excitement of weekly installments through finale to DVD archive—clearly describe the first pole, the origin point, but with no apparent transit to a destination. Although the experience of an unfamiliar episode—an hour of anticipation, tears, joy, and anger, which encourages the viewers to question what they know, strengthens or challenges their spiritual faith, invites them to sympathize with villains and believe in the inexplicable— could fit within this structure of oppositions, cosy re-encounters with a familiar show would be a more difficult case to argue.

The answer lies in a revisiting of what pilgrimage means. The case of Lough Derg is a particularly extreme example of physical deprivation and committed faith, but the performance of apparently endless stations, devotions, and circuits on jagged rock and in rain, with only lake water and dry bread for consolation, offers its pilgrims a remarkable feeling of comfort. Lough Derg is a center for Irish nationalism, and many of those who make the devotional trip are overseas Irish, connecting, though they have left their everyday environments behind, with a powerful sense of homeland. Turner quotes a 1944 volume on the pilgrimage that stresses the deep pleasures in the physical punishment: "Most pilgrims develop for this rocky island and its harsh routine an affection that really defies explanation. Again and again they return to it with a gaiety, an uplifting of the heart, a profound sense of relief, in short the very sentiments proper to homecoming after life-long exile" (Curtayne, quoted in Turner 1969: 124).

This experience of pilgrimage as a homecoming—a sense of rejoining a community, even if the individual travels far from home—is, Turner notes, also central to other cultures, such as the Guadalupe pilgrimage with its importance to Mexican ethnic identity (1969: 125); we might consider the Islamic *hajj* to Mecca in the same context. However, the feeling of belonging to a community is not confined to nation and race. Sandvoss, writing of football supporters and media followers, suggests that fandom "best compares to the emotional significance of the places we have grown to call 'home,' to the form of physical, emotional *and* ideological space that is best described as *Heimat*" (2005a: 64).

The association of a sacred place of fandom with belonging helps contextualize the practice and experience of fan pilgrims. The visitors to Graceland in King's 1993 account "have travelled thousands of miles, from Japan, from Europe and now from Russia" but now experience "a feeling of shared purpose" in candle-lit vigil and quiet devotion, where Elvis impersonators "greet each other solemnly" (King 1993: 102–3). Similarly, Doss describes Graceland as "the most visible public place where they can comfortably and collectively express their private feelings for Elvis" (1992: 90). The Lewis Carroll Society of Great Britain returns regularly to Charles Dodgson's birthplace in Daresbury and grave in Guildford: though reserved, their testimonies are invested with emotional connection. "One gets a bit closer to the man and his time by being in places associated with him"; "Seeing where it all began, Daresbury Parsonage, was very affecting" (Brooker 2005a: 282).

They depart from their own habitus and the frameworks of everyday life, but those who travel to the homes or final resting places of Presley and Carroll experience their destinations as familiar, safe, places of communion and reassurance. The terms Morinis associates with the two poles of pilgrimage's origin and destination should therefore be adjusted: though the destination point does carry, as Morinis suggests, the values of "perfect ideal," that ideal can also be bound up with the "familiar," the "known," the "human" and "social" (1992: 26).

In Sandvoss's conception of *Heimat*, the feeling of belonging can operate at a conceptual level, as well as in physical space. The latter offers a deeper, more intense experience—offering "the rare opportunity to relocate in space a profound sense of belonging which has otherwise shifted into the textual space of media consumption"—but *Heimat* can also signify a "symbolic, personal space" (2005a: 64). So, just as football fans describe both their club (as a concept) and its stadium (the physical place) in the same terms of security, stability, and warmth, so entering the textual world of *The X-Files* can provide what Sandvoss terms a "mobile *Heimat*," less profound than standing where Mulder stood and inserting oneself into the fiction, but nevertheless a sense of returning, of immersion in a place of belonging, that fits the broader definition of pilgrimage.

During this research, I undertook a journey of my own. Despite my own initial resistance to Aden's treatment of TV viewing as metaphorical travel, a revisiting of pilgrimage's connotations—combined with the testimonies of viewers engaged in the same fandom as Aden's respondents—convinced me that this ritualized, immersive TV viewing common to fan practice can qualify as "symbolic pilgrimage."

As a final note, I would go further, and suggest that "symbolic pilgrimage" is more than just a subcategory of or poor cousin to "real," geographical journeys, offering a fainter taste of the same sensations and a shallower sense of connection. In fact, symbolic immersion and psychological leaps of faith are integral to many, perhaps the majority, of geographical media pilgrimages. When a fan visits Union Station, Los Angeles, it takes significant imagination and investment to transform this busy, modern railway hub into the dingy police headquarters of *Blade Runner*. Hills admits that the Vancouver sites of *X-Files* pilgrimage are "banal: a back-street alleyway, a university building, a shopping precinct escalator" (2002: 149). Cavicchi describes Springsteen fans visiting an ordinary house in New Jersey: "No big deal, you know. Could have been anyone's house. (pause) But it was Bruce's house" (1998: 171). Even Graceland, Doss observes, is a "mundane mansion," unremarkable in itself: "well, gee, Graceland's not that grand and Elvis's guitar-shaped swimming pool is awfully teeny" (1992: 23). These places are made special for the most part through their symbolic value, serving as a physical, earthly focus for something greater and intangible. This is what Sandvoss, drawing on Edward Relph, calls "'other-directedness,' places not experienced in and for themselves but in reference to absent codes and symbols" (2005a: 58). The alley, the grave, the stadium, the station may seem mundane to non-fans; but once the pilgrim has made the geographical journey, he or she makes an internal leap ("this is where Deckard stood . . . this is where Carroll lies") that completes the connection and enables communion. Just as a fan may "travel" metaphorically without moving to a place of belonging, so fans who travel physically may well, at their destination, still have a symbolic journey ahead of them.

12

From Smart Fan to Backyard Wrestler
Performance, Context, and Aesthetic Violence

Lawrence B. McBride and S. Elizabeth Bird

Prologue

I was backstage[. . . .] Stu burst in the doors after his match, his head streaked with blood. No one could see where the wound was. After cleaning him off, I realized that the wound was negligible—barely a half-centimeter long[. . . .] Since he was appearing later in the show, we helped him dress it with yards of gauze which were then decorated with theatrical blood[. . . .] I found out later that Stu had bladed during the match, and that he had not told anyone beforehand, except his opponent. He didn't even tell me about it as I wiped the blood from his bald head. Another layer of deception was laid down as an outrageous bandage soaked in fake blood was used to cover a real cut. I began to realize that I lacked the heart to survive in a field in which reality was so fragmented. There was much to wrestling that I still didn't understand. (Lawrence B. McBride, Summer 2001, Bloomington, Illinois)

Introduction

The 1990s saw the proliferation of backyard wrestling federations, inspired by the showmanship of professional, televised wrestling, but operated locally and autonomously by young, mostly male wrestling fans performing on family property. Backyard wrestlers build their own rings, use trampolines as rings, or simply spray paint a square on the ground, where they perform free for audiences of schoolmates and friends. The development of backyard wrestling depended as much on the availability of cheap, portable technology, such as camcorders, as it did on the existence of the spectacle of professional wrestling. How fans became wrestlers, operating in their own, self-constructed reality, is the subject of this chapter.

The backyard wrestling phenomenon illustrates the complexity of wrestling as a mass-mediated cultural phenomenon, operating on multiple levels of spectatorship and performance. This chapter draws from ethnographic research by McBride with two local wrestling promotions (such groups are called independent wrestling federations, or indy feds) that began as backyard groups: the Chicago area's Lunatic Wrestling Federation (LWF), and Fucked Up Wrestling (FUW), which operated in central Illinois. We show how fans, grounded in a media/audience spectator aesthetic, become active producers and performers themselves.

Wrestling as Ritual

Today's pro wrestling is the most recent manifestation of a century-old American tradition that has reconfigured itself often, adapting to the circus side-show, the saloon/vaudeville circuit, the first urban sports arenas, the earliest one-camera live television, then cable, then the Internet. Throughout, the show's core element has been a distinctive style of ritualized combat taking place in a space resembling a boxing ring. The word "ritualized" is appropriate, in that the performers assume alien identities within the tight delimitations of the wrestling show. These identities, called "gimmicks," are the morally significant agents in the plots of wrestling shows, which involve cheating villains ("heels") and honest heroes ("babyfaces"). But the spectators' performance of credulity in the face of the fantastic nature of the display is the primary element that qualifies the show as "ritual," distinguishing it from contemporary sports (Barthes 1972; Morton & O'Brien 1985). As Jenkins (1997) points out, pro wrestling can also be productively interpreted as melodrama, of a kind specially tailored to the male imagination. To point out that wrestling is fake is to miss the point; to suspend judgment and play along is to begin to enjoy it.

Nevertheless, wrestling, and by extension, its fandom, is one of the most denigrated forms of popular culture. Twitchell (1992) groups it with a few other genres as epitomizing the carnivalesque "trashing of taste" in American culture. Commentators decry the way televised wrestling validates the hegemony of class (Freedman 1983), gender and sexualities (Jhally 2003), or ethnicities (Lincoln 1989; Mondak 1989). Woo and Kim (2003: 361) conclude that wrestling's "anti-social content" ("aggressive acts, rule violations, and glamorization of violence") may influence young people to become violent and antisocial. Inherent in these critiques is the assumption that wrestling fans routinely take the staged contests at face value. It is not our intention to dispute the presence of violent, sexist, racist, and generally "antisocial" imagery in professional wrestling. However, wrestling is not monolithic; we argue that both scholars and social critics have missed many layers of meaning and experience, particularly those of backyard wrestlers, indy wrestlers, and Smart Fans (discussed below) where complex distinctions operate between spectators and performers, real and unreal. Backyard wrestling is an integration of productive practice and an aesthetic bound to a specific fandom context.

The Rise of Backyard Wrestling

To explain the structure of backyard wrestling federations, we invoke a participant's account, describing how a federation was formed and revealing both the broader context of pro wrestling and the way specific fan behaviors such as backyard wrestling have meaning in that context. In Spring 2000, McBride interviewed "Billy Whack," a young man who performed as the ring announcer and color commentator for the LWF, while observing a training session at "the Factory," LWF's rental space in a complex of small warehouses in Mokena, Illinois. One wall was a huge garage door, which was open. Most of the space was taken up by the ring, and in the deepest part of the room, behind the ring, a couch and some chairs were arranged around a TV and VCR. In the ring, young men performed drills, repeating the same moves over and over.

Whack described how LWF began. One summer in the early 1990s, he and some friends gathered at home to watch Wrestlemania, an annual Pay-Per-View wrestling show staged by the WWF (later WWE). Afterwards, the fans went out to the yard, and "somebody stuck four sticks in the ground and put a crappy rope around, and we just jumped around like idiots. We're all winded and sore and tired, and we weren't even doin' any moves, just punchin' and kickin' and jumpin.'" This odd diversion was captured on videotape. The next day, the young man who would become Billy Whack watched the tape with a friend:

> It was the worst, poorly lit, crappy[. . . .] And, I'm like "Wow [. . .] this is pretty cool." And then me and him came to the idea that we should try to organize this, do it a little bit better, maybe write a little story line, come up with some characters[. . . .] Let's call it the Lunatic Wrestling Federation. So my parents were going away for a weekend, so I ran out there and we put four poles in the ground, put these little clamp lights up and we jumped around like idiots and videotaped it, and we had the little bell and every- thing. We brought in more people; and that's what we did for the summer of '93.

The summer of 1994 saw more backyard LWF shows, now featuring a ply- wood ring built by the wrestlers. Winters were spent planning and writing future shows and storylines. The year 1995 was a breakthrough one, with the opportunity to stage a show on a ten-acre property belonging to a friend's parents:

> So we figured, let's try to promote this[. . . .] We handed out fliers at the high school. And we had like 350 people show up [. . .] we had lights and little cameras and everything. We were getting to be really good. Well, we were saving our money, let's just buy a wrestling ring. We spent everything we had, which was about four thousand five hundred bucks[. . . .] They delivered it, set it up. We jumped around like idiots. You see a recurring pat- tern. We said let's trademark everything: we have these names, we have these gimmicks, we had these ideas. And let's start putting on real shows. So we planned for a whole year and in October of '97, we had Bloodbath '97 at the Romeoville rec center. Like ten bucks a head, and we were makin' money and we couldn't believe it[. . . .] Then we found we had to get a promoter's license, and take out an insurance policy just for the night on the audience, rent the venue, and a DJ, for the music equipment. We were finding out it was pretty costly. It just gets crazier each day, like I never know what's going to happen next. I've met tons of wrestlers and the people I've met through this, [gestures behind him to the students] we're running training camp on Wednesdays, we're doing shows, we're about to get a TV deal. We have an actual TV camera crew come out and film it, edit the tape, we sell the tape, [and] we're about to start sellin' merchandise off our web site.

The FUW began in a similar way in Bloomington, Illinois, in 1999, when spontaneous wrestling broke out as a few young fans were watching RAW on TV. Soon a committed group of about twenty 18–21-year-olds, most of them male, was devoting significant resources to FUW, practicing, buying costumes and props, and eventually paying dues to support the costs of promotion and insurance. When the group folded in 2003, it had performed in bars, the county fairgrounds, and the local National Guard Armory, charging anywhere from five dollars to fifteen dollars for admission. Neither the LWF nor the FUW turned a profit in the long term despite their eventual popularity.

Backyard wrestling federations are to World Wrestling Entertainment (WWE) what garage bands are to world-famous rock bands. Despite the staggering disparity in production values, all groups work in the same idiom: they write storylines and create original characters, who perform the same style of ritualized wrestling. Backyard wrestlers do not simply parody or role play the WWE, but develop their own scenarios, even when they have no consistent fans of their own, using camcorders to record and then critique their performances.

Within wrestling culture, backyard wrestling emerged alongside and within the context of the "Smart Fan" phenomenon. When McBride first met FUW wrestlers, they stated immediately that the most important thing to know about wrestling was the difference between Marks and Smarts. Smarts are "Smart to the business," while Marks appear to believe in the authenticity of the competition—Smarts see them as the stereotypical "dupes" imagined by wrestling's critics. Smarts approach the genre of wrestling as would-be insiders, while Marks root unreflexively for the most popular faces. Smart fans possess truly incredible amounts of knowledge about the history of wrestling, including wrestlers' real names and career histories, how various promotions began and folded, who won every Wrestlemania ever. Smart fan informants defined a Mark specifically as someone who responds to wrestling in the way intended by the people who write the storylines (the bookers), describing Marks with statements such as "Kids are Marks" or "We were all Marks when we were kids." Smarts view Marks with scorn.

Interested in the behind-the-scenes action of WWE personnel decisions and the process of scripting the televised shows, Smart fans parallel many other familiar fan cultures (Hills 2002), whose members are as much interested in movie studio politics and the strategic maneuvers of contract negotiations as in movies or TV shows themselves. Fully cognizant of the staged nature of wrestling, Smarts follow the WWE not just to see the shows, but to keep track of what "the Fed" is doing. Generally, backyard wrestlers considered themselves Smarts; however, their "readings" of the televised productions of the large promotions were not wholly ironic, in the self-conscious sense of some other consumers of "trash" media (see Bird 1992). Even though these fans' enjoyment of televised wrestling was occasionally preempted by their critical attitude, they respected the WWE as the elite level of the wrestling world, appreciating the artistry of the productions.

Smart fans also call themselves Internet fans. As noted by many scholars, the Internet has opened up a new world of communication for fan cultures (see Bird 2003; Hills 2002; McKee 2001b), which also coincided with the appropriation of other communications technology, such as the video technology central to backyard wrestling, and the techniques of building rings and staging. Smarts voraciously consume information on insider websites, referred to as "dirt sheets," which also leak results. When McBride met his FUW research participants, they would already know what was going to happen on Monday night televised wrestling, including match outcomes. Beyond reporting on the major wrestling promotions, dirt sheets also report on the indy feds, and the Internet provides an arena for Smart fans to meet and establish tape-trading relationships. Smarts and backyard wrestlers devote hours to watching tapes of independent wrestling federations from around the country, as well as Japanese and Mexican wrestling shows, old-school wrestling (from before cable TV), and the much-coveted shoot interviews, in which wrestlers would appear out of character and share humorous and harrowing stories about life in "the business."

Today's young people are often disapprovingly characterized as the "media generation." However, media saturation does not necessarily mean total subjection; media participation may produce rich intertextual productivity (Drotner 2000). For decades, fan cultures have translated Smart spectatorship into shared storytelling through fan fiction, conventions, and dramatic recreations (Bacon-Smith 1992; Bird 2003; Jenkins 1992). The presence of a portable camcorder in a household hosting a large group of young fans watching WWE might be the decisive factor in the transition from play to production that we see in the LWF and FUW stories. The idea to "try to organize this, do it a little bit better" came to countless, isolated groups of young wrestling fans first watching themselves on tape—the recording, playing, critique, and exchange of tapes is as much part of the backyard wrestling phenomenon as the matches themselves. And the Internet was the medium that defined the further development of these groups. Online, the young fans could learn tricks of the business, such as "blading"—secretly cutting their own scalps during matches to create the illusion of having been "busted wide open." Using Abercrombie and Longhurst's (1998) fan typology, Smart fans could be defined as "enthusiasts," while backyard wrestlers have moved to become "producers," although generally emerging from and remaining in the Smart fan position.

Aesthetics and Contexts

By the time the Smart aesthetic in wrestling developed, the WWE had for years been distancing itself from the pretense of being a real sport, decreasing the physicality of its wrestling in favor of fantastic character development and storylines. Although the wrestling done at all three levels (national, indy, and backyard) fits within the same idiom, a qualitative difference among the shows is evident. The typical Monday night cable wrestling shows consisted of more talking and skits than actual wrestling, while indy shows are generally action packed, with more intense moves. There is a basic economic factor explaining this. When fully professional wrestlers are severely injured, they can suffer serious financial loss and carefully planned storylines can be disrupted. For indy wrestlers, however, paychecks are not as substantial; many view wrestling as a hobby, and almost all have day jobs. In that context, more risks are taken because, as at an "indy rock" show, it is the quality of the performers' and audiences' experience that is most important. In the backyard, many risks are taken, and the risks are compounded by lack of training. Yet FUW wrestlers argued that there is no excuse for being stupid and taking terrible risks, and certain moves, particularly the "pile driver," were banned in the FUW.

   In backyard wrestling, some kids have taken such risks with their bodies that the phenomenon has been sensationalized by mainstream media as a horror story about deviant youth (e.g. Reilly 2001). However, risk is part of the idiom common to all three levels of wrestling. Wrestlers see wrestling moves as falling along a scale that runs from low-risk to high-risk. Low-risk spots include punches and kicks, and submission-style wrestling. Being thrown through a table is a high-risk spot. Ranged between the extremes are seemingly hundreds of variations of "hurrican-ranas," "moonsaults," and "suplexes." Generally, low-risk spots have less potential for pain and injury.

When, in 1994, regional promotion Eastern Championship Wrestling changed its name to Extreme Championship Wrestling, it embraced what became known as the "hardcore" style. This meant that in some matches the face/heel distinction was deemphasized, and the action centered around extremes of violence, generous use of weapons, and copious amounts of (real) bleeding. The pick-you-up-and-slam-you-down moves were still there, but there might be thumbtacks or barbed wire spread around the ring. ECW crowds would chant "ta-ble! ta-ble! ta-ble!" as they waited for the inevitable slam-through-a-wooden-table move. Folding step ladders also became integrated into hardcore-technique ECW wrestling shows. Instead of jumping off the top rope to crush an opponent, wrestlers might reach under the ring and retrieve one of these ladders, to gain altitude for higher flight.

FUW wrestlers made it clear there was a limit to the acceptability of hardcore wrestling, beyond which was "garbage wrestling," seen as hardcore and bloody, but artless. They believed hardcore elements were best used sparingly, within the context of a good match. Good wrestling was supposed to look as if it hurt, but as far as possible, pain was to be controlled. The use of hardcore spots and weapons in the FUW reflected this. Getting hit on the head with a steel chair (a chair shot) looks brutal, makes a loud noise, but doesn't hurt too much, relative to the spot's effect on the audience.

Smart fans fueled the success of ECW and the indy wrestling scene, which in turn shaped the dominant aesthetic among Smarts and backyard wrestlers. This aesthetic was not centered on violence or bleeding; Smarts avidly sought out tapes of old American shows featuring what became known as "old school" wrestling, which mainly involves a seemingly infinite repertoire of ingenious submission holds. Japanese and Mexican wrestling, highly valued by Smarts, has evolved to include a much more intricate, stylized, and gymnastic set of high-flyer moves.

Among Smart fans and backyard wrestlers, high-risk moves are more valued, because they understand this behavior as a form of generosity. The generous wrestler will give his all in a performance to ensure a dual outcome: the match will be spectacular, benefiting the fans, and each wrestler will make his "opponent" look good, helping him "get over with the fans." Generosity in wrestling is a major theme in wrestler Mick Foley's (1999) memoir. Foley describes how selfish wrestlers, on the receiving end of a high-risk move, will be more concerned with avoiding injury than with making the wrestling look convincing. This prevents the wrestler on offense from looking powerful, and thus does his career little good. While the ideal in pro wrestling is a balance of concern for safety and willingness to absorb punishment, both are needed in a good match.

Smart fans, most of whom have read Foley's book, understand this ideal. Thus, unlike Marks, who are mostly content to go along for the ride, Smarts often form strong emotional attachments to those wrestlers who go to the greatest lengths to bear the burden of the performance. For instance, according to this aesthetic, the FUW research participants considered the famous Foley vs. Terry Funk "exploding ring match" of August 18, 1995, in Yokohama, Japan, to be "one of the greatest of all time" (see Foley 1999 for a full account). Foley and Funk were each badly burned in the match, for which the ring ropes had been replaced with barbed wire, and the ring rigged with firework-like explosives. At one point, Foley hit Funk in the head with a metal step ladder; Funk then pushed Foley off that ladder into the barbed wire ropes, as Foley was preparing to dive down onto Funk, leading with the elbow. Foley won the match:

> While I celebrated, Terry was placed in an ambulance and rushed to the hospital. It was truly a touching scene as the adoring crowd reached out just to touch him, and chanted his name. Terry had done me a gigantic favor. Terry had only lost a couple of matches in the last decade in Japan, and a victory over the Funker was a huge milestone. Terry Funk [. . .] had just given me a hell of a gift. (Foley 1999: 337)

Thus, without the ideal of the generous wrestler, the hardcore aesthetic would indeed be meaningless violence. As to why Smart fans took the ideal to heart so completely as to begin wrestling in hardcore style in their backyards, we submit that the essence of wrestling must be experienced first-hand to be fully known. At a performance, the anticipation of the match, the crowd's noise, and the impact of the moves will trigger what wrestlers understand as an "adrenaline," or "fight or flight" response, which mitigates pain, and which arguably constitutes an altered state of consciousness. This response allows them to withstand a level of physical punishment (falls from high balconies, deep lacerations, serious burns, and so on) that shocks those not initiated into wrestling fandom. When wrestlers achieve this state, they can perform in seemingly superhuman ways, allowing wrestling to become truly spectacular; this altered state can become the motivation to continue (for an extended discussion, see McBride 2005). Backyard wrestling, then, is a fan culture based on physical experience in a way rarely if ever described in the literature on fans, although perhaps closest to Grossberg's (1984b) discussion of the physical experience of rock music fandom. The experience was described by FUW wrestler "Dre" following a match in which he had been "powerbombed" through a table, a spectacular move that shattered the table and caused a huge crowd reaction. "It just felt so good. That table just exploded," commented Dre, adding later, "You know, when we're in the ring it's like a trance we go into." Another interviewee, South Florida indy wrestler Mark Zout, commented, "it just gets your blood pumping in a different way, and it's almost indescribable the rush you get" (McBride 2005: 69).

In spite of media condemnation of backyard wrestling as pure viciousness, appealing to the very worst in young people, Smart fans and backyard wrestlers subscribe to their own standards of behavior. They will discuss the appropriateness of certain approaches, as well as their disgust for stereotypical views of their sport. For instance, a column posted on the site "Obsessed with Wrestling" described backyard wrestling as "the very slap in the face of professional wrestling" that has "idiots buying into it like a cheap reason to go to school to 'meet chicks.'" The column's author, Brian Bertrand (2004), was referring primarily to cheaply made tapes of violent wrestling that featured multiple props. A fan responded that Bertrand

> has based [his criticism] on what is seen in the "Best of Backyard Wrestling" tapes, and has never seen what else has been done. Being a backyarder myself, I cannot say that I have ever hit anyone with a light-tube, used fire, or ever jumped off a roof onto someone in four years[. . . .] The only reason the public believes backyard wrestling is wrong is because they have only seen the brainless idiots who have no skill beating each other with weapons[. . . .] All backyard wrestlers take pride in what they do. You bashing what people have put so much work into perfecting makes us look like idiots, which we are not.

Others joined in, describing the artistry of their moves and the rules that govern the experience:

> I became involved in backyard wrestling when I was twelve years old[. . . .] I was anxious beyond belief, but soon realized that these new found friends

of mine were very much like me. I had never been exposed to backyard wrestling before, but I'm certainly glad that my first experience was with these gentlemen [...] competitive, but sports oriented, not violent. It was a great experience and gave me much of the confidence I was lacking in my earlier life.

Of course backyard wrestling is violent. Indeed, as we emphasize, the managed, performed pain is an integral and motivating part of the experience. We can see how the hardcore idiom within wrestling is the expression of the refinement of the physiological pathway to wrestling consciousness and peak wrestling experience. The realness of the spectacle runs away with the pageantry, as real weapons cause real injury, doubtless releasing the "adrenaline" that is repeatedly referenced by wrestlers as a goal. Nevertheless, the experience is not uncontrolled, mindless viciousness, as critics suggest.

Conclusion

The "meaning" of American wrestling is so often taken to lie at the surface, inscribed with a conventional, reactionary symbolism of racism, sexism, and jingoism, and thus meriting widespread condemnation. For instance, Sut Jhally, discussing the effect of televised wrestling, shows little appreciation for any kind of active fan participation: "Wrestling's target audience [...] can't reach the distance necessary to view wrestling with a critical eye. 'The audience, young boys especially, think it's real,' Jhally says" (Souza 2002: n.p.). Here, Jhally asserts that wrestling fans "can't" coherently critique wrestling—that the youthful fans "think it's real." He also claims there have been backyard wrestling-related deaths; none of these assertions are true. The picture suggests benumbed youths mindlessly buying into this clearly corrosive imagery. This "cultural dope" theory of the audience has been effectively dismantled when it comes to most media-reception situations, yet wrestling fans as critical readers seem hard for critics to grasp. Smart wrestling fans indulge in elaborate criticism of wrestling (see Lipscomb 2005 for a discussion of websites), often showing a sophisticated grasp of nuance, and playing with the notions of reality and unreality. We would not deny that Vince McMahon's WWE glorifies images and themes that are disrespectful and harmful to women, gays, and minorities—but this in itself is often a subject of Smart discussion and ridicule. But the

WWE is not the beginning and end of wrestling, and by contributing to this misperception, Jhally and other critics misunderstand the more creative and variable worlds of indy and backyard wrestling. Even Jenkins (1997), who has a more nuanced understanding of wrestling as melodrama, does not see the producerly potential in wresting that he has identified among other fan groups.

Ethnographic studies of media audiences and fans reveal dimensions of experience that social criticism does not. A mass-mediated cultural phenomenon such as wrestling is sustained by the interaction of physical, productive practices within the context of a socially learned aesthetic. Audience ethnography can access the specific knowledge of the mediated phenomenon—the interaction of producer-fan practice and fan values. In the case of the wrestling audience, the behavior patterns of wrestling shows in general, and backyard wrestling in particular, are meaningful in the specific contexts of Smart fandom versus Mark fandom. We argue that the backyard wrestling "ritual" was replicated so uniformly across the nation not solely because children were imitating what they saw on television but because a certain productivity was enabled by a particular configuration of material culture (video cameras and trampolines, cable TV and Internet service) that was available relatively uniformly. The wrestling experience offered something even more than active fandom, in that it allowed participants to explore the limits of physical sensation that goes far beyond the spectator role. Grossberg (1984b) describes the yearning of young people to *feel* through music, in an alienating world of images: "I'd rather feel bad than feel nothing at all." Wrestling offers a similar rush of feeling—controlled, almost ecstatic pain that cuts through mundane and often alienating "reality."

Part IV

Fan Audiences Worldwide
From the Global to the Local

13

Global Fandom/Global Fan Studies

C. Lee Harrington and Denise D. Bielby

When we were asked to submit a chapter on global fandom, we said "sure."[1] We put the idea aside for several months, came back to it, and began to wonder what we had gotten ourselves into. What, we asked ourselves, does the term "global fandom" even mean? Does it mean studying the meaning of "fan" in different parts of the world? Does it mean studying how fans in different countries all respond to the same "global" text? Does it mean studying import/export trade patterns and how fans in one cultural context respond to texts from another cultural context? Given our own uncertainties, we decided to pose these questions to scholars who conduct fan research in different parts of the world. This chapter is thus about the *status* and *possibilities* for global fandom and global fan studies, and is based on email interviews with sixty-five scholars.

Our exploratory study is framed by four overlapping debates. Most obviously, it is framed by debates over cultural globalization, since media consumption[2] is "perhaps the most immediate, consistent and pervasive way in which 'globality' is experienced" (Murphy & Kraidy 2003: 7). Until recently, there has been a clear distinction between global media studies taking a macro political economic approach and the more micro (text-based) media reception research more commonly associated with cultural studies. In the latter approach, scholars have spent the last two decades exploring the effects of border crossing by both texts and persons; that is, the reception of imported media by local audiences (e.g. a Chilean in Chile watching *Desperate Housewives*) and the reception of "home" media by dislocated audiences (e.g. someone from the United States traveling in Chile watching *Desperate Housewives*) (see Ang 1985; Harrington & Bielby 2005a; Juluri 2003a, 2003b; Liebes & Katz 1990; Milikowski 2000; Naficy

1999). The focus of this approach is typically the effects of imported texts on national and cultural identities.

Given rapid advances in technological distribution and evolving formal trade agreements, fan studies scholars have recently turned from the study of imported media to the notion of "global" media texts and internationally dispersed audiences. For example, the International *Lord of the Rings* Audience Research Project directed by Martin Barker (http://www.lordoftheringsresearch.net) includes globally dispersed viewers (over twenty-five thousand to date) as well as globally dispersed research teams, and facilitates a variety of audience and fan studies analyses (both qualitative and quantitative). The project allows for within-country and cross-cultural comparisons of audience response to the film. Furthermore, the open (online) discussion of the research process, unfortunately still rare in academia, encourages collective reflection about the difficulties and limitations of such a project. Other global media texts ripe for scholarly investigation include the Eurovision Song Contest, which launched in 1956 and currently has thirty-nine countries participating, and the recent Live 8 concerts in Canada, France, Italy, Japan, South Africa, Russia, England, and the United States, which allow for a unique opportunity to study cultural (music) globalization explicitly framed by larger political and economic events (the G-8 meetings in Scotland, July 2005).

Crane argues that media reception theory

> requires modification to be useful in today's complex global environment. Understanding the public's responses to global culture in different countries and in different settings in those countries necessitates a broader reconceptualization of reception theory, one that goes beyond focusing entirely on the audience itself and instead examines the relationships between the imported culture and the national culture, as well as the roles of cultural entrepreneurs. (2002: 18–19)

Indeed, global media reception studies are slowly moving (back) to central questions of culture, power, and ideology more typically associated with a political economic approach.[3] In the context of fan studies, for example, Sandvoss (2003) engages explicitly with debates over cultural, political, and economic globalization in his empirical study of football fandom. He examines how television "provides the cultural and social basis of the globalization of football fandom" by both reflecting global structures and acting as an agent of globalization (2003: 82, 86). In another approach,

Juluri (2003a, 2003b) studies the reception of music television in India in the context of globalization as an everyday experience. Posing the central question, "What does it mean to be a global audience?" he writes, "The reception of music television in India is [. . .] not so much about a 'global' text and a 'local' audience [. . .] but instead about the construction of a new sense of the 'global'" (2003b: 119–20). Our own project here is geared, in part, toward an understanding of scholars' conceptualization of fandom in the context of globalization.

The second debate framing our study surrounds the question of who, what, and where is the media audience (see Mosco & Kaye 2000). Originally an industrial (marketing) term linked with the rise of commercial radio broadcasting, the concept of the audience quickly became one of the central ideas in mass communications research. The concept began to destabilize in the late 1980s, however, as scholars recognized the extent to which media are embedded in everyday life and the extent to which we are all living in a mediated culture, both researchers and research participants. As Bird asks, "if we cannot define an audience, is it effectively impossible to study it?" (2003: 4). This notion of "elusive audiences" has been critiqued, however, by global media scholars. For example, Juluri argues that "the study of globalization and media needs to turn its attention to the media audience, not merely as a commercially constructed aggregate of viewers, or partially disembodied subjects of global modernity, but as the point at which media are made meaningful and effectivized" (2003a: 9). He questions, "what does it mean for us as scholars to bow to postmodern recognition of the impossibility of total knowledge [of the audience] precisely at that moment when millions of people across the non-Western world have only begun to become global [. . .] audiences?" (2003b: 218).

Most scholars approach the embeddedness of the media in everyday life as a hurdle rather than a barrier to empirical research, which brings us to the third debate framing our project: methodology. Traditional social science methods such as interviews, surveys, and focus groups are criticized for their inability to fully capture the experience of mediated lives (see Alasuutari 1999a), and in the context of fan studies are seen by some as unable to fully tap into the inarticulacy of fan pleasures (Hills 2002). Ethnography is argued to be the ideal way to study contemporary media audiences, though research claiming to be ethnographic is often anything *but*. The classic anthropological model of long-term on-site fieldwork represents a major challenge to media and fan studies, and has undergone scrutiny throughout the academy for its us/them, researcher/Other dichotomization (among other reasons). In addition, as Kraidy and Murphy (2003) note, ethnography's commitment to *depth* seems to clash with the *breadth* needed to fully comprehend processes of cultural globalization. Indeed, it is somewhat ironic (and confusing) that media studies turned to ethnography precisely when the "ethnographic crisis" was unfolding in anthropology. The sometimes paralyzing debates over the role of ethnography in the study of global media (see Algan 2003) are revealed in overlapping and often contradictory discussions of passing ethnography (Couldry 2003), auto-ethnography (Hills 2002), virtual or cyberspace ethnography (Bird & Barber 2002), multisited ethnography (Marcus 1998), mediation ethnography (Tufte 2000), and translocal ethnography (Kraidy & Murphy 2003), among others. In reference to the latter, Kraidy and Murphy write,

> ethnography's importance lies more in its capacity to comprehend the articulation of the global with the local, than in its supposed ability to understand the local in isolation of larger-scale structures and processes. A translocal ethnography builds on that to focus on connections between several local social spaces, exploring hitherto neglected *local-to-local articulations* [. . .] the idea of a *translocal* ethnography is born out of the paradox that in times of globalization, a rigorous ethnography *must be local and at the same time cannot only be local.* (2003: 304; original emphasis)

Kraidy and Murphy's recent book *Global Media Studies* (2003) represents a major effort to reconceptualize the role of media ethnography in understanding globalization.

Finally, and relatedly, our project is framed by the ongoing debate about researchers' presence or self-reflexivity in data collection and/or published findings. As Jenkins (2001: n.p.) points out, "the value of ethnography is not ultimately that it allows you to talk to 'the real' but that it introduces notions of dialogue and accountability." While academia in general privileges the critical distance of the academic "expert" vis-à-vis his or her "object" of study, there are obviously different and evolving traditions throughout the academy. Generally speaking, cultural studies expects self-reflexivity, and as it is the widely assumed home of fan studies (though this is debatable), scholars—perhaps *especially* those adopting ethnographic techniques—are expected to make their fannish presence, identities, and pleasures known. This is not unproblematic, of course, as Hills's (2002) and others' discussions of scholar-fans, fan-scholars, and "legitimate" knowledge(s) attest. When we wrote our book on soap opera fandom in the early 1990s (Harrington & Bielby 1995), it frankly did not occur to us to declare our own fandom in print, in part due to our training in mainstream sociology, in part due to where fan studies was at that time, and in part due to the way we construct our own personal fan identities.

As we discuss below, the question of self-reflexivity remains a concern for fan scholars in research and publication. It is also a concern of scholars evaluating the possibilities of a truly "global" fan studies. In her critique of U.S. fan studies, for example, Meehan (2000) suggests that when scholars "share the taboos" of the groups they study, it "may prevent them from placing US fandoms in the context of US culture and from exploring the degree to which fandom's values and fan experience are shaped by dominant ideology" (2000: 74). Fan scholars' "insider" status and own identities thus make it difficult, Meehan suggests, for them (us) to perceive and analyze the relevant cultural contexts shaping fan activities and identities.

These four related debates—centered on cultural globalization, defining the media audience, methodology, and self-reflexivity—thus serve as the conceptual framework for our exploratory study of global fandom and global fan studies. We describe our data and methodological approach below, followed by a discussion of key research findings.

Project Design

Our research is based on email interviews with scholars who study and/or write about fans. All participants received email invitations to participate in the study. If they responded affirmatively, the survey (available in English and Spanish) was emailed to them for completion. Our methodology involved modified snowball sampling; we initiated some invitations to participate in the study, and participants were asked to recommend others. The invitation was also forwarded to several listservs with our permission. We followed through on all of the recommendations (we did not screen anyone out), so the pool represents people who *we* think do fan studies and people who our *participants* think do fan studies. Our goal was not to include everyone in the world who conducts fan research (an impossible goal) but to attract the most globally diverse pool possible given our language restrictions.

TABLE 13.1
Selected Traits of Fan Studies Scholars (n=65)

SAMPLE	PERCENT
Male	46%
Female	54%
1–4 publications on media consumers/fans	34%
5–100+ publications on media consumers/fans	42%
Other	7%
Humanities scholars	20%
Social science scholars	45%
Interdisciplinary studies scholars	26%
Business (sport) management scholars	6%
Other (e.g. education, movement science)	3%
SCHOLARS WHO	
Define fandom primarily as ìinvestmentî	38%
Define fandom primarily as ìengagementî	20%
Emphasize no single dimension of fandom	32%
Emphasize affective dimension of fandom	18%
Primarily emphasize affective/behavioral dimensions	17%
Emphasize research question or goal as definitive	11%
Emphasize ideological dimension of fandom	3%
SCHOLARS WHO	
Are fans of what they study	63%
Humanities scholars	78%
Social science scholars	67%
Interdisciplinary scholars	46%
Business (sport) management	25%
Acknowledge their fandom in data collection	44%
Humanities scholars	62%
Social science scholars	44%
Interdisciplinary scholars	85%
Business (sport) management	0%
Acknowledge their fandom in publications	42%
Humanities scholars	71%
Social science scholars	44%
Interdisciplinary scholars	71%
Business (sport) management	0%

We emailed 104 surveys to potential participants and received sixty-five completed responses for a 63 percent return rate (very respectable within sociology). The survey consists of twenty-seven questions focusing on participants' involvement with fan studies research and their perspectives on a range of fan-related issues. We attempted to word the questions such that they could be easily understood by non-native English speakers, but we did not always succeed. We note that this study of scholars was in fact a study of scholarly produced *texts,* as we worked wholly with the written (emailed) surveys. Following a grounded theory approach, this study is directed toward developing an understanding of participants' perceptions of the status and possibilities of global fandom and global fan studies, as revealed through the written surveys. The methodology was designed to capture both variation and depth in participants' responses.

Our sample includes thirty males and thirty-five females. Most are faculty and graduate students who conduct academic research, though several fan fiction writers also participated. Our participants conduct research and writing projects in twenty different countries, though North America is overrepresented, constituting 49 percent of the sample (n=32).[4] English is the primary language of publication, though Spanish, Chinese, Russian, Korean, German, Finnish, and Dutch are also represented. Participants' level of experience, discipline of training, and methodological approach vary. For example, 85 percent of the sample reports at least two years' experience conducting research on media consumers and/or fans, with 29 percent reporting eleven or more years. Eighty-three percent of the sample has published in the area of media audiences/consumers/fans, with 42 percent having five or more publications (one participant has over one hundred publications). A total of thirty-six different disciplines of training were reported, representing the social sciences (e.g. mass communications, sociology, clinical psychology, anthropology), humanities (e.g. English literature, philosophy, folklore), business (e.g. sport management), and interdisciplinary fields such as cultural studies, African studies, and Japanese studies. This variety in educational background is reflected in the wide range of methodological approaches participants bring to their scholarship, including textual/literary analyses, psychoanalysis, experimental and quasi experimental design, surveys, interviews, focus groups, participant observation, virtual ethnography, archival research, discourse analysis, performative/narrative analysis, polling methods, and historical research, among others.

Please note that, given space constraints, we opt to focus in this chapter on summary (descriptive) findings, with plans to examine several issues in greater depth elsewhere (e.g. Bielby, Moloney, & Harrington n.d.; Schimmel, Harrington, & Bielby n.d.). Our discussion below focuses on three key findings. First, we discuss participants' understanding of fans vs. consumers, dimensions of fandom, and the fan studies "canon." Second, we discuss self-reflexivity in media fan research. Finally, we explore the possibilities for global fandom and global fan studies. Given confidentiality agreements, no names are used; we identify participants by code number only.

Understanding Fans

We asked participants to distinguish between consumers and fans. Their responses confirmed dominant conceptualizations in the (Western) fan studies literature.[5] Many view fans and consumers as existing on the same continuum (e.g. Abercrombie & Longhurst 1998), with fans distinguished primarily by their degree of emotional, psychological, and/or behavioral *investment* in media texts (38 percent of participants emphasized this aspect of fandom) and/or their "active" *engagement* with media texts (20 percent emphasized this aspect; see table 13.1). Participants also referred to issues of community, sociality, self-identification, and regularity of consumption in distinguishing fans from consumers. Consider the following responses:

> One could say that in the "first world" nations everyone is a media consumer. We all constantly consume media artifacts [. . .] to obtain information, for pleasure and relaxation, or simply to channel our frustrations and anger[. . . .] A media fan is obviously a media consumer but one who develops a personal attachment to a particular media artifact or "star" and actively engages in a multiplicity of levels of creation that transcends or could even transform the "original" text, character, or star persona. (Participant #7)

> I see no real distinction though I am fully aware that orthodox representations work—often quite insidiously—to figure the two as very different indeed[. . . .] [M]uch of the critical interest and value of fandoms stem not from their status as a distinctive thing apart [. . .] but from their very ordinariness [. . . .] [F]ans are simply consumers that take their practices or media consumptions seriously and mobilize them in ways that are perhaps a little more spectacular and overt than other consumers but whose uses of media aren't qualitatively different. Thus any distinctions are, to my mind at least, of degree rather than kind. (Participant #47)

We also asked participants to identify which of the following dimensions is most significant for understanding fans: intellectual, affective, behavioral, or ideological. Nearly one-third (32 percent) feel that no single dimension is more important than others (i.e. all are relevant), almost one-fifth (18 percent) identify the affective dimension as most important, about another fifth (17 percent) believe that a mixture of (though not all) dimensions take precedence (most emphasize affective and behavioral dimensions), and slightly more than one-tenth (11 percent) believe the answer depends wholly on the research question and/or goal. We note that only 3 percent believe the ideological dimension is most important, which raises interesting questions in terms of Meehan's (2000) critique of ethnography, ideology, and cultural awareness in U.S. fan studies (see below). A number of participants identified additional dimensions they feel are crucial to an understanding of fandom but were omitted from our forced-choice question, including cognitive, aesthetic, psychological, and socio-cultural dimensions.

General consensus over the meaning(s) of fandom is echoed by consensus over the dominant stereotype of fandom—the all-too-familiar (to Western scholars at least) loser/lunatic image (Jensen 1992). Participants point to modifications of this stereotype, however, based on historical era, cultural location, and object of fandom:

> Complete geeks. Fortunately, we now have self-proclaimed Geek Peter Jackson on our side and he's got a trunkload of Oscars. I think in the US the last decade has given the notion of Geekhood some residual coolness. Gen X are children of the 70s, and we understand camp like no other generation[. . . .] [Y]ou've seen what we watched on TV, what we wore to grade school, the lunchboxes we had! [. . .] [P]art of the generational requirement of Gen X is to have your own pet corner of fandom that you can hold close to your heart and call your own. (Participant #30)

> [I]n Finland we do not have such prejudices concerning fans as "freaks" as in the US. This may partly boil down to language: in Finnish the term "fani" (fan) does not associate with "fanatic" nearly as closely as in English and perhaps other Indo-European languages[. . . .] [T]here is less need for fandom studies to defend fans. (Participant #21)

> Like much of the modern, Western world, the stereotypical image of the media fan in Australia remains a fairly negative one[. . . .] Such an image is of course inflected variably by social differences such as gender, age, race, sexuality, and so on[. . . .] [T]he straight male sports fan, far from being a pilloried figure, is rendered all-but-normative, whereas the "housewife" lover of TV soap, the adolescent girl fan of a teen idol, or the queer devotee of a Hollywood star is regularly coded as socially pathological or deficient. (Participant #47)

In general, then, our participants' understandings of fandom and its stereotypes confirms the extant literature.

Finally, we explored the idea of an emergent fan studies canon by asking participants to identify the most important publications on media consumers and/or fans, the most influential scholars, and the publication outlets perceived to be most receptive to fan studies research. The five most important publications (in descending order of significance) are identified as follows: Henry Jenkins's *Textual Poachers* (1992), Lisa A. Lewis's *Adoring Audience* (1992) and (tied for second) Matt Hills's *Fan Cultures* (2002), Camille Bacon-Smith's *Enterprising Women* (1992), and Janice Radway's *Reading the Romance* (1984). In terms of the most influential scholars, three tiers emerged (clearly, this is awkward terminology). The first tier (most influential) is occupied solely by Henry Jenkins. The second tier of influence is occupied (in alphabetical order) by Camille Bacon-Smith, John Fiske, Matt Hills, Janice Radway, and Dan Wann. The third most influential group of scholars identified by participants includes (in alphabetical order) Nicholas Abercrombie/Brian Longhurst, Ien Ang, Will Brooker, Lawrence Grossberg, C. Lee Harrington/Denise D. Bielby, Constance Penley, and Jackie Stacey. Finally, participants identified the following publication outlets as most receptive to manuscripts on fans (in alphabetical order): *Journal of Sport Behavior,* Routledge, Sage, and *Television & New Media.*[6]

To briefly summarize this section, scholars agree that a range of dimensions should be taken into account in studying fandom, with the affective dimension singled out as particularly important. Participants also point to an emergent fan studies canon, as noted above. In the following section we discuss scholars' perceptions of the need (or lack thereof) for self-reflexivity in the research and publication process.

Self-reflexivity

As discussed in the introductory chapter to this volume, Henry Jenkins (2001) identifies three generations of Western fan scholars and encourages recognition of the historical context that shaped their authorial or fannish presence in their research. The question of self-reflexivity is an issue in media studies defined broadly, of course (as well as many other areas of the academy), and is central to scholars' efforts to develop the appropriate methodology for global media studies (see

Murphy & Kraidy 2003). We asked participants whether they themselves are fans of what they study (Hills's scholar-fans, 2002), and if so,
whether they acknowledge that in data collection and publication.[7]
Almost two-thirds (63 percent) of participants are indeed fans of what
they study, though less than half (44 percent) self-identify as fans in
data collection and only 42 percent in published articles. Their explanations for acknowledgment (or lack thereof) focus on methodology,
discipline of training, institutional status, and cultural location, among
other reasons:

> I expect it from a scientist to acknowledge his/her own position towards the
> research object (which for me is the fan as well as the media) and I would
> expect it from myself. Besides, I think it's very easy to find out if a
> researcher is a fan himself by reading his work—whether he mentions it or
> not. It makes a big difference. (Participant #22)

> Certainly anyone who looks at my bio would know I am a consumer and
> producer of, for example, science fiction. I make no apologies for that in
> any of my writings. But I don't waste valuable scholarly time on personal
> confessions, either[. . . .] It's no surprise US citizens often write US history,
> either, or French citizens French history, or Catholics Church history. The
> work should speak for itself. (Participant #48)

> I do not acknowledge that I am a sport fan in published articles. Of course,
> much of our publishing occurs in journals dedicated to examining aspects
> of sport and exercise. Most of the people who do research in these areas are
> also fans of the sport they research. It is almost as if you had to acknowl-
> edge that you breathe. (Participant # 3)

> [Mass Communication] in Korea tends to expect a positivist, objective
> research. The inter-subjective, interpretive researches of qualitative studies
> or cultural studies have often faced severe criticism in terms of objectivity
> and verification. (Participant # 46)

We mapped responses on self-reflexivity to both disciplinary heritage
and cultural (geographic) location. In terms of the question "Are you
yourself a fan of what you study?" over three-quarters (78 percent) of
those trained in the humanities responded "yes," along with two-thirds (67
percent) of social scientists, nearly half (46 percent) of those trained in

interdisciplinary fields, and one-quarter (25 percent) of those trained in business (sport) management. In response to the question "do you acknowledge that in data collection?" nearly two-thirds (62 percent) of humanities scholars who are fans of what they study responded "yes" along with almost half (44 percent) of social scientists. The vast majority (85 percent) of those educated in interdisciplinary fields responded affirmatively to this question, although none of those trained in business (sport) management did. Finally, in response to the question "do you acknowledge that in published articles?" the vast majority of humanities scholars and those trained in interdisciplinary fields who are fans of what they study responded affirmatively (71 percent of each group), while less than half (44 percent) the social scientists did, and none of those trained in business (sport) management. (We found sport fan scholars differing from other participants on a range of issues; see Sandvoss 2003; Schimmel, Harrington, & Bielby n.d.).

To examine self-reflexivity and cultural (geographic) location, we began by separating participants into two groups. While not wanting to reify presumed distinctions between the "West" and the "Rest," we were at the same time precisely interested in how our own socio-cultural location (as U.S.-born-and-trained scholars who read only English-language publications) has shaped our understandings about fandom and fan studies in ways that may—or may not—be shared by colleagues in other parts of the world. Prior work has suggested that central foci of Western fan studies—in notions such as pleasure, autonomy, individuality, freedom, leisure, etc.—must be understood in terms of the larger cultural context rather than taken for granted as inevitable features of fan experiences. For example, Meehan (2000) argues that the emic (insider) status typical of U.S. fan ethnographies contributes to scholars' underengagement with issues of ideology:

> For fans, leisure time is spent in fandom, work time in the "mundane world" of nonfans. An emic approach accepts this division as authentic, lived experience and thereby as a unique feature of fandom. Thus, emic ethnographers overlook the constructedness of "leisure time" and the role that dominant ideology plays in that construction. (Meehan 2000: 75; see, however, Sandvoss 2003)

Indeed, we reiterate the finding noted above that only 3 percent of our participants perceive the ideological dimension of fandom as most significant. While self-reflexivity represents just one way in which cultural location might impact scholars' analyses, it offers important insight into how trajectories of research might develop differently in diverse global contexts.

As the term "Western world" has no single international or academic definition, we elected to follow a common (albeit problematic) practice by separating participants into two groups, one including scholars and fan fiction writers from North America, European Union member states, Australia, and New Zealand (Group 1), with our participants from Brazil, Chile, India, Israel, South Korea, Malaysia, Puerto Rico, Russia, South Africa, Taiwan, and Turkey comprising the second group (Group 2). Similar percentages of scholars from these groups (77 percent and 73 percent, respectively) report being personal fans of what they study, but fewer (74 percent) Group 1 scholars acknowledge that fact when collecting data as compared to Group 2 scholars (88 percent). In response to the question "do you acknowledge that in published articles?" 60 percent of Group 1 scholars who are fans of what they study respond "yes" compared to 100 percent of Group 2 scholars. In short, Group 1 scholars are only *slightly more likely* to be fans of what they study—but, if they *are* fans, they are *considerably less likely* to acknowledge that in data collection and/or published articles (particularly the latter) than scholars working in other parts of the world. What factors related to cultural context might lead to this finding? How does this help create different fan studies around the globe, particularly given Meehan's (2000) hesitations noted above?

In sum, most of our participants are fans of what they study though whether they reveal this in data collection and publication varies, depending in part on disciplinary heritage, cultural (geographic) location, and power/status dynamics. In the following section we examine the status and possibilities of global fandom/global fan studies.

Global Fandom/Global Fan Studies

Earlier we listed the various methodologies used by participants in their own research. We also asked, "What would be the ideal methodological design for a study of 'global fandom'"? We received a number of responses along the lines of, "Good God. I'm not even going to try to answer this" (Participant #1) and "Yikes! Start with Tylenol on hand" (Participant # 24). To ask about appropriate methodological design implies, of course, that a thing called "global fandom" even exists.[8] As our participants note, this assumption is debatable:

I do not know if "fandom" is a globally representative category to general-ize—would fans of *Sex and the City* or *Star Trek* in suburban USA fall into the same category of fandom as a working class peasant fan of [the actor] Chiranjeevi in rural India? I doubt it. (Participant #2)

Filling in this questionnaire, I'm starting to find the empirical category "fandom" quite useless [. . .] so if you want to globalize it you'd end up in many compli-cated debates about what constitutes a "fan" in, say, Sydney, and in Tehran, and in Helsinki. [J]ust study "global" consumption patterns. (Participant # 4)

I think [global fandom] is too broad a category; there are specific move-ments that can [be] discussed intelligently and smaller stories that can be constructed[. . . .] Right now, we're in a place where all kinds of fandoms are now communicating and merging—tv fandoms are talking to anime vidders are in contact with role play gamers, but those are all separate genealogies[. . . .] I worry that they'll be swept together and important his-tory erased. (Participant # 34)

The study of consumer culture or fandom should be studied in terms of every specific cultural, social, historical and political context. To carve out a "global methodological design" may not help, but on the contrary may sup-press the cultural and social differences around the globe, which is the exact opposite of what cultural studies and its interdisciplinary ideals strive to achieve—to demonstrate the different social and cultural varieties and compositions in people's lives. (Participant #35)

Indeed, in a brief summary of sport fan research, Lee suggests that cul-tural context is a key factor distinguishing sport fan communities from one another:

In the world of soccer, the hooligans, particularly the "English model," have embodied the idea of the pathological and dangerous fanatics[. . . .] Differ-ent types of societies have produced other types of fans [. . .] such as the Danish roligans, the Italian ultra, and Scotland's Tartan Army. These fan groups take on characteristics specific to the social and political conditions within which they arise. (2005: 197)

Most of our participants *do* believe in the concept and possibility of global fandom (and global fan studies), though many share the cautions noted in the quotations above. They propose a variety of methodologies to empirically access global fandom; some approaches, mostly in sport fan studies, are heavily quantitative:

> A longitudinal quasi-experimental design that measures participants' identification with at least three different teams across different sports as the independent variable and has multiple measures of psychological health. Have at least six different measurements of both the independent variable and the dependent variables. (Participant #3)

Others are largely Internet based:

> Virtual ethnography would be the most efficient way to compare and contrast modes and methods of fandom around the globe. A combination of observation (e.g. of fan-created Web sites, fan fiction, fan art) and participant observation (in chats and bulletin board discussions) could be used. Obviously this would entail a multilingual and computer literate research team. (Participant # 17)

Most participants indicate the necessity of a multisited, collaborative research project that is methodologically diverse. They emphasize a social-scientific focus with particular emphasis on ethnographic methods, though several made impassioned pleas for the continued relevance of literary/textual analyses. As one can imagine, this sets the stage for an extremely complicated research design:

> [O]ne way that might be efficient without having one national or regional perspective dominate would be to have researchers from different areas of the world design projects; then everyone looks at the designs so that all researchers know what the others are doing. Then, as the projects are completed individually, a joint publication could emerge in which the collaborators work to thread together the projects based on their original goals. (Participant #24)

> It's a very interesting goal [. . .] but I think it would inevitably neglect many methodological angles and leave major occlusions, and perhaps necessarily falsify the subject in some ways because of the difficulty of finding researchers who are adequately embedded in all the various local formations and languages[. . . .] Overall, I think it would require a collaboration

between multiple researchers with a shared sense of purpose and divergent regional specializations as well as divergent specializations within the study of fandom[. . . .] [I]t would have to be social science oriented, and I think the most interesting results would be descriptive, followed by analysis along political economy and globalization lines. (Participant # 26)

One of the scholars participating in the International *Lord of the Rings* Project shares the following insights:

I would have to say that on paper, the design for [the LOTR] study looked almost perfect: combination of marketing strategies and merchandising, large survey (both online and offline), and interviews. From participating with this project, I have learned that a survey of this size should be designed and pre-tested very carefully, and that a project such as this would require a firm and consistent theoretical background[. . . .] [T]he design would be such that the researchers would be strongly encouraged to cooperate in transnational groups, otherwise the project runs a severe risk (as did [. . .] the LOTR project) of reifying the nation state. (Participant #57)[9]

These responses speak to the notion of translocal or multisited media ethnography discussed earlier, as well as to the research agendas proposed by Kraidy and Murphy: "First, global media scholarship must make *a commitment to empirical research* to complement its theoretical arguments[. . . .] Second, we advocate that global media studies *embraces real interdisciplinarity,* because the complexity of globalization and its multifaceted process require diverse expertise" (2003: 306; original emphasis). Fan studies' emergent global focus suggests that the above agendas are shared by both fan studies and global media studies, thus potentially bringing these literatures together in a new way.

Conclusion

As an initial effort, our exploratory study met with some challenges. For example, we underestimated the amount of time it would take to complete the survey, which seemed to irritate some participants (never a good research outcome!). In addition, our attempt to find the most accessible terminology possible, combined with the lack of followup opportunity, meant that miscommunications occurred (e.g. participants did not always understand our questions). Relatedly, disciplinary divisions within fan studies revealed themselves in that the terminology we as sociologists use to describe empirical research on fans and fandom (e.g. research "participants," media "consumers," etc.) was considered problematic by some of those who completed the survey. An unexpected phenomenon occurred wherein several participants did not directly answer our questions but instead replied, "Read my book," or "Look at my webpage." In part, this probably reflects the unexpected length of the questionnaire and/or the desire by published authors to not repeat themselves in gruesome depth, but as researchers who have interviewed other groups of professionals before, this was a first for us. Finally, a significant limitation of our project is that the survey was available in only two languages (English and Spanish), which certainly limits any research findings purporting to be "global" in nature.

Despite these limitations, our study points to fruitful areas for continued research. Findings suggest general consensus on some aspects of fan studies (e.g. the meaning of the term "fan"), indicate continued lack of consensus in others (e.g. expectations of self-reflexivity), and raise interesting questions for fan studies scholars: how have etymological differences shaped the public image of fans and fandom in different parts of the world? Where and with whom are fan scholars exchanging ideas (see Murphy & Kraidy 2003: 11), and how has that shaped different trajectories of fan studies? Why do scholars seem to place so little emphasis on the ideological dimension of fandom? How can we more fully explore the relationship among disciplinary training, cultural location, and self-reflexivity in fan scholarship? How should key assumptions in Western fan studies— about the importance of pleasure, say—be understood in other cultural contexts (see Meehan 2000)?

It is difficult to address the importance of these questions because we have no way of knowing the extent to which our sample is representative of the field, which raises epistemological questions. For example, in our discussion of self-reflexivity we separated participants into two groups, with Group 1 comprised of "Western" scholars and Group 2 comprised of scholars in other parts of the world. Fully 80 percent of our participants are located in Group 1. Consider too that the emergent fan studies canon we identified included *only* Western scholars, publications, and publication outlets. Finally, consider the 63 percent return rate on our email survey. While this is a perfectly satisfactory rate for sociological research, we were enthusiastically awaiting completed surveys from scholars who would have helped extend the global reach of our project (including scholars from Uganda, Kenya, Ecuador, China, Zimbabwe, Zanzibar, Bolivia, Mexico, and Nepal). Did these potential participants not understand the survey questions? Did the questions not capture fan studies as they know it? Did our questions focus, as Meehan's (2000) critique might predict, too much on individualistic fan experiences and too little on the political economy of fandom that might be more recognizable to other groups of scholars? The answers to these questions might tell us something significant about the global location of the history and development of fan studies . . . or it might tell us something about the methodological limitations of our project. At this point, we honestly do not know which.

Ultimately, the most important finding of our study is scholars' concerns about what might be gained or lost by assuming that "global fandom" even exists. We asked participants "how would you *study* global fandom?" with the hope of revealing their assumptions about what it actually *is* (see opening paragraph). The diversity of their responses, however, speaks to a notable lack of clarity regarding the existence and/or nature of global fandom, and thus, about the possibilities for global fan studies. We hope this study is the beginning of a fruitful conversation to that end.

Notes

1. We thank Andrea Parks for her assistance with data entry and preparation of transcripts; Kimberly Schimmel for her assistance in identifying potential participants and for feedback on prior versions of the manuscript; and our participants for their time and effort in completing the surveys.

2. We define the term "media" broadly here to include television, sport, music, movies, literature, and so on. Some of our participants study mediated fandom (e.g. fans of televised music or sport) while others study nonmediated fandom (e.g. fans of live music or sporting events). We acknowledge that this broad definition might be controversial within some areas of the academy.

3. A full examination of the history of reception studies is beyond the scope of this manuscript; for recent discussions, see Alausuutari (1999a), Bird (2003), and Meehan (2000).

4. Countries represented in the sample include Australia, Belgium, Brazil, Canada, Chile, England, Finland, Germany, India, Israel, Italy, South Korea, Malaysia, the Netherlands, Puerto Rico, Russia, South Africa, Taiwan, Turkey, and the United States.

5. See Hills (2002) and Sandvoss (2005a) for a review of the major sociological and psychological approaches to fans and fandom.

6. These survey items were open-ended questions. We have included here the most frequently identified publications, persons, and publication outlets.

7. As one participant points out, however, the general expectation of self-reflex-ivity in fan studies does not extend to scholars who are *non*-fans or *anti*-fans of what they study. Why are scholars expected to "confess" their (our) pleasures but not displeasures? (Participant #59)

8. It further implies, in reference to our prior discussion, that a global media *audience* exists. Juluri asks, "[W]hat would cultural studies have to say about something called the global audience? The marketing-oriented definition of the global [TV] audience as a billion people all over the world watching the Olympics or *Baywatch* is clearly not the answer[. . . .] [B]ecoming a global audience may be seen not only as the outcome of cultural production on a worldwide scale by giant media conglomerates, but as a moment of situated struggle over what constitutes the world for the audience" (2003b: 120).

9. A number of participants cited the LOTR project as one of the most ambi-tious efforts to date, though some argue that the type of data being collected does not adequately distinguish between fans and other audiences, and does not allow for the richness of fan experiences to be explored. However, in a series of presenta-tions about the project at the 2005 International Communication Association meetings, it seemed to us that findings made contributions to both fan studies and audience studies (broadly defined).

14

Between Rowdies and *Rasikas*
Rethinking Fan Activity in Indian Film Culture

Aswin Punathambekar

Let us begin by examining two recent moments of fan activity surrounding Indian cinema. On October 8, 2005, A. R. Rahman, the renowned film music director, performed in Bangalore as part of a worldwide tour. The entire concert was managed by fans who volunteered their services for everything from ticket sales to stage construction to crowd management. As part of their effort to gain recognition as the "official" Rahman fan club, they also decided to present Rahman with a gift—a montage, composed of thumbnail images of all his album covers, which formed the contours of his face. Faced with the prospect of buying expensive software, these fans (who run a design company called 3xus.com) went on to develop their own software. After many sleepless nights of painstaking coding, they finally got to meet Rahman and present the gift. A few days later, they learned that Rahman liked the gift and had displayed it in his studio in Chennai. This story of fan activity went largely unreported in mainstream media.

Little more than a month later, Amitabh Bachchan, the enduring superstar of Hindi cinema, was hospitalized and had to undergo surgery. Not only did media outlets cover every detail of Bachchan's hospital stay and subsequent recovery, but many instances of "fan devotion" were also recorded. Citing several examples of fans organizing prayer sessions in cities worldwide, Chopra writes, "fans routinely gather outside Mr. Bachchan's home in suburban Mumbai for a *darshan,* or sighting, but that is the least of it: some have sent him paintings of him done in blood, presumably their own" (Chopra 2006: 1).

It is perhaps not surprising that mainstream media coverage of Bollywood ignores fan activity except when it seems obsessive or pathological—"paintings in blood" certainly makes more sensational copy when compared with a group of highly educated, technically skilled fans who discuss Rahman's music on an Internet newsgroup. Indeed, when one raises the question of fan activity surrounding cinema, the standard response, among academics and film journalists/critics, is to point to Tamil and Telugu film cultures where fan associations devoted to former stars like M. G. Ramachandran and N. T. Rama Rao have played pivotal roles in these stars' political careers. As the editor of *Filmfare* explained, "you'll find crowds outside Bachchan or Shahrukh Khan's house. But never that level of passion as you'd find in the south. There is no organized fan activity around Bollywood. No one asks Shahrukh to float a political party or threatens to commit suicide just because his film flops!"[1]

In this paper, I argue against framing fan activity in Indian film culture in terms of devotional excess or in relation to political mobilization in south India. I suggest we shift our attention away from the cinema hall and heroes like Amitabh Bachchan to the realm of film music and the figure of the music director. This move will force us to take into account how cinema, as an object, is constituted in fundamental ways through convergence with other media. In other words, developing fan activity surrounding film music as an entry point entails rethinking the history of cinema's publicness as a history of cinema's intersections with various "new" media (radio, TV, Internet, and mobile phone), and thereby adds to the mapping of different cinematic spaces that projects such as "Publics and Practices in the History of the Present" (www.sarai-net) have initiated.[2] Such a reconceptualization of cinema's publicness will also help us steer away from treating fan activity as epiphenomena of formal politics and transitions in the political sphere proper. This is necessary not only to chart the way fan activity operates in relation to Bollywood but also to acknowledge and begin accounting for fan activity in south India that may have no connections whatsoever to political parties and electoral campaigns. Following this, I argue for a reassessment of the figure of the fan and the need to dismantle the binary of *fan-as-rowdy* versus *fan-as-rasika* and, instead, locate the "fan" along a more expansive continuum of participatory culture.[3] I conclude the essay by situating this paper in relation to academic calls for fan studies to "go global," and posit that it is just as critical, if not more, for studies of media globalization to focus on fan activity. In fact, examining fan communities that cohere around film culture in India might make valuable contributions to our understanding of the emergence of Bollywood as a global culture industry.

Music Directors and Fan Identification:
The Case of A. R. Rahman

Among other elements that distinguish a popular Indian film from, say, a Hollywood film, the one that is cited most often is the presence of at least five or six songs with seemingly no direct connection to the narrative. Songs, often choreographed into elaborate dance sequences, have been an integral part of popular Indian cinema ever since sound was introduced. As Majumdar further explains, "film songs and song sequences have their own circuit of distribution, both official, or industrial, and unofficial [...] they permeate the aural environment of India's public spaces, from markets and festivals to long-distance buses and trains" (Majumdar 2001: 161). The commercial value of film music has also meant that music directors have occupied a key role in the industry from the very beginning.[4]

Music directors have been central to developments and transformations in practically every aspect of the process—lyrics, expansion of orchestras and introduction of instruments from around the world, singing styles (the transition from actor-singers to playback singers), and, from the perspective of producers, responding to and shaping audience tastes (Arnold 1991). In fact, from the early 1940s, producers have been giving prominence to music directors. Film songs became a central component of prerelease publicity of films, and advertising began emphasizing the music director. Arnold points to a practice that continues to this day: major producers began to select commercially successful music directors to work on their new productions (1991: 206). Having their names displayed prominently on posters, billboards, and gramophone record sleeves, and radio shows such as the nationally popular *Binaca Geet Mala* (on Radio Ceylon), led to the construction of what Majumdar terms "aural stardom" (2001).[5] Over the years, songs came to be associated with music directors (and playback singers) just as much as with actors/actresses lip-synching on the screen.

A. R. Rahman started his musical career as an ad-jingles composer and emerged as a music director in the 1990s—first in Tamil cinema and post-1995 in the Bombay-based Hindi film industry. While translations of his work for Tamil-language films such as *Roja* (1992, dir. Mani Ratnam) and *Bombay* (1995, dir. Mani Ratnam) were highly successful nationwide, it is with *Rangeela* (1995, dir. Ramgopal Varma) that Rahman made his mark as a "national" music director. Rahman's nonfilm projects have also been highly successful—

for instance, his 1997 album *Vande Mataram,* released to coincide with the fiftieth year of Indian independence, sold millions of copies worldwide.

There are at least two things to keep in mind that set Rahman apart from other important music directors. First, projects such as *Vande Mataram* (1997) that involved Rahman in music videos, promotions via MTV, Channel [V], and other music shows on satellite television established him as the first music director in India to have a strong *visual* presence in addition to the aural stardom conventionally associated with music directors. In fact, Rahman figures prominently in posters advertising "Bollywood tours" worldwide—his performativity, in other words, extends beyond recorded sound.

Second, his rise coincided with the Bombay film industry attracting mainstream attention in transnational arenas, in main part due to the Indian diaspora's close ties to cinema. This led not only to an expanded audience and fan base but also to visibility generated in "world music" circles (Talvin Singh's music from the Asian Dub Foundation in London, for example) and to composing music for international projects such as *Bombay Dreams* (2002) and the stage version of *Lord of the Rings: The Return of the King* (2006). The multiple boundaries that Rahman (and his music) traverses—linguistic (Tamil-Hindi-English), religious (Hindu converted to Islam), regional/national, diasporic, and global—are strongly reflected in the online fan community.

The Rahman fan community is an online newsgroup that was formed on January 1, 1999, and today involves nearly eight thousand five hundred members from twenty-six different countries (arrfans.com). This is a space that brings together, for instance, fourth-generation Tamil-Malaysians, second-generation Indian-Americans, Indians in Gulf countries like Dubai, middle-class youth in urban India, and a growing number of non-Indian fans.[6] Embedded as citizens in disparate ways, each fan brings her/his own linguistic/regional background, experiences of varying racial/ethnic politics, religious affiliations, and different registers of knowledge and affiliation with India and "Indian" culture to bear on her/his engagement with Rahman's music (and Indian cinema in general).

The primary activity that defines this group is a detailed discussion of Rahman's music. This involves translating and evaluating lyrics, the use of different instruments and musical arrangement, songs' place in the film narrative, song picturization (and choreography), playback singers, and so on. Like other fan communities around the world, Rahman fans also monitor print publications, radio and television shows, and different websites for news and trivia about their star. The community includes people who work with Rahman on a professional basis, who have played a key role in getting this fan community recognized as Rahman's official fan club. Over the last two years, fans based in different cities around the world have begun meeting off-line to extend discussions conducted online, to help organize Rahman concerts, and, in some cases, to form informal bands and perform Rahman songs.

Enabled by the Internet, constituted by individuals from different parts of the world, driven by an interest in film music that reaches across the world, the Rahman fan collective clearly is formed at the junction of many border-crossing dialogues. It is important, therefore, to also note how interactions are influenced by broader technological, economic, and political changes. For instance, the last decade has witnessed the film and music industry, new media companies, and the Indian state engaging in attempts to curb "nonlegal" media practices that include sharing of films and film music. Relying on stereotypical notions of "rowdy" fans who operate in the shadowy bylanes of cities like Bangalore and Kuala Lumpur, media organizations and nation-states tend to view fans' appropriation of music as deviant acts and rely on a "prohibitionist approach that seeks to protect intellectual property at all costs" (Ford 2006: 3; Liang 2005).[7] Treating spaces like the Rahman fan community as online extensions of neighborhood stores that sell mp3 collections for a fraction of the cost of a CD tells us little about how fans broker consensus on what constitutes "legal" sharing and appropriation of Rahman's music. Examining the many discussions Rahman fans have had on intellectual property, CD pricing mechanisms, availability of Rahman's music in different parts of the world, legality of sharing background music from films for which Rahman has composed the score, monitoring ftp sites that circulate Rahman's music, etc., is crucial if we are to understand how online fan communities have emerged as a crucial node in a larger realm of "porous legality" (Liang 2005) that defines Indian cinema's circulation around the world.

What I wish to suggest here is that, over the years, the Rahman fan community has emerged as a "zone of engagement" (Tsing 2005) where individuals, media technologies and institutions, and broader cultural and political forces participate in the construction, contestation, and negotiation of Indian cinema's place in a transnational cultural sphere. However, before we examine the formation and social dynamics of such zones, we need to rethink our understanding of fan activity surrounding Indian film culture. It is this problematic that the rest of the chapter will tackle.

Beyond the Cinema Hall: Reconceptualizing Publicness and the Fan

Sivathamby provided what is perhaps the earliest articulation of cinema and the public sphere in India. He argued that "the cinema hall was the first performance centre in which all Tamils sat under the same roof. The basis of the seating is not on the hierarchic position of the patron but essentially on his purchasing power. If he cannot afford paying the higher rate, he has either to keep away from the performance or be with all and sundry" (1981: 18). As Srinivas notes, this "formulation can be read as pointing to the democratic possibilities of cinema" (forthcoming: 20). While there was a certain mode of policing this "democratic" space (e.g., seating codes, from the "gandhi class" all the way up to "dress circle"), this does "permit us to conceive of the cinema hall as a kind of public institution that had no precedence in India" (Srinivas forthcoming: 20).

Following this early formulation, scholars have approached the problematic of cinema's publicness by focusing on a range of filmic and extra-filmic sites with varied theoretical lenses: (1) Indian cinema as a "site of ideological production [. . .] as the (re)production of the state form" (Prasad 1998: 9), (2) Indian popular films as social history (Virdi 2003), (3) in terms of spectatorship and democracy (Rajadhyaksha 2000), (4) in terms of censorship (Mehta 2001; Vasudev 1978), and (5) in terms of stardom (Majumdar 2001). While these studies grapple with the idea of how cinema relates in complex ways to the civic and the political, fan practices have not been the focus of systematic research. The two notable exceptions here are Srinivas's pioneering work on fan associations in Andhra Pradesh (2003) and Dickey's work in Tamilnadu (1993).

Dickey locates fan activity at the intersection of the formal realm of politics and civil social activity (conducting charity work, organizing blood donation campaigns, and performing other "social services"). Building on scholarship on Tamil cinema that has examined the relationship between the construction of stardom and the politics of mobilization (Pandian 1992), Dickey provides a very useful ethnographic account of this aspect of fan activity in Tamilnadu. She does, however, ignore the possibility of fan activity that might not necessarily be "public" in the sense of there being a neighborhood fan association that meets at street corners, at tea shops, or outside cinema halls. Indeed, her analysis circumscribes fan activity in Tamilnadu as that defined by working-class (often lower-caste) male youth in visible, public spaces.

In his pathbreaking work on the Telugu film industry, and viewing practices in the state of Andhra Pradesh more broadly, Srinivas complicates Dickey's analysis and theorizes fan activity as being structured by a dialectic of devotion and defiance (2000), as a struggle between fan expectations and the industry's careful management of the star persona to derive maximum mileage from fan activity. Focusing on one major star, Chiranjeevi, Srinivas situates the formation of fan clubs in Andhra Pradesh in relation to a broader history of subaltern struggles (*dalit*/untouchable movements, for instance) and forces us to consider fan practices as a domain of political activity that does not fit within classical liberal accounts of citizenship and political representation, but one that has clear links to a politics of mobilization around linguistic/regional identity (Srinivas 2000).

While he has written that we also need to understand the political nature of fan associations beyond their "linkages with the politics of linguistic/identity nationalism," he maintains that fan activity is political mainly because it "develops around the notion of spectatorial rights." He writes,

> The cinema exists because of my presence and for me. Further, the "I" at the cinema is always a member of a collective: *we make the film happen*. Anyone who has watched a Chiranjeevi or Rajnikanth film knows exactly what I am talking about. Not only do these stars address spectators in rather direct ways (including by looking at the camera) but seem to perform according to "our" demands. (2003: n.p.; original emphasis)

Even as he exhorts us to examine the various "webs of public transactions" involving cinema, and to rethink what constitutes the "political" beyond the narrow sense of the term, Srinivas's analyses remain bound by one particular, highly visible mode of fan activity and the film industry's perception and management of such activity. He goes on to say that "much work needs to be done across the spectrum of activities and organizations that fade into the cinema hall at one end and the political party at the other" (2003: n.p.).

In the light of Indian cinema's flows worldwide, the question of who comprises the "we" in the cinema hall and what "our" demands might be complicates the notion of "spectatorial rights" (Rajadhyaksha 2000). For it would be difficult to maintain that a third-generation Tamil Malaysian fan of Rajnikanth is positioned as a spectator in precisely the same way as a fan in Tamilnadu or, for that matter, Japanese fans who watch subtitled prints. The notion of spectatorial rights also does not help us explain the kind of activity that fans of A. R. Rahman are involved in, as we saw earlier. While opening up an important line of inquiry, Srinivas's analysis needs to be extended in at least two directions.

The first question we need to address is, Are the two poles of the spectrum—the cinema hall and the political party—useful analytic categories to begin with? If we were to consider film music, a component of films that circulates in the public realm much before and long after the film itself does, we would be forced to consider the radio, the television, the Internet, and cell phone networks as sites constitutive of the publicness of cinema as much as the cinema hall itself, if not more.

Consider the story of Rameshwar Prasad Bharnwal, a resident of Jhumri Tilaiya in the state of Bihar, who has mailed nearly three *lakh* (300,000) request cards to radio stations for nearly two decades, and at least ten cards a day to *Binaca Geet Mala* when the show was broadcast on Radio Ceylon (Krishnan 1991). Bharnwal, a member of a radio listener's club that discussed films, film songs, and requests to be mailed, recalls sending nearly one hundred requests for popular songs of the time. Shows such as *Binaca Geet Mala, Chitrahaar* and *Showtheme* (on state-regulated Doordarshan), *Videocon Flashback* (on [V]), and *movie zones* (on sites like IndiaFM.com) are all key nodes in a mediated public culture shaped not necessarily in the cinema hall, by the screen. I propose that a focus on fan activities that emerge at the intersection of film and "new" media opens up the possibility of rewriting the history of Indian cinema's publicness as a history of media convergence, and as a history of fan activity that does not necessarily "fade into the cinema hall at one end and the political party at the other" (Srinivas 2003: n.p.).

The second question concerns the image of the fan that we derive from a focus on the space of the cinema hall and its surroundings, or fan associations of stars like Rajnikanth and Chiranjeevi: obsessive, male, working-class, and rowdy. The "excessive" behavior that marks viewers in the front benches of cinema halls, what Liang (2005: 371) calls the "protocols of collective behavior"—whistling and commenting loudly, throwing flowers, coins, or ribbons when the star first appears on the screen, singing along and dancing in the aisles, etc.—is routinely cited as what distinguishes fans from the rest of the audience. Further, the publicness of fan associations' activities—celebrating a star's birthday or one hundred days of a film, organizing special prerelease functions, adorning street corners with giant cutouts of the star, decorating theaters where the film has had a successful run, etc.—and press coverage of such activities have further served to both marginalize and circumscribe fan activity as undesirable, vulgar, and at times dangerous. As Srinivas, drawing on Dhareshwar and Srivatsan's analysis of rowdy-sheeters, writes,

> The fan is a rowdy not only because he breaks the law in the course of his assertion or his association with criminalized politics—the fan becomes a rowdy by overstepping the line which demarcates the legitimate, "constructive," permissible excess, and the illegitimate [. . .] as far as the "citizen" is concerned, the fan is a blind hero-worshipper (devoid of reason) and a villain. The rowdy/fan is an agent of politics which is de-legitimized. (2000: 314)

Fans, in other words, are imperfect citizens in aesthetic, socio-cultural, and political terms. Middle-class constructions of norms of excess are, without doubt, designed in part to maintain hierarchies of cultural production and taste. I would further argue that the *fan-as-rowdy* is constructed in semantic and social opposition to the idea of the *fan-as-rasika*—rowdy fans of the actor Rajnikanth as opposed to *rasikas* (connoisseurs) of the renowned Carnatic musician M. S. Subbulakshmi, for instance.

Where, then, do we position film music fans, like the members of the radio club in Jhumri Tilaiya, who wrote hundreds of letters to Ameen Sayani, the famous anchor of *Binaca Geet Mala,* expressing their admiration of singers like Talat Mahmood and Geeta Dutt? In what terms do we describe the desires and attachments of thousands of "respectable" English-speaking middle- and upper-middle-class men and women who constitute the primary readership for magazines like *Filmfare?* How do we account for shows on Channel [V] or MTV-India that were designed to tap into urban youth's "obsession" with Hindi cinema? And finally, how do we make sense of online life-worlds of fans in diverse locations worldwide who design websites devoted to film stars, maintain blogs, write detailed reviews, create ways and means to share music, and come together as online and offline communities on the basis of shared attachments to film culture?

I argue, therefore, that we need to move away from meanings derived out of experiences based in the cinema hall and/or linkages to political parties, and place the "fan" along a more expansive continuum of participatory culture (Abercrombie & Longhurst 1998). Yes, there are rowdies and *rasikas*. However, denying the existence of several other sites and modes of participation, and continuing to relegate fan activity to the fringes of a transnational public culture shaped so strongly by cinema, will not only sustain cultural hierarchies but will also mean turning a blind eye to the many important ways in which cultural and political identities are being shaped in "new" media spaces today. Let me clarify right away that I am not advocating an exhaustive mapping of different modes and levels of intensity in being a "fan"—that would be both impossible and theoretically pointless. I propose that we treat the "fan" less as a subject-position taken up by individuals in different locations, and more as a dynamic construct that is industrial, textual, and social. In other words, I am suggesting that we begin to examine how the "fan" (and fan activity) operates within a certain circuit of cultural production, in this case, the convergence between film and "new" media in the Indian context. How do media producers who develop "interactive" content for new media understand "fans," and how is this understanding translated into practice? In what ways do "new media" texts invite and structure fan activity? What does an examination of an A. R. Rahman fan community tell us about the many new and complex relationships among cinema, new media technologies, and social lives?

This shift towards examining the "fan" as a construct that is not eternal and essential but, rather, as shaped equally by industry practices, textual properties of film-based content that flow across multiple media, and social interactions in identifiable fan communities is vital if we are to appreciate and understand the centrality of spaces of participatory culture such as the Rahman fan community to the larger problematic of the emergence of "Bollywood" as a global culture industry.

Conclusion: Fan Studies Meet Global Media Studies

I began this chapter by introducing a fan community that has cohered around a film music director, A. R. Rahman. Building on a brief description of the formation and activities of the Rahman fan community, I have argued that a focus on fan activity surrounding film music will help us rethink the history of cinema's publicness as a history of media convergence, and also to stop considering fan activity solely in relation to political mobilization. By focusing attention on fan activity, I also seek to add to studies that have pushed film scholarship beyond formalist concerns with the text and opened up other entry points into understanding our experience with cinema (Hughes 2003; Liang 2005).[8] Following Stephen Hughes, I would even suggest that once fan activity is "taken as a necessary part of film history, we must rethink how we construct Indian cinema as an object of study" (2003: n.p.). In this concluding section, I wish to situate this chapter in relation to calls for fan studies to "go global," and what it means to focus on Bollywood now.

Scholarly literature on fan activity has emerged primarily from Anglo-American contexts and experiences. This literature has moved from talking about fans as infringers/poachers (Jenkins 1992) to analyzing how fans today operate as lead users, surplus audiences, grassroots intermediaries, the "long tail," performers, content generators, and even future talent for media companies (Jenkins 2006). As Jenkins argues in his recent work, fan participation has become an integral component of contemporary media culture, and both academics and industry professionals are interested more in terms of models of participation (2006: 246). Given how media flows from other parts of the world have influenced Anglo-American media texts, industries, and audience expectations over the past decade, it is not surprising that scholars who study fan activity are calling for fan studies to "go global," to begin to include accounts of fan activity in "non-Western" locations. Further, given "Western" media's current fascination with Bollywood, and the gradual development of Bollywood as a legitimate area of inquiry in academic locations in countries like the United Kingdom and United States, extending fan studies into a new and fascinating realm of non-Western popular culture would certainly seem timely. But I would argue that fan studies "go global" with great caution lest the faulty assumption that "non-Western" media are still tethered to the boundaries of their respective nation-states be reinforced. As several scholars and commentators have pointed out, simply because a circuit of media flow does not include countries like the United States or the United Kingdom does not make it less global.

To begin with, radio shows like *Binaca Geet Mala*, videocassettes of film songs that circulated throughout South Asia, the Middle East, and many countries in Africa, satellite TV channels that beam Indian films and film-based programming around the world, and, now, Internet portals dedicated to Indian cinema are all evidence that, historically, the cultural geography of fan activity surrounding Indian cinema has always been global. Fan communities that cohere around various aspects of Indian cinema also tell us that we need to think beyond the "national" as the most important scale of imagination and identity construction (Curtin 2003). Over the last decade, it has become clear that the creation of Bollywood properties—films, music, apparel, web portals, mobile games, etc.—is an enterprise that takes place in many locations around the world, and involves people with affiliations and stakes that criss-cross varied regional, national, and diasporic boundaries. Bollywood, in other words, cannot be understood in terms of a "national" cinema industry limited to the boundaries of the Indian nation-state or restricted in its imagination by rigid definitions of "Indianness." By continuing to limit Bollywood to notions of "Indianness," we risk neglecting attachments that do not follow lines of ethnicity or nationality. We need to recognize that a focus on transnational fan communities (Rahman fans, for example) will help us better understand how media circulate and get hinged to varied aspirations around the world, and, crucially, how Bollywood, from a "non-Western" location, has begun claiming the status of a "global" culture industry.

Notes

1. Personal interview with Shashi Baliga (Editor, *Filmfare*), November 14, 2005. Also see http://kollywood.allindiansite.com/g/60ta.html.

2. Http://www.sarai.net/aboutus/projects/old&new.htm.

3. The term "*rasika*," derived from an aesthetic theory (*rasa*) of performance, connotes a highly developed sense of appreciation of various art forms. "*Rasika*" can be roughly translated as "connoisseur." The term is most commonly associated with religious devotion, and classical music and dance forms.

4. Film music records account for 61 percent of the ten billion-rupee music industry in India. See http://www.contentsutra.com/blog/_archives/2005/5/12/810890.html.

5. Majumdar argues that "it is necessary [. . .] to theorize an aural conception of stardom to account for the dual pleasures and recognitions in song sequences, a concept of stardom in which even the absence of glamour and the invisibility of playback singers can be regarded as defining features of their star personas" (2001: 171).

6. The moderator of the group informed me that over the last two years, over 50 percent of new subscribers have been non-Indians.

7. See, for example, http://in.rediff.com/movies/2005/apr/04ficci.htm.

8. Also see http://www.sarai.net for an overview of projects that map transformations in media and urban life in India.

15

Beyond Kung-Fu and Violence
Locating East Asian Cinema Fandom

Bertha Chin

In 2005, for the first time in history, the Venice Film Festival both opened
and closed with Chinese-language films, Tsui Hark's martial arts epic,
Seven Swords, and Peter Ho-Sun Chan's musical, *Perhaps Love,* respectively. Meanwhile, a number of major American and European cities each
have annual film festivals dedicated to showcasing talents from East Asian
countries like Hong Kong, China, Korea, Japan, and Taiwan, providing
fans with a variety of genres apart from martial arts (*wuxia*) and gangster
films popularized by the likes of Tsui Hark and John Woo in the eighties,
and a string of horror films marked by the onset of the release of Hideo
Nakata's *Ringu* (1998) to Western audiences. Festival billings aside, Chinese-language films like *In The Mood for Love* (2000, dir. Wong Kar Wai),
Hero (2002, dir. Zhang Yimou), *2046* (2004, dir. Wong Kar Wai), and most
recently *Kung Fu Hustle* (2004, dir. Stephen Chow) have been made widely
available for Western audiences.

These films, screened outside the periphery of film festivals, suggest
that there are demands for Asian-language films—often considered as cult
cinema due to the film genres that are exported overseas—among Western
viewers. Matt Hills argues that the "distinctiveness required for cult status
is [. . .] partly based on such films' cultural-textual differences from the
'mainstream' of Hollywood productions, given that a sense of what is marginal often has a national-contextual specificity, with the 'foreignness' of
some [. . .] film genres rendering them marginal [and cultish] in markets
outside of their country of production" (2005c: 161). As Jancovich et al.
add, this "supposed difference from the 'mainstream' (although they may

in fact be the mainstream of their own culture) [. . .] often involves an exoticization of other cultures" (2003: 4).

There has been plenty of academic work surrounding fan cultures that has offered us a glimpse into American and British fans' social and cultural world, and many such studies are conducted within the context of the Internet, where fans have been congregating to conduct their activities. However, work surrounding the reception of East Asian popular culture by Western audiences or Asian migrants located in the United States, United Kingdom, or Australia is limited. As Darling-Wolf suggests, "few analyses have focused on texts produced and/or consumed outside the US. Even fewer have considered the significance of fan culture on an increasingly global scene, fostered in particular by the advent of the internet as a tool for intercultural, and potentially worldwide, fan activity" (2004: 507).

My curiosity regarding this topic stems from ongoing research on fan fiction fandom and my personal interest in East Asian cinema, especially Hong Kong (HK) cinema (which will be used as the main example here), and its reception and treatment as cult cinema in Western countries. When I was growing up in Malaysia, these films were marketed and treated as "mainstream" along with major Hollywood productions, unlike the cult status they achieved in the United States as early as 1973, when three HK martial arts films topped the U.S. box office chart. The minimal fanfare those films provoked led Desser to conclude that those films appealed "not to mainstream audiences struggling with the legacy of the Vietnam War, but precisely to those subcultural, disillusioned, disaffected audiences who had opposed the war or who were more radically and generally alienated from much of mainstream culture" (2003: 186).

At the same time, being a Malaysian-born Chinese educated mostly in Australia and the United Kingdom, and having minimal comprehension of the Chinese language, not to mention other East Asian languages, limits me to fan sites and Web forums where English is the preferred, and main, language used. This leads me to wonder if, first, fan cultural theory is transferable between cultures when the object of fandom is produced in a different cultural and national context; second, if East Asian cinema is consumed the same way by fans in Asia and in the West (or if this is possible to determine at all with the Internet blurring national boundaries); and third, if cultural identity in any way determines the performance of fan identities.

This chapter, though a largely experimental and introductory endeavor, is an attempt to "de-Westernize" fan studies by shifting the emphasis away from American and European popular cultural texts and focusing on texts produced in East Asia. Within the scope of this chapter, however, I am interested in the reception of East Asian cinema within a Western context, specifically the question of whether its classification as cult cinema leaves it "vulnerable," as Jancovich et al. point out, to "exoticization," especially when these films are discussed (in English) and viewed within the cultural context that may be "foreign" to the culture within which the films were produced. What I am also interested in exploring here is whether fan cultural theory creates, and assumes, a homogenous fan culture, so much so that it might not necessarily allow us to explore the possibility that other (fan) identities exist, influenced by the social, cultural, and national contexts in which the objects of fandom are produced. These questions will be examined in relation to existing work on East Asian fandom, but I will also make use of some fan data from an ongoing project for illustrative purposes.

Fandom in an East Asian Context

Current fan cultural theory such as that offered by Jenkins (1992) and Baym (2000) presents a complex social network of fans who not only exhaustively discuss the texts and the meanings they might derive from the characters and the texts but also go on to make use of these texts creatively, participating in what Fiske terms fan "textual productivity" (1992: 37). Some of these fans write fan fiction and poetry, make music videos and fan films, and circulate the finished products for review and consumption within the fan interpretive community.

However, with the rising popularity of East Asian popular culture, non-media scholars are also showing an interest in what has preoccupied fan scholars for the last two decades. As Kelly states, "we now recognize that the forms and practices of music, sports, comics, film, fashion and other areas of leisure and consumer culture are just as essential to fully understanding Japan as its factories, schools and politics" (2004: 2)—an observation that undoubtedly resonates with other East Asian countries as well.

Most fan studies conducted within an East Asian context are concentrated on fans of Japanese popular culture. For instance, the popularity of Japanese *manga* and its fandom has introduced readers to terms such as *yaoi*, "an acronym for the phrase 'Yama nashi, ochi nashi, imi nashi' (No Climax, No Resolution, No Meaning)" (Thorn 2004: 171), coined in the eighties within the specificity of Japanese comic/*manga* conventions to define a range of amateur *manga* that shares some similarities to the largely textual slash fiction.[1] This particular fan practice has extended from *manga* to include anime texts in recent years, and has spread to fans outside of Japan too.

Rather than working through the angle of fan resistance favored by some Western scholars (Jenkins 1992; Tulloch & Jenkins 1995), these East Asian scholars propose the concept of "intimacy," which "impels individuals to act in ways that go beyond the bounds of self to seek greater communion with the object of their adoration" (Yano 2004: 44). According to Yano, this drive to seek intimacy revolves around knowledge of mundane details about the stars that only fans would know; a relationship with the star as well as with other fans; and the experience of meeting the star, or otherwise physically expressing their adoration, which results in "pounding heart, loss of consciousness, or tears[. . . .] This bodily engagement authenticates the fan-star relationship as real by virtue of those tears and cheers" (2004: 45). This sense of intimacy is centered on the fan relationship to the star rather than a specific cultural text or event, and this intimacy "informs future decisions of consumption so that each decision is made within the framework of fandom" (2004: 48).

On the other hand, Kim Hyun Mee argues that fans are "trained" through their actions and languages: "they must wear the same clothes, shout the same slogans, and show contained passion[. . . .] They try to maintain 'grace' as fans that are worthy of the star's status by abstaining from talking back or cursing when attacked by rival fan clubs, upholding order and calm, and cleaning up after events" (2004: 44). Through their "selfless" acts, they gain and retain a sense of intimacy with the stars by upholding the star's status and reputation in public. Kim's exploration was of the world of female soccer fandom, but again, the emphasis appears to be on stars rather than cultural texts or events. Despite the fact that these female soccer fans were attending a public event such as the 2002 World Cup, their responsibility was to the star and by extension, the star's fan club. A similar trend can be observed in fans' review of pop star Leon Lai's recent concert in HK, where they discuss upholding Lai's reputation as a top Asian entertainer and philanthropist by being on their best behavior and respecting guest performers at his concert (i.e., not walking out during the guest performances and shaking hands with guest performers even if fans would rather experience that physical contact with Lai himself).[2]

Even when fans are part of a mass audience—the comic convention, the soccer stadium, the rock/pop concert—the emphasis is on fans' "personal" relationship with the star. Most scholarly work on fans that has emerged from the West stresses the active participation of fans in production and consumption, suggesting that there is a resistance of sorts to the official culture. Recent works on fans within an East Asian context, however, seem to depict different approaches to the concept of fandom and celebritydom, suggesting that the national and cultural context within which texts or objects of fandom are produced may be an important factor to consider.

HK Cinema in a Western Context

Leon Hunt wrote that "HK cinema has largely been theorized in terms of the hybrid, the transnational, the postmodern and the postcolonial" (2003: 157–58). While film production in the former British colony has been on the decline due to threats from rampant piracy and competition from other East Asian countries, the 2005 Venice Film Festival's choice of book-end films confirms the contribution of HK filmmakers to the world of international cinema, which has been exporting home-grown talent to Hollywood since the emergence of a new HK cinema in 1982 that saw the premiere of internationally recognizable names like Tsui Hark, Ann Hui, and Stanley Kwan (Abbas 1997). Action superstars like Bruce Lee and Jackie Chan, and directors and martial arts choreographers such as John Woo and Yuen Wo-Ping are no longer the only household names, as more and more stars and films are "brought over" from underground cult status to the mainstream. Their collaborations with Hollywood have also made their previous work, made in their country of origin, easily available to admirers in the West. Just as a successful Hollywood remake of East Asian films will provide "a platform for the cult text's wider availability" (Hills 2005c: 164), the success of a star or a director will provide similar opportunities for his or her previous work to become more accessible to fans internationally.

"With few exceptions, films made in HK are all part of the mainstream; all make use, to the full extent that their budgets allow, of established stars, established genres, and spectacle" (Abbas 1997: 20). Even Wong Kar Wai, who makes "superhip movies the international art-house set loves for their languorous rhythms, their gorgeous-garish visual tones, their iconizing of alienation, their pioneering of a sultry cinematic language" (Corliss 2004), makes use of popular genres such as martial arts (*Ashes of Time*, 1994), the gangster film (*Fallen Angels*, 1995), and melodrama (*In The Mood for Love*, 2000) in his films. While action films "are undeniably important for the HK film industry" (Abbas 1997: 19), they only represent one side of HK cinema, albeit a side with which most international fans are comfortable and familiar. However, as Abbas argues, it is undeniable that these action films put the HK film industry on the international film map, resulting in the export of its talents and skills, not to mention securing the cult status of its films among fans worldwide even when it remains part of the mainstream cinema around Asia.

However, unlike American television, where the lifespan of a popular show can last many years and where spin-offs can continue the legacy of a cult show such as *Star Trek*, films do not possess the same kind of "longevity." Characters rarely last beyond one or three films, at the most. The absence of a weekly or daily serial means that character and plot development occurs over the length of the film—an average period of two hours—as opposed to the character and plot development in a TV show, which can continue over years, making it easier for fans to become emotionally attached to the show's characters and their relationships. For fans who are involved in textual production such as fan fiction writing, this longevity allows them to build a meta-text of background information for the plots and characters.

On the other hand, general fan fiction sites like Fanfiction.net frequently offer stories based on film characters.[3] If there are any instances of fan fiction to be found based on HK productions (whether film or TV dramas), they are usually "real actor" or "actor-centric" fictions. "Actor-centric" fictions are, not unlike some form of "real actor fiction," popular and widely accepted among some fan fiction circles. In these "actor-centric" fictions, actors or pop idols are positioned in a fictional universe created by fans, playing original characters that may be based on an amalgamation of characters from their past or latest films and TV dramas.

The "actor-centric" fictions and the range of scholarly work that emphasizes East Asian stars suggest that the climate of fandom in East Asia is particularly idol-driven rather than character-driven. Just as their television dramas, often "young people's stories of love, work, friendship and consumerism [in East Asian cities]" (Hu 2005: 171)—or "trendy dramas" as they are mostly known, a cultural form that has no Western equivalent, according to Darling-Wolf (2004: 524, note 6)—feature "multitalents" (Darling-Wolf 2004: 510), stars who juggle a television, film, and music career, the HK film industry is also dependent on these pop idols to sell and promote a film. For example, for nearly two decades, superstar Jackie Chan had to hide the fact that he had fathered a son for fear that the announcement might affect his fame. "Japanese girls, for some reason, are among his (Chan's) most obsessively loyal fans, and, largely for fear of upsetting them, he keeps quiet about his many romantic involvements" (Dannen & Long 1997: 3). We constantly return to the figure of the star (such as Jackie Chan and Leon Lai) as the object of (Asian) fan adoration rather than a specific filmic text or genre. Even within the space of the Internet, websites and forums are mostly geared towards an actor rather than a film.[4]

This is not to say that this factor presents a marked difference between East and West. Rather, it is possible that the national and cultural structure of the industries influences the way fans perform their identities (such as maintaining proper conduct to achieve a form of intimacy with the star—a practice that is probably more common in Asia than in the West). While movie stars in Hollywood rarely cross boundaries between films and TV, most stars in Asia are required to sing and act for both film and TV at the same time, even at the height of their careers.[5]

HK Cinema Fandom in the West

However, does this emphasis shift when East Asian films are discussed in English-language forums and being simultaneously viewed as "foreign cinema" in a cultural and national context that differs from that in which the films were originally produced? In a popular English-language discussion forum dedicated to the HK auteur, Wong Kar Wai,[6] for example, discussions were concentrated on the director himself, his various works, his artistic techniques in filmmaking, and his long-time collaborator and cinematographer, Christopher Doyle, rather than the stars and Asian pop idols Wong has a penchant for casting in his films.

Indeed, when questioned about the appeal of East Asian cinema, fans praised the following features:

> The variety and originality of many films and stories. It doesn't seem as overused and dumbed down as so many western media products. Plus, pretty Asian people. (Orca)

I like the realism. Not every movie has a happy ending. I believe there's often more depth to the characters and their stories. (Rutju)

[A]s a white European, I really enjoy the obvious sense of geographical and cultural distance, because the pleasure is kinda twofold: moments which are very different are enjoyable because I'm learning something new, and moments which are very familiar are enjoyable because that familiarity is surprising and reassuring at the same time. (Seven)

While some audiences based in the United States and United Kingdom are introduced to East Asian cinema through anime fandom—"the language (in anime) struck me, and I found out that [. . .] live action films from the east offered the same intricate, interesting storylines, with innovative effects and ideas" (Orca)—some grew up watching HK films and Sammo Hung's *Martial Law* on television, while others stumbled onto the films by accident, or were introduced by friends who were already fans of martial arts or gangster films from HK. The arrival of DVD technology also helped introduce more films to these fans as the technology allowed them to borrow DVDs of East Asian films from friends who have a more extensive collection.

Fans at this forum, however, do not express a feeling of being marginalized as a result of their interest: "[O]riginally, when I first exposed myself to Asian cinema, I felt like I was very different, and nobody knew what on earth I was talking about when they asked me what my favorite films were. But it has grown far more mainstream now, good enough for me to strike up conversations with many people at work" (Orca). Kungfuchemist agreed, stating "now that Hollywood has co-opted the style of Asian films, there seems to be a new interest in where these influences came from. So I see those who were once marginalized becoming the people on the cutting edge, as it were." Seven similarly argues, "I can still participate in discussions of mainstream culture if I have to, so I think of my 'extra' interest in Asian cinema as 'elite' rather than 'marginalized' knowledge." Their participation in the fandom and their interest in East Asian cinema create a feeling that they are more "elite," as Seven testified, than other fans or casual audiences. In a sense, these fans possess "popular cultural capital" (Fiske 1992: 33) that puts them in the forefront of an ongoing trend that is popularizing East Asian cinema in the West, even if these films are considered part of the mainstream in the East Asian region.

What Next?

Susan Napier has remarked that the cult phenomenon of anime in the West (mostly the United States) has been characterized not so much by the genre's eroticism but by its exoticism. "The fan's interaction with the cultural object is deeply engaged, transcending issues of national boundaries, content, style, or ideology, and it cannot be subsumed under any one-note description. The fact that anime is a Japanese, or at least non-American product, is certainly important but largely because this signifies that anime is a form of media entertainment outside the mainstream, something 'different'" (2001: 242). And fans, as Seven testified above, take their interest, whether in anime or in East Asian cinema, as a sign of "elitist taste" that is different from the norm that the West is familiar with, an accumulation of popular cultural capital that will set them apart from their peers and from "official culture."

Jancovich et al. have warned of the dangers of "exoticization" when the cultural object, in this case East Asian cinema, is produced within different national and cultural contexts. The fan data provided have certainly touched on the difference East Asian cinema provides to the alternative they are familiar with. But rather than focus on the cultural and geographical distance of the East from the West, fans have instead concentrated on the popular cultural capital they accumulate as a result of their interest, and the sharing of popular cultural capital with their friends. The so-called "exoticism," as suggested by Napier, is its "un-Americanness," its difference from the "mainstream," but for the fans themselves, it is a sign of their "elitist taste."

As we have also seen briefly in this introductory paper, the concept of celebritydom and fandom appears to work differently in East Asian cultures, where rather than a strong focus on characters from a popular text, the emphasis is on the pop idol. The region's actors multitask as singers and TV stars, and fans would support the actor's films, music, or TV serials in order to achieve a form of intimacy with the star. While fan cultural theory thus far provides remarkable insight into fans' social and cultural worlds, it is still dominated by texts that are produced in the United States and United Kingdom. Furthermore, these explorations are largely of fans of TV texts, and a more extensive look into film fans may be useful in this case. On top of that, the national and cultural contexts within which these texts are produced, and the cultural identities of fans, are also important factors to consider.

The shortcomings of fan cultural theory are revealed in this case, as the current range of work assumes a homogenous fan culture dominated by American and British texts and methods of production and consumption. Work on fans emerging from East Asia provides a different take that might better equip scholars in examining media fans, particularly in the current technologically dependent world.

N O T E S

1. On important differences and tensions between *yaoi* and slash, however, see Thorn (2004).

2. The discussions can be found at http://invisionfree.com/forums/Worldwide_Leon_Fans/index.php?showtopic=829.

3. Obvious examples like *Star Wars, Harry Potter,* and the *Lord of the Rings* film series aside, *Pirates of the Caribbean,* which at date of writing is just a single film, has the most fan fiction at 7,012 stories stored on the archive.

4. General Web forums do exist, but many—such as the Asian Cinema Forum (http://www.acfmovies.com/board/index.php)—serve more as a forum for down-loading films via peer-to-peer Internet protocols such as BitTorrent than as a space for discussing films.

5. This warrants a further investigation that could combine a more in-depth look into film fans that is, unfortunately, beyond the scope of this paper.

6. The forum can be accessed at http://www.wongkarwai.net.

16

Han Suk-kyu and the Gendered Cultural Economy of Stardom and Fandom

Anne Ciecko and Hunju Lee

Examining the chronological development of star performance within a body of films, together with concomitant extradiegetic incarnations, provides critical access to the meaning-making work of fandom and star construction within particular cultural moments. Composite constellations of star texts can guide fan behaviors and interpretive processes, and encourage dialogic engagement with societal attitudes and consumer practices. Therefore, grafting the career of a film star such as Han Suk-kyu—until recently, the biggest box-office draw and highest-paid actor in South Korean cinema—onto a grid of national vicissitudes and socioeconomic changes offers a very intriguing cultural case study of contemporary Korean cinema, celebrity, and audiences—and of popular discourses of masculinity. Focusing mainly on Han Suk-kyu's career on and off the movie screen from 1997 onwards, the narrative of Han's stardom that we reconstruct and analyze is a story about industry shifts and gendered cultural trends, and, most critically, fan/audience expectations and frustrations: Korea's top male star decided, at the pinnacle moment of his screen appeal in 1999–2000, to take a prolonged movie-acting hiatus. When he returned to the big screen, cultural tastes of the movie-going public (especially the desired demographic of younger audience members) had shifted enough to radically diminish Han's star currency. In this chapter, we investigate the understudied Korean star/audience dynamic through the following cultural phenomena: movie-screen absence coupled with media presence, the regulation of affect in Korean male star performances, popular Korean perceptions of ideal masculinity and their relationships to domestic film genres, and the rise of consumer nationalism and cinematic spectacle.

Han Suk-kyu's filmic career growth corresponds with economic recovery in South Korea. After a start as a voice and TV-drama actor, he became a huge movie star during the period of the Asian financial crisis, bringing box-office magic/industry clout to his leading-man roles. Until recently, his films have likewise been associated with the creative reinvention of genre conventions and the rising surge of commercially viable contemporary Korean cinema. Ultimately, Han's career trajectory sheds some light on the complexly entangled workings of industry trends and consumer behavior.

Han's Absent Presence

During the highest point in Han's stardom, his film texts actively directed fandom. However, Han Suk-kyu's "comeback" film, *Double Agent* (2003, dir. Kim Hyeon-jeong), the first movie produced by a company he formed with his brother, Him Pictures, was largely rejected by audiences. The rationale Han had offered for leaving the movie screen at the height of his star currency was to recharge his creative batteries and reemerge a better actor (see Choi 2000; *Cine 21* 2002).[1] However, his entrepreneurial foray into movie making apparently left his fans feeling betrayed, as one aborted "home" production after another led to a much-longer-than-expected delay. Meanwhile Han continued to appear as a fixture in commercial advertisements on television and in print. He and his brother also at that time launched a website and a script-development service.

Instead of providing the necessary *Contact* with his fans (to quote the title of one of his successful romance films, ironically about a cyber-relationship), this website and the one for *Double Agent* failed to provide the necessary interactivity (indeed, the whole marketing campaign for *Double Agent* seems to have been the result of major miscalculation). According to figures from the Korean Film Commission, *Double Agent* ended up ranking only a very disappointing #19 for the year (2003).[2] Other rankings during the time of Han's hiatus and return to the big screen also showed ominous signs of discontent. The results of a survey of 124 directors and producers published in *Daily Hankook* actually found Han Suk-kyu in the #1 position—as most overrated actor (Park 2001). The reason given for this choice was Han's overattachment to money and a lack of diversity in his roles and performances after 1998's *Christmas in August* (dir. Hur Jin-ho). Another survey published in the *Daily Chosun* ranked Han the #13 Korean star in terms of audience appeal (D. Lee 2003)—although he had held the #1 spot just one year before. In the alchemy of Han's star making (and arguably diminished star currency), timing has been crucial. Questions of temporality have been critical to the cultural timeliness of Han's film narratives and performances, the strain of extended screen absence (even when the star has remained "present" through other mediations), audience/fan perspectives, and the trends of popular culture's constructed masculinities.

Han's stardom as a cultural phenomenon connects to both consumer behaviors and cinematic expressions of gendered representation and nationalism in South Korea. At the peak of his popularity, Han's often-celebrated "realistic" and "natural" screen acting differentiated him from other male stars' exaggeratedly comic and hypermasculine styles (S. Lee 2003). The rise of Han Suk-kyu's stardom actually corresponds with growing audience fatigue with such male stars' performances, and a preference for Han's emphasis on ordinary, everyday behaviors and gestures and very subtle (rather than over-the-top) facial and vocal modifications invoking the inner workings of characters' minds. However, during Han's off-screen period, industry trends and consumer tastes swung towards sensationalistic genres (horror, thriller, raucous comedy) and favored Han's male star "competitors" (including Song Kang-ho, Sul Kyung-gu, and Choi Min-sik), known for their ability to transform into myriad characters, and avoid typecasting. New, younger male stars also emerged, essentially positioning Han (now in his early forties) as part of an older generation.

Han Suk-kyu's movie personae in leading roles from 1997 to 1999 were marked by a relative fixity, consistency, and constancy—which potentially made the rupturing effect of his screen absence all the more apparent for a desiring audience. However, his years of self-imposed exile from the big screen were marked by an intense visibility in advertisements via other consumer culture vehicles.

Han Suk-kyu's endorsements have included television and print ads for products for tele- and cyber-communications, a bank, familiar beverages, a furniture company, an oil company, and men's professional attire. Han's hawking is a selling of "capital as a kind of brand loyalty to the advertising company" (Marshall 1997: 195). This had a potentially two-fold result: Han appeared more loyal to the corporate advertisers than to film fans, and he diluted his own brand power. This phenomenon is arguably exacerbated by the fact that Han's advertising persona is so similar to the ways his movie image is read by Korean audiences, and even the ways the perceived "stability" of his personal life continues the process of star identification. Rather than just being Han Suk-kyu, however, the "star" of the advertisements is clearly a man who's working for the money—and not a "pure" movie star (see Gallagher 1997). At the same time, as is the case for a number of Asian male stars, Han's advertisements are profoundly self-reflexive, and his films have become increasingly so (Ciecko 2004). The largest and most important Korean companies, such as Samsung electronics, LG Oil Company, and SK Telecom, selected Han Suk-kyu to be their celebrity spokesman on the basis of his "image."

A series of Han's ads for SK Telecom also function as friendly public service announcements about where and when to turn cell phones off, counseling viewers on proper protocols for public use. Another SK Telecom ad appeals to national pride and support for the Korean soccer team, depicting Han leading the victory chant. Costars from his films have appeared with him in television and print ads, adding an intertextual *frisson* of recognition for Korean audiences, and further blurring his real/reel image. (The TV commercials have even used snippets of music used in Han's films.) For example, one Maxim coffee ad that aired during the time of Han's big-screen hiatus featured his female costar Ko So-young from *Double Agent*, who plays a flower shop worker who receives a romantic surprise from gentleman Han. In one television commercial from the LG Caltex Oil series, Han drives a truck and saves the day by helping push to safety a busload of children stuck on a railroad track. Throughout these advertising images, Han frequently greets his viewers with his trademark benevolent smile.

Further blurring boundaries, the off-screen Han Suk-kyu behind the diegetic personae has been depicted in the Korean media as a model of the "good Korean man": husband, father, lover—loyal to the woman who had loved him since before he was a star. Qualities of restraint, reticence, moderation, and emotional self-control are consistent traits of Han Suk-kyu's movie characters—and valued traits in "traditional" Korean society's construction of masculinity. In an interview, the actor has himself admitted that "many people say they can see me in my performances (my characters) because my performance [style] is to draw a character into myself instead of letting myself assimilate with the character" (Y. Kim 2003). Korean audiences have viewed many of Han's characters as extensions of his real-life personality. For his devoted female fan base, Han Suk-kyu frequently offered an idealistic version/vision of a sincere man seeking and giving absolute, constant love. However, Han's characters are continually experiencing a "crisis" of masculinity, resulting from their apparent passivity; and according to a Korean film critic, this contained style of performance limits the diversity of Han's screen selves and gives the audience a sense of constancy (In 2002). His male heroes are often hostages bound by social structures oriented toward material values and hierarchies dominated by the gangster boss's order; a national system with conflicting ideologies (North/South Korean relations in the espionage thrillers); and lost, unrequited, or destined love.

The Economy of Emotions

On the movie screen, Han Suk-kyu's film characters frequently have limited choices and repressed personalities, and do not possess the power to manage their own lives. They are marked by tensions around the restraint of affect, and inability to intervene in the forces of fate—both in their inability to fight and alter societal forces, and in their personal human relationships. For example, as Makdong in *Green Fish* (1997, dir. Lee Chang-dong), Han is a young, confused man, newly discharged from the army, who returns home and is drawn into the underworld. He is increasingly driven by economic urgency, urban entanglements, and the dissolution of his family. In the delicate melodrama *Christmas in August,* Han Suk-kyu plays a dying photographer who contains his despair, sadness, and panic in the face of imminent death; but Han deftly—and indirectly—enables his audience to glimpse and recognize the hidden emotions through his reserved performance, an outward cheeriness betrayed by a wan smile. The film that solidified Han's box-office appeal for female audiences immediately predates the new era of the Korean blockbuster. *Christmas in August* was released in January 1998, following on the heels of Han's 1997 surprise hit, *The Contact* (dir. Chang Yoon-Hyun), which directly targeted contemporary Korean women. In the 1997 annual report on his *www.koreanfilm.org* website, critic Darcy Paquet (n.p) suggests, quoting the movie's producer, an even more specific audience of working women or "office ladies"—a term that connotes (mostly) single women between twenty and forty years of age. Like *The Contact, Christmas in August* successfully appealed to female audiences through a quotidian romantic narrative featuring a repressed thirtysomething male—calmly resigned, vulnerable (although striving to maintain an upbeat façade), and, indeed, terminally ill. The fledgling romance he develops with one of his customers is both tender and decidedly platonic.

Christmas in August was a watershed moment for Han's career. Like *The Contact* and to a certain extent the special effects–laden reincarnation fantasy *Ginko Bed* (1996, dir. Kang Je-gyu) before it, *Christmas in August* creates a small, intimate space for the female spectator, one that appears to have been shut down in the blockbuster era. We want to qualify this assertion with the reminder that we are not reductively equating the romance genre with female audiences (or suggesting they are by definition excluded from other genres). Such gender codings are evident in the casting, star performances, and marketing of these films—the representational gender politics within and outside narrative cinema. *Christmas in August* swept the Korean Film Awards with recognition for best film, direction, cinematography, and a best actress award for Shim Eun-Ha for her role as Da-rim—a slightly impetuous performance that plays off Han's character, Jung-won's forced optimism.

However, the gender politics turn ominous in Han's next film, the spy thriller *Shiri* (1999, dir. Kang Je-gyu), the film that broke South Korea's then all-time box-office record and Han's first full-fledged Korean blockbuster. His character, Yu Jung-won, a South Korean secret agent, finds out that his lover is actually a North Korean terrorist involved with a plot to blow up buildings around Seoul, including a stadium where the "reunification" soccer game is being played. Financed by the *chaebol* Samsung Group, *Shiri* employed state-of-the arts special effects, and an unprecedented marketing campaign, contributing to the acceleration of Han's star "capital" and the fixing of his flawed hero image. *Shiri* also was a landmark in post–economic crisis, post–IMF bailout terms: it sunk Hollywood's *Titanic* (Ciecko 2002). In *Shiri*, Han's character discovers the betrayal late in the game and is forced to confront the truth about his lover and the fact that he has inadvertently enabled the deaths of many people. At the end of the film, the tormented Yu Jung-won faces off with his now-exposed sniper/fiancée, and again Han reveals the conflicted emotions on his character's face. In *Shiri*, Han is also cast against the charismatic actors Choi Min-sik and Song Kang-ho, who, respectively, play a North Korean terrorist, Park, and his secret agent partner, Lee. Han's character, Yu, is positioned with each in a relationship that challenges him to reconsider codes of brotherhood, the masculine melodramatic bonds that pervade contemporary Korean blockbusters.

Han's character is again tricked by a woman in 1999's graphic murder mystery, *Tell Me Something* (dir. Chang Yoon-Hyn). Detective Cho is a rather hardened cop with a tarnished reputation, who ends up working on a serial killer case; he gradually warms to the attractions of a faux-innocent woman who turns out to probably be a murderer. Han's re-pairing with actress Shim Eun-ha (his girlish costar from *Christmas in August*) serves to underscore his character's inability to intervene, to "act." His disempowerment is visually underscored in the very last aerial shot of the film, which has him duped, horrified, and literally crawling on his hand and knees.

Although its spy-thriller genre recalled Han's biggest screen hit, *Shiri*, his comeback film, *Double Agent*, finally released in South Korea in January 2003, did not meet the expectations of audiences or critics—nor, arguably, did it compensate them for the long wait. The Korean film industry since 2000 has been geared towards revamped genre films targeting young audiences—especially fantastic movies like horror films, historical dramas emphasizing spectacle and action and giving expression to new displays of nationalism (including growing anti-American sentiment), Korean teen comedies adapted from Internet fiction, and showcases for exaggerated physical performances (Heo 2002). In addition to a wave of newer, younger stars, the mercurial and volatile screen personalities of male stars (including Han's peers) have "clicked" with younger audiences—much more than Han Suk-kyu has been able to do. Even the website for Han's comeback vehicle, *Double Agent*, lacks the ludic sense of pop culture play that younger audiences have come to demand. Meanwhile Han's star image appears all the more static.

Double Agent tells the story of a North Korean who deceptively defected from North Korea to the South to work as a spy, but was dumped by both the North and South Korean governments after his engagement in double espionage was exposed. The film also includes a side narrative of a romance (first a sham, then the real thing, a rather tepid relationship) with a fellow female espionage agent. The based-on-a-true-story narrative of *Double Agent* ostensibly fits into a category that includes political thrillers like *Silmido* (2003, dir. Kang Woo-suk) and *Taegukgi* (2004, dir. Kang Je-gyu)—the latter a Korean War film made by the director of *Shiri*, the most expensive Korean production ever and current box-office record holder. However, *Double Agent* did not share these films' savvy marketing blitzes and audience appeal. Lacking also the new "spectacular nationalism"[3] of these recent hit films, *Double Agent* focused instead on the male protagonist Lim Byung-ho's psychological conflicts, his inner struggle as he cannot choose between the two countries in the divided nation. (In an interview, the actor himself expressed anxiety about his performance style and the restrictions demanded by the role, and appraised the potentially audience-alienating choices he made as a producer [see Y. Kim 2003]).

The Commodification of Gender

Another factor that impacted the reception of Han's comeback was the Korean audience's changing perceptions of ideal masculinity. Contemporary young men are increasingly less inclined to identify with the traditional father image of the self-sacrificing, uncomplaining, yet take-charge man who earns for his family, and is hesitant to express feelings, even when experiencing intense pain and sadness.

Recent Korean cinema has witnessed the rise of the male antihero, a representation connected with the state of the Korean economy and unemployment and disaffection among the youth. Additionally, both young women and men in their teens and twenties reportedly covet the "flower boy" (see Nam 2001) image that pervades Korean popular culture: the cute and cuddly (even androgynous) male that women can imagine caring for, like a pet. This boy-toy becomes a kind of commodity for female consumption, sexual objectification, and voyeuristic desire. The prototype is slim, fashion-conscious, and pretty in a way that connotes gender and sexual ambiguity. Further, although largely unrealized in contemporary films that tend to relegate women to minor roles, a potentially greater range of popular cultural representation of the modern Korean woman is present, allowing for a fluidity of gender signifiers—a more masculine feminine. In a modified version of these gendered images, the sensationally popular (and frequently imitated) teen comedy *My Sassy Girl* (2001, dir. Kwak Jae-young, based on an Internet novel) depicts a submissive and sensitive young man enthralled by a troubled, domineering-yet-charming (and self-described melodrama-hating) young woman. Among older male actors, Han Suk-kyu's peer, Song Kang-ho, has been particularly adept at conveying comic personae in a variety of film genres, from the raucous amateur wrestler slapstick of *Foul King* (2000, dir. Kim Ji-woon) to the darkest-of-dark humor of the hit-torn-from-the-headlines thriller *Memory of Murder* (2003, dir. Bong Joon-ho).

Nevertheless, many contemporary Korean films reinforce, while a few critically challenge, the dominant ideology of gender. For example, in the morally ambiguous and controversial *Happy End* (1999, dir. Chung Gi-woo), Han Suk-kyu's peer actor, Choi Min-sik, plays an emasculated unemployed househusband, a TV drama watcher and reader of novels with an adulterous wife. His "feminized" character is presented and por-trayed in an increasingly sympathetic manner that almost justifies his explosive final act of violence. In *Take Care of My Cat* (2001, dir. Jeong Jae-eun), a rare Korean feature focused on female characters and directed (and written) by a woman, a group of five female friends all experience employment frustrations and limited options for career mobility. The most balanced female character in the film (and the best "friend") is the most nonconformist in her rejection of conventional codes of femininity; indeed, the entire film rejects the narrative necessity for romantic fulfill-ment. *Happy End* finished the fifth-grossing Korean film at the domestic box office the year of the blockbuster thriller *Shiri. Take Care of My Cat* barely made a dent at the box office, while a male gangster drama called *Friend* (2001, dir. Kwak Kyung-Taek) claimed the top spot for the year and made domestic box-office history, with the story of four young men whose lives are affected by the criminal underworld.

While the blockbusters of the new millennium draw in audiences across gender lines, they do not specifically acknowledge the female spec-tator. In these films, there has been a mass mobilization of masculinized nationalism; the disturbing result is a demonization and dehumanization of women in the Korean blockbuster, or in another extreme, a removal from the cinematic public sphere (S. Kim 2002).[4]

Consumer Nationalism and Spectacular Masculinity

Recent English-language scholarship on Korean cinema supports our asser-tions about the popular cinematic representations of masculinity in con-temporary films, displays of nationalism, and national identity formation. In his book on Korean cinema and masculinity, Kim Kyung Hyun (2004) makes the crucial point that tangled cultural discourses have profoundly impacted gendered screen images—from negotiations of Confucianism, democratization, industrialization, militarism, and postcolonialism—and includes a compelling reading of Han Suk-kyu's role in *Green Fish*. He sug-gests that Han's performance, a powerfully measured characterization in this gangster film/family melodrama, proved his mettle in leading roles and opened up "serious parts in thrillers and blockbuster actions films like *Shiri* and *Tell Me Something*" (K. Kim 2004: 50). (However, Kim does not mention Han's film *Christmas in August*.)

The coauthors of *Korean Film: History, Resistance, and Democratic Imagination* distinguish between the realism of 1980s films and the "escapist films" of today (Min, Joo, & Kwak 2003: 183). This movement from a retro-realism toward a new spectacularity is echoed in our Han Suk-kyu case study. The rise of Korean blockbuster culture, we assert, corresponds with the rise of Korean film audiences who display status-minded gender politics of consumption and "consumer nationalism"— the latter referring to the South Korean government's attempt to regulate (feminine-coded) excessive consumption of imported consumer goods; frugality and "buying Korean" therefore became configured as desirable traits and actions (Nelson 2000). The post–economic crisis creation of the domestic blockbuster is predicated on a sense of supporting Korean movie making, based on increasingly globalized—and masculinized—perceptions of production and entertainment value. However, in this case, the ideal consumer/audience member for current contemporary Korean cinema has been constructed as a "vital" young man, with a thirst for excess. The moment of the idealized female spectator recognized in Han's romances such as *The Contact* and *Christmas in August* seems to have passed. While melodrama remains deeply integral to virtually every Korean popular film, the highest-grossing Korean films overall nationwide for 2003 (the year *Double Agent* was released) and the first half of 2004 were lavish male-centered war films. While female characters do appear, they are very minor figures; the central focus is on codes of brotherhood and the masculinized mise en scène.

In contrast to the Korean period films of the past focusing on political conflicts and social problems, the current historical movies emphasize action and visual style. Further, they serve as vehicles for new expressions of nationalism, and the spectacularity that marks blockbuster-era Korean cinema. This flexible genre encompasses films like the Korean/Chinese coproduction *Musa: The Warrior* (2001, dir. Kim Sung-su, at the time the most expensive Korean film ever made), a historical action drama dealing with war and reunification during premodern times with beefy star Jung Woo-sung as a fourteenth-century superhero. Other films attend to more recent Korean history such as the Korean War and the subsequent Cold War era stained by ideological conflict within the divided nation, between

South Korea and North Korea. Released in December 2003, *Silmido* quickly broke domestic box-office records with a story based on the sensitive historical fact that from 1968 to 1971 in South Korea, male criminals were secretly trained on an island for a special mission to infiltrate North Korea and kill Kim Il-Sung. However, when the relationship between South and North Korea changed from acute conflict to a mood of reconciliation, the South Korean government decided to kill the trained hitmen. After *Silmido*'s smash success, the Korean War drama *Taegukgi* set a new record for both production cost and box-office receipts. In the film, Korean heartthrobs Jang Dong-Gon and Won Bin play two biological brothers, both forced to become soldiers, whose fate and future is shattered by the Korean War. Each of these relatively young actors (born in 1972 and 1977, respectively) have done commercial endorsements for myriad trendy products and have had roles in hugely popular television drama serials. However, they also are exemplars of *Hanryu*, or Korean wave stars, who have found huge youth audiences throughout East and Southeast Asia for their TV and film work. They represent a key component of the cultural economy of contemporary Korean cinema—its perceived viability not only through the domestic audience/fan base, but also through the increasing outflow of films and star popularity beyond the borders of the nation.

The phenomenon of the popular war film is a contemporary one in South Korea, compatible with concurrent quests for festivalized expression of national identity, especially among the youth (evident in public expressions of nationalism such as street celebrations after World Cup victory and anti-American demonstrations). Historical events in these films are shown primarily through stylized hyperreal war images achieved through special digital effects. However, films such as *Silmido* and *Taegukgi* also rely strongly on sentimentality and discourses of family and loyalty to convey a sense of tragedy, while *Double Agent* largely contained its drama within the character played by Han Suk-kyu. While the recent South Korean political actioners have orchestrated pyrotechnic gunpowder and flag-waving displays out of the ashes of history, Han's long-anticipated comeback, *Double Agent,* although based on a true story, failed to spark with his monochromatic performance and representation of generic elements, as well as gender politics. *Double Agent* serves as a vehicle for Han's subtle, psychologically motivated shape shifting, as his character assumes different identities but reveals the same solid core; the movie neglects to deliver some crucial ingredients of the blockbuster formula and the "new" Korean male star. Han's overextended absence from the movies served as a metaphorical defection from mass audiences, betrayed by his entrepreneurial and extradiegetic marketing of his star brand in a manner that registered an excessive investment in his own image. The pre-release hype around *Double Agent* was countered by ultimate consumer disappointment in the star's seeming inability to reinvent and recharge himself. Upon his screen return, Han's apparently devalued star currency and fan attraction is thus connected to a rigid actorly display of masculinity (not to mention hubris) that is—by current Korean standards—devoid of satisfactory spectacle.

But on an optimistic note, Han's actorly capital and potential fan/audience appeal are not yet completely depleted. His subsequent films of the new millennium, *Scarlet Letter* (2004, dir. Byun Hyuk), *The President's Last Bang* (2005, dir. Im Sang-soo), *Mr. Housewife* (2005, dir. Yun Seon-dong), and *Umlanseosaeng* (2006, dir. Kim Dae-woo) demonstrate some diversified strategies for maintaining screen longevity that does not rest exclusively upon blockbuster box-office receipts: willingness to embody unsympathetic characters, supporting roles and shared leads, and playfully deconstructive gender representations. Such resourcefulness may be ultimately rewarded by fans who are willing to appreciate the generative possibilities of textual versatility.

NOTES

1. All original translations from Korean-language sources in this essay are by Hunju Lee.

2. This box-office ranking data for 2003 is provided by the Korean Film Commission, http://www.kofic.or.kr.

3. The term "spectacular nationalism" as conceptualized by Hunju Lee refers to blockbuster films that deal with historical events through spectacular images.

4. For a study of the evolution of Korean masculinity in relation to militarism and disengaged from feminized domesticity, see Moon (2001).

Part V

Shifting Contexts, Changing Fan Cultures
From Concert Halls to Console Games

17

Loving Music

Listeners, Entertainments, and the Origins of Music Fandom in Nineteenth-Century America

Daniel Cavicchi

After having attended the opera four nights in a row in 1884, 24-year-old Lucy Lowell chastised herself by writing in her diary, "I suppose it can't be good for a person to go to things that excite her so that she can't fix her mind on anything for days afterwards" (Lowell 1884: April 19).[1] Lowell was the daughter of Judge John Lowell and a member of one of the first families of Boston. While many young women of her social standing spent their time attracting appropriate male suitors by acquiring rudimentary skills in singing and piano playing or self-consciously showing themselves off in the boxes of the city's growing number of concert halls and theaters, Lucy eschewed such social intrigue and instead became truly obsessed with onstage sound and spectacle. She attended performances by almost every touring opera and symphonic star that passed through Boston, every rehearsal and concert of the new Boston Symphony Orchestra, and many local festivals, band concerts, and musical theater productions. In the seven volumes of her diary, which she wrote between 1880 and 1888, she wrote page after page of description about her experiences of hearing music. She only mechanically mentioned attending singing lessons on Mondays and Thursdays; she sometimes referred to expectations about her own socially mandated performances with disdain. "Had a dinner party for Miss Tweedy. Mabel + Hattie were the other girls, John Howard Messers, G. D. Chapin, L. Pierce + R. Loug, gentlemen," she wrote in 1880. "I had to sing in eve'g. Bah!" (Lowell 1880: January 28).

Lowell was not alone; since the mid–nineteenth century, increasing numbers of young people in America's rapidly growing cities had formed a unique and sustained attachment to the world of public concerts. People had listened to music before the 1850s, of course; indeed, concert going was an activity that a member of the elite in the United States had had the leisure to indulge at least since the American Revolution. But before mid-century, attending a concert more often than not meant attending a special event that was as much social as musical, an opportunity for people in a community to come together in a ritual space. During the 1850s, increasing numbers of national tours by professional virtuosos, supported by new systems of concert management, enabled people to develop new ways of acting musically that were centered less on amateur performance among friends in the privacy of one's home than on regularly witnessing professional performers in public halls. Young "music lovers," like Lowell, constituted a group that, for the first time in American history, was able to shape its musical experiences entirely around commercial entertainments like concerts, theater, and public exhibitions.

In this chapter, I will outline the ways in which the practices of music lovers not only transformed America's musical life, setting the ground for a late-nineteenth-century music business based on listening technologies like the phonograph, but also provided models for cultural consumption that would be adopted and extended in twentieth-century mass culture, particularly by those we today call "fans." For several years, I have studied the diaries, scrapbooks, and letters of people living in the nineteenth-century urban United States in order to learn more about how they understood music. Scattered widely in state and private archives, many of the materials have not been studied as evidence of musical life. Together, however, they offer powerful evidence that, while fandom is often characterized in media studies as a product of mass consumer culture in the twentieth century, the basic practices associated with fandom—idealized connection with a star, strong feelings of memory and nostalgia, use of collecting to develop a sense of self, for example—precede the development of electronic "mass communication" technologies. Music loving suggests that fandom's origins may have less to do with diffuse and private consumption through modern electronic media than with shared modes of participation in older systems of commodified leisure.

Reframing Musical Experience

Cities in the United States had slightly different trajectories for developing new entertainment markets and commodifying musical experience, based on the idiosyncrasies of geographical location, demographics, and religious influences. Boston, for instance, first created markets around making music, including sheet music publishing and instruments sales, thanks to a Puritan prohibition on theater that was not repealed until 1797 and whose effects lingered long after. Overall, however, markets focused on hearing music developed in most eastern cities by the 1850s. Pleasure gardens, theaters and concert halls, taverns, museum stages, and minstrel shows—all increased in number between 1840 and 1870 in cities like New York, Philadelphia, Boston, Charleston, and New Orleans. Concert programs, once one-sided announcements of song titles, became, after the Civil War, multipage, stapled documents with advertisements for soap, shoes, corsets, and pianos, alongside the usual list of songs to be performed. Performers themselves became commodities for sale, advertised in circulars and managed by entrepreneurs who carefully manipulated artists' repertoires, schedules, and appearances (Gottschalk 1881: 122).

Along with musical entertainment came a shift in understanding about what music was. Before 1800, music had primarily existed either as a private amateur pastime, made among friends and family, or as an elaborate public ritual, either in street parades or at church services. One could love it, but its embeddedness in social functions made more likely that one loved that which the music enabled. But commodification encouraged an attachment to music's own singular effects. Concerts and public performances, especially, segmented musical experience into distinct phases of production (composition), distribution (performance), and consumption (listening). Understanding musical experience as a thing that one could anonymously purchase and consume must have been an extraordinary idea for people used to having to painstakingly make sounds, through singing or playing, in order to have "music" in the first place. The purchase of instruments and music, the lessons, the rehearsals, the mistakes, the labor—all that was separated out, given to others, and made invisible, so that one could, if he or she so chose, simply engage in the act of hearing, of audiencing. Not only could people indulge in regular, timed, and relatively reliable music performances but also, by "just listening" to those performances, they were able to encounter music anew.

One part of the appeal of the seemingly endless stream of virtuosos at midcentury, for example, was the extent to which each performer surpassed expectations about what was possible in musical performance. As a critic wrote about Edward Seguin's first appearance in the opera "Andie; or, The Love Test," at Boston's Tremont Theater in 1838, "The moment Seguin opened his mouth, one universal gape of astonishment infected all, such was the wonder produced by his magnificent organ" (quoted in Clapp 1968: 376). William Cullen Bryant noted that concerts could even surprise the most jaded of audience members, as happened during a concert by pianist Leopold De Meyer in 1846:

> A veteran teacher of music in Buffalo, famous for being hard to be pleased by any public musical entertainment, found himself unable to sit still during the first piece played by DeMeyer, but rose, in the fullness of his delight, and continued standing. When the music ceased, he ran to him and shook both of his hands, again and again, with most uncomfortable energy. At the end of the next performance he sprang again on the platform and hugged the artist so rapturously that the room rang with laughter. (Bryant & Voss 1975: 438)

An important consequence of such encounters, for listeners, was a new and heightened awareness of the personal qualities of performers. In a time when romantic ideas of a core individual self were taking hold and, in romantic relationships, people were striving to achieve an intense "sharing of selfhood" (McMahon 1998: 66), the act of loving music often idealized identification with performers, similar to the communion nineteenth-century romance readers often felt with characters and with authors. Especially after repeated encounters with the same performer, music lovers often began to feel a strong and uniquely charged connection to that performer's unchanging, "inner" self. In fact, the word "star" signified this attitude. First used as theater slang in the 1820s (*Oxford English Dictionary* 2005) and often applied after 1850 to designate the new "system" of theater production that focused on traveling virtuosos rather than local stock troupes, a star was not just an actor or a singer but a unique person whose presence transcended any one role, burning brightly through the artificial masks of the stage.

Many stars of the nineteenth century—Ole Bull, Anna Thillon, Anna Seguin, Marta Alboni—inspired music lovers to understand their listening experiences as part of a continuing and reciprocal relationship with a specific performer. However, the first music star to be widely associated with such feelings of personal connection was Jenny Lind, the Swedish opera singer who contracted with impresario P. T. Barnum in 1850 to tour the United States. Lind had been an opera star in Europe in the late 1840s, famous for her roles, but in her concert tour she was promoted by Barnum as "simply Jenny." In fact, Barnum shrewdly hyped her simplicity, innocence, and humility as a contrast to both the alleged immorality of the theater and her own otherworldly singing talent. As historian John Dizikes put it, "People searched her appearance and especially her face for clues to that inner person [. . .] she would begin hesitantly, nervously, and then: her talent would come to the rescue, her voice, almost as though it existed independently of the body which contained it, would gush out in crystalline splendor and convert a precarious moment into an ecstatic one" (1993: 133).

In diaries and letters, Lind's audience members emphasize Lind's personal character. William Hoffman, a clerk who was in the crowd awaiting Lind's arrival in New York in 1850 and who showed up several times with the crowds outside Castle Garden, hoping to get inside but stymied by the high ticket prices, nevertheless repeatedly copied newspaper reports about her personal qualities in his diary, concluding that "her great powers of benevolence speak for her the most enviable qualities of soul that any being ever could possess" (1850: September 21). Henry Southworth, a twenty-year-old New York City store clerk who, like Hoffman, participated in the welcoming crowds and sought to get a glimpse of her at her hotel, described his experience of hearing her sing in terms of her character: "I cannot express my delight and wonder in words, she is indeed a wonderful woman, she sings with perfect ear and is at home, in everything she does" (1850: September 13). Lind even seemed to heighten auditors' awareness of their own selves. Caroline B. White, in response to hearing Jenny Lind in Boston, wrote, "I have heard her! The wonderful Jenny! And though language itself has been exhausted in her praise—it seems to me too much cannot be said, *such* a volume of *such sounds*—singing, clear melodious— can any one listen to them and not feel one's aspirations glow warmer, loftier, holier, than ever before?" (1851: November 22).

Aside from being "star-struck," music lovers were also attracted by the sheer novelty and power of auditory experience. Part of the excitement of attending concert halls was experiencing music with a mass of people; diarists often commented on the fullness (or emptiness) of the house at a performance and of the roar of the crowd at the finish of pieces or in demand of an encore. Likewise, music lovers were enamored of hearing someone confidently project his or her voice or the sound of his or her instrument into a large auditorium, a unique and memorable acoustic situation. Even business directories for cities like Boston and New York touted the magnificence of their halls for audiences. For example, one Boston directory for 1860–1861 glowingly described the city's Music Hall, built just six years earlier, in terms of its structural characteristics, including its ceiling "45 feet above the upper balcony," the seventeen unique, semicircular windows "that light the hall by day," the hall's capacity of one thousand five hundred people on the floor, and the fact that "the whole has been constructed with special reference to the science of acoustics—a consideration of the utmost importance in a building intended as a music hall" (*Sketches and Business Directory of Boston* 1861: 109).

Concertgoers themselves were careful to note in their diaries the qualities of the halls they had attended, from Lucy Buckminster Emerson Lowell (1845: October 29) noting the "intense perfume" of the straw-filled seats in Boston's new Howard Athenaeum to William Hoffman (1850: November 19), who, after finally attending a Jenny Lind concert, wrote in his diary mostly about the "size and finish" of New York's Tripler Hall. Indeed, music lovers learned the acoustic properties of various halls so as to position themselves to best hear the music coming from the stage. Joseph Sill was thrilled when he was able to obtain a box for a John Braham performance where, as he commented, "we were so close to him that his softest tones were heard" (1840: December 2). In contrast, Lucy Lowell was none too pleased when she was forced to sit in the balcony of Boston's Apollo Theater where "the orchestra + chorus sounded all blurred" (Lowell 1884: April 30). Henry Van Dyke, writing in 1909, described the ways in which an imagined music lover thought of his seat as a secret treasure, chosen explicitly for its acoustic properties:

> The Lover of Music had come to his favorite seat. It was in the front row of the balcony, just where the curve reaches its outermost point, and, like a rounded headland, meets the unbroken flow of the long-rolling, invisible waves of rhythmical sound. The value of that chosen place did not seem to be known to the world, else there would have been a higher price demanded for the privilege of occupying it. (1909: 5–6)

Again and again, listeners talked about hearing a performance as an astonishingly physical experience. Music lovers' profound emotional attachment to stars in part came from attending fully to the physical presence of the virtuosos who performed onstage—to the power and quality of their voices projected from the stage to the dexterity of their bodies as they manipulated instruments. In response to opera, especially, music lovers often expressed overwhelming visceral ecstasy, imagining music "filling their souls" to the point of losing composure, something that was experienced as excitingly dangerous and quite cathartic within the behavioral strictures of middle-class Victorian culture (Rabinowitz 1993). Walt Whitman, in *Leaves of Grass,* drawing on his own fascination with New York opera in the 1840s, described music listening as a kind of sexual communion: "A tenor large and fresh as the creation fills me / The orbic flex of his mouth is pouring and filling me full." Music "convulses" him, "whirls" him, "throbs" him, "sails" him, and "wrenches unnamable ardors" from him. He is "licked," "exposed," "cut," and "squeezed" by waves of orchestral sound (1982: 54–55).

Reorganizing Music and Daily Life

Having such an intense attachment to concert performances was sometimes difficult for music lovers, since the desire for musical sound could only be satisfied periodically. Even then, concerts were finite events, and the memories of musical experiences often seemed to recede and disappear, especially after only one hearing. How could one keep heard music—and the feelings created by it—alive over time?

The longing for music was satisfied, in part, by music lovers seeking out as many musical performances as possible. The number of musical experiences one could have in any given week depended on many factors, including the number of theaters and halls in the vicinity, the length of the concert season (typically October to May), and, of course, the availability of cash needed to purchase tickets or subscriptions. But many music lovers, even without money, found ways to experience music. Walt Whitman, when not at the opera, lingered outside churches and halls, listening to the music from the street. Others, like clerk Nathaniel Beekley (1849), sought out music four or more nights a week during Philadelphia's concert season and, in addition, attended both Catholic and Protestant church services on Sundays in order to hear music.

Repeated hearings of the same piece could help to fix the music in one's mind. In the 1850s, it was customary for touring performers to complete a "run" of shows in the places they visited as long as audiences kept coming, so as to accommodate all who wished to see them and to increase profits. And it was common in the antebellum era for audiences to attend multiple (and often all) performances in the same run, especially if the music was complex enough to merit such attention (Preston 1993: 59–61). George Templeton Strong, for example, regularly attended every performance of pieces that he liked, commenting that "I never can satisfy myself about music till I have heard it more than once and have ruminated on it, marked, learned, and inwardly digested it" (Lawrence 1988: 318). Music lovers engaged in these practices enthusiastically and often lamented in their diaries that they could not hear a piece *more* often than a run of performances allowed. As Lucy Lowell pined about Wagner's "Ring Trilogy," "O dear how I should like to hear it all over again + again + go to Beyreuth! I wish I could spend next winter in Vienna + go every night anything of Wagner's is given" (Lowell 1884: April 16).

Another way to keep the music alive between performances was to literally reproduce the music through amateur performance. While concert going cultivated behaviors and values that were different than those held by amateur performers, the two expressions of musicality tended to reinforce one another: concertgoers often turned to the piano to reproduce the pieces they had heard and amateur performers found themselves drawn, as audience members, to the virtuosity of the professional stage. This was a phenomenon that instrument and sheet music entrepreneurs knew well. Ads for sheet music began appearing in concert programs as early as the 1850s, touting "full translations" of pieces heard that night in concert. In 1849, the ever-popular Germania Society even distributed the sheet music to one of their original pieces, arranged for piano, to the women in their audiences, with the implication that they would use the music to remember the performance. It was appropriately called "Ladies Souvenir Polka" (Newman 2002: 163).

When not reliving musical experiences in some way, many music lovers worked to extend their audience experiences beyond the concert hall. Those caught up in "Lindmania," for example, vied to capture glimpses of Lind not simply in performance but also outside of performance, arriving in a steamship at the wharf, standing on the balcony of her hotel room, traveling through the streets in her carriage. If they had the resources, music lovers would also travel to sites associated with various performers and composers. The "grand tour" of Europe, a requisite coming-of-age event for wealthy Americans in the 1800s, often turned into a much-saved-for pilgrimage for music lovers. Alice Drake, a young piano student from Colorado, made a voyage to Weimar, Germany, in the 1890s and promptly sought out the house of the recently deceased Franz Liszt, quizzing the house's caretaker, and playing on Liszt's pianos, a thrill she recounted by writing in her diary, "I never tho't I would ever do that!!" (1897: October 26).

In addition to such pilgrimages, music lovers used their personal diaries and journals to extend their musical experiences. Music lovers had, fairly early on, created a new descriptive vocabulary to articulate the feelings they had while concert going. Older generations of American audiences had typically experienced music with a mild pleasure. "It was very satisfactory" or "we had a pleasant time" were common phrases for describing concert experiences. In fact, before 1850, people tended to describe their musical experiences with the phrase "we had some music," blandly lumping any sort of musical activity into a descriptive category not worthy of further comment, like the weather. But concertgoers after the 1850s often described their musical experiences with far more personal specificity.

Diaries in the nineteenth century were often used as memory devices, helping writers to remember who they had met at parties or from whom they had received gifts, for instance, so that they might reciprocate in the future. In terms of music, however, the function was not so much social as psychological, satisfying a longing for more. Some music lovers attempted to fix on paper every moment, every feeling, during a concert to the extent that their diaries were not so much mnemonic tools as stand-ins, indices, for the performances themselves. Thus Lowell could write in her diary after the last concert of the Boston Symphony in 1886, "I feel so desolate at thinking that this is the last, that I shall dwell on each detail, to lengthen out the enjoyment" (1886: May 29).

In all, such recording encouraged self-conscious knowledge and comparison of how it felt to hear and see various performances and performers over time. One could, in effect, "collect" and arrange concerts just as one would collect and arrange phonograph records. Sheet music binders, personal collections of sheet music arranged and bound in leather, were a corollary to this sort of activity; binders—often with the collector's name embossed on the front cover and handwritten marginalia that evaluate or describe the feelings evoked by the pieces—clearly served as a summary of an individual's taste and experience in music. With the growth of the music press at midcentury, including regular reviews and the use of lithography and photography for circulating images of musical stars, scrapbooks supplanted diaries and sheet music binders as music lovers' most useful tool, able to contain descriptive writing, clippings of reviews, and images.

Redefining Normal Participation

What were the consequences of this activity? Music lovers were well aware that their engagement with music was different from that of other audience members. Simply by becoming regular attendees of musical performances of specific forms, or by particular groups, or in particular concert halls and churches, music lovers began to distinguish themselves from others in the audience through their uniquely focused and comparative engagement with the music. Indeed, criticism of early music loving emphasizes the strangeness and potential pathology involved in a singular focus on a performer or performance. William Clapp, for instance, described the mania created by ballerina Fanny Elssler's visit to Boston in 1840 as a disease that trumped every other event in the city:

> It was "Elssler" on every side. She was dreamed of, talked of, and idolized; and some wag having circulated a report that "Fanny" would take an airing in her barouche, quite a gathering took place on Tremont Street. Boston was not alone in this ovation, for the ladies from Boston to Philadelphia, all wore Elssler cuffs, made of velvet with bright buttons. In every store window articles were displayed flavoring of the mania. Elssler boot-jacks, Elssler bread, etc. etc., were to be seen, showing how violent was the attack of *Fannyelsslermaniaphobia*. (1968: 368–89)

A Boston satirist calling himself "Asmodeus" wrote a pamphlet that thoroughly lambasted the citizens of Boston for their extraordinary enthusiasm about Lind's 1850 concerts:

> For two long weeks, did I hear nought in my rambles, by night or day, in barber shops and work shops, in beer shops and stables, in hotels and private domicils, from Beacon Street to the Black Sea, all the cry was, Jenny Lind and Barnum, Barnum and Jenny Lind! Soon I met my ancient and respected friend Pearce, so full of madness and music that he rushed through the streets with the fearful velocity of an escaped locomotive.

Hold worthy friend, quoth I, whither so fast?
He gazed wildly at me for a moment, then shouted as he run—Jenny
Lind and Barnum! Barnum and Jenny Lind! (Asmodeus 1850: 12)

Clapp's use of the fake medical term "Fannyelsslermaniaphobia" was
not unfounded; the activities of music lovers had earlier been recognized
by the medical establishment as a pathology called "musicomania."
Though it had been known for centuries that music could produce powerful psychological and physical effects, a phenomenon that was used for
treatment by medieval physicians (Gouk 2004), in the nineteenth century
the effects of music acquired potentially negative connotations. The association of music with "mania" first appeared in the United States in 1833 in
the *New Dictionary of Medical Science and Literature,* which described the
condition as "a variety of monomania in which the passion for music is
carried to such an extent as to derange the intellectual faculties" (Dunglison 1833: 64). Musicomania fell out of use by 1900, and it is not clear that
anyone was actually treated for the disease, but during the nineteenth century, the term found its way into everyday discourse as an alternative
name for music loving, and references to the condition were sprinkled
throughout novels and essays between 1850 and 1870. It was even
employed by music lovers themselves to jokingly refer to their own concert hopping.

If joking was one response to music loving, a more ominous response
was an increasing association of the excessive behaviors of music loving
with the divisive caricatures of class politics at midcentury. Depictions of
music lovers in the press often featured disorder, with an emphasis on
crowd violence, lack of control, and metaphors of savagery or animalism,
characterizations that fit with growing middle-class disdain for the social
chaos created by immigration and urbanization. As early as 1843, William
Cullen Bryant described an audience in such terms, saying, "The concert
room was crowded with people clinging to each other like bees when they
swarm, and the whole affair seemed an outbreak of popular enthusiasm"
(Bryant & Voss 1975: 438). Boston Brahmin Caroline Healey Dall described
her experience of a Jenny Lind concert as if she had just visited the
cramped quarters of an inner-city tenement:

No one could conceive a more horrible crowd. Dark windows looked into
the offices, and in no way could fresh air be obtained[. . . .] When I heard
the cry for water, air, open the windows &c.—who come as from desperate

dying men—in choked voices—I felt what must come. I made several calm attempts to get out, but there was no possible means of egress, and a disappointed crowd were storming without[. . . .] We saw bonnets torn off—women trampled on, men falling in tiers of five or six. I have seen crowds before, but I never imagined what a suffocating crowd would be. (1850: October 30)

In response—and borrowing from ascendant ideologies of romanticism, as well as "refinement"—idealist middle-class reformers introduced a new way to "love" music in the 1860s. Instead of passionate attachment to a performance, they proposed what might be called a "classical" appreciation: ritualized, reverent, intellectual attention to the unfolding of a composition or work. If antebellum music loving proposed focusing audience attention on performance as a way to challenge the informal socializing of theater culture, this new form of engagement proposed to refine music loving even further by removing the spontaneity and showmanship of live performance that might lead to obsession or spontaneous emotional display. Those promoting this reform found it necessary in a culture that seemingly had been taken over by the excessive spectacles of mass commercialism. True appreciation of art was not about purchasing tickets to experience virtuosic curiosities but rather about encountering the timeless beauty of a composer's work.

Social historians have noted that such a "disciplining of spectatorship," as John Kasson put it, is emblematic of postbellum ideologies of genteel refinement and taste and of the emergence of powerful class divisions in the United States after 1850 (Butsch 2000; Kasson 1990; Levine 1988; McConachie 1992). That this reorientation was based on new class associations is apparent in the changing nature of audience criticism. If the initial criticism of music loving was simply about being *too invested* in music, by the close of the century, accounts of audiences were more often about being *too invested in the wrong ways and for the wrong reasons.* William Althorp, a classical music reformer and critic, in a long essay in the *Atlantic Monthly* in 1879, specifically compared the approaches of "refined" musicians and "ordinary" music lovers:

A musician, after listening to a great work, does not, as a rule, care to have it immediately repeated[. . . .] But when the ordinary music-lover hears a piece of music that particularly pleases him, he generally wishes to hear it over again; he will listen to it day in and day out, until he gets thoroughly

sick of it, and never wishes to hear it more. He sucks and sucks at his musical orange until there is nothing left but the dry peel, and then throws it
away. (1879: 150)

Antebellum criticisms of Elssler or Lind "mania" identified temporarily
excessive musical behavior as wildly inexplicable and in a way that left
"normal" musical behavior unstated; it was simply understood how one
should behave. But in the late 1870s, Althorp was careful to associate excessive musical behavior with lack of discipline and education and to provide
his readers with an alternative position, all through metaphorical language
that provide cues of social class. He associated the musician with connois-
seurship, deference, and judgment, and the music lover with sensualism,
immediate gratification, and boorishness. Such distinctions would shape
discourses of musical audiences for the next century.

Music Lovers as Fans

"Fan" is a term that only came into widespread use in the early twentieth
century, when mass consumerism, based on new systems of marketing
and communications, was transforming the industrial West. Not only did
media technology create a temporal and spatial separation between performers and audiences in the market; it also gave audiences the ability to
create affective engagement with performers or products by enabling people to experience, repeat, and study such "texts" in the intimacy of their
home, and incorporate them into the fabric of their daily life. That fan
studies has become a growing field in media studies is not surprising; the
rise of fandom as a self-aware consumer movement (exemplified by fan
"clubs" in the 1920s and 30s) seems to coincide with the hegemony of
media entertainment, especially film and music.

However, given the murky etymology and meaning of the term "fan"
(Cavicchi 1998: 38–39; Hills 2002: ix-xv), it may be more useful, in thinking
about the history of fandom, to start not with the emergence of the
descriptive term "fan" but rather with the existing patterns of behavior
that the historically contingent term was meant to describe. As I have
argued elsewhere (Cavicchi 1998: 4–6; 2004), there is evidence of fan-like
practices among people participating in the commodification of urban
leisure in the industrial West before 1900, including the readers of mass-
produced books, opera lovers, urban theater goers, and the members of

fraternal baseball clubs. Music culture, in particular, is useful for beginning to open up the history of fandom because it was at the forefront of both twentieth-century media technology (in the form of both recording and broadcasting) and nineteenth-century urban entertainment (in the form of commodified performance and mass-published texts) and thus provides linkages between what typically have been perceived as different eras of audience behavior.

Just as fans of the twentieth century were faced with new relationships—with performers, with musical texts, and with each other—created by the advent of recording and broadcasting, music lovers of the nineteenth century wrestled with the shift of such relationships in the development of commercialized music culture. In urban America during the 1840s and 1850s, musical experience became no longer only something shared by a congregation or community in the local rituals of a church service, dance ball, or military muster; it had become also a tangible product, made by those who were musically gifted, and easily exhibited and purchased by anyone with cash. The commodification of music in concerts particularly highlighted the process of exchange between performer and audience and the ways in which hearing could become a form of consumption.

Like mass communication technologies, nineteenth-century commercial concerts brought extraordinary access to music for many Americans. However, structurally, such access in both eras was based on an audience anonymity and ephemerality that limited music's ability to signify deeply shared values and experiences. Fans and music lovers represent those who have refused to accept the anonymity and limited involvement of audiences necessitated by the large-scale commercialization of musical experience; they both instead seek to creatively imbue their participation in musical life with a lasting personal connection and depth of feeling. The ways in which modern fans create significant affective involvement in popular culture—including close listening, Internet discussion, pilgrimages, and collecting, among other activities—have numerous parallels in the culture of nineteenth-century music lovers. When the star system unmoored performers from localities and exaggerated their professional skills in the 1840s, music lovers sought to understand stars as authentic people with whom they had an intimate bond. While most people returned to their daily lives after concerts ended, music lovers actively extended their audience role beyond the purchased frame of performance by seeking out music in churches and homes, by attempting to see stars in the street, by making pilgrimages to significant sites, by performing their favorite pieces on home instruments, by collecting sheet music, and by meticulously recording descriptions of their listening experiences.

Not only are individual behaviors parallel, but the functions of those behaviors in their respective contexts are also similar. Scholars have argued that modern fandom is always in some ways an "improper identity" (Hills 2002: xii), often interpreted as a "pathology" (Jensen 1992). According to the frameworks of exchange in the new market economy, music-loving behaviors were likewise abnormal; music lovers did not abide by the equation of a ticket for a performance but sought rather to go beyond and around it, much like the alternative "shunpikes" that had turned up in the 1830s, snaking illegally around toll gates on many states' newly built roadways. Not surprisingly, critiques of music loving were based on lovers' thwarting of the norms of the market: music lovers' rejections of the frameworks of capitalism meant that they had to be either sick, suffering from a mania, or unaware of correct social behavior—that is, without "taste."

I don't wish to discount the significant transformations wrought by the mass media in the twentieth century. But as Jonathan Sterne (2003) has shown, even revolutionary inventions like the phonograph only became possible in the first place thanks to previous shifts in the ideological frameworks of science, social class, and the self. In the same way, twentieth-century music fandom became possible with previous changes in the norms and practices of participants in the world of commodified music. Music lovers, as witnesses to the beginnings of the commercialization of popular culture in the nineteenth century, were among the first to assume the role of the audience-consumer and to create the strategies many use today for understanding the world of stars, merchandizing, and spectacle.

Note

1. Use of unpublished archival materials in this essay courtesy of the American Antiquarian Society, the Historical Society of Pennsylvania, the Massachusetts Historical Society, the New York Historical Society, and the Library of the School of Music, Yale University.

18

Girls Allowed?
The Marginalization of Female Sport Fans

Victoria K. Gosling

Sport is historically a male cultural practice. It is (and it seems always has been) predominantly played and watched by men. However, in recent years there has been a significant increase in the number of female participants in, and fans of, sport. With women's sport participation on the increase, coverage of sport in the mass media is rising, and with some changes in relation to gender roles and expectations, it is becoming more common to find women with an interest in, or even a passion for, sport. However, women continue to be marginalized both in fan communities and in academic research and literature on sport fans. What little has been written on female sport fans has been produced mostly in relation to changes in the nature of sport audiences, and more specifically, the rise in number of female fans has often been viewed as evidence of the embourgeoisification of certain sports (such as soccer in the UK) and the marketing of these to more middle-class, family-based audiences. In an earlier paper Crawford and Gosling (2004) suggest that there exists little consideration of women's everyday experiences of being a sport fan, limiting our understanding of what being a sport fan means to many women. Building on this earlier paper, this chapter offers a critical consideration of the existing literature on female sport fan culture, and in doing so, offers a basis for future research into the everyday experiences and identities of female sport fans. This chapter, drawing on existing literature and our work on British ice hockey fans, therefore considers the case of female fans of sport and their continued marginalization from sport and supporter communities.

The Position of Women as Sport Fans

As Giulianotti (2005: 80) writes, "gender stratification within sport began early." As far back as the ancient Greek Olympic games, women were barred from participating in, or attending, sporting events (Guttmann 1986). Up to the late nineteenth century, "sport" primarily (if not exclusively) consisted of masculine pastimes such as blood and combative sports (Gorn & Goldstein 1993). With the codification of many sports in the late nineteenth century, Victorian masculine ideologies such as the ideal of the muscular Christian gentleman became formally set within modern organized sports (Mangan 1986 cited in Giulianotti 2005). However, there is a long (though often marginal) history of women as sport fans. Even in ancient Greco-Roman times, there were frequently certain sporting events that allowed women to participate in the proceedings and attend as spectators—though these were certainly less common than the events of their male counterparts.

In more modern times, there are also numerous examples of women standing alongside their male contemporaries watching and avidly following sport. For example, Haywood (1996) suggests that female fans have always attended professional soccer (association football) matches in the UK, though not always in large numbers. In particular, between the two world wars the number of female spectators attending soccer in the UK grew. With more women taking an active role in the First World War, gender roles began to change and afterwards the increasing respectability of football, with improved grounds and behavioral standards, allowed more women to become involved as fans (Haywood 1996). Furthermore, with the more liberal social climate of the 1960s, the attendance of women at football matches increased. England's World Cup win in 1966 allowed the game's image to be reconstructed, and more female fans were actively targeted, with television coverage offering women instruction on football rules such as the offside rule. Such changes in attitudes and increased television coverage of football encouraged more women to follow the sport as fans and take it up as players, leading to the establishment of the Women's Football Association in England in 1969 (Woodhouse & Williams 1991).

Being a sport fan can be very important for many women, just as it is for many men. Sport (for both men and women) can play an important role in defining individual identities: who we are, where we come from, and which social groups we belong to. Furthermore, Crawford and

Gosling's (2004) consideration of British ice hockey audiences highlights the important networking opportunities that this can provide for women. Ice hockey, as with other sports, can offer women an opportunity to "hang out" and be with other women (and men) in a public place, and for some women this provides an opportunity to develop new friendship networks and meet other female fans, as exemplified in comments made by "Leslie" (female, aged seventeen):

> [W]e sit in one block, so we know most of the block and like, you see people around like, it's good[. . . .] And my friends go and we got to meet other people, and it just, it's like a big group of us, we didn't know each other before. We just know each other as the Storm gang . . . we, where we sit we call it the "barmy army," [block] 109's barmy army. (cited in Crawford & Gosling 2004: 484)

Dell (1998: 105) also suggests that sport fandom can be empowering for women, helping them to challenge dominant gender roles: "Women successfully insisted on watching televised wrestling two or three times a week and then openly admired the parade of male bodies that filled the screen, transgressing the roles set out for them as wives and mothers."

However, women remain restricted from attending most mass spectator sports due to cultural expectations and gender discrimination. Women continue to be more restricted in their leisure choices and opportunities than men (Deem 1982, 1986; Shaw 1994; Wearing 1998). This is due to numerous social factors, such as women's limited presence in many "public" places, economic constraints, limited leisure time, and social expectations of women's location and roles within society, such as domestic and caring responsibilities. As Davies (1992: 173) suggests,

> Although I now live ten minutes walk from the Dell in Southampton, I've not yet made it to a single League game. Even if the Dell were to install crèche facilities, the demands of four-year-old Scarlett and one-year old Harry, plus a part-time job, leave little spare time and energy to devote to the live game.

Women's childcare responsibilities not only restrict their attendance at sport, but when children are taken along in family units to sport events, women continue to be marginalized by the expectation that they will perform the role of primary carer in these public settings (Day 1990).

It is also evident that the nature of many sports and sport venues has restricted women's access as spectators. Increased concerns about football hooliganism in the 1970s in the UK saw a dramatic decline in women attending live soccer matches. Likewise, many sports and sport venues are the sites of overt sexism and aggressive masculine behavior. Though undoubtedly sexism and aggression are not solely encountered in sport, it does seem that sport provides a legitimate site for expressions of "hypermasculinity," and Williams[1] (cited in Coddington 1997: 81) argues that this is one of sport's major appeals to many male fans:

> Many [men] want to be overtly sexist and racist. They need to have this exaggerated sense of their sexuality to defend themselves from potential accusations that they are not real men. English men are very unsure of their sexual identities and, consequently, have to reaffirm themselves as real men by talking about women in a way that is derogatory.

It is also the case that in the past mass spectator sport venues lacked adequate facilities (such as women's toilets), and most were dated and dangerous places and therefore uninviting for many women, especially those who wanted to bring young children along. As Davies (1992: 175) eloquently puts it, "Presumably, football wouldn't be football without someone peeing on your head. Well, lads, if that's what you want, you can keep it. And I'll just stick to my TV."

However, more importantly, sport has remained ideologically a male domain. As Dworkin and Messner (2002: 17) suggest, "organised sport was created in the late nineteenth and early twentieth century by and for White middle class men to bolster a sagging ideology of 'natural superiority' over women" and has continued to constitute a male-dominated domain both for participants and supporters. As Whelehan (2000) suggests, women's progression into these male enclaves has been a very slow and difficult process.

Women therefore have traditionally constituted a minority at most mass spectator sports. However, it is evident that in recent decades there have been significant changes within the nature of many contemporary sports, most notably what Giulianotti (2002: 28) refers to as "hypercommodification." In particular, there has been a shift towards refocusing many sports towards more affluent family-based audiences, rather than the traditionally masculine (often working-class) profiles of many mass spectator sports, such as soccer, rugby league, and baseball. As Crawford (2004: 97) writes,

> [I]t is the contemporary nuclear family unit that has become the focus of both consumer society and social regulation. Increasingly, consumer goods, such as the "family-ticket," "family-meal," "family-pack," are targeted towards this basic unit of consumer society. It is [at] the family-unit, both in the home and outside of it, that consumption is increasingly aimed, and likewise, it is towards this audience that many contemporary sports and sport venues (along with many other forms of entertainment) have increasingly marketed themselves.

As Fink, Trail, and Anderson (2002) suggest in their study of female and male fans of men's and women's intercollegiate basketball in the United States, female fans are more likely to consume sport-related merchandise and are more likely to stay loyal to their team. Similarly, Coddington (1997) asserts that many female soccer fans in the UK are extremely dedicated in their patterns of support, and as Woodhouse (1991) highlights in her survey of Football Supporter Association members, a larger proportion of female soccer fans were season ticket holders and were also strong attenders at away soccer matches, suggesting that women are a potentially lucrative and underexploited market for sport clubs.

This targeting of women has proved particularly successful in North America, where Fink, Trail, & Anderson (2002: 9) outline that 46 percent of the Major League Baseball (MLB), 46 percent of National Football League (NFL), and 38 percent of the National Basketball Association (NBA) fan base is female. They argue that such growth may be the result of marketing strategies that have targeted female fans. For example, the NFL launched a series of seminars entitled "football 101" to teach women more about (American) football, and in 2000 over twelve thousand women attended. The NFL suggests that these seminars were a success, as they led to a 5 percent increase the following year in the number of women watching the Super Bowl on television, taking the viewers to forty million women (McCarthy cited in Fink, Trail, & Anderson 2002: 9).

However, this association of female sport fans with the increased commercialization of sport has often led to the neglect of issues of gender and sport fandom in favor of discussions of the "embourgeoisification" of sport. Jones and Lawrence (2000) suggest that many studies of sport fan culture have either considered fans as a homogenous mass or focused almost exclusively on issues of supporter violence. For instance, Free and Hughson (2003) criticize previous studies of soccer hooligans, such as those by Armstrong (1998), Giulianotti (1991, 1995), and King (1998) for paying little or no attention to issues of gender.

Furthermore, a large proportion of the literature on sport fans (such as Redhead 1997; Rinehart 1997) has often adopted a value-laden reading of fans who attend live sports events as more "authentic" and "participatory," as opposed to "passive" "armchair" supporters who follow sport via mediated sources such as television. Hence, as women are often more likely to follow sport via the media, it is they who are most likely to be deemed "new consumer fans" (King 1998) or "passive" fans (Redhead 1997). Therefore, they are more likely to be labeled as "inauthentic" in their support. Here parallels can be drawn to Thornton's (1995: 105) work on rave (sub)cultures, where the "commercial" ("mainstream" music) becomes feminized, while the "hip" and "authentic" is viewed as masculine and "the prerogative of boys." As Davies (1992: 169) wrote of her experience of being a (female) soccer fan who primarily follows it on television,

> I would argue that the "true supporter," as defined by the footballing estab-
> lishment—and also, sadly, by some of the alternative, fanzine culture—is by
> and large a man. The devoted lad who is rooted to the terraces, season after
> season; who may well cancel his wedding day, should it coincide with a
> Cup-tie; who could name a first-born after first team players; and who is
> capable of struggling with relegation over lager and curry. After years of
> struggling with institutionalised sexism, we women fans have learnt that as
> long as we adopt these norms of fan culture, we *may* make the grade. Those
> unable or unwilling to become "ladesses"—or, indeed, for us at home look-
> ing after the lads' children and cooking the lads' sausages—the only way we
> can participate in the game we love is to watch it on the telly. And make no
> mistake: we do love the game.

Though the increased marketing of sport towards women and the proliferation of sport-related merchandising and media have potentially eroded barriers to sport in the home, it remains the case that most live mass spectator sport audiences are male dominated (Sandvoss 2003). The Sir Norman Chester Centre for Football Research (SNCCFR) suggest that female attendance at soccer in England has increased from as low as 5 percent in the 1980s to around 15 percent in the late 1990s (Haywood & Williams 2002). If we accept this argument (though these findings have been contested by Malcolm, Jones, & Waddington 2000), it still signifies a vast underrepresentation of female spectators at soccer, and this pattern is replicated at most male mass spectator sports around the world.

As Goffman (1968) argues, visibly different minority groups often see their position and presence within a group both questioned and challenged. The stigmatization of these "others" leads to the challenging of their authenticity as "real" members of a group or community. Therefore female fans of male mass spectator sports often find that their authenticity as "real fans" is questioned by other (most often male) supporters and that they are labeled as "uncommitted" to their team (Woodhouse & Williams 1999). As Brimson and Brimson (1996) outline in their "lads" book on soccer,

> women like football [soccer], they don't love or worship it[. . . .] For them, any game is just an event, but for men it's a dream of what could, and damn it, should have been. (cited in Woodhouse & Williams 1999: 60)

Crawford (2004) suggests that sport supporters follow a moral career path as they are socialized and taught to adopt and conform to the social norms of the existing group. As Back, Crabbe, and Solomos (2001: 77) indicate in relation to ethnic minority supporters of English soccer, an "entry ticket" involves much more than a financial transaction, as fans must learn to "articulate and master the implicit cultural codes that police the boundaries of acceptance." Back et al. apply the work of Bauman (1998a) and argue that boundaries of inclusion and exclusion within a given community are mediated through cultural terms and therefore supporters must gain the correct "cultural ticket" to be accepted. Therefore, more visible differences such as skin color or gender that deviate from the "norm" of the supporter group may lead to women and ethnic minorities being excluded from full membership or participation. As Rowlings (1992: 164) wrote of her experiences of growing up as a female soccer fan,

> Whether I was really accepted, I am now not sure. I could argue a point of view and had therefore to be taken notice of[. . . .] But I knew I was considered an oddity—unlike any of the girls in my class and clearly something that the boys were unused to dealing with. As I grew older, I found that this uncertain position remained especially when first meeting people and sharing my love of the game.

However, it is possible that increased levels of female participation in sport as well as the increased number of "new" and "imported" sports may provide more opportunities for women to attend live sport events.

Women, Sport Participation, and "New" Sports

It is evident that the number of women participating in organized sport has significantly increased in recent decades, and most notably in many traditionally "masculine" sports such as soccer. For instance, in England in 1989 there were only 263 women's clubs and around seven thousand players, but by 1997–1998 this had increased to one thousand seven hundred women and girls teams with around thirty-four thousand registered players (Haywood & Williams 2002). In Britain in 2002, soccer overtook netball as the most popular sport for women, and the FA boasts that "football [soccer] is now the top female sport in England" (FA 2003). In "hockey nation," Canada, 28 percent of girls now play soccer compared to only 6 percent who play ice hockey (Hong 2003). In China, soccer is also one of the fastest-growing female sports. In the United States, there are over 8.5 million known soccer participants; in Africa, there is the African Women's Championship in Nigeria; and there has been a soccer revolution in North and South America, Asia, Africa, and Australasia—making soccer a sport that women play all over the world (Hong 2003).

Studies of attendance patterns at women's sport events, such as Woodhouse's (2001) survey of those attending women's international soccer matches in England, would seem to suggest that these are attended by a much higher proportion of female fans than most male mass spectator sports. However, though there are some success stories, such as the popularity of women's soccer in the United States, women's participation in traditionally masculine sports such as soccer still tends to attract significantly smaller audiences. Furthermore, Woodhouse's (2001) survey indicates that 87.2 percent of those who attended these international soccer matches either had themselves, or were attending with someone who had, a friend or relative who was playing. This indicates that women's soccer (certainly in England) is not yet attended in large numbers by a wider audience with a general interest in the sport. It is also apparent that women's sport participation continues to receive significantly less media coverage than male-dominated sports (Duncan & Messner 1998). Hence, fans (both male and female) of women's sport are frequently provided with less access to information about these sports and fewer opportunities to feel part of, or participate in, sport fan communities.

However, the increased globalization of sport, and in particular the promotion of certain "new" or "imported" sports into countries that have no (or little) traditional (masculine) culture associated with these, such as soccer in North America and basketball and ice hockey in Europe, may provide more opportunities for women to attend these sports in more equal numbers. For instance, Hofacre (1994: 26) has suggested that the introduction of professional soccer into the United States has provided an opportunity for female fans to attend this sport on a more "equal footing" with men—as soccer in the United States lacks the tradition and male domination of other sports such as baseball and American football. Likewise, Crawford and Gosling (2004) indicate that the rise in popularity of ice hockey in the UK in the 1990s saw men and women attending this sport in relatively equal numbers.

Free from the "baggage" of the masculine history and traditions of these sports, "newer" or "imported" sports can much more easily be targeted towards "family" (i.e. women and children and not just men) audiences. Sports such as ice hockey and basketball in the UK have been sold much more as a form of "family entertainment," as indicated, for example, by Dave Biggar, the former director of marketing of the British ice hockey team the Sheffield Steelers and, later, the (British) Manchester Storm and (American) Hartford Wolfpack:

> We pitched it [ice hockey] as "it's great. It's this, that and the other . . . and oh, by the way, it's a hockey game." And the nice thing is you'd get mom, dad and the kids would arrive, the kids had been bribed in the first place to come, 'cause we'd given them a free ticket or they'd seen it, and we'd created this hype[. . . .] I mean, we just created hype out of nothing. (cited in Crawford 2002: 28)

Though women frequently attend sports such as ice hockey in the UK in almost equal proportions to men, this does not necessarily mean that women are accepted by other (most notably male) fans as "legitimate" (Crawford & Gosling 2004). In interviews with British ice hockey supporters, Crawford and Gosling reveal that the attitudes of many male supporters indicate that women continue to be seen as "inauthentic" in their patterns of support, most notably cast into age-specific roles as "mothers" who are there to look after the children, "girlfriends" who are there with partners, or "silly young girls" who are there to "lust after the players." For instance, "John" (male, aged thirty) criticizes young female fans, stating,

They sit there talking all through the game, and when they score a goal they don't even get up. We've sat there and the girls are in and out, in and out, and for me they are just there to look at the players, they're not interested in the game are they? They just have a giggle, you know what I mean? You can't concentrate with someone chatting away. It's obvious what they've gone for. (cited in Crawford & Gosling 2004: 486)

Such comments, Crawford and Gosling (2004) argue, emphasize the belief (and unease) of male fans that women attend male mass spectator sports merely to "swoon" over the players. Women fans are therefore viewed as inauthentic and not dedicated enough in their support. Although it may be the case that some female supporters may have been attracted to sport, and in particular soccer, by the ways in which players such as David Beckham are packaged and sold today (Woodhouse & Williams 1999: 61), Hinerman (1992) suggests that most fan activities involve some level of fantasy, and this is not necessarily a sign of less dedication. As Van Zoonen (1994: 98) highlights, it is "the patriarchal will to maintain power" that dictates that it is wrong to look lustfully at the male body, and it is the *male* gaze that dominates sport presentation (see Rose & Friedman 1994). Therefore male mass spectator sports in both the mass media and the live event are primarily targeted towards a male audience (Cooper-Chen 1994). The presence of women fans therefore threatens the "male gaze," as women become the observers and men the objects of the gaze, and men may find this incredibly unnerving (Whelehan 2000).

Significantly, Crawford and Gosling (2004) found no evidence to imply that female fans were any less dedicated in their support or less knowledgeable about the sport they followed. On the contrary, many were quite keen to assert their credentials and knowledge as "real fans." As Coddington (1997: 79) highlights in relation to female soccer supporters, many women "tend to take their footballing [soccer] commitments very seriously, precisely because they have a nagging feeling that they are on trial."

Conclusion

This chapter has offered an overview of existing literature on female sport fans and suggests that this is still a relatively underdeveloped area of research. In particular, it has argued that there is very little understanding of what it means to be a female sport fan and how this is located in women's everyday lives and therefore offers a basis on which to conduct further research.

It has been, and continues to be, a slow and complex process, but the number of female sport fans is rising. However, drawing on research by Crawford and Gosling on British ice hockey fans, this chapter has argued that even when women do attend sports in equal numbers, they are still frequently excluded from supporter "communities." Therefore, women continue to be restricted in their patterns of attendance at live sport events due to their socially ascribed roles as mothers and wives and due to the often masculine and aggressive nature of some male mass-spectator sports. Furthermore, those who follow sport via the media have often been deemed inauthentic in their patterns of support.

Women's marginal position within sport fan cultures means that their legitimacy as sport fans is often questioned, even though there is some evidence to suggest that women may be more dedicated and loyal to the sports they follow. This questioning of authenticity and loyalty could simply be seen as an expression of men's fears over women invading their traditionally masculine space; however, it plays an important role in marginalizing female fans.

Being a sport fan can play an important role in constructing women's identities and in providing women and girls with access to social networks of other fans. In addition, it may be used to subvert dominant gender roles. Therefore, what remains missing from the research is the role that sport fan culture can play in women's everyday lives, and in particular its significance in challenging gender roles and empowering women. Dell (1998) has highlighted the role that wrestling can have in challenging dominant gender roles, but debates on female sport fan culture need to engage more closely with questions of gender power relations, in a way similar to that which Bacon-Smith (1992), Jenkins (1992), McKinley (1997) and others have done in relation to media fan cultures. It is only then that we can gain a better understanding of the gendered power relations that envelop contemporary sport fan culture.

NOTE

1. No reference given.

19

Customer Relationship Management
Automating Fandom in Music Communities

Tom McCourt and Patrick Burkart

Fan cultures receive much attention in contemporary media studies, and for good reason. As social and cultural phenomena, they offer researchers a chance to observe seemingly pure play—authentic and often charming self-disclosures and shared identities among enthusiastic participants. However, cultural industries increasingly are seeking to rationalize and routinize these expressions of identity and solidarity in online contexts in the hopes of reducing uncertain demand (Burkart & McCourt 2006). Since consumers face an ongoing avalanche of products in the form of recordings, videos, and texts, it is imperative that marketers steer the right items to the right consumers at the right time. Discovering affinity groups, and tapping into their searching and sharing operations, has become a lucrative business. "Word-of-mouth is an incredibly powerful discovery tool for music fans," according to eMusic's COO, David Pakman. "Our new 'neighbors' and 'top fans' features deliver the virtual equivalent of that. For the first time, a music service will introduce you to your musical 'neighbors' and kickoff a more personal way to discover new music" (Choicestream 2004).

The major record labels are tethering online spaces to their newest digital distribution channels (Burkart & McCourt 2006). The "automation of fandom" denotes their management of virtual communities through sponsored online "hosts" and automated content software that defines and controls each fan's online "experience." As they attempt to displace informal fan sites, their legal strategies have also hampered open file sharing and threaten the "relative anonymity and diversity of public criticism"

(Bielby, Harrington, & Bielby 1999: 1) characteristic of online fanzines. The automation of fandom reduces prospects for music fans' autonomy as it also pulls the rug out from under their self-organized communities.

The music industry anticipates that online music distribution will grow in the double digits for many years to come. Recent sales figures from iTunes and other online music service providers validate digital distribution as a preferred mode of delivery over physical CD shipments. However, the need to effectively market music becomes more acute in cyberspace as recordings shed their physicality and, in many ways, their corresponding value (McCourt 2005: 249). Customer Relations Management (CRM), based on personalization systems, seeks to build brand loyalty by creating online "experiences" tailored to customer preferences and sending personalized content to consumers. In addition to its purported ability to identify customers who have affinities for particular products, CRM is useful for cross-promoting the product lines of partner companies or subsidiaries. But CRM's greatest strength may be its ability to identify an individual customer's value to the company or firm. Through CRM, one bank discovered that 20 percent of its customers created all of its revenues, while the other 80 percent were "destroying value" through the labor costs required to process their transactions (London 2001: 10). As the music industry makes the transition from hard goods to digital files, the value of customer profiles traded among online portals, affiliates, and advertisers rises accordingly.

Types of CRM

Online music buyers typically access such systems through a "portal" or "My Service" interface, which allows them to customize the information they receive, including news, messages, recommendations, and billing notices. These systems recognize and track returning customers; the more the customer uses the service, the more accurate its suggestions become. Such systems assemble marketing dossiers in the process; this information, about both individual and general consumer behavior, can be used to hone in-house marketing efforts and also can be traded between corporate divisions or sold to outside interests. Direct mail firms and the U.S. Postal Service have used similar software for decades to sort information into databases that can be rented and sold. In the online music industry, personalization systems fall into three categories: collaborative filtering, which suggests content based on the user's purchasing history and volunteered comments from the user and others; human-based genre/mood matching, in which experts classify and categorize individual music tracks into logical groupings; and "listening machines," which analyze the actual wave forms of recordings to compare their melody, tempo, harmony, timber, and density.

Collaborative filtering is intended to serve as an automated equivalent to "word of mouth." The navigation patterns, purchasing history, and volunteered feedback of users are compared to each other, with recommendations based on the resulting matches. An early experiment in a collaborative filtering system, a 1992 project of Xerox PARC called Tapestry, was soon followed by the GroupLens project, which tracked each item a user rated along with a score for preference (Reidl, Konstan, & Voorman 2002: 5). It then estimated which users were "good predictors" by finding similarities between user tastes, and then used these "good predictors" to find new items to recommend. The first music collaborative filtering system, Ringo, was created at the MIT Media Lab in July 1994. One user described the service:

> What Ringo did was simple. It gave you 20-some music titles by name, then asked, one by one, whether you liked it, didn't like it, or knew it at all. That initialized the system with a small DNA of your likes and dislikes. Thereafter, when you asked for a recommendation, the program matched your DNA with that of all the others in the system. When Ringo found the best matches, it searched for music you had not heard, then recommended it. Your musical pleasure was almost certain. And, if none of the matches were successful, saying so would perfect your string of bits. Next time would be even better. (Negroponte & Maes 1996: n.p.)

The founders of Ringo launched Firefly, a commercial service, in 1996. Users registered for a Firefly "passport" on the company's website and rank-ordered artists on a list. The site then looked for those with similar tastes (which Firefly termed "trusted neighbors") and made recommendations. In addition, users could visit the home pages of their "trusted neighbors" on the Firefly website and engage in correspondence. One writer reported, "The concept was neatly logical: users would rate and review music, building a grand cross-referenced database of musical tastes. The more you told the system what you liked, the more Firefly would be able to make specific recommendations based on what *other* users liked"

(Brown 2001). However, Firefly was unable to develop a successful business model, and pieces of its technology were sold to Microsoft and Launch.com in 1997 (Brown 2001).

Amazon.com implemented "Bookmatcher" on its website in 1997. Customers filled out forms indicating their interests, and the system matched them with book lists tailored to their entries. Bookmatcher required more time from users than most were willing to give, however, and Amazon now uses implicit data from previous purchases, which feed into its "New For You" and "Recommendations" features. Recommendations result from algorithms based on customer ratings as well as the buying patterns of customers who placed similar orders. To reduce errant data, users can exclude purchases from their "dossiers" (Stellin 2000: C8). For example, a purchase of Boxcar Willie for your sister-in-law can be excluded from your Goth or techno-laden profile, if you do not want the system to characterize you as an admirer of "the world's favorite hobo" (Willie 2004).

An ambitious example of the human-based genre/mood matching systems, at least to judge from its name, is the "Music Genome" project of a software company called SavageBeast (as in, "music soothes the . . ."). Its music experts sorted thousands of recordings according to a variety of attributes, or "genes," such as rhythm, lyrics, and instrumentation (Clark 2000: B1). On October 31, 2001, SavageBeast introduced what it called the "Celestial Home Jukebox," a system for organizing files, building playlists, and soliciting recommendations. Among other things, the "organization" function scans one's collection, renames and retags files with metadata, and places them in playlists according to genre, instrumentation, mood, rhythm, tempo, vocal style, etc. Users can also select "seed songs" from which the program will create playlists. The program also provides links to retailers (Music Industry News Network 2001).

User interfaces vary among human-based services, but most make recommendations based on reactions to a series of song clips. Users of failed startup Music Buddha created a "musical fingerprint" by choosing for each clip a recognizable genre such as jazz, rock, or classical, which they then narrowed into "smooth jazz" or "heavy metal." They then chose from a limited number of lifestyle or mood options offered on a menu, such as "tattoos and pool cues" or "celebration of women." After auditioning a selection of eight- to ten-second song "hooks," users indicated whether these clips matched their preferences. At the end of this process, Music Buddha produced names of recordings the user might like, and opportunities to buy the recordings or add them to a "favorites" list (Brown 2001: n.p.). The CEO of Music Buddha likened the result to "the mix tape that the boyfriend gives to the girlfriend[....] That is the oh-wow moment we are trying to replicate" (Clark 2000: B1). Other systems, such as Media Unbound, iTunes, and MusicMatch, combine collaborative filtering with "expert" classification. MoodLogic.com allows users to "search by characteristics such as 'romantic R&B songs from the 1970s,' and visualize them graphically with elements called 'mood magnets'" that have been collaboratively identified by its users (Clark 2000: B1).

Listening machines, on the other hand, are fully automated. In the CantaMetrix system, for example, a computer analyzes a source track's waveforms for melody, tempo, harmony, timber, and density, and then retrieves similar recordings. Listeners may select a mood on the interface, such as "happiness," and stream preselected tracks. Such systems have long precedents. According to Joseph Lanza (1994), Muzak president Waddil Catchings originated the idea of coding each song in the Muzak library according to rhythm, tempo, instrumentation, and ensemble size. The results were then piped into munitions factories during World War II to flatten out work efficiency curves.

These systems are increasingly integrated with industry-created virtual communities, which can include message boards and chat as well as "lighter" interactive options such as list sharing. For example,

> Playlist Central is an online Rhapsody community where you can find playlists to listen to and add to your collection, or publish your own playlists to share with the world. E-mail your Playlist Central finds and creations to your friends, or post them on your blog. Friends can download Rhapsody and enjoy 25 free plays a month as well[....] My Rhapsody gives you a central place for personalized recommendations from the Rhapsody editors, once you've entered your favorite genres. (Rhapsody 2005: n.p.)

Rhapsody allows subscribers to email their playlists to others; if the recipient also is a Rhapsody subscriber, he or she can click on an attachment, which will play the recordings from the sender's playlist. iTunes introduced a playlist function in October 2003, when it solicited playlists from musicians, and also offers "iMix," in which users publish playlists that can be rated by others, as well as "Party Shuffle," which automatically chooses songs from a user's library. Yahoo Music promotes its "personalization & community" features in the same fashion:

Leveraging the more than three billion song, artist and album ratings of Yahoo! Music fans, Yahoo! Music Unlimited will generate personalized homepages and recommendations based on perceived tastes and subscriber community ratings. As users rate more songs and add to their digital collection by importing music from CDs, downloads, etc., subscribers discover new music through recommendations made by other Yahoo! members who have similar music tastes. (Yahoo! 2005: n.p.)

Problems with CRM

CRM is available commercially on various platforms, and many companies "roll their own" or augment outsourced applications with their own personalization software. When CRM techniques become standardized, they will probably develop variations of Nielsen and Roper reports with detailed, real-time information on consumer behavior. Although CRM is improving its surveillance, collaborative filtering, and reporting ("business analytics") functions, however, these systems have failed to realize the success predicted by their developers. A 2003 study by Forrester Research reported that "[o]f the 30 million people who used a personalized retail site [in 2002], only 22 percent found it valuable" (Kouwe 2003: D2). One problem inherent to collaborative filtering is "cold start": when making matches, a company needs a large group of consumers who have made a large number of purchases before it can predict future choices. A related problem is the "popularity effect." As one executive said, "The holy grail [of CRM] is to be able to capture all the customer's interactions in detail and get smarter about what *not* to recommend. . . . We can recommend very well. Knowing when not to bother someone is much harder" (Guernsey 2003: G5). Thus, systems err on the side of false negatives (not offering music you might like) rather than false positives (offering music you might not like). This inherent conservatism results in predictable choices. According to one critic of the Firefly service,

> The service would rarely, if ever, break out of the mold of mainstream bands and recommend fringe music you'd never heard of before. And if your tastes strayed across numerous niches—say, you liked country and pop and techno, but weren't particularly devoted to any one genre, Firefly was equally problematic; the odds of finding a community of users with identically eclectic tastes were slim. (Guernsey 2003: G5)

A similar concern was raised about GroupLens, which has been used by Amazon.com, CDNow.com, and Music Boulevard. A music critic wrote,

> Just because I like a particular jazz musician such as Sonny Rollins—and I do—doesn't mean I want to hear everyone who sounds like him. Sometimes I want to hear music unlike anything I've heard before and no recommendation engine will be able to find those elusive musicians for me. I won't even be able to say what I want, or what I like, unless I hear it. (Jossie n.d., n.p.)

These systems share the weaknesses of contemporary radio market research practices such as "callouts," wherein listeners evaluate snippets of songs, or "hooks." Given such a limited sample, listeners respond favorably to familiar music while rejecting works that are unfamiliar. Such systems decrease the likelihood that listeners will be exposed to unfamiliar genres and develop new tastes and interests. Filtering systems, similarly, can know only what the user already likes, and they are further restricted by the arbitrary parameters imposed by coders.

Human-based genre/mood classifications, such as the Music Genome Project, are no less problematic. A comprehensive set of genre definitions and mappings is impossible to establish. Genre classification is an intensely subjective process, and continuously proliferating and evolving categories compound the problem. "Mood" classification is even more subjective. For example,

> When MoodLogic's database was searched for all songs with the mood "aggressive," the system comes up with relatively mild fare[. . . .] CantaMetrix [in comparison] responded to the same word with snarling tracks by Black Sabbath and System of a Down. But when asked to find songs similar to Eric Clapton's recording of "Hoochie Coochie Man," CantaMetrix suggested a sweet song called "God Only Knows" by some female gospel singers called the Martins, and the country classic "I Saw the Light" by Hank Williams. (Clark 2000: B1)

Ultimately, autorecommendation systems attempt the impossible. Tastes are not fixed; they are plastic and highly subjective. Yet these systems are built on the assumption that tastes are objective, mechanical, knowable— that tastes are easily reduced to mathematical formulas. Such systems "[take] the stunning breadth of choices and boils them down to a limited number. In doing so, filtering fails to unearth the incredible diversity of our tastes, the quirkiness inherent to being human" (Smith 2000: 5). Music portals construct these online "fan clubs" exclusively to promote consumption; the Rhapsody system excludes group communication except for exchanges of playlists. Their automated personalization software inverts the dynamics of informal, "bottom-up" websites created by artists or fans by funneling visitors into "digital enclosures" of continual surveillance and analysis.

Andrejevic (2003: 141) notes, "The value of a cybernetic commodity exceeds its production cost [when] the minimum of convenience or customization required to induce a consumer to relinquish personal data or to submit to detailed forms of monitoring" has been achieved. In the absence of tangible commodities such as CDs and DVDs, the support structure itself (in this case, cyberspace) becomes the commodity. It will be controlled not by users but by cultural industries that create value through transactions, or the process of circulation. To compensate for the lack of hard goods, and to rationalize their intrusion into privacy, digital cultural providers tout greater selectivity, personalization, and community as "value-added" features. These measures are increasingly necessary as consumers pick and choose single releases, rather than bundled collections, from a growing volume of material.

Combining CRM and virtual communities makes good marketing sense, because these virtual communities emulate the organic solidarity of music fan cultures, and analyzing fan interactions improves the recommendation power of CRM's data-mining software. Yet these communities, while supposedly communal, require their participants to be individuated and isolated. The personalization of CRM furthers media trends towards narrowcasting that have long driven cable and satellite television and now drive satellite radio. You have to pay for access, and you get something ever narrower; eventually, you get a "channel" heard only by yourself. Such micro-segmentation, however, has social costs. As one observer noted, "The music may be speaking right to me, but it's alienating being a niche market of one" (Goldberg 2000: n.p.). Critics contend that "iTunes is about music as a commodity; Napster was about music as mutual experience. iTunes is about cheap downloads; Napster was about file sharing—with sharing the key word" (Jenkins 2003: n.p.). Napster enabled users to discover new content by browsing shared folders, but such coincidental collaborative filtering is unlikely with new "authorized" digital music sites like iTunes, and even second- and third-generation network and service sites like KaZaA and Gnutella, which lack Napster's sense of community. As Napster morphed into Napster II, music fans decried the loss of community: "What I loved about Napster was the ability to connect, often in the wee hours of the morning, with total strangers who shared my tastes and interests and to discover new music, which I would never have heard otherwise" (Jenkins 2003: n.p.).

In real communities, whether in physical space or cyberspace, members share affinities, interests, and needs; this commonality is recognized and mediated by the members themselves. Overseers or overlords of a fan community attract suspicion, and may even be ousted as members, if the fan community does not first disperse. In contrast, online cultural distributors construct the *appearance* of community, while largely denying members the ability to communicate or otherwise interact directly. Playlists from different services are incompatible, user behavior is inconsistent, and metadata may be missing or incomplete. While celebrity playlists or endorsements may serve a valuable function for marketers, they are constructed to support a public persona. Merchandisers also may abuse playlists as they seek to get rid of excess hard goods inventory (Kouwe 2003: D2).

As online fan communities supersede music scenes linked to places, these communities in turn will develop into "walled gardens" of online shops and light virtual communities moderated and policed by distributors. Internet visionaries see the online universe governed one day by an "adaptive Web" that will conform to the needs of its users, rather than vice versa (Gray in Wellman 2002: 96). Yet present digital delivery systems are profoundly indifferent to those needs. They strengthen norms of consumerism and quiescence; they have permitted the entertainment industry—the consciousness-making sector—to resolve its crises of production and consumption at our expense. CRM subjects us to unprecedented surveillance and manipulation. Participants have so little control of the terms of their membership that the intimate information they are required to surrender may be transferred without notice to anybody. In the process of squeezing value out of participation, these systems atomize fans and subject them to "monitored mobility" (Andrejevic 2003: 142) within the system. Intrusive online agents demanding personal information and pushing advertising and media on us will give us all the harried feeling of airport travelers, funneled through an enclosed media fun-house where we are repeatedly required to identify ourselves, and our privacy and our property exposed to search and seizure.

Online cultural distributors create "audiences" by isolating their users and reaggregating them into a manufactured community of atomized streamers and downloaders. The purpose is to encourage more consumption, faster production cycles by creators, and more disposable culture. You use it once and throw it away; you are thinking about, and paying for, not this song or that artist, but the virtual machine that delivers a reliable stream of pleasure to you alone. Aside from the corporate-controlled "communities" enabled by CRM, online cultural distributors lack common spaces and public forums for sharing tastes and experiences, further alienating fans from their music, from each other, and ultimately from themselves. The fan "scenes" vital to the creation of culture become moribund as their rituals for sharing and social spaces for group identification are supplanted by cultural industries seeking to automate fandom. On both the individual and collective levels, CRM furthers the reification of culture.

20

Playing the Game
Performance in Digital Game Audiences

Garry Crawford and Jason Rutter

Research into audiences and their engagement with cultural texts has often followed a trajectory established by Morley (1980), Hobson (1982), Radway (1984), Ang (1985), and Hermes (1995), namely, an emphasis on the consumption of routine—if not mundane—texts in everyday, often domestic, environments. Its sizable contribution to cultural studies has, in no small part, been the means by which this emphasis has opened up the study of the rich variety of practices, knowledge, and discourses that audience members bring to their involvement with everyday cultural texts. Conversely, the research trope that appears to be developing around much of the study of digital games has emphasized the spectacular (e.g. King & Krzywinska 2002), the out-of-the-ordinary (e.g. Kennedy 2002), the place of digital games in a canon of "art" (e.g. Jenkins 2005a), or possible links to aggressive and violent behavior (see Bryce & Rutter 2006).

This chapter explores the validity of such assumptions by situating digital gaming within a broader socially situated context. We provide a brief introduction to the consideration of digital gaming and gamers as an audience and argue that the literature on media audiences and fans provides useful theoretical tools for understanding the use of digital gaming in patterns of everyday life. In particular it is argued that the concept of "performance" allows parallels to be drawn between the literatures on gaming and on fans/audiences, which allows for an understanding of how game-related performances and interactions can extend beyond the game interface. Furthermore, we suggest that the inclusion of gaming within debates on audiences and fans can expand our understanding of audience engagement with "texts."

Digital Gaming

Though the origins of digital gaming can be traced back to the 1950s, it was not until the late 1970s and 1980s that digital gaming began to develop as a leisure industry. It was during this period that arcade games such as Pong, Asteroids, Pac Man, and Space Invaders were first produced, along with machines designed for the home, such as the Video Computer System (VCS) from Atari, Nintendo's Famicom, the Vic-20, and Commodore 64, along with various (often unlicensed) clones of Atari's Pong. Today, entertainment software and digital gaming are a major international leisure industry worth in excess of $21 billion (ELSPA 2005). The largest entertainment software market is the United States, where in 2003 continuing growth made the games industry worth in excess of $7 billion (ESA 2004).

However (contrary to popular belief), digital gaming is not restricted to male adolescents. The North American–based Interactive Digital Software Association (IDSA 2002) suggests that 55 percent of regular console gamers and 60 percent of computer gamers are over the age of thirty-five. While digital gaming is by no means a level playing field when it comes to gender (Bryce & Rutter 2003; Crawford & Gosling 2005), Fromme's (2003) study of over a thousand German school children suggests that almost a third of girls claimed to "regularly" play digital games (55.7 percent of boys), with only 2.2 percent of the children surveyed having never played a digital game.

Although access and experience related to digital gaming vary across demographics, digital gaming has developed into a common leisure practice for a wide range of individuals. Given the increased popularity of games, it is reasonable to question what the everyday practices are that have become established and associated with being a digital game player.

Digital Gamers: Players or Audience?

The textual (often narratological) emphasis commonly evident in work on digital games along with a focus on the disruptive possibilities of games technologies has meant that rather than being understood as an "audience," much of the literature on gaming continues to situate gamers as individual players. Despite notable contributions to the understanding of gaming as a social and situated practice (such as Schott & Horrel 2000; Yates & Littleton 2001), there remain often implicit assumptions about digital gaming and the engagement with a certain piece of technology. These are often encoded in a range of metaphors, from "immersion" (Murray 2001), "being there" (Newman 2004), and "relationship" (Aarseth 1997) to more almost-symbiotic approaches. Within such frameworks, there is little in the way of understanding elements of the gaming experience that are not limited to the actual playing of the game itself. Here, there are few tools for understanding gaming as consumption, as leisure, as social. The almost absolute emphasis on the individual player means that there is a marginalization of the possibility or importance of a digital games audience. Moreover, where research has engaged with digital gaming across digital networks, ranging from the local physical connection of game consoles to massively multiplayer games played via the Internet and, more recently, gaming across mobile phone networks with portable devices (Moore & Rutter 2004), there has been a tendency to see these networks as technical innovations, rather than extensions of established social practice and routines.

However, both quantitative and more ethnographically oriented work is increasingly highlighting the limitations of focusing merely on the individual gamer and game. Research undertaken for the Interactive Software Federation of Europe (ISFE 2005) suggests that 55 percent of gamers play with others, and, similarly, academic research by Wright, Boria, and Breidenbach (2002), Crawford (2005a), and Jansz and Martens (2005) supports the idea of gaming as a social activity.

It is notable that even culturally oriented work on gaming has not yet fully engaged with possibilities for developing an understanding of audience as a frequent and important element of playing digital games. For example, though Kline, Dyver-Witherford, and De Peuter (2003) draw on the language and literature of "active audiences," they use this language merely to highlight the way individual gamers can adopt "oppositional" readings to games, and include no understanding of how these readings are located within the social interactions and everyday lives of gamers. There has been a lack of research on the meanings and motivations associated with gaming, the place of gaming within everyday routines, their relation to identity, their position as a nexus for a range of consumption practices, and their frequent extension into conversations, social interactions, and performances away from the gaming environment.

The reluctance to align digital gaming discussions with those of other media users originates in the assumption that it constitutes a significant and marked departure in media forms and practices that cannot necessarily be understood using the same theoretical tools or literature as "older" media forms, such as television. For instance, Kerr, Brereton, and Kücklich (2005) question whether digital games can be understood as a "text" in the same way as analogue media forms (such as television, radio, and cinema) can, as, unlike these, digital game narratives are often dynamic and fluid.

However, Kerr et al. themselves recognize that the degree of fluidity (i.e. user-determined choices) within a game should not be overemphasized. In particular, the level of "user control" or degree of "interactivity" a user has with, or over, digital games has been questioned by numerous authors (such as Gansing 2003; Palmer 2003). Palmer (2003: 160) suggests that new technologies are frequently introduced and sold to the market by means of the rhetoric of their increased "user-control." However, the user's level of control or interaction with the medium is still restricted by not only the limitations of technology but also the aims of the designers and manufacturers, and the ideologies behind these aims.

As the "interactive" potential of games has often been overemphasized (and underconceptualized), so too has the linear nature of other texts. Numerous authors have suggested that older media forms, rather than being seen as static, need to be understood as dynamic and fluid. De Certeau (1984) and his followers have highlighted the way the reader of a text (be it a book, a film, or a television show) introduces a fluidity into its meaning and social significance through individual interpretations. Furthermore, Sandvoss (2005a) suggests that the object of media fandom, be this even one film, cannot be understood as a singular static text, as what fans consume will involve not only their own reading of this text but also that of others, along with what has been written about the text and further textual productions associated with it (such as fan fiction).

This separation and distinction of digital games and gamers as *significantly* different from other media forms and their users is paralleled in much of the literature on sport (and in particular soccer) fans in the UK. Writers such as Taylor (1992) and Redhead (1997) have suggested that soccer fans are different and distinct from consumer or other fan groups, often drawing on romanticized ideas of soccer fans as tied into a more "authentic" and "traditional" (read: masculine working-class) culture than consumers (read: female and/or middle class). However, both Sandvoss (2003) and Crawford (2004) suggest that such an approach greatly restricts the understanding of these groups and limits the range of theoretical tools that can be applied to the consideration of them. We suggest that the separation of digital gamers from wider debates on media audiences, fan cultures, and consumption does this too. Likewise, though some writers on fan culture (such as Hills 2002) claim to offer a "comprehensive overview of fans" (cover notes), they have been guilty of focusing primarily (if not solely) on media fans, at the expense of other forms of fan culture, such as sport (Sandvoss 2003).

We wish to suggest that there is an underexplored similarity between fan and gaming cultures and, more pertinent to our interest, the ways in which being involved in the gaming experience is linked to a rich intertextual and transtexual web of other texts and practices. Furthermore, recognizing the similarities and interconnections between fan and gaming cultures allows for a more fully formed understanding of the interaction between "users" and media "texts." Audience activity is not just the preserve of a few "exceptional" fans or gamers, but rather a range of possible activities and levels of engagement with texts. Gaming, probably more than any other media form, allows us to challenge the boundaries (as set out by authors like Jenkins 1992) between "ordinary" and more active fan readers, and allows fans and gamers to be located within wider discussions of audience behavior (also see Sandvoss 2003).

Below, we develop this notion and in particular highlight the parallels that can be drawn between the "performativity" of both game players and media audiences.

Gaming Performativity

Many sociological considerations of both media audiences (such as Abercrombie & Longhurst 1998) and fan cultures (Hills 2002; Sandvoss 2005a) have highlighted the proliferation and saturation of media forms within contemporary society that has concurred with, and helped to bring about, a change in contemporary media audiences. Abercrombie and Longhurst (1998) suggest that the mass media increasingly impinges on and saturates contemporary society in a "mediascape" (Appaduari 1990) that, as with the landscape beneath our feet, often goes unnoticed but is fundamental in shaping the world around us. This mediascape provides a resource that individuals draw upon in their social performances. As a result, "being a member of an audience is no longer an exceptional event, nor an everyday event[;] rather it is constitutive of everyday life" (Abercrombie & Longhurst 1998: 68–69). That is to say, we live in an increasingly narcissistic and "performative society" where individuals will draw on the media as a "resource" (such as informing the way they dress, speak, or act) in constructing their social performances.

Likewise, new media technologies, such as the Internet and digital gaming, contribute to contemporary mediascapes, providing resources individuals draw on in their everyday lives. Kerr et al. highlight performance as a key component and analytical tool in understanding the nature of and pleasures obtained from digital gaming:

> New media are seen to possess a performative aspect, insofar as they allow for and foster the users' experimentation with alternative identities (Turkle 1995). This is true for computer games as well as internet chat rooms etc. The pleasure of leaving one's identity behind and taking on someone else's identity is regarded as a key pleasure in digital games. (2004: 15)

Gameplay can involve significant elements of performativity (Eskelinen & Tronstad 2003) and frequently involves participants taking on and acting out specific roles. In particular, Rehak (2003) suggests that digital gamers constitute both participants and spectators in the games they play, playing out roles in these games and in turn observing their in-game performances. Digital games frequently allow gamers to play with their identities and to imagine themselves in different social and/or fantastic situations, though even the simplest of games (such as Solitaire or Tetris) involve the gamer performing certain in-game actions, such as moving cards or falling blocks.

However, where others have focused on in-game performances, we wish to argue for an understanding of gaming performance within a wider social, cultural, and media audience framework. For example, for Kerr et al. (2004: 13), a key feature of gaming performativity is that this "is separate from everyday life." However, clear distinctions between a "virtual" gaming world and "real" life are problematic. Bryce and Rutter (2001) argue that gamers are not "absent" but constitute active participants within the games they play, and suggest that digital gaming can involve "virtual," "psychological," and "physical" presence for gamers, all of which are "real." Hence, the fantasies and performances constructed in digital gameplay will be shaped and informed not only by the nature of the game but also by the gamer's "out-of-game" social identity and interests. While gamers may wish to experiment with identities, avatars, and new in-game experiences, it is pragmatically apparent that they cannot do so in a rewarding fashion without drawing upon the language, knowledge, and experiences they have when not playing the game.

Though many game-related performances are physically solitary and take place "in-game," Sandvoss (2005a) argues that most fan performances (such as those of sport or other media fans) are performed for and to the fans themselves. Both the literature on fans and the literature on gaming identify the importance of individual escapism and fantasy, such as games or sport fans imagining themselves in the action of "the game" as a character or player. However, as with the performances of fans, those of gamers can extend beyond the intrapersonal.

In particular, multiplayer games allow in-game interaction with other human players. This can simply involve competing against a human opponent, such as in a sport game like Pro Evolution Soccer or FIFA, or sending messages and engaging in synchronous talk with other online players in first-person shooters (FPS).[1] More elaborately, this can take the form of performances, such as dressing and adapting characters in massively multiplayer online role-playing games (MMORPGs), which the player may then use to interact with other human players—sometimes "in-character."[2] For some players, in-game performances with and to other players can constitute a (if not *the*) key focus or object of their gameplay. For example, King and Borland (2003) discuss a group of fifteen players of the MMORPG Ultima Online who together bought a (in-game) tavern and set up an acting troupe who performed plays (such as Dickens's *Christmas Carol*) to other players. Indeed, Wright, Boria, and Breidenbach go as far as to argue that the value of gaming is not to be found in the game text but in the way it is performed within a social context:

> The meaning of playing Counter-Strike [an online FPS] is not merely embodied in the graphics or even the violent game play, but in the social mediations that go on between players through their talk with each other and by their performance within the game. Participants, then, actively create the meaning of the game through their virtual talk and behavior borrowing heavily from popular and youth culture representations. Players learn rules of social comportment that reproduce codes of behavior and

established standards of conduct, while also safely experimenting with the violation of these codes. (2002: n.p.)

Indeed, gamers' performances and interactions will frequently extend beyond the in-game experience. At the simplest and most obvious level, gamers will interact and often perform to those they game with. For instance, Crawford (2005b) highlights the way gamers will often celebrate key victories or successes with, or to, the people they play with (or those around them). An example of this are the comments made by "Mark" (male, twenty-three, graduate student, UK) in relation to playing the football management game Championship Manager:

> It gets very emotional but . . . very frustrating game as well, it's crazy. I remember I won . . . first time I won the FA Cup [in the digital game Championship Manager] 'round my mates at midnight. Don't know, I wouldn't usually do, I mean his parents were asleep, I woke his dad up I got so excited and you know, crazy. It's weird like that . . . it has this hold over you. (cited in Crawford 2005b: 256–57)

It is the significance of the "nongaming" encounter as an important element in the enjoyment of digital games that is highlighted by Jansz and Martens (2005) in their survey of gamers attending LAN events.[3] They found that although these heavy gamers corresponded in many ways to the stereotype of the male, teenage, single gamer who still lives at home, their prime motivation for attending these events was for the face-to-face social interaction found there. Similarly, the interview-based work of Swalwell on LANners stresses the centrality of social interaction for a group of gamers. She writes,

> Most acknowledge that the sociality of the event is one of the best aspects of a lan. To "have a chat and a beer"[. . . .] Lanning's social nature is so strongly espoused amongst lanners that one player, Martin, announced in email correspondence that gaming exclusively online was anti-social, using the negative label "lamer" to refer to those "who just play on the net." (2003: n.p.)

Furthermore, game-related social interactions and performances may also extend beyond sight of the games screen (or LAN event), as conversations and friendship networks based around gaming continue into other social domains. For instance, Crawford (2005b) suggests that many gamers will frequently discuss games and gameplay with family, friends, or work-mates, away from the gaming screen.

Gamers may exchange tips or gaming solutions or cheats, or gaming add-ons or modifications ("mods"), which they have produced them-selves—all demonstrating (performing) their game-playing and/or pro-gramming abilities to others (see Mactavish 2003). Jenkins (2002) also suggests that gamers can sometimes draw on the games they play to con-struct stories and narratives, which they recount to others. Moreover, these social performances can extend beyond face-to-face communication, as the Internet has proved a useful medium for gamers to construct and share gaming solutions, add-ons, updates, and mods, as well as fictional stories or "fan art" based upon gaming narratives. Illustrations of this include the official website of the MMORPG World of Warcraft (www.worldofwar-craft.com), which features a section on fan art, while the official SI Games website (www.sigames.com) has a stories discussion board for players of the Championship Manager series to recount their gaming stories and exploits. This parallels the productivity of fans of other media forms as particularly highlighted in the followers of science-fiction television series such as *Star Trek* and *Doctor Who* discussed by Jenkins (1992).

Moreover, gameplay can also act as a resource for social performances that are not based exclusively on gaming. In particular, knowledge and information gained from digital gaming can be used to inform conversa-tions or social interactions based around other subject matter. This is par-ticularly facilitated by the high levels of "intertextuality" evident in many games.

Intertextuality is evident in a range of media forms, including novels, television, and film, where the understanding or "decoding" of any one text may often refer to, or even require, the understanding of another text or texts (Rutter 1998). However, Marshall (2002) suggests that media inter-textuality is particularly apparent in new forms of media, such as digital gaming, which frequently draw on the narrative of, or make reference to, other texts. As Murray and Jenkins (n.d.) wrote,

a high proportion of the digital media on the market are second-order phe-nomena, adaptations of texts that gained their popularity through film and television. In a horizontally integrated media industry, characters, plots and images move fluidly across various media, participating in what Marsha Kinder (1991) has called the entertainment supersystem.

In particular, digital games are frequently based upon television series (such as *The Simpsons*) or films (such as *Star Wars*), which add additional elements and narratives to these existing texts. A notable example of this is the digital game Enter the Matrix, which includes cinematic scenes and gameplay that follows a narrative that runs parallel with (and helps inform the understanding of) the final two films in *The Matrix* trilogy. There is likely to be a considerable crossover between fans of particular media texts and gamers, which enables individuals to draw on gaming texts in wider (non–game-related) social interactions and performances.

Crawford (2006) discusses how the game series Championship Manager is frequently drawn on by many of its players as a resource in conversations about soccer. Of the twenty-nine Championship Manager gamers he interviewed, twenty-five indicated that information and knowledge derived from this games series would frequently be used to inform conversations and social interactions about soccer. As indicated by "Shaun" (male, age and occupation unknown, email interview, UK),

> Yes I used to love trying to impress my work mates with my knowledge of relatively unknown foreigners [footballers], never letting on that it was all gained from buying them in CM. (cited in Crawford 2006: 509)

This example illustrates how the performativity of gamers can be socially located and drawn on as a resource in wider, everyday, social interactions; it also identifies parallels with other fan and audience groups (in this case soccer fans), emphasizing the importance of not establishing (false) distinctions between "types" of audiences, which may in practice share many similarities and even membership.

Conclusion

This chapter has sought to highlight the location of gaming in wider social practices and in particular, its role in facilitating and informing social performances. Though taking a partial view of digital gaming can make it appear a solitary activity, it is important to recognize that even individual gamers bring their social, cultural, and psychological selves to the games they play. Numerous games and gaming platforms facilitate in-game social interactions, such as playing with others online or in-person, and it is these social aspects to gaming that many find its most appealing feature.

Beyond these in-game (or in-front-of-the-game) interactions, gamers will also frequently carry aspects of their gaming lives with them into other social arenas. Many gamers will frequently discuss games, swap and trade information, or produce game modifications that they exchange with others. Games can also provide resources and information that can be drawn on to inform social performances and interactions not directly related to gaming, such as the conversations of sport or media fans.

Many writers on sport and media fan culture and digital gamers have sought to emphasize both the exceptional nature of these "communities," as well as their distinction from other fan groups and/or audiences. What such distinctions fail to address is the frequency with which individuals engage with, and combine and draw on, a variety of different texts, and they also ignore other, wider bodies of literature that may be of benefit in understanding these communities.

In particular, the social and performative aspects of gaming draw attention to the similarities and parallels with other media audiences and fan groups, and it is the literature and debates on these that we suggest can provide new and fruitful avenues in the research on and consideration of gaming patterns and practices. In particular, comparisons and links to the literature on fans and media audiences allow greater recognition and understanding of how digital gaming performances and interactions occur, not just at the level of the gamer/game interface but also at the level of wider social significance.

NOTES

1. See Wright, Boria, and Breidenbach (2002) for a discussion and taxonomy of the performance of in-game talk within games such as Half Life.

2. Some MMORPGs, such as World of Warcraft, have "role-playing" areas or servers, where the players are discouraged from stepping out of character or discussing "real-world" subjects.

3. LAN parties are events where gamers bring their own computers to attach to a temporary Local Area Network (LAN) in order to play with/against each other both as individuals and in teams. These events can vary in size from a few friends meeting at one of their homes to several hundred gamers congregating for several days over a long weekend and playing around the clock. The largest organizer of such events in the UK is Multiplay (www.multiplay.co.uk).

Part VI

Fans and Anti-Fans
From Love to Hate

21

Fan-tagonism

Factions, Institutions, and Constitutive Hegemonies of Fandom

Derek Johnson

Disharmony has long held a contradictory place in studies of fandom and cult television.[1] While early works like Bacon-Smith's *Enterprising Women* (1992) stressed unity within fan communities, Jenkins's *Textual Poachers* acknowledged rifts among fans, producers, and even other fans, stressing the "passions that surround[ed] disputes" (1992: 130). However, Jenkins too deflected attention from conflict and dissent, emphasizing the consensual and positing that "disagreements occur within a shared frame of reference, a common sense of the series' generic placement and a tacit agreement about what questions are worth asking" (137). As Jenkins later explained, he "accented the positive" to distance fandom from perceptions of it as immature, deviant, and ultimately immaterial to academic study (Harrison 1996: 274). While tactically advantageous, this initial focus on consensus and unity underplayed the constitutive centrality of antagonism and power to television fandom.

Since then, Tulloch and Jenkins (1995) have shown that science fiction series attract heterogeneous fan groups with varying interests, diverse reading practices, and unequal positions of stature within the community. Baym (2000) and MacDonald (1998) have examined the internal hierarchical structures that frequently make fandom a site of exclusion. Externally, Gwenllian-Jones (2003) examines tensions between communities and institutions over unauthorized interactions with corporately owned intellectual properties. While these accounts begin to emphasize inequalities of power relative to fan culture, media studies would benefit from more expansive theorizations of constitutive, hegemonic antagonisms beyond the "moments of friction and dispute" that characterized *Textual Poachers* (Jenkins 1992: 132). Instead of conceiving of antagonism as momentary aberration within unified consensus, I propose that ongoing struggles for discursive dominance constitute fandom as a hegemonic struggle over interpretation and evaluation through which relationships among fan, text, and producer are continually articulated, disarticulated, and rearticulated.

Focusing on the cult television series *Buffy the Vampire Slayer* (1997–2003), this chapter argues that power-laden discursive struggles play a constitutive role in structuring the fan-text-producer relationship.[2] Through communicative contributions to websites, newsgroups, and bulletin boards, factions of *Buffy* fans construct competing "truths" about the series, its producers, and its relationship to fandom, endeavoring to fix fan identity in respectively advantageous ways. Discussions of the program erupt across a range of online venues, some dedicated exclusively to *Buffy*, others to the works of series creator Joss Whedon, and others to television at large. My sample, collected during the 2001–2002 and 2002–2003 seasons, is neither exhaustive nor does it confirm monolithic, representative attitudes within a singular, generalizable *Buffy* fan community. Rather, in the interaction of opposing factions operating *within* individual communities in defined virtual spaces, this study evidences antagonistic competition between discourses of interpretation and evaluation.[3]

The significance of these struggles for discursive hegemony becomes apparent when considered in terms of the relationships between fans and textual structures discussed by Jenkins (1992) and Hills (2002). Hills coins the term "hyperdiegesis" to denote the consistent continuity that makes cult narratives like *Buffy* cohere overall as ontologically secure worlds (2002: 138). Hyperdiegesis provides audiences with constant, trustworthy, supportive environments for productive practices like discussion, speculation, and fan fiction. While hyperdiegesis is a quality of the primary text, Jenkins's "meta-text" is a tertiary, fan-made construction—a projection of the text's potential future, based on specific fan desires and interests (1992: 97). But diverse, divergent fan interests—generated from the same hyperdiegesis, but leading to different meta-textual conclusions—cannot, I argue, be met by any singular, canonical iteration of the series. Events in hyperdiegetic continuity that please one fan or interest group conflict with competing meta-textual interests of another. Co-present meta-texts, therefore, necessarily exist in opposition. Competing meta-textual evaluations of hyperdiegetic states will therefore play a crucial role in structuring the antagonistic ways fans relate to one another, producers, and the text.

Ultimately, this chapter proposes that practices of cult television fandom be considered in terms of "fan-tagonism"—ongoing, competitive struggles between both internal factions and external institutions to discursively codify the fan-text-producer relationship according to their respective interests. To illustrate, I will explore discursive conflicts, first within fan communities and, second, between fans and producers of *Buffy*.[4] At both levels, competing interests advocate rival "truths" that codify and recodify fandom within continually contested parameters. While factionalized internal interests vie for discursive hegemony, forces external to fan practice exercise their institutional power to define and delimit relationships among audience, production, and text. The struggles of fan-tagonism not only produce tertiary interpretations and evaluations but also (as I will show) encode contending constructions of the "normative" fan-text-producer relationship into the primary television text. Antagonisms external and internal to fandom structure its practices, with fan and institutional interests competing to establish dominant meta-textual interpretative discourses while legitimizing specific audience relationships to the industrial production of the hyperdiegetic text.

Fan Factions and Aesthetic History

Though acknowledging diverse interests within fan groups, Tulloch and Jenkins stress the importance of shared, restricted meaning making, arguing that a "unified interpretative position is what makes fans a cultural unit, an interpretative community" (1995: 108). In the absence of institutional power, these interpretative communities wield discursive power "to write the aesthetic history of the show—dividing [it] into a series of 'golden ages' and 'all-time lows'" (1995: 145). But if, as Hills argues, communal schism occurs over "favourite characters, actors, periods in a series, films in a franchise, or according to differences in fans' interpretative strategies," the process by which competing interest blocs attempt to secure this aesthetic consensus comes into question (2002: 62). How do inequalities of status and textual interest give way to unified interpretation? Alternative positions and tastes must somehow be silenced so that divergent interests within a community can be unified as hegemonic interpretative consensus.

Within discussions of *Buffy*, interpretative schism frequently occurred in response to the visibility of "shippers" (short for "relationshippers"), fans whose meta-textual conception of the series advocated the romantic coupling of specific characters and whose ongoing pleasure depended in part upon sustained diegetic potential to spark or preserve those romances. While shippers are not limited to cult series, *Buffy* offered numerous dyads to create such interest: Buffy/Angel, Buffy/Spike, Buffy/Riley, Spike/Angel, etc. Shippers often inhabit specialized online communities and discussion venues, but this multiplicity of romantic permutations regularly puts shipper interests in competition within larger *Buffy* fan communities.[5] Although some pairings proved more popular, the inability of the producers' official hyperdiegetic construction to satisfy all these shipper interests created grounds for struggle. While meta-texts coexisted paradigmatically, canonical hyperdiegesis could only syntagmatically fulfill one of them at a time. Thus, when the Buffy/Spike relationship began in season six, the text foreclosed on meta-textual hopes for reunion with previous love interest Angel (or Riley). Thus, debates over hyperdiegetic developments erupted to negotiate the incompatible interests of concerned fans.

Some concerned fans, however, opposed any pairing. Endorsing alternative taste cultures that devalued romance as soap opera convention, these fans introduced further meta-textual incompatibility—intensifying existing antagonisms. As one particularly vitriolic fan wrote,

> There's nothing like wanting to rant and whine about the pathetic state *Buffy* [. . .] has sunk into only to open a message board [. . .] filled with a thousand "This is the best eva because Spike+Buffy 4eva!!!" dumb posts from 'Shippers to make me want to brain myself with a blunt, barbed metallic cleaver to end the pain.[6]

This fan demonstrates passionately, if impenetrably, that fans do not easily agree to disagree—differing opinions become co-present, competing interests struggling to define interpretative and evaluative consensus. While Buffy/Spike shippers welcomed developments furthering that relationship, others articulated such episodes, incompatible with their meta-textual conception of the series, to a decline in quality. Continuing his diatribe, the same fan claimed,

'Shippers don't care that the plot is non-existent, the pace plods, and everything sucks[. . . .] It doesn't matter that Spike tried to rape Buffy [. . .] [in]
a shocking show of lack of continuity and lazy writing [. . .] because 'Shippers know that Spike and Buffy belong together. Just like how Angel and
Buffy belong together [. . .] [E]veryone ends up talking about baby names
while genuine fans flee in terror.

Coyly demonstrating an inability to reconcile hyperdiegesis with meta-
text, this critique imposes a discursive framework not just on *Buffy*'s aesthetic history but also on *Buffy* fans at large. The equivalence posited here
of nonshippers and "genuine fans" raises the stakes of the debate past textual evaluation to include the proper aesthetic orientation of fan to text.

Discursive attempts to retrospectively define golden ages and all-time
lows aggravate this fragmentation of antagonistic fan communities. In
constructing aesthetic histories, different factions foreground elements
from the hyperdiegetic past that most strongly support their meta-textual
interests, contrasting them with unsavory elements that do not—knowledge claims that, if reiterated, produce norms to either invalidate the
series' status quo or legitimate it within a tradition of quality. During
2002–2003, for example, many fans constructed the recent season six as
Buffy's aesthetic nadir—a truth claim contested by others in a debate
tellingly entitled "Season 6 was the biggest piece of shit ever."[7] This critical
deliberation placed individual seasons—and fans who valued them—
within hierarchies of taste. According to one fan, "to say that Season 6 was
good is almost to dishonor those seasons that were actually good," elabo-
rating that *Buffy*

started out as a groundbreakingly great television series. [In Season 6], for
whatever reason, they decided to fall back on Soap opera clichés [. . .] [giv-
ing] the Up yours to the old school fans who would have loved a return to
normalcy[. . . .] That isn't even going into the long term damage to the
"heart" of the series that various arcs suggested.

Professing adoration for the series' past, the author nevertheless claimed
that "old school fans" had been shortchanged by recent plot developments
that veered from their shared meta-textual interests. Because supposedly
shared desires for "normalcy" had been foreclosed upon by narrative
developments, the author perceived a failure in ontological security, in the

somehow truer hyperdiegetic "heart" of the series in which he or she had become invested—an investment devalued by recent episodes.

Proponents of season six's meta-textual promise, however, launched their own attempts to reify it as a golden age within an alternative aesthetic history. One fan wrote, "Overall season 6 was the most experimental season of them all. A lot of the experiments failed, I'll admit, but a lot of them succeeded with flying colors." Another supporter, attacking a detractor, blasted, "I think you're an arrogant narcissist [. . .] [F]orgive me for not taking seriously your hackneyed, uncreative argument, which by the way has been argued all over the Internet." The evaluative struggle again enlarged, forwarding truth claims not just about season six but also about competing factions of fans. For both sides, "true fan" status necessitated appreciation of one aesthetic, one prescribed evaluative relationship to the text.

Brooker describes similar struggles between "gushers" accused of uncritically accepting drivel and "bashers" charged with gratuitous harshness. Such hostile interpretative stalemates fragment online fan communities into splinter groups with "their own strongholds [. . .] where they consolidate and preach to the choir" (2002: 95–96). Only in rupture could the antagonisms of Brooker's *Star Wars* fans produce the unified consensus of interpretation observed by Tulloch and Jenkins. For the *Buffy* fans observed here, however, "common sense" consensus of interpretation vis-à-vis season six formed hegemonically in debate, where a dominant discourse was legitimated before dissident secession became necessary. Detractors incorporated alternative interpretative values until most agreed that season six "had some of the best ideas of the entire series, but the way they were written was just awful." Even the staunchest season six supporter backpedaled: "this post has made me reconsider my opinion of season 6 as a whole [. . .] I can say that I enjoyed this season more than any other, but I can no longer say it's the best." Those whose meta-textual interests meshed with season six (like Buffy/Spike shippers, for instance) could continue enjoying that season the most, but they lost the battle to legitimize truth claims about its excellence as dominant discourse. Their tastes were subordinated within a hierarchical, hegemonically consensual, group meta-text.

Not all *Buffy* fans, however, consensually accepted season six as a low point in the series; this discussion only evidences the process by which antagonism constituted a single unified reading formation. Although season three compared favorably in 2002–2003 to season six, elements of the former were framed when first aired as "a SLAP to the face," guilty of "turning our beloved show into crap."[8] Thus, fan interpretation is constantly shifting, never unified or maintaining the same valences over time. Despised eras may later become beloved if they retrospectively satisfy the meta-textual desires of dominant fan interests. This extended analysis of aesthetic debate is therefore representative not in the judgments it contains, but in the process by which those judgments were met. Consensus of interpretation legitimated some meta-textual constructions and evaluative discourse at the expense of marginalized others. By discursively framing textual history, competing power blocs attempt to fix the meta-textual projections that can be made from the hyperdiegetic text in the future. Reiterated over time, these antagonistic debates form a habitus, generating not explicitly declared rules and norms but reasonable, common sense behaviors that reproduce the dispositions most favorable to it (Bourdieu 1999: 110). By reinforcing certain textual contingencies as desirable, fan consensus reproduces tastes predisposed to those particular interpretations. Although golden ages change, factionalized fan interests can provisionally install certain evaluations as hegemonic common sense through antagonistic, intracommunity discourse. By constructing consensual legitimizations of a particular season or storyline, the habitus of fan discourse encourages future interpretations to evaluate narrative elements against a privileged meta-text. The interpretation of the cult text in the future is made to appear as the extension of a supposedly consensual and objective view of the past.

Fan Activism: Vilifying the Producer

While fan-tagonism structures hegemonies of textual interpretation, internal struggles to empower factional meta-texts often expand to challenge the discursive and productive monopolies of institutional forces outside fandom—often those in the industrial sphere of hyperdiegetic production. Corporate producers' creative choices often delimit the range of interpretation possible within fan meta-texts, authorizing some but denying others. While audiences can, via fan fiction, adapt the text to marginalized interests, they can also challenge corporate producers by constructing interpretive consensuses that delegitimize institutional authority over the hyperdiegetic text.

Early studies of television fandom engaged with external fan-producer antagonisms more openly than internal fan schisms. In Jenkins's view, fan fiction "involves not simply fascination or adoration, but also frustration and antagonism[....] Because popular narratives often fail to satisfy, fans must struggle [. . .] to find ways to salvage them for their interests" (1992: 23). But salvage is not always possible. This antagonism moved into the institutional sphere when Jenkins's *Beauty and the Beast* fans, finding their meta-textual interests foreclosed upon, advocated the cancellation of the series—only a season after fighting to renew it. *Doctor Who* fans launched similar campaigns to "'save the programme' from its producer" (Tulloch & Jenkins 1995: 160). The producers of these series either eliminated narrative elements in which dominant fan factions had become invested, or else introduced new ones that prohibited significant meta-textual contingencies, therefore compelling some fans to defy their authority with what Pam Wilson calls "narrative activism" (2004: 337).

But like *Star Trek*'s Gene Roddenberry, *Buffy* creator Joss Whedon is often deified by the fan base. As an auteur, Whedon's authorial signature linked *Buffy*, spin-off *Angel*, and even the diegetically autonomous *Firefly* in an intertextual relationship (sometimes referred to as the "Whedonverse" or "Jossverse"), reinforcing the hyperdiegetic coherence of those worlds by promising consistency, continuity, and quality within and between texts. The ontological security he provided caused some fans to "agree with Joss that he knows what's best for our own good better than we do."[9] So if the author figure can so defuse fan discontent, where does fan-tagonism come into play?

Enter perceived pretender to the throne, executive producer Marti Noxon, whose collaboration with Whedon challenged the hyperdiegetic security of auteurism. While Whedon nurtured fledgling series *Firefly*, Noxon faced scrutiny and distrust while managing *Buffy*'s sixth season in his stead. The aforementioned hegemonic reading formation that devalued season six worked simultaneously to delegitimize Noxon's productive authority and privileged relationship to the text. Many fans vilified Noxon: one Frequently Asked Questions list insisted she was "widely considered the Devil,"[10] with some fans dubbing her "Marti Noxious." Mirroring evaluations of season six in general, criticisms of Noxon condemned her production of "angsty and depressing episodes" akin to melodrama and soap opera.[11] While it is unclear whether such critics were unwilling to accept a woman as Whedon's show-running successor, the female Noxon was nevertheless assigned the blame for the series' perceived dalliances in devalued, feminized storytelling forms (despite the series' prior melodramatic leanings). Even fans who admired Noxon held her, for better or worse, responsible for both the quality of that season and any problems perceived during Whedon's absence. "I actually think that she 'gets' these characters better than Joss does," opined one fan, "which is why I was so surprised at how bad season six was with her at the helm."[12]

Not all disgruntled fans delegitimized Noxon in such a direct, constructive manner. One fan authored a *faux* studio press release announcing Noxon as the next "Big Bad" (*Buffy*-speak for each season's recurring narrative antagonist):

> It was easy to make the audience hate [Noxon]. We purposely planted innumerable inconsistencies into the weekly scripts, making the characters act very, well, out of character. According to Noxon, "They hate me. They really do. I've managed to tick off the Angel fans, Spike fans, the Willow fans [. . .] pretty much the whole lot of them[. . . .] Just check out some of the posting boards[. . . .] So, I guess I'm doing a good job. I mean, I'm the one Big Bad you just can't defeat."[13]

Highlighting a number of hegemonic (if often unduly severe) fan discourses surrounding Noxon, this critique charged her stewardship with breaking continuity and, thus, harming the narrative's hyperdiegetic coherence. Perceiving a diversity of fan factions each disgruntled and alienated by Noxon's productive control, this text evidences a potential point of commonality for a hegemonic consensus of interpretation between competing interests all feeling equally betrayed. These sentiments did not go unrecognized: "I get such hate mail, you wouldn't believe," echoed Noxon (Gottlieb 2002).

Fan attitudes toward Noxon, therefore, suggest a struggle for discursive and productive authority between fans and producer. By calcifying perceptions that Noxon had illegitimately taken over and sullied the series, these fans worked to negate her authority in support of their own metatextual interests. Because they so denied producerly and narrative competency, we might be tempted to call these viewers "anti-fans"—a term Gray proposes for audiences who approach texts in negatively charged, uninterested, or irritated ways (2003: 71). However, the militancy of these *Buffy* viewers remained symptomatic of fandom, not of anti-fandom in its own right. Though Gray importantly identifies alternative modes of audience engagement, anti-fans who hate a program (without necessarily viewing it) must be differentiated from disgruntled fan factions who hate episodes, eras, or producers because they perceive a violation of the larger text they still love. Fans may follow programs closely, even when meta-text and hyperdiegesis become so divergent that one would rather see the series end than continue on its displeasing current course. Fans may hate the current status quo, but their intense feelings and continued contribution to fan discourse stem from pleasurable engagement with the diegetic past. Negative discourse in these instances compartmentalizes dissatisfaction with part of the text so fans may continue enjoying other elements of it.[14]

Fan factions maneuver to secure extra-textual, intracommunal interpretative dominance, but also to counter external threats to their interests posed by institutions, declaring their own authority in legitimizing cultural production and audience relationship to it. Each power bloc, formed around factional meta-textual interests, competes to wield enough discursive power within the community to mobilize appropriate challenges to the productive power of outside institutional/industrial forces. But given the unequal resources available to antagonistic fans, is the battle for authority over the fan-text-producer relationship one that any faction can hope to win? If producers like Noxon are the Big Bad, as some fans contend, what special powers work to prevent their defeat?

The Author Strikes Back: Disciplining the Fan

While besieged producers sometimes defend themselves in online fan forums, they also enjoy privileged means of answering challenges to their discursive, producerly authority. Corporate counterdiscourses discipline and reorient the relationship of fans to textual production, reinscribing unruly audiences who produce their own texts—both fan fiction and tertiary critiques—within consumptive roles that more efficiently translate fandom into corporate profits. Corporate producers intervene in the struggles of fan-tagonism by reasserting their productive dominance, reframing "normative" fandom within "proper" spheres of consumption.

This response often manifests as legal action. Issuing injunctions against online fan productions, *Star Wars* producer George Lucas is "in the ironic position of reclaiming control over an Empire, [. . .] stamping out 'rebel' interpretations such as slash fiction or films that infringe copyright" (Brooker 2002: 88). But his Lucasfilm, Ltd. is not the only corporation to serve cease and desist orders. "The Slayer's Fanfic Archive," a *Buffy*-oriented site, was similarly shut down by Twentieth-Century Fox in 2003.[15] As Consalvo remarks, fans respond to these studio tactics by removing links to official corporate sites and organizing media blackout days that withhold the free advertising provided by fan sites (2003: 78–79). Arguably, such tactics only inconvenience media corporations; moreover, fans confronted by corporations are financially unable to mount a corresponding legal defense (Jenkins 2000: 104). Brooker (2002), Consalvo (2003), and Gwenllian-Jones (2003) have all also noted the assimilative tactics employed by studios; fans who migrate to official sites—submitting to institutional rules and surveil- lance—receive amnesty from corporate lawyers. Yet these legalistic mea- sures target only those fan uses of copyrighted intellectual property that challenge corporate productive and distributional hegemony. Because copyright law cannot curb consumer dissent, alternative strategies must rejoin the challenges represented by fans' discursive power to construct aesthetic histories of corporate production.

To this end, the television text itself has been mobilized to narratively construct "acceptable" fan activity—bolstering extra-textual legal mea- sures by building critiques of unruly fans directly into the text that sup- ports unauthorized discursive activity. Thus, while defiant fans made her a villain, Noxon concurrently oversaw the narrative construction of fans as the Big Bad in *Buffy*'s sixth season. Fancying themselves super villains ("like Dr. No"), unpopular geeks Warren, Jonathan, and Andrew become "The Evil Trio," the season's ongoing threat to Buffy. Instead of bringing the apocalypse, like most Buffy nemeses, these weak, ineffectual, pathetic villains complicate Buffy's attempts to manage greater (arguably soap- operatic) real-world problems. What distinguishes these flaccid antago- nists, however, is their intertextual referentiality to cult texts. Trapping Buffy in a looped sequence of time in the episode "Life Serial," for exam- ple, they draw parallels between their actions and those featured on cult series from which they effectively poach:

> Andrew: I just hope she solves it faster than Data did on the ep of *TNG*
>   where the *Enterprise* kept blowing up.
> Warren: Or Mulder, in the *X-Files* where the bank kept blowing up.
> Andrew: Scully wants me so bad.

Tailored to fan sensibilities, these characters make references that audi- ences with memories of these *Star Trek* and *X-Files* episodes alone would appreciate.

Simultaneously, however, such recognition implicates viewers in the deviance articulated to the Trio's social otherness and inappropriate rela- tionship to media texts. The Trio's obsessive interest in *Star Wars* col- lectibles evidences their status as undisciplined consumers amassing trivial knowledge and possessions—an alterity that recalls their prior transgressions of social norms. In the fifth season, Warren had built a submissive robotic slave to replace his flesh-and-blood girlfriend Katrina. After attempting suicide in season three, the eternally friendless Jonathan reconfigured the universe in season four's "Superstar" to make himself the center of Buffy's world—demonstrating a fannish proclivity for unauthorized manipulation of the hyperdiegesis.[16] Though Andrew debuts in the sixth season, he is established as the brother of a previously encountered teen deviant. These outcasts' pathetic villainy therefore derives from substitution of constructs—robots, parallel universes, and media texts—for normative interpersonal relationships. The only chance these infantilized men have for a nonrobotic, hetero-normative sexual encounter lies in placing a spell on Katrina in the episode "Dead Things." When this rape fails, and Warren kills Katrina, the articulation of fandom, social violation, and transgressive alterity calcifies, only reinforced by the devotion shown to Warren by an increasingly demasculinized and suggestively homosexual Andrew. Even as Buffy and Xander protect Andrew from unjust death at the hands of Willow in "Two to Go," they demasculinize him for demonstrating his fan knowledge (in this case, a triple *Star Wars* reference):

> Andrew: You think your little witch buddy's gonna stop with us? You saw her! She's a truck driving magic mama! We've got maybe seconds before Darth Rosenberg grinds everybody into Jawa Burgers and not one of your bunch has the midichlorians to stop her!
> Xander: You've never had any tiny bit of sex, have you?

Amid the "growing up" theme of season six, the fan status ascribed to Xander in prior seasons is interestingly reduced and transferred to these new characters. In condemning fannish behavior, adult Xander understands the social unacceptability of filtering reality through fantasy texts. Xander no longer makes fan references without some kind of conscious self-deprecation to mark himself off from the Trio and thus from fan deviancy. Noxon characterizes the Trio as "trying to do anything to sort of shortcut having to do adult things, like getting a job or going to school" (Sci-Fi Wire 2002). Career and heterosexual relationships thus prevent Xander from being similarly constructed as deviant fan—unlike the Trio, whose inability to form relationships outside of cult media articulates fandom to immaturity, instability, and even the violations of rape.

While embodying cult fandom in general, the Trio also narrativizes *Buffy* fans specifically. Despite their relative insignificance, these powerless fans attempt to insinuate themselves into larger (narrative) on-goings. In posing challenges (like the time loop) that produce diagnostic knowledge of Buffy's abilities, the Trio plans to redirect her attention—and that of the series—away from soapy, real-world dilemmas and towards a more fantastical direction of their meta-textual choosing. While referencing other series at the diegetic level, their extradiegetic role is as stand-ins for outspoken *Buffy* fans. Tom Lenk, the actor who plays Andrew, explains, "We're playing what the truly obsessive *Buffy* fans would be [. . .] the writers have told us that we're basically them personified" (Topel 2002). As part of the industrial discourse working to constitute a disciplined fandom, the Trio reinforces the hegemonic "truth" that fans should be disregarded, mocked, and even feared as obsessive, socially deviant outcasts.

These representations further inhibit fandom's discursive productivity by disarticulating fans from storytelling practice and rearticulating them to compliant consumption. In season seven, Andrew (sole surviving member of the Trio) becomes Buffy's prisoner-yet-pseudo-ally. In "Storyteller," Andrew's fan practices expand from referentiality to unauthorized narrative production; he effectively authors a fan video about Buffy (and, extradiegetically, *Buffy* the series), filtering narrative events through his own interpretative perspective. Andrew also rewrites his own history, excusing his crimes while also embellishing his prior villainous prowess. His sexuality still uncertain, Andrew identifies with Anya, rather than Xander, as he films a romantic conversation between the two. This unruly storyteller is ultimately confronted by Buffy (at knifepoint over the Hellmouth!) and coerced into abandoning these textually productive practices: "Stop! Stop telling stories. Life isn't a story," Buffy commands, demanding that Andrew discontinue his interpretations of the hyperdiegetic past. To be redeemed and socially rehabilitated, deviant Andrew must cease and desist—give up storytelling and submit to the narrative as the authoritative Buffy experienced it.[17] His eventual redemption is punctuated by his transformation from sexually ambiguous nerd into confirmed heterosexual, suave sage, and trusted ally. Appearing on spin-off *Angel* the next season ("The Girl in Question"), a changed Andrew offers Angel and Spike advice about "moving on" before departing with a beautiful woman on each tuxedo-clad arm. Though he still references cult texts, Andrew, like Xander, has replaced fandom with a new social discipline—seemingly that of watcher-in-training.[18] Andrew's redemption thus promises a more proper, passive, socially acceptable fan consumption.

Deployed within larger institutional discourses, the Trio's reformation of fan-text-producer relationships should not be mistaken as the malicious response of a single producer like Noxon. Leyla Harrison, a recurring character on the *The X-Files* (named in memory of a prominent fan fiction author), similarly enforces boundaries between the fan and textual productivity. Though a "fan" of Mulder and Scully, untrained Agent Harrison settles for reading reports of their exploits, rather than contributing to them. Even the *Star Trek* franchise, whose generic conventions prohibit overt acknowledgment of contemporary fandom, manages to pathologize unauthorized narrative production. Lt. Barclay, a recurring character on both *The Next Generation* and *Voyager*, is repeatedly disciplined for his addictive, unhealthy use of holodeck technology to appropriate the regular characters in virtual reality narratives. Although Hayward (1997) and Jenkins (2002) suggest that interactions between industry and audience enabled by television and new media convergence might blur the lines between production and consumption, characters like the Evil Trio allow television institutions to redraw that line and increase its resolution, rearticulating distinctions between normative audience and Othered fan, professional and amateur, producer and consumer.

Conclusion

This struggle to consensually legitimate competing knowledge claims about fans, cult texts, and their production—fan-tagonism—operates discursively to constitute hegemonies within factionalized fan communities. But internal constructions of communal interpretative consensus comprise just one front on which the war for hegemony is waged; we must also look outward since it is in the productive authority of external corporate institutions that the greatest power is mobilized. Fans attack and criticize media producers whom they feel threaten their meta-textual interests, but producers also respond to these challenges, protecting their privilege by defusing and marginalizing fan activism. As fans negotiate positions of production and consumption, antagonistic corporate discourse toils to manage that discursive power, disciplining productive fandom so it can continue to be cultivated as a consumer base. Here I have added to our catalogue of the corporate arsenal a textual strategy through which producers work to subordinate fans to their discursive authority. However, while textual representations like the Evil Trio constitute an institutional bid to circumscribe fan activity, that textuality is negotiated in turn via interpretative and evaluative debates within fandom that, through their own redefinitions and reevaluations, keep antagonistic, discursive struggles for hegemony in play. As one writer observes of the Trio, "The controversial nerds were either loved or hated by the fan base. Some adored their comedic riffs on everything sci-fi and geek-based while others were irritated by the exact same thing" (DiLullo 2003). Thus, as the Trio and other textual manifestations of the external, institutional dimension of fan-tagonism enter into fan aesthetic historiography, they promise to inspire the same kind of internal, factional fan schism explored at the outset.

Whether through interpretative, legal, or narrative measures, fan activity is discursively dominated, disciplined, and defined to preserve hegemonies of cultural power at local or institutional levels. Ultimately, the multidimensional, antagonistic dynamics of cult fandom demand that we avoid utopian models of fan community and productive participation, and engage more directly with the constitutive negotiations of hegemony.

Notes

1. Thanks to Julie D'Acci, Henry Jenkins, Jonathan Gray, Ron Becker, and Aswin Punathambekar for their helpful comments and insights on various drafts of this piece.

2. Theorizing fan-text-producer relationships complicates audience-text relationships as discussed by Nightingale (2003), accounting for both productive and consumptive fan practice and, following Gwenllian-Jones (2003: 174), industrial strategies designed to maximize audience involvement.

3. While relaxing limitations on group dynamic and generating alongside greater diversity of membership more disagreement and antagonism, online communication has not *introduced* conflictual relationships to fandom. Though insufficiently emphasized in previous scholarly work, real tensions, anxieties, and disputes were evidenced in offline fan relations (see Jenkins 1992: 187–91; Bacon-Smith 1992: 229). We might, however, still interrogate the amplifying or foregrounding effect of the Internet.

4. In addition to the dimensions of fans vs. fans and fans vs. producers, other dynamics of conflict could be similarly explored (fans vs. academics, for example).

5. Although I distinguish between larger fan interests, communities, and competing factions within them, the boundaries of discrete interest groups do not prohibit individual fans from enjoying "dual citizenship" or visiting other com-

munities; like-minded, consensual groups rarely operate in isolation without (antagonistic) interaction at a larger level. Thus, we might think of the larger fandom as a site of struggle just as we would the individual communities.

6. "Damn the 'Shippers," retrieved 2 May 2003 from http://mrsg.lunarpages. com/tv/shippers.html.

7. "Season 6 was the biggest piece of shit ever," 5–6 July 2002, retrieved 2 May 2003 from http://fireflyfans.net.

8. "Why is Joss turning our beloved show into crap?" 6 October 1998, retrieved 2 May 2003 from alt.tv.buffy-v-slayer.

9. "The Remote Controllers," 20 October 2002, retrieved 2 May 2003 from http://www.whedonesque.com.

10. "Opinion FAQ," retrieved 2 May 2003 from http://www.slayage.com/ articles/000057.html.

11. "Had an Idea," 4 November 2002, retrieved 2 May 2003 from http://firefly fans.net.

12. "Season 6 was the biggest piece of shit ever."

13. Headline: "Season Big Bad revealed (soilers) [sic]," retrieved 2 May 2003 from http://www.btvs-tabularasa.net/list/taraflash.html.

14. Jenkins recognizes this compartmentalized disappointment in his often overlooked chapter on *Beauty and the Beast* fans (1992: 132).

15. See Chilling Effects (http://www.chillingeffects.com) for more accounts of media corporations taking legal action against fan producers.

16. Larbalestier (2002) discusses Jonathan as a textual embodiment of Buffy fans.

17. Andrew briefly relapses in the later episode "Dirty Girls," including a fight to the death with Mr. Spock in his history of rogue vampire slayer Faith. Andrew was, however, sternly reprimanded.

18. The need to cultivate enthusiastic media consumption makes it counterproductive for corporate discourse to entirely rehabilitate the fan. See Gwenllian-Jones (2003).

22

Untidy

Fan Response to the Soiling of Martha Stewart's Spotless Image

Melissa A. Click

In 2002, I set out to study Martha Stewart fans in hopes of understanding Stewart's popularity in the United States at a time when women seemed to have more choices outside the home than ever before. My public calls for focus group participants drew fans I could not easily recognize as such. For me, this raised the question, What is a fan? The insider trading scandal Martha Stewart was involved in during the time period in which I conducted my interviews, October 2002 to October 2005, added a layer of complexity to my study of Stewart's fans. The scandal drew immense media attention that impacted both her celebrity and her media texts, many of which were amended to extract her presence or canceled outright.

Interestingly, the interviews I conducted with audience members of *Martha Stewart Living* revealed that fans were drawn to at least two distinct aspects of this text: Martha Stewart *the celebrity,* and *the ideas* created by Martha Stewart. As I argue below, an important component of the criticism of Stewart, and the positions her fans took as a result of this criticism, is the tension between femininity and feminism in U. S. culture; Stewart's text and persona raise questions about what an American woman can or should be. Thus, the ways in which Stewart's audiences respond to her and her media texts reveal the ways in which Stewart's blending of traditional and contemporary ways of being a woman provoked both praise and condemnation.

There is much to be learned from studying fans who do not fit traditional descriptions. Indeed, in doing so we move closer to creating a fuller picture of the ways audiences respond to media texts. In this essay, I explore the ways in which my experiences with *Martha Stewart Living* audiences raise a number of fruitful questions for further explanation about our understanding of fan behavior, the ways in which fan positions might change over time, especially in response to changes in their favored text, and how fan readings of texts reflect and impact social values.

Martha Stewart Living Omnimedia

By the time I began my focus group research in 2002, Martha Stewart Living Omnimedia was a $295-million-a-year business (Carr 2003: C5). As the highly visible focal point of her media texts, known to fans simply as "Martha," Stewart built a wildly successful business based on her own good taste. Fans could consume Stewart's advice for living through a number of formats, all of which carried nearly identical messages: books, magazines, television, radio, newspaper, and the Internet.[1] Stewart's lifestyle advice drew a huge audience; when my project began, Martha Stewart had sold more than 10 million copies of her more than thirty-four books, and the combined readership of Stewart's magazines was 10 million readers (Tyrnauer 2001: 398). Stewart's daily television programs drew 1.67 million viewers (Fine & Friedman 2003: 1). Her Kmart line included five thousand products and earned $1.6 million in sales in 2001 (Tyrnauer 2001: 398). In 2002, Martha Stewart was without question a savvy businesswoman who had successfully constructed a public personality as a trusted advisor who strove for perfection and promoted impeccable taste.

As a result of Stewart's visibility as an expert in matters of high taste, a perfectionist in the home, and a successful businesswoman, her image was repeatedly critiqued in U. S. popular culture. Underneath many of these critiques lay the ways in which Martha Stewart's subject matter in her media texts (images of domestic perfection), when combined with her public persona (a divorcee with seemingly strained personal relationships), confused gender norms. Furthermore, Stewart's media texts, in many ways, catered to women who work in their homes, yet Stewart, as one of the most powerful businesswomen in the United States, had very little time to lead the domestic life she detailed. Popular critiques of Stewart hinted at or aimed to demonstrate that her public persona was only a façade—and behind that façade was an entirely different person. However, in early 2002, none of the reports about Stewart's alleged imperfections was weighty enough to topple her image as a know-it-all good girl.

What I find intriguing about Stewart as a public figure is that since her rise to popularity in the mid-1990s, she has been a public figure that audiences simultaneously love *and* love to hate; as a result, some audience members feel reluctant to consider themselves "fans" because of Stewart's public persona and its ridicule in the media, and the degree to which Stewart's messages focus on the commonly undervalued realm of the domestic. However, many nevertheless value the emphasis Stewart places on every intimate detail of "homekeeping" and the empire she built in the process; they feel that Stewart elevated the role of the homemaker in U. S. culture. Interestingly, these "reluctant fans" were drawn to Stewart's texts, yet readily distanced themselves from Stewart the celebrity.

Analysis of Stewart's texts and audiences became more complicated by two events in 2002: first, the publication in April of the unauthorized biography *Martha Inc.* by Christopher Byron, which portrayed Stewart as "a foulmouthed, manipulative shrew who dumped her husband for, among other transgressions, not stacking the firewood *just so*" (Naughton 2002: 36, original emphasis); and second, the allegations in June that Stewart improperly traded her shares of ImClone stock in December of 2001. These events, in Stabile's words, marked the beginning of "a reversal of fortune that the US news media aggressively and delightedly chronicled" (2004: 315).

NBC turned Byron's biography into a movie-of-the-week, which aired in May 2003 and depicted Stewart as "a backstabbing, egomaniacal control freak" (O'Connell 2003). Stewart was indicted on nine federal counts in June 2003. Her trial began in January 2004 and ended with a conviction in March 2004. After her conviction, Stewart's name on her flagship magazine *Living* was reduced in size, and her presence in the magazine virtually disappeared; distributor Viacom dropped Stewart's syndicated TV show altogether (Tyrnauer 2005: 178). In early 2005, Martha Stewart Living Omnimedia announced a record loss of $60 million in 2004 (Naughton 2005: 36).

Byron's biography and the ImClone scandal fractured Stewart's seemingly spotless image and drew incredible media attention. As Shaw suggests, Stewart's public persona played a significant role in the media's treatment of Stewart's troubles: "because she peddles perfection, when she screws up she is all the more attractive as a target of ridicule" (2003: 57). Complicating matters, Stewart's indictment, trial, and conviction coexisted with media coverage of a number of corporate scandals at Enron, Tyco, WorldCom, Adelphia Cable, and Global Crossing. These arguably more egregious cases drew much less media attention, and as Stabile found, far fewer mean-spirited accounts: "The language used to describe Stewart's demise manifests a spiteful gleefulness—a tone strikingly absent from coverage of [the individuals at the center of other corporate scandals]" (2004: 324).

Importantly, the prominence of Stewart's legal troubles in the media and the public debate over the fairness of her treatment—both in the courtroom and in the media—provoked Martha Stewart's audience, encouraging the once reluctant to take a stand on Stewart's presumed guilt or innocence. As my focus group interviews progressed, discussion of Stewart's own media texts took a back seat and my project shifted to examine the media coverage of the events that tarnished Stewart's image and to explore the positions people took to explain Stewart's indictment and conviction. What follows is an account of two important groups in Stewart's audience and the ways in which the ImClone scandal made the distinctions between the two groups less clear.

Method

The research I discuss is based upon a focus group interview model in which I gathered data about audiences' relationships to and feelings about Martha Stewart and her media offerings through open-ended discussion with groups of participants (see Lewis 1991; Lindlof & Taylor 2002; Lunt & Livingstone 1996). I conducted a pilot focus group interview in April 1999 and eight additional focus group interviews between October 2002 and July 2004. In total, I interviewed thirty-eight people.[2]

Each group meeting was audio recorded for transcription purposes, and the transcripts were examined for similarities and dissimilarities in both what was said and what was not said in each group. In my analysis, I uncovered general patterns and made comparisons to see if and how the differences in demographic characteristics and exposure to Martha Stewart within and across groups affected group members' attitudes toward Martha Stewart and Martha Stewart Living Omnimedia. However, one of the most interesting aspects of my research was the ways in which the participants related to *Martha Stewart Living* and Martha Stewart, and the ways in which these relationships changed in response to the ImClone scandal.

Martha Stewart Fans?

One of my most difficult—and most basic—research tasks was determining who was a Martha Stewart fan and what that meant. Of the thirty-eight interview participants, twenty-five participants responded "yes," and six responded "no" when asked whether they considered themselves to be a fan of Martha Stewart. Seven hesitant respondents answered "don't know," "not really," "quasi," "yes/no," "to a certain extent," and "undecided." Even more intriguing, many of the respondents who replied that they were not fans of Martha Stewart knew more about Stewart's personal life and media texts than those who responded that they were fans of Martha Stewart; and the participants who responded that they were fans of Martha Stewart repeatedly expressed ambivalence when discussing Stewart and her media texts.

Making sense of the positions the interview participants took required that I reexamine the term "fan." Jenkins offers one definition: "one becomes a fan not by being a regular viewer of a particular program but by translating that viewing into some type of cultural activity, by sharing feelings and thoughts about the program content with friends, by joining a community of other fans who share common interests" (1988: 88). Many of my interviewees were regular viewers, but not all of them felt comfortable taking part in public activities or discussions about Stewart, and none of them shared that they were part of a community of other fans. Were they still fans?

Tulloch and Jenkins differentiate between fans and followers, suggesting that fans are "active participants within fandom as a social, cultural and interpretive institution," and followers are "audience members who regularly watch and enjoy [media texts] but who claim no larger social identity on the basis of this consumption" (1995: 23). This distinction comes closer to explaining the identifications of my interview participants; but through the course of my interviews, it became increasingly clear that many of the people I interviewed in Stewart's audience were both "active participants" and regular consumers, yet they adamantly disliked Stewart and did not call themselves fans. Where do they fit in?

Gray calls attention to two important, and often overlooked, types of fans: "anti-fans" and "non-fans." "Anti-fans," he argues, are those "who strongly dislike a given text or genre, considering it inane, stupid, morally bankrupt and/or aesthetic drivel" (Gray 2003: 70). Though they evaluate a text entirely oppositely from fans as commonly defined, Gray suggests that anti-fans may be as intimately involved in texts as fans, and may be similarly organized and visible. "Non-fans," on the other hand, are those "who do view or read a text, but not with any intense involvement" (Gray 2003: 74). Unlike fans and anti-fans, non-fans may experience the text from a considerable distance and thus while they may enjoy a text, they "watch when they can rather than must" (Gray 2003: 74). Gray's offerings help to explain those who adamantly oppose Stewart and those who are not sure if they are Stewart fans. However, like fans and followers as described above, anti-fans and non-fans are clear-cut and separate categories. Some of the audience members I interviewed described that their feelings for Stewart changed as the ImClone scandal progressed. Can one audience member exhibit differing fan characteristics, and how do we account for changes in fandom over time?

Hills persuasively argues that fandom is not a "thing" but is instead performative (2002: xi). He suggests that a question that audience researchers have not yet addressed is "what fandom does culturally" (Hills 2002: xii). This echoes Jensen's claim that "fandom is an aspect of how we make sense of the world, in relation to mass media, and in relation to our historical, social, cultural location" (1992: 27). The people I interviewed may or may not be fans—and their fandom no doubt changed with time and the progression of the ImClone scandal. Importantly, the ambivalences Martha Stewart fans expressed as they put down and took up new fan positions in response to ImClone demonstrate that being a fan is a complex experience affected by the social contexts in which a text exists.

While my interview participants were drawn to *Martha Stewart Living* as a text, the ways in which they viewed the television program, read the magazine, and responded to Martha Stewart in general differed.[3] While I hesitate to construct separate fan groups, a distinct pattern of fanship did develop as my interviews progressed. In my research, I have found two different groups in Stewart's audience that I believe might be called "fans": those who are drawn to Stewart's texts and products for their perceived high quality and their beautiful presentation, but disassociate from her persona (*Living* fans); and those who are drawn to public debate over Stewart's persona and read her media texts as a way of watching for cues about Stewart's "true" persona (Martha fans). The line between the two groups is fuzzy, however, and fans' identifications are not static—they moved quite a bit over the course of the ImClone scandal.

Living *Fans*

The first group I discuss are the fans who prefer the information Stewart delivers through her various media texts (almost all of which share the title *Living*) to her public persona. *Living* fans are drawn to Martha Stewart because of their interest in what she does and how she does it; but unlike fans as traditionally understood, they distance themselves from Stewart's persona in response to public criticism of her actions—whether in response to criticism of Stewart by members in the small group interview, in response to their own experiences with or beliefs about Stewart, or in response to media stories about Stewart.

What I heard repeatedly from the people I interviewed is a sense that their feelings about Stewart's texts sometimes are separate from their feelings about Martha Stewart the celebrity. *Living* fans were drawn to *Martha Stewart Living* not for its host, Martha Stewart, but for its content. Candace[4] clearly articulates this: "it's not her personality, because I find that she's kind of phony in a way[. . . .] The show, the presentation and what she does I'm interested in, but her personally, there are others on the Food Network that I prefer to her." Beatrice likewise explained, "I don't really watch her, I watch what she's doing."

Despite their selection of *Martha Stewart Living* based on the content of the show, most participants said they watch more to observe than to actually undertake the projects Stewart offers. Again and again, interviewees described Stewart's programs and periodicals as an outlet for relaxation and escape. Of Stewart's television programs, Karla conveyed, "There are beautiful things on it, it's relatively mindless, I don't have to think a whole lot." Delores suggested that the magazine takes her "away from all the stuff in my life, it's relaxing."

Even though fans of Stewart's media texts do not often undertake Stewart's projects, they do collect information on tasks that they may want to undertake at a later time. Grace reported that she has "a ton of magazine clippings that I will put to use one day." Hailey similarly offered that she and her spouse clip information deemed useful from Stewart's magazine: "we cut out the articles that we think are going to be useful and we do have a giant binder in the house that we do use."

While *Living* fans take great pleasure from watching and reading Stewart's texts, many of them are reluctant to share their interest in Stewart with others, in part because of the public criticism of Stewart. Carole revealed that she used to be less open about her interest in Stewart than she now is: "I was sort of like a closet Martha Stewart devotee for a long time [. . .] I was so stupid about it and then I decided 'this is ridiculous,' but so many people I knew were really discouraging about her." When discussing his interest in Stewart, Aaron confessed that "I love to talk about her, and I think she's fascinating, and part of me feels really pathetic, too, that I read her." Rachel is so guarded about her feelings for Stewart that she did not even tell anyone that she was attending my interview: "I kind of like her stuff, but I wouldn't tell anybody necessarily and that's the straight up truth."

A few participants disclosed that their friends and family teased them for their interest in Stewart. Carole is teased by one of her daughters: "She's one of those really practical people [. . .] and she works [. . .] and it's a little too much for her, she laughs at that, good natured, but you know." Pamela reported that sharing her interest in Stewart with friends and family sometimes "elicits a giggle or an eye roll." Mary reported that her two sons think she is "psychotic" for taping Stewart's television programs and keeping a well-marked collection of videotapes.

Despite the possibility for teasing or scorn, a few fans openly maintain their interest in Stewart; these *Living* fans use humor to reference their interest in Stewart in daily contexts. Lane, a clergywoman, disclosed that she has referenced Stewart in her sermons: "if I talk about [. . .] how people get stressed out before the holidays and we want everything to be perfect, I'll confess to having been in the 'Martha Zone.'" Mary relayed that she often quotes Stewart to others: "I say it to everyone, it drives my family to distraction. I say it to people at work [. . .] 'Oh, that's a good thing, like my friend Martha will always say.'"

In sum, *Living* fans are drawn to *Martha Stewart Living* for its content and beauty. They admire Stewart's expertise, attention to detail, and professionalism. While they use the text to relax or escape, and collect the information contained in the text, *Living* fans do not necessarily undertake the projects Stewart demonstrates. Many *Living* fans suggest that they are fans, yet they can be reserved about their interest, in part because of the public ridicule of Martha Stewart. Only a few are such strong fans that they do not care what others think of them. In many ways, criticism of Stewart, and the impact it has on *Living* fans, shames them into silence about their interest in domestic activities. If, as I argue, the controversy around Martha Stewart reflects the push-and-pull relationship between femininity and feminism, the reluctance of many *Living* fans to openly own their interest in *Martha Stewart Living* suggests that the devaluation of the domestic sphere continues.[5]

Martha Fans

The next group of fans I felt I could identify as such were, unlike *Living* fans, less interested in the *information* Stewart conveys through her media texts than they were in Stewart's *persona*—as constructed through both media texts and her very public persona as a celebrity. Many of these fans made fun of Stewart and/or adamantly disliked her; however, like Gray's anti-fans, they were intimately familiar with Stewart's life and her media texts.

Many Martha fans regularly watched Stewart on television, read her magazines, and followed stories about Stewart in the popular press. Unlike the *Living* fans, they described their interest in Stewart as connected to Stewart as a celebrity, not the ideas that she offers. Correlated with the degree to which these fans were conflicted or adamant in their dislike of Stewart, their reactions to her ranged from amusement to hatred. Nadia offered that she found Stewart to be humorous: "I like watching her shows, they're somewhat entertaining and it is just hilarious watching her [. . .] it's just a trip to me." Abby reported that in Stewart's television shows "there was a tone that was patronizing, there was an edge that was just like, I wanted to say 'F.U.' to her."

Martha fans used media stories and gossip to help construct their opinions of Stewart. Maggie used what she read in Jerry Oppenheimer's 1997 unauthorized biography of Stewart to develop a position on Stewart's personal life: "I think she [. . .] keeps in touch with her sister and the biographer tried to paint a very negative picture of her as a mother, but I think she's very close to the daughter, they do things together and then, then friends, I think she has a pretty rich social life." Rachel shared that she watched NBC's May 2003 made-for-TV movie, *Martha Inc;* she described it as portraying Stewart as "really bitchy" and "super non-forgiving."

Many interviewees reacted to what they perceived as a rigidity in Stewart. Kira described Stewart as "a bitch on wheels." Jackie described Stewart as "elitist" and "arrogant." For Rachel, Stewart has an "arrogance" as if she's "the standard," which she explained makes it "hard for me to watch the entire thing because it's just her half the time and there's no, there's no room for flexibility at all."

Despite the fact that these "fans" do not sound much like fans, many are regular viewers and readers of Stewart's media texts. Interestingly, many participants watched Stewart's television show just to watch Stewart's behavior, especially with guests. Sarah's description of her motivation was similar to several participants' reasons for watching Stewart: "I'm more interested in her as a person than anything she does, so, I'm just fascinated to see how this dour, creepy woman, what's she going to be like on her show today?" The interest of the guest segments for these viewers lies in the challenge of Stewart's authority, especially because she is self-constructed as an expert who has a vast knowledge and performs tasks perfectly. Aaron described that he enjoyed segments in which Stewart interacted with a guest; he felt this is when one could see Stewart's "true" persona: "when she interacts with other people [. . .] you kind of see this iciness in her that you always hear about in her."

Unlike *Living* fans who reported that they watched *Martha Stewart Living* to relax and escape, Martha fans reported amusement, irritation, or anger when watching the show. Janice insisted that she "mouths off" at Stewart while she is watching her program. Maribel reported that she sometimes phones her friends when she is watching Stewart on television to share her amusement or frustration, "I'll call people when I'm watching Martha Stewart and be like 'Oh my God that idiot's at the miso factory, you've got to see this,' and then my friend Sara's at home, and she pulls on the TV and she's like, 'What a fuck-wad!'"

While the Martha fans are drawn to Stewart for different reasons than the *Living* fans, they similarly are devoted in their interest in acquiring information; instead of collecting and treasuring Stewart's texts, they read biographies and parodies of her, and create or seek information critical of Stewart. Emily reported that she writes parodies of Stewart's "projects that may or may not be worth the effort" and emails them to her friends and her mother. A number of the interviewees enjoyed parodies of Stewart on *Saturday Night Live;* Rachel related that these parodies "are really funny, just because she goes on and on about the little particularness [sic] of certain things." Several respondents discussed taking pleasure in a series of published parodies by Tom Connor. Olivia mentioned that the parody she owns "portrays her as real, very difficult to work for; she's literally beating up the waiters and waitresses at this wedding she's catering and the people that are working for her."

Unlike *Living* fans, Martha fans are drawn to *Martha Stewart Living* to observe and critique Martha Stewart. They dislike Stewart for what they perceive as arrogance and hostility, especially as these behaviors play out with guests on Stewart's TV show. To Martha fans, Martha Stewart is a joke; they are provoked to respond to the text. Martha fans are more likely to share their interest in Stewart with others, yet their interest lies in critiquing Stewart the celebrity. The critiques of these fans are, no doubt, part of what keeps *Living* fans silent about their interest in *Martha Stewart Living*. The draw for Martha fans, at least in part, is to question Stewart's authority; as a result, the lifestyle advice she offers can be demeaned and ignored. Martha fans' debates over Stewart's worth are expressions of the conflict between women's roles in and out of the home. Martha fans' critiques of Stewart position her interest in and attention to the domestic as trivial. Thus this group prioritizes women's empowerment outside the home as more relevant to U. S. women's lives.

ImClone

My interviews with fans spanned nearly the entire time in which the ImClone matter was unfolding. Each interview allowed me to "check in" with Stewart's fans to gauge their reactions to the ImClone situation as it progressed. While most of the fans I interviewed did support and defend Stewart's actions through ImClone, some of the respondents rebuked Stewart for getting into trouble. However, despite their criticism of Stewart's role in the ImClone scandal, both the *Living* and the Martha fans were supportive of Stewart and were likely to express that Stewart had been treated unfairly.

Fans' feelings about Stewart's treatment softened their feelings for her and made them more sympathetic to Stewart as a celebrity. As aforementioned, the allegations, indictment, and conviction of Stewart unfolded at the same time major corporate scandals were unfolding at Enron, Tyco, and WorldCom, among others. Many fans referenced these scandals and used them as a benchmark for judging Stewart's alleged crimes. Every interviewee expressed, in differing degrees, that Stewart's crimes were lesser in comparison. Pamela offered that Stewart's case was "small potatoes" compared to the other corporate scandals. Tom offered, "Martha Stewart, that was pennies compared to what's going on, she just got a raw deal."

Those who believed that Stewart was treated unfairly referenced the public's negative opinions of Stewart to explain why she might have been an easy target; this is an interesting move for Martha fans, most of whom had previously participated in the negative constructions of Stewart. A few fans suggested that the media's appetite for scandal influenced some of the publicity around the case. When asked to explain why she felt the allegations about Stewart's stock sales were unjust, Grace replied, "I think the media eats up the idea of Martha Stewart doing something wrong." Max also referenced what he believed was the media's constant focus on the details of Stewart's life: "it was just blasted all over, [...] I think it goes back to people like to see the perfect fall or like to see someone that's this far up and knock them down a few pegs." Some fans argued that hatred of Martha Stewart blew the ImClone scandal out of proportion. Aaron, for example, suggested that Stewart "was made a scapegoat, you know, there were a lot people that always hated her and they were looking for any excuse they could to burn her at the stake, so to speak; and I think this was the perfect opportunity to do that. Or try." Abby similarly stated that she felt that Stewart had "been targeted, people have gone after, people really hate Martha."

A number of participants felt gender discrimination was at the heart of the supposed mistreatment of Stewart. Nadia emphasized that she thinks it is "clear" that Stewart was targeted "because she's a woman." Karla maintained that the treatment of Stewart "reeks of sexism." Abby saw the treatment of Stewart as a reprimand for being too powerful: "You want power? We're going to punish women of power. You want to have this big empire? You're going to get punished."

Importantly, many of the Martha fans were so angered with what they perceived as mistreatment of Stewart through the progression of the ImClone scandal that some who had previously had negative feelings about Stewart softened their positions. Rachel, who had previously said she had difficulty watching Stewart because she seemed arrogant, now said, "I feel bad for her and everything [...] I just don't want to listen to the media say 'yes, this is deserved of her' because I really wonder, is it?" Jackie, who had previously called Stewart "the bitch of life," expressed that she felt Stewart was treated unfairly in comparison to male corporate executives: "I resent how she's being handled as opposed to the way, like, Kenny Boy Lay, and Skilling and all those folks [are being treated]." Abby was perhaps the most sympathetic of all of the non-fans; soon after Stewart was sentenced, she reflected upon the changes in her feelings about Stewart:

> I like her more now, I'm much more sympathetic and empathetic to Martha
> now, much more so. Now my thoughts about Martha Stewart are more

about that she's been targeted as a strong dynamic woman in a sexist society [. . .] I want to like rescue her.

When I asked *Living* fans if their feelings about Stewart would change if she was found guilty, almost all of them said no. Candace explained her position this way: "she's not my moral compass, I'm just going to her for information and I like the way it's presented." Nadia, who answered my question after Stewart had been found guilty, also maintained that the decision did not change her position about Stewart "at all"; she said, "I would still watch her show, yeah I don't care. If it's on when she's out of jail, I'll watch it."

Through the ImClone scandal, *Living* fans and Martha fans amended their positions on *Martha Stewart Living* and Martha Stewart. *Living* fans finally articulated their frustration with the negative public construction of Martha Stewart. Whereas the impact of this negative construction had previously made them reluctant to communicate their interest in Stewart's media texts, the public discourse about Stewart's alleged mistreatment through ImClone gave them courage to discuss their interest in her. Martha fans, partially responsible for the negative public construction of Martha Stewart, softened their critiques of Stewart and supported her by critiquing the U.S. legal and media systems. As both fan groups rallied around Martha Stewart, the distinctions between them became more unambiguous.

Conclusion

Ang, in her study of *Dallas* fans who expressed both love and hate for the show, offered that hating and loving are "only labels people stick on the way in which they relate in general to the programme" (1985: 13). These labels, far from being unambiguous descriptions of fan positions, relate to the ways in which viewers react to a text. Ang argued that inevitably viewers' experiences of a text are "ambivalent and contradictory" (1985: 13). In my study of *Martha Stewart Living* audience members, I found exactly the ambivalence Ang described. I was able to isolate two distinct audiences: one who loved Stewart's texts and one who hated Martha Stewart; however, in neither case were these categories stable—conflicted fans moved between both groups, especially as the ImClone scandal progressed.

Interestingly, when Martha Stewart, and her texts as a result, were threatened with legal action and received incredibly negative media attention, the differences between the groups lessened and they both rallied to support Stewart against what they believed was unfair treatment. This movement in response to real threats to *Martha Stewart Living* and Martha Stewart suggests that it may not be useful to study fans as stable categories, but instead it may be more useful to study what fan beliefs and practices mean and how they function culturally. In this case, the fan positions taken before ImClone suggest that the public devaluation of the domestic sphere was strong enough to keep *Living* fans silent. The negative popular construction of Martha Stewart as a celebrity, in part because she did not clearly perform gender roles fitting of a powerful public U. S. woman, aided this process. Ridicule of Stewart, an activity practiced by Martha fans, thus served to discipline Stewart's power and delegitimize the focus of her media texts, namely, domestic information and projects. Both fan groups changed their positions in the context of the ImClone scandal, in which Stewart's perceived power was reduced and she was positioned as a victim; both fan groups believed Stewart was mistreated and thus rallied to support her.

Fan positions and media texts are never stable or final. Studying audiences as classifiable groups keeps us from understanding the ways in which audiences adapt to texts over time. In March 2005, Stewart was released from Alderson Federal Prison for Women to incredible media fanfare; it seems that punishment made Stewart a more likeable figure. Stewart spent the five months of her house arrest planning a comeback. In September 2005, she launched two new television shows: *Martha,* a live reworked version of her daily show, and *Martha Stewart: The Apprentice,* a spin-off of Donald Trump's *Apprentice.* Martha Stewart and her media texts continue to evolve, and her audiences will also as a result.

Notes

1. Because the various formats through which Stewart delivers her messages are quite similar, I refer to each of these formats as one unified text, *Martha Stewart Living*. Indeed, almost all of the different formats share this moniker, and the skill with which Stewart repackages information from one format for another has been duly noted (Tyrnauer 2001: 398).

2. Though I do not have the space to list participants' demographic characteristics here, I interviewed participants from a range of demographic characteristics, including sex, race, class, and sexual identity.

3. Though not the focus of this essay, elsewhere (Click forthcoming) I examine

the important impact of fans' genders, classes, sexualities, and races on their relationships to Martha Stewart.

4. The names of the people I interviewed have been changed to conceal their identities.

5. Twenty-three respondents shared that they considered themselves to be feminists. The strength with which respondents claimed feminism contributed to the positions fans took on the gendered messages produced by Martha Stewart's persona and her lifestyle suggestions yet seems to have no bearing on whether respondents were *Living* or Martha fans—feminists were equally distributed in both groups.

23

The Anti-Fan within the Fan

Awe and Envy in Sport Fandom

Vivi Theodoropoulou

Anti-fans are people with clear dislikes.[1] They are people who, for a variety of reasons, hate or intensely dislike and have strong negative views or feelings about a certain text, genre, or personality (Gray 2003). This chapter looks at a particular category of anti-fans: those whose status as such is defined by the fact that they are fans. It looks at the anti-fan within the fan. It aims to demonstrate cases where fandom is a precondition of anti-fandom and to illuminate instances when for a fan anti-fandom is given and set. These are cases where two fan objects are clear-cut or traditional rivals, thus inviting fans to become anti-fans of the "rival" object of admiration. It suggests that under such circumstances, a fan becomes an anti-fan of the object that "threatens" his/her own, and of that object's fans. Thus, when A and B are the opposing fandom objects, fans of A are anti-fans of B and of B's fans, and vice versa.

The chapter argues that such anti-fans emerge whenever binary oppositions are established between two fan objects. It proposes that this kind of anti-fandom is fostered particularly in the realm of spectator sports and is embedded in the nature of such sports that promote incessant competition and ranking. Inspired by Thucydides (1920 [431 BC]), it applies the term "αντίπαλον δέος" ("*antipalon deos*") to argue that it is a series of emotions such as fear, admiration, respect, and envy for the *opposing threat* that cause hatred and anti-fandom of this kind. More importantly, it demonstrates how fans participate in such bipolar structures.

The focus of the chapter is on football. It explores fans of the two most popular and famously rival clubs in Greece, Olympiakos and Panathinaikos. The two clubs have shared a deep rivalry since their founding. Olympiakos is the *opposing threat* and *counterforce* to Panathinaikos and vice versa. This rivalry is one of the classic and most acknowledged bipolar structures in European football,[2] with the two teams being considered mutually exclusive and antagonistic fan objects. Based on a series of interviews and group discussions with fans of the two teams that took place in spring 2005,[3] the chapter exemplifies the conditions and provides a definition of such anti-fandom. It suggests that the emotional investment in anti-fandom is significant to the construction of fan identity. It concludes that bipolar oppositions act as the definitive mechanism of distinction to the outsider and enable identification with the team. In this sense, and by emphasizing the importance of identification against the rival, the chapter suggests that anti-fandom may also work as a form of language, structured, like language, through binary oppositions.

The Concept of the Anti-Fan

Even though popular culture and fandom literature have been looking at instances when audiences feel uncomfortable with or ambivalent about given genres or texts (see Alters 2003; Barker & Brooks 1998; Barker, Arthurs, & Harindranath 2001), Jonathan Gray (2003) was the first to categorize the practice of (actively) disliking genres, texts, or personalities as "anti-fandom." Anti-fans do not dislike popular texts for nothing. On the contrary, they are often familiar with their objects of dispassion and aware of the reasons for their dislike. According to Gray, "anti-fans must find cause for their dislike in something. This something may vary from having previously watched the show and having found it intolerable, to having a dislike for its genre, director or stars; to having seen previews or ads, or seen or heard unfavorable reviews" (2003: 71). The discussion of anti-fandom has thus far outlined moral and ethical objections, and textual and class considerations, as the most essential underlying principles of opposition to texts and personalities. Be the text *Television without Pity* postings (Gray 2005), *The Simpsons* (Alters 2003), or David Cronenberg's film *Crash* (Barker, Arthurs, & Harindranath 2001), it is predominantly the moral value of the text as interpreted and received by the reader that triggers anti-fandom.

However, there is another anti-fandom cluster that, so far, has not been discussed or examined in fan culture studies in much detail: anti-fandom caused and triggered by fandom. This type of anti-fandom encloses cases where the dislike of object A results from liking object B; where the hatred for something is dictated by the love for something else and the need to protect the "loved one."

In this sense, the anti-fan is the person who hates the fan object of another fan for the simple reason that this object is in direct, straightforward, or historical competition with her/his own object of admiration. This way, an anti-fan is always a fan. I would like to suggest that binary oppositions between fan objects are a precondition for such cases of anti-fandom. The two competing objects have to be in an outright rivalry with each other. Often, this means that the competence and skills of the two objects, which are in direct competition, are near equivalent (or perceived to be near equivalent), and it is this equivalence that makes the opposing fan object a threat to the fan's object and makes her/him an anti-fan.

Sport genres are the perfect place for anti-fans to be "produced," because one of the central meanings of sports is competition. TV and music genres perhaps do not provide such anti-fans with the same ease. On TV and music, the competition is not direct, and the competing objects are less frequently mutually exclusive. However, in cases of textual proximity, binary oppositions that invite anti-fandom may be established. *Star Wars* fans' dislike of *Star Trek* is a recorded case (Brooker 2002).

This concept of the anti-fan emerged in my early study on fandom and everyday life. All participating sports fans expressed their hatred for the opponent of their object of affection that they considered the biggest threat. Whatever bipolar oppositions were constructed (Manchester United vs. Arsenal, Manchester United vs. Liverpool, Olympiakos vs. Panathinaikos), the underlying principal was a feeling of awe for the "rival" (Theodoropoulou 1999).

"*Antipalon deos*" is the notion behind the conceptual framework of this anti-fan definition.[4] Thucydides (1920: 3.11.2) used the term to signify the state of *reciprocity of apprehension* between the members of the Athenian alliance. According to him, an alliance depends upon balanced fear that is rooted in a stable balance of power among its members (see Crane 1998: ch. 7). The use of the term has been extended in modern Greek to also express the mutual fear between opponents, enemies, or adversaries that ensures unity and cohesion in the interior of the rival camps, and a state of balance between them (Babiniotis 1998). It is the "counterforce," "counter-awe," or "opposing threat" to something that guarantees the balance of power.[5] Prior to Thucydides, Homer (1999) used the word "*deos*" (awe) in his writings to denote the (physical) fear during a fight,[6] while, after Thucydides, the ancient Greek lexicographer Hesychios summed up the meaning of the term as undying "fear and respect" (Chantraine 1964).

The notion of anti-fandom I propose entails a similar sense of fear and respect for the object that acts as counterforce to an object of admiration. The fact that something is good enough to be a counterforce to a fan object is what creates a balance of fear and makes an anti-fan. The conditions that make Olympiakos the counterforce to Panathinaikos are historically specific and long lasting. A brief overview of the formation and evolution of Greek football will provide the context within which such bipolar oppositions have been created.

A Brief Socio-Historical Overview of Loathing

Sandvoss (2003) argues that cultural practices such as football fandom cannot be examined in isolation from their historical context, or the socio-historical and economic framing of football itself. As elsewhere, football in Greece follows and reflects the historical and sociopolitical circumstances of the country.[7] Overall, both football and football fandom have been organized and developed since the first decade of the twentieth century on the basis of socio-historical characteristics such as social class, descent, origin, cultural traditions, neighborhood, district organization, and composition of towns (Bogiopoulos & Milakas 2005).

In the period between the two world wars and because of imbalanced growth, a "parochial rivalry" between city and periphery started to manifest throughout Greece. The bipolar oppositions Athens-Piraeus and north-south are indicative of a phenomenon that was encountered throughout the country: the geographical rivalry between the bourgeois cities and towns and the periphery. It is anchored in the fact that the bourgeois centers gathered the economic, political, and administrative powers of the country and people from higher socioeconomic strata, while the rural areas and the periphery of towns were populated by the working class and refugees, isolated from the action and the "center." Such bipolar rivalries were gradually transfused into football. In this class rivalry, whose essence is refracted through geographical and "land-planning" reflections, rests the primary reason for the rivalry between the eternal bipolar opposition of Olympiakos-Panathinaikos[8] (Bogiopoulos & Milakas 2005).

Panathinaikos was formed in 1908 when its ancestor team POA (Athens Football Club) was founded. The club acquired its current name PAO (Panathinaikos Athletic Group) in 1924. The Group is based in Athens and, as the name indicates, represents the whole of Athens municipality (pan-Athena). It has green as its color and the trefoil as its emblem, and alternative name. Even though the group's athletic activities go beyond football to other sports, it is the football team that is the group's pride and joy. Olympiakos Fun Club of Piraeus (OSFP) was established as an athletic association in 1925 out of the merger of two sports clubs based in the port of Attica, Piraeus, situated only a few miles away from the Athens center. It is the team of the wider area of Piraeus. As with Panathinaikos, despite Olympiakos athletic association having expanded into many sports, it is football that dominates. The team's color is red and its emblem is the laurel-wreathed head of an athlete, to correspond with the Olympic idea denoted in its name. The alternative to the team's name is "Thrylos," the Greek word for "legend."

Both clubs display an impressive hall of national trophies. The sweeping majority of Greek championships and cups in the history of the Greek football league have been won by either of the two teams. Olympiakos has overall performed better in pan-Hellenic tournaments and won more national championships and cups, while Panathinaikos has a more impressive course in Europe, with participation in more European tournaments such as the European Champions Cup, the UEFA Cup, and European Champions League.

Since the beginning of their history, the two teams have been constructed as *opposing threats* to one another. Panathinaikos was founded first. The class rivalry between the capital city of Athens and the labor neighborhood of the port of Piraeus, as well as the geographical proximity of the two areas, which was always inviting comparisons between the two, and perhaps magnifying the differences, made the middle-class circles of Piraeus feel disconnected from the capital. In particular, Olympiakos was not only founded so that the Piraeus working-class people and harbor workers could find outlets to sports and leisure but also so that its upper-middle-class founders could have the satisfaction of creating a *principal antithesis* to Panathinaikos of the urban center, of gaining prestige, and of measuring up to the Athenian middle-class society. It was the Piraeus middle class, their aspiration of upward social mobility and success, that led them to the creation of Olympiakos, as the foil to Panathinaikos. The historical backdrop to the rivalry is a class division and a sense of parochialism between the teams' fans, along with the fact that both teams have traditionally been the major contenders of the Greek league, always constituting a threat to one another.

Since its professionalization in the 1970s, Greek football has gradually become more commercialized and commodified. The competition and antagonism between the two teams has been strengthened. However, some of the distinctions between what could in older times have been considered "preconditions" of fandom for the two teams, such as residential proximity, or social and economic stratification, have, by all means, weakened. You do not have to be a resident of Athens or middle class to support Panathinaikos; you do not need to be working class or living in Piraeus to be a fan of Olympiakos. Both teams currently enjoy a pan-Hellenic fan base and aficionados from any walk of life.

Negatively Constructed Difference as a Means of Identity Construction

However, even though bonds of socioeconomic background and locality are not as relevant as they used to be, current fans of both teams essentially reproduce and preserve stereotypes and distinctive marks rooted in the original social class difference of the earliest fan base of Panathinaikos and Olympiakos. Thus the fan identity is socially and culturally constructed in the sense that a fan and her/his fan identity is defined in relation to her/his anti-fan and all the socio-historical baggage the counterforce carries. Despite the changes in particular conditions, the history of both teams and of their fan groups is still imposing identity positions. Fans are well aware of these, take them up, and incorporate them—albeit in a more modern frame of thinking—in their forming and defending of their fan identity. On top of that, the *"antipalon deos"* ethos is preserved and intensified by the strong antagonism and lasting good performance of the two clubs and by the efforts of the management to sustain the binary opposition. Thus, the contemporary identity of the one club and its fan base is still defined in relation to the other.

Currently, then, and as my interviews confirmed, Panathinaikos's fans frame themselves as of upscale aesthetics and quality of behavior, critical and demanding of their team and its management, and confident. Olympiakos's fans in their self-representation, on the other hand, give more value to commitment and sentiment, are more passionate, and support their team actively by going to the football matches. They are the blue-collar fans. These characteristics are ridiculed when taken up by the anti-fans. Olympiakos fans paint Panathinaikos fans, their anti-fans, as being lazy and spoiled, not going to the field when their team is going through a bad season, as pretentiously intellectual, and as not being "masculine" enough. Meanwhile, according to Panathinaikos, Olympiakos's fans are sexist chauvinists, hot-blooded thugs, and hooligans. The following abstract of a focus group is indicative of the barriers fans set to distinguish themselves from "rival" fans. The dialogue between Tom, a fan of Panathinaikos, and Aspa, a fan of Olympiakos, highlights and magnifies the perceived difference between the two teams' fans:

> Tom: Well, Panathinaikos' fans, we are different. We are fans. Olympiakos' are fanatics. I mean, we've got humor, we can take a joke, we're not as aggressive as they are. How can I say it? We're classy.
>
> Aspa: You're fags!
>
> Tom: Because we're demanding and picky? Because we're not a herd like you are? Because we can reason and argue and don't resort to beating people up?
>
> Aspa: You're not committed. We'd never leave empty seats when Olympiakos plays. We'll go and shout our hearts out for our team!
>
> Tom: That's because you're hungry! I understand. You're starved for success. You didn't have that satisfaction as many times as we did. We're well fed darling, with victories and European participation.
>
> Aspa: You're not a true fan! You don't know how to support your team. Come on! Everybody knows you're "couch fans." As long as you have a TV set!
>
> Tom: At least we can be critical of our team and administration. We can say no to the manager, we don't follow orders, we don't get paid by the owner to be religious supporters, we're not employed by our team! We love it unconditionally!
>
> Aspa: Surely your team pays for your doctors and shrinks!

What both Tom and Aspa try to do with this fast exchange of words full of irony and clever remarks is to make clear what they are like mainly by implying what they are not. They are making statements about their fan identities. As Woodward explains, identities are formed "in relation to other identities, to the 'outsider' or in terms of the other: that is, in relation to what they are not. The most common form in which this construction appears is in binary oppositions. Saussurean linguistic theory maintains that binary oppositions—the most extreme form of marking difference—are essential to the production of meaning" (Woodward 1997: 35). And clearly, within the binary opposition between Olympiakos and Panathinaikos, fan identities are constructed "through a hostile opposition of 'us' and 'them'"(Woodward 1997: 30). Through this bipolar structure, fans conceptualize their fan identity and make sense of their fandom. They do so in a negative fashion as they discriminate themselves from the anti-fans through stereotypes about themselves and negatively constructed and exaggerated difference about the rivals. In a way, then, just as binary oppositions are for de Saussure (1974) part of the logic of language and thought, so they are for anti-fans the structure through which they make identity statements and communicate what they are and, crucially, what they are not.

Defending and Protecting Fan Identity

It is important to note that dialogues and discussions like the above are frequent among fans of the two "eternals," and most of the time take place in an antagonistic but also playful and teasing fashion. Sports fans, in fact, take great pleasure in talking and arguing with anti-fans. They enjoy participating in a "game," as they call it, of exchanging witty lines with their "rivals" and take up a contest of who will defend and prove that her/his fan object is better. Be this a contradiction or not (Hills 2002), they become particularly emotional when talking about the object that they are anti-fans of or when talking about the anti-fans of their fan object. They do not want to participate in such teasing games when their team loses, and they express their hatred for the "opponent" of their object of affection, while doing their best to "belittle" anti-fans and consequently "uplift" and reaffirm their own fan identity. This is their ultimate aim.

Alec, a fan of Panathinaikos, explains his pattern of calling up his best friend, who is an Olympiakos supporter, when Olympiakos loses a match. "Of course I will make him suffer. Of course I'll call the little bastard up and make sure he confesses and admits how horribly they played. And, yeah, I know he won't. But I'll be going on and on and explain in every technical detail all their mistakes and he's bound to feel like shit after that." It is interesting that fans of the two teams perform their fandom differently among fellow fans and among anti-fans. They are honest with each other and critical of their team as a group of fellow fans. When anti-fans are present, the situation is different. They would do their utmost to defend their team and fan object choice and refute the critics. Alec explains that he would never admit in front of an anti-fan that Panathinaikos did not play well, even if it was a friend of his. He would just say that "the team played as good as it could, but due to unexpected factors it lost the game." When asked why, he responded that the anti-fan has bad intentions: "It's one thing to make good intentioned critique and another to give your opponent the opportunity to exterminate and make fun of you. They just wait for you to make a mistake and then hit you. So I would not give them the satisfaction." The discussion goes on:

> Interviewer: But this is what you say you do to your friend, who's Olympiakos, no?
> Alec: Yes. But the point is, I am right. He is wrong!
> Interviewer: And again this is what he or any rival fan of yours would also say when criticizing Panathinaikos.
> Alec: Well, that's the name of the game!

It is becoming clear, with respect to protecting and defending their identity and fan object, that fans as anti-fans know they are "performing," that they have knowledge of what their role is, and that it changes depending upon the "context of performance." It is also clear that fans of both teams employ the same practices and are not so different in enacting their fandom after all. They play a game that offers them psychological unbending and relaxation, aiming to impose their superiority by belittling the rival.

Fans of both teams also perform emotionally charged behavior of this kind in the field as spectators of matches between them. They do not attend the match only so that they can support their team but also so that they can humiliate the rival. They have intense reactions, shout obscenities, get extremely upset and passionate, and sometimes become aggressive. Their chants against each other are legendary for their vulgar language full of sexual connotations, and heavy swearing. The most classic but also humiliating chants, according to fans' testimonies, are the parodies of the teams' anthems. These are sung by anti-fans in the rhythm of the original team anthems but with different lyrics. The new composition of Panathinaikos's chant goes, "Panathinaikos, queer, fanatic queer, Panathinaikos, eternal champion of transvestites." It causes a chain reaction of "Olympiakos, your great team, fuck your Piraeus and your mother's pussy." It should be mentioned that swearing is a culturally constructed habit of Greek fans. They tend to escape through swearing rather than beating and violence. Such behavior and the use of sexist language is not unexpected, within a crowd. The "machismo" phraseology embedded in their chanting is a Greek particularity of precapitalist values of sexism and subordination to the powerful male. Both teams' fans in their game of chants adopt a traditional and outdated rhetoric and claim superiority by competing as to who will assert their masculine identity.

Overall, either through everyday talk and socializing or through in-field interaction as spectators, anti-fans employ the practice of belittling the rival as an "identity boost"–seeking mechanism, and so as to protect their fan object. Social identity theorists argue that people want to protect and maintain a positive social identity (Tajfel & Turner 1979, in Wann & Thomas 1994). Thompson argues that the stigmatization associated with some fan activities and the feelings of self-doubt it might evoke urge fans to formulate special groups and communities where they can find reassurance (Thompson 1995) and safeguard their identity. Sport fandom, and practices of football anti-fandom in particular, one could argue, provide not only mechanisms to safeguard one's fan identity but also ways to gain a great deal of "identity boost" and self-esteem. This is the purpose that the process of belittling or humiliating the rival fan serves for the opposing teams' fans.

Conclusion

This chapter proposes a new way of looking at the concept of anti-fandom. The anti-fan is first and foremost a fan, and resorts to anti-fandom so as to protect her/his fan object from the threat its "counterforce" poses. It suggests that in cases of extreme antagonism between two fan objects when binary oppositions occur, fans love to hate the "opposing threat," and use their anti-fandom as a form of communication and language.

The case study discussed reflects a condition of our times, where football fandom, because of the commercialization and commodification of the sport, increasingly adopts a populist expression of the antagonism ethos of late capitalism. Largely this ethos is about ridiculing the rival, about winning, being powerful, being the best. Fans take up and reproduce the values of antagonism in their construction and expression of fan identity. A worthy rival arouses fear, awe, respect, and envy. It intensifies the antagonism. It intensifies fans' urge to feel superior.

In the particular case study of Olympiakos and Panathinaikos anti-fandom, this modern socio-cultural condition coexists with two Greek particularities of older times: the conflict of the urban bourgeoisie and the working classes of early capitalist Greece, and the premodern Greek development of a "macho" masculine identity that goes back in time, but is still adopted in football. Both these elements are still affecting the way anti-fandom is expressed and experienced. It is suggested that it is the mixture of such elements with the long-lasting and ever-growing antagonistic ethos that makes such an explosive and vibrant opposition and case of anti-fandom as that of Olympiakos-Panathinaikos.

Concerning anti-fandom in particular, it needs to be said overall that thinking about anti-fans in the way proposed here opens up further questions. For instance, we might ask, By which mechanisms are binary oppositions between two fan objects constructed, and why? Under what circumstances may such a concept apply to other fields of popular culture, like TV and music genres? And, with sports, could a further elaboration and enrichment of this concept and of the elements that condition its appearance help to draw insights in cases of excessive sports-fans behavior or hooliganism? A further elaboration of such a notion of the anti-fan is certainly needed, so that we might better contextualize and theorize it. Pursuing such a task can lead to a better understanding not only of the role of anti-fandom to the identity positions of the fan, but more generally of fandom's expression and appropriation.

In memory of my supervisor, Professor Roger Silverstone

NOTES

1. I would like to thank my interviewees for their thoughts and time. Heartfelt thanks go to Giota Alevizou, whose contribution at various stages of this chapter has been immense, and immensely appreciated. Many thanks also go to Yiorgos Chouliaras and Yiorgos Lellis for sharing their expertise on the meaning of ancient Greek texts and terms with me. I am grateful to the editors for their comments and feedback.

2. Along with rival couples of Barcelona and Real Madrid in the Spanish league, AC Milan and Inter Milan in the Italian, FC Celtic and Glasgow Rangers in the Scottish, and others.

3. Interviewees were recruited through acquaintances and snowball sampling. Two focus groups and four informal, semistructured interviews with fans of Olympiakos and Panathinaikos were conducted. Fans of both clubs were present in the group discussions and asked to talk about their love and hate, so that the interaction between anti-fans could be assessed. The playful nature of group talk among anti-fans and the aggressive/defensive mode adopted was an indicator that the context of fandom and anti-fandom talk and behavior affects what is disclosed and how. This assumption was confirmed by individual interviews with participants in the first group conducted at a later date, where fans presented a more solemn and candid face regarding their anti-fandom. In total, twelve fans were interviewed.

4. See also http://www.perseus.tufts.edu/cgi-bin/ptext?doc=Perseus%3Atext% 3A1999.04.0034&query=chapter%3D%2311 and http://perseus.mpiwg-berlin.mpg. de/cgi-bin/ptext?doc=Perseus:text:1999.01.0200&query=book%3D3%3Achapter% 3D11%3Asection%ED2.

5. For instance, USSR was the counterforce to the USA during the Cold War.

6. See Homer (1999), book 7, line 479, on "*chloron deos.*"

7. The first seeds of football development are to be found in the formation of urban centers like Athens, where Panathinaikos was formed in 1908. After World War I, financial growth and urban center development began. The forming of city centers and the composition of towns were crucial factors in football growth, with Olympiakos being established in 1925 as the team of the Piraeus port and the prime rival of the capital city's team. Key to football growth was also the influx of Greek refugees from Asia Minor who looked for ways of getting incorporated into their old homeland. They played a crucial role by forming teams like the Athletic Union of Constantinople (AEK) and the Panthessalonikian Athletic Club of Constantinople (PAOK).

8. But also of Aris-PAOK in Thessalonica.

24

A Vacancy at the Paris Hilton

Jeffrey Sconce

Those who dismissed the ludic nihilism of Jean Baudrillard's later works—his final resignation in the face of hyperreality's triumph, his refusal to advocate on behalf of any illusory remnant of subjectivity, his concretization of evil in the encroaching logic of the object—should refer to a string of simulations reported in November of 2005, a month that—if history still existed—would no doubt figure prominently in its demise. As Iraq continued to explode and thousands of refugees from Hurricane Katrina found themselves cut off from the last crumbs of government assistance and public memory, celebutante Paris Hilton and three members of her roving entourage left a Hollywood nightclub to take their existential maw on the road. Hoping to outwit the paparazzi, Hilton's boyfriend/chauffeur Stavros Niarchos—presumably out of reflex more than logic—threw a coat over his head and then promptly rammed Hilton's $162,000 Bentley into the back of a truck. Naturally, they fled the scene, only to later be briefly stopped by the LA police. Despite an on-camera confession by one of the passengers that he "was the only one sober," the police looked the other way and allowed the merry band to continue their night/week/month/life of menacing all honest working folk who might stand between them and a good time. The following day a spokesperson for the LAPD denied accusations that the quartet had received "special treatment," while Hilton's publicist noted, "It's all very upsetting as you might imagine. But the important thing is at the end of the day what seems to be going on here is that Paris is the only victim. She's going to be stuck with the tab of repairing that car" (Whitcomb 2005).

By inviting us to imagine that any amount of money might actually matter to Hilton, perhaps her publicist thought he had contained the incident by appealing to the average schlub's empathy for the common "fender bender," as if Hilton's boyfriend had cracked up a '74 Gremlin backing into a Burger King dumpster. Such heroic efforts at populist spin were negated a few days later, however, when Hilton and Niarchos made their way to Las Vegas, whereupon Hilton, while purchasing some $4,000 worth of lingerie (and for maximum PR effect, a bullwhip), lost control of her pet lemur, Baby Luv. The lemur proceeded to run amok in the store before at last turning on Hilton herself (no doubt to the cheers of the store's staff and patrons). Meanwhile, back at the hotel, the terror of encroaching boredom provoked Stavros and his buddies to activate the hotel's sprinkler system, damaging twelve other rooms on their floor. Trading in levels of embarrassment and shame that would kill mere mortals, the couple remained in their protective bubble of wealth and self-absorption, and soon Paris, Stavros, Baby Luv, the bullwhip, and the $4,000 in lingerie were on their way back to Los Angeles, no doubt to find a replacement Bentley, or failing that, perhaps a car that runs on the boiled blood of nuns and orphans.

Of course, it is easy to take cheap shots at Paris Hilton; in fact, it is necessary—her entire career depends on it. In a culture that refuses to have any meaningful debate over issues of social and economic inequality, Hilton gamely serves as the stupid rich girl America loves to hate, not necessarily because she is rich and stupid but because she so wantonly violates certain unspoken protocols of fame. Americans take inequalities of birth, wealth, and opportunity in stride; but in a cultural economy where fame is inexorably replacing talent as the coin of the realm, a nagging, residual Protestant work ethic still expects fame to be earned the old-fashioned way—through excellence in some form of criminal, political, athletic, or artistic practice. So annoyed was *Daily News* gossip columnist Lloyd Grove at this injustice that he devoted an entire column to swearing off reporting Paris Hilton "news" ever again. "The arc of Paris' 'career'—from rich, witless party girl to rich, witless party girl with a television show—is an insult to the American sense of fairness: the idea that you get ahead by working hard, playing by the rules and acquiring a skill of some sort," he grouses (Grove 2004: n.p.). As Grove's disgust suggests, most Americans have learned to tolerate trust-fund kids as an annoying side effect of capitalism, but when the insanely overprivileged refuse to enjoy their wealth and leisure in private, demanding instead that we must bear public witness to their privileges as "talent" or "allure," they transgress a much more powerful moral boundary, one that has allowed the fabulous and the drably normal to survive in nervous harmony for hundreds of years.

But herein lies the evil genius of this object we have come to know as the Paris Hilton, and why only the theoretical armature developed by Baudrillard over the past twenty-five years is equal to the task of "explaining" her continuing presence on the contemporary mediascape. For years, Baudrillard's work has been facilely dismissed as ignoring the real world, overvaluing sign and simulation, and thus avoiding meaningful intervention into some leftist fantasy of a nonexistent public sphere. But honestly, what model of political economy, psychoanalytic demystification, or reception analysis is up to the challenge of *explaining* Paris Hilton? In assuming that Hilton enjoys "illicit" or "unjust" fame, we begin the search to uncover an underlying cultural, social, or psychoanalytic mechanism that would recuperate the Hilton phenomenon as a fleeting and perhaps curable pathology. But what secret is there to "uncover" in a figure whose entire existence has always been predicated on performing constant visibility and who circulates through all media (Grove's column and this article included) as an object of depthless fascination? "She's the perfect Bush-era heroine, because she's all style and no content," opines a snarky Naomi Wolf in the pages of *Vanity Fair,* making a stab at Baudrillardian posturing and yet still attempting to ground Hilton in some fantasy of historical determination. Even more off the mark is Camille Paglia, who in the same piece asserts, "People want to be soothed right now, and there is something about Paris Hilton that's soothing" (Smith 2005: 280). Paglia assumes here that most Americans *like* Paris Hilton, when in fact, the vast majority of her media exposure is framed as negative irritation (strange that Paglia would confuse the two). Much more appropriate are Baudrillard's comments at the beginning of *Fatal Strategies:* "Things have found a way of avoiding a dialectics of meaning that was beginning to bore them: by proliferating indefinitely, increasing their potential, outbidding themselves in ascension to the limit, an obscenity that henceforth becomes their immanent finality and senseless reason" (1990: 7). Fame and anonymity, style and content, talent and ineptitude, justice and injustice: how could we expect any of these binaries to adhere or correspond in the current mediascape? And what better way to conceptualize Hilton than as a bored object "in ascension to the limit," a metonymy (but not a symptom) of the media's ongoing proliferation into "senseless reason"?

Part of the vertigo here no doubt stems from the public experiencing a form of "the bends," unable to surface from the real at the same velocity as the bright and shiny objects of simulated fame. For example, we had all made our peace with those peculiar celebrities who are "famous for being famous," figures who appear to have little or no talent, and yet through sheer saturation become public institutions. Hilton, on the other hand, gives us the first celebrity who is "famous for being famous for being famous"; or, to put it more succinctly, *meta/meta-famous.* In so doing, she diabolically moves the already highly simulated institution of celebrity one step closer to complete obscenity—that is, toward a final annihilation of fame's traditional trade in depth, mystery, and fantasy into a "more visible than visible" display of perpetual celebrihood as self-evident surface (Baudrillard 1990: 55). Hilton's strategy has been to leverage her wealth, privilege, ignorance, and lack of talent in such a manner that *she might become famous for wanting to be famous **based** on her wealth, privilege, ignorance, and lack of talent.* Thus, every blip she makes on the mediascape, be it yet another magazine cover or facetious public concern over her missing Chihuahua, only further accelerates a vicious circle of fame, wealth, and entitlement that in turn generates its own media gravity, attracting more exposure, opportunity, fame, wealth, and entitlement. It is a brilliant strategy for negotiating the media end-times—a perpetual motion machine of hype—and further confirmation of Baudrillard's contention that today "the entire critical problematic of the media revolves around this threshold of tolerance for the excess of obscenity" (2003a: 29). In this paradoxical scenario, the more the public professes to hate Paris Hilton for her "fake" celebrity, the more *truly* famous she becomes, every detail of her life buttressing a Chinese finger-trap of envy and loathing. The more the public wants her to disappear, the more visible she becomes.

Perhaps this is why Hilton is wise enough to devote most of her energy to wrecking Bentleys, terrorizing lingerie shoppers, and milking brief engagements to fellow millionaires named Paris—the viral media attention to such hijinx is not a side effect of her fame in the entertainment industry but rather serves as the prerequisite that allows her to find "real" work in front of the camera; indeed, from her infamous "sex tape" to the panic that gripped young LA in the wake of her stolen PDA, Hilton's "backstage" career has proven far more important to her persona than her "legitimate" turns as the star of *The Simple Life,* a briefly ambulatory corpse in *House of Wax,* or a bikini-clad burger-huckster for Carl's Jr. In fact, it is doubtful such a radical experiment in simulation as Paris Hilton could take place without the concurrent proliferation of the lucrative offshoots of the culture industries that now thrive wholly on stoking the red-hot obscenity of Hollywood's glitterati. While the tabloids have always been a factor in the industry, the current explosion of these ancillary Hollywood sites, from the traditional print rags to TV's *Extra* to the web's Gawker.com, has at last created a textual space coequal to the products of the entertainment industry. Much more than a mere supplement, these sites have moved from providing biographical background and gossip to creating an autonomous textual arena that is often more compelling in its dramaturgy than the bland recycled product proffered by the studios and television networks. The implications of this shift could not be more profound. Somehow, Hollywood has managed to go from producing actual entertainment to creating venues for the public to bear constant, almost mandatory witness to celebrities entertaining themselves (how else are we to explain *Access Hollywood, MTV Cribs,* and *Ocean's Eleven,* texts ostensibly aimed at different audiences and yet united in their ritualized performances of narcissism?). In this respect, Hilton has realized the dream of every transvestite who ever passed through the gates of the old Warhol factory system: simulate glitz, glamor, and attitude, and a career will follow, not necessarily one that involves creating any actual art or media, but rather, a career that involves endlessly recreating one's self for attention and consumption. Blissfully unencumbered by Warholian irony or East Village poverty, however, Hilton has succeeded where Holly Woodlawn and Candy Darling failed (one can only imagine the levels of irony that would be at play had Warhol lived to meet and interview Hilton). Only a highly capitalized and thoroughly naïve bid for such narcissistic spectacle could really hope to succeed. In the wake of Warhol, in the wake of Duchamp, any number of art hipsters might have let a lemur loose in a lingerie store as a self-conscious gesture of avant-garde agitation, but only a walking simulation of fame like Hilton—pure surface evacuated of all interiority—could actually succeed in achieving such sincere affectation so effortlessly.

Erotic Capital

Hilton's ability to convert all forms of exposure into continued hype is a testament to the way today's meta/meta-famous, like cockroaches, have become immune to the forces that formerly would have killed the merely famous. Bad publicity, overexposure, naked careerism, candid glimpses of condescension, decadence, and hypocrisy: in the past such "negatives" would have eventually overwhelmed a celebrity's ability to maintain credibility with the public. For Hilton, of course, these qualities are the very foundation for her larger public career. No doubt much of this persona was indelibly established by the release of Hilton's "sex tape" just before her mass media debut in *The Simple Life*. Waggishly titled *One Night in Paris*, the film documents an hour or so of sex between a then 19-year-old Hilton and 32-year-old Rick Salomon. For many years, young women in Hollywood had to worry that cheesecake or "art modeling" photos from their starving past might return to haunt them once they had settled into a comfortable character and career before the movie camera. Such photos are almost always more humiliating for what they say about the celebrity's former class status than for the revelation of any private flesh. What beautiful actress would really be humiliated by the exposure of a famous and well-compensated bosom? Much worse is the glimpse into the actress's desperate and hungry past, when the economics of flesh, lens, and desire were much more naked in their circuitry. Hilton, of course, has never struggled or starved, so the arrival of her sex tape—in advance of any career and in absence of any deprivation—has a much different pornographic effect. Not up to the technical or performance standards of professional San Fernando porn, the tape is less a "hot lifestyles of the rich and famous" than a rather clinical document about the sexual practices of the young, privileged, and bored (perhaps most jarring to viewers [and Salomon] is the moment a jaded Hilton interrupts the proceedings to answer a cell phone call, thereby validating Jerry Seinfeld's claim that a cell phone at dinner [or in the bedroom] says to everyone involved, "I've got other options"). The press has reveled in stories of Hilton's embarrassment over the tape, but truth be told, her career would never have flourished without this shadow porn text (whether actually seen or just acknowledged) in place to underwrite her arrival on American television.[1] It is difficult to say how much the widespread downloading of the Hilton sex tape inflated the numbers for her subsequent television debut on Fox. One thing is for sure: it created a rather unprecedented reading protocol for *The Simple Life* and for the rest of her public career, inverting the chain of desire that traditionally informs the Hollywood imaginary. While generations of old spent years fantasizing about what their favorite starlet might look like nude, Hilton's triple-X debut will forever make the public wonder what this party girl/amateur porn actor might look like if she could act, or sing, or do anything other than shop. Getting the sex and nudity out of the way up front has allowed Hilton to pursue her quest for absolute blankness unencumbered by any residual public desire or even interest in exposing her more authentic or real "private" self.

Hilton is thus an excellent subject for all manner of speculative play in that her blank surfaces can be read as either empirical evidence of total vacuity or as a sang-froid performance of studied detachment. Compare, for example, two famous quotations by the meta/meta-famous. On her reality marriage fiasco, *Newlyweds,* Jessica Simpson famously asserted one day that "Chicken of the Sea" was in fact chicken. That's just stupid.[2] But when Hilton arrives in Altus, Arkansas, and says to the locals, "I've always heard that people hang out at Wal-Mart. What is Wal-Mart? Is it, like, they sell wall stuff?" (*The Simple Life,* episode one), her bafflement is both stupid and brilliantly condescending. Hilton acts like she might be naïvely outraged at her treatment by the press from time to time, implying she is sincerely stupid and sincerely hurt at being called stupid. But then she will stage a revolutionary stunt like appearing in P Diddy's "Vote or Die" campaign only to then "forget" to vote in that year's election. What better way to remind her public that their hollow pursuit of political embetterment, like their pursuit of meaningful entertainment, has now been completely absorbed within the meta/meta-famous's kingdom of absolute simulation? After all, why *would* Paris Hilton need to vote, or even entertain the plebeian fantasy that voting was actually important? Titillating photos of her wearing only a "Vote or Die" t-shirt are a sexual tease, certainly, but they are much more effective as a spectacle of eroticized apathy, a way of capturing the icy sexiness that only the absolute detachment of wealth, privilege, and apolitical boredom can provide. That's hot because it is so bitterly and brutally cold.

Hilton's unique performance of meta/meta-fame may imply that this phenomenon is wholly confined to her gender, age, and class. But there are in fact many roads to such hyperreal status. Consider, for example, the plight of Kevin Federline. If Hilton's persona plays with that familiar line in the aristocracy dividing the highly decadent and the highly dumb (a trope dating back, no doubt, to the golden age of syphilitic insanity), Federline instead works the territory of the self-deluded goober moron, a meta/meta-famous celebrity who seems to truly believe he possesses incredible talent (Hilton, to her credit, would appear to understand she is famous only for her fabulousness). Indeed, the Hollywood Hills are now littered with people who are famous for being famously deluded. As is well know to tabloid readers, an obscure Federline had fathered one child and was expecting a second with ex-*Moesha* star Shar Jackson when he uncere-

moniously dumped his starter family to attach himself to pop tartlet Brit-
ney Spears, whom he subsequently married. Endlessly parodied and
attacked as an irresponsible, lazy, gold-digging hillbilly freeloader, Federline finally fired back through his art, releasing a rap single in late 2005
titled "Y'all Ain't Ready." The track stands as an unwitting and witless
anthem for the meta/meta-fame generation, Federline bragging that he
hopes to soak the public for "about 2 mil" in record sales while reminding
everyone that he enjoys frequent sexual congress with Spears. When the
single leaked out as an mp3 on the Internet, critics were quick to agree,
"No, we ain't ready." Inevitable comparisons were then made to Vanilla Ice,
formerly the gold standard in walking white-rapper punch lines. Such
comparisons, however, misread the full audacity of Federline's gesture.
Vanilla Ice at least understood he needed to feign some form of biographical street-cred in order to succeed as a white rapper, inventing an elaborate story of his life in the 'hood to cover for his suburban Dallas
upbringing. Federline, on the other hand, simply offers his own
meta/meta-famous status as sufficient cause for railing against the hurtful
persecution of the meta/meta-famous:

> I'm starrin' in your magazines
> Now every day and week
> Back then, they call me K-fed
> But you can call me Daddy instead

We may not understand him now, but in the future it appears we will all
be his bitch.

Throughout his rap, Federline accuses his detractors of not being able
to handle his "straight 2008" sense of style, reminding us that the
meta/meta-famous typically wage their warfare against the mundane populace on the terrain of consumption and style, proving once again that the
culture wars, whatever their putative left-right politics might be, are in the
end almost always about clashing taste formations. This was most evident
in the series architecture for Hilton's big media debut in Fox's *Simple Life*.
Tellingly, in its first iteration, the series began with the idea of flying yokels
to Beverly Hills to be humiliated for misunderstanding the etiquette of
valet parking, thereby reversing the folksy critique of the original *Beverly
Hillbillies* into lifestyle pornography for everyone living west of La Brea
Boulevard. Faced with preemptory criticism of this concept (coming in
large part from those last great defenders of the real—Southern Senators),

Fox retooled the show around Hilton as a vehicle for showcasing her superficiality and condescending snobbery. Season one took Hilton and her accessory friend Nicole Richie from their pampered LA environs to work on a farm in Arkansas. A classic of the new cultural wars, the entire series hinged on sorting out which taste culture the viewer would find more repellent—young Hollywood in all its narcissistic stupidity or regular working people condemned to a life of eternally nonfabulous boredom. The dirty little secret here, of course, is that the show—despite its putative placement of Hilton and Richie as the butt of the joke—was in fact structured for profound polysemy. At stake in the series were two visions of America's future: in one, everybody under the age of thirty lives in LA and no one can remember how to milk a cow; in the other, the heartland masses storm southern California and return with the cast of *The OC* on the ends of their pitchforks.

Hilton's talent for both conspicuous consumption and, even more importantly, passing conspicuous judgment on the consumption of others testifies to how the contemporary culture of celebrity has so radically inverted previous criteria for talent and creativity. If Hilton does have a talent, it is as a master semiotician of LA trend mongering. Surveying our recent crop of Hiltons, Federlines, and Simpson sisters, it is clear that the desire to become a star today is no longer attached to any fantasies about public admiration for one's unique talent or a creative body of work (films, music, etc.), but appears increasingly to be wholly a function of transforming oneself into an unvarnished object of envy, and thus an arbiter of appropriate taste. The signifiers of fame have become so completely detached from expressive talent that any residual investment in "creativity," "genius," and/or "depth" has long since evaporated from the scene (twenty years ago, Rupert Pupkin in his most pathetic fantasies of fame and fortune still wanted to be a good comedian). In this respect, "talent" now appears increasingly to rest on an ability to reflect leisure, pleasure, and discrimination back to the masses in the form of idleness and spectacular consumption. As Hilton's career demonstrates, her entire persona depends on her signature *inability* to do or contribute *anything* productive, making her fame the most pure and tasteful of all. In fact, since her entire persona depends on performing the role of a talentless and parasitical socialite whose only desire is to consume and be consumed as famous, then it necessarily follows that Hilton's "success" in any given endeavor—music, TV, film, animal husbandry—would sully and thus threaten to undercut the entire foundation of her career.

Once upon a time, fame used to at least go to the trouble of masquerading as talent, or at least craftsmanship. Fifty years ago, Marilyn Monroe was apparently so tortured by the public's refusal to take her seriously as an actress that she sought out Lee Strasburg, Arthur Miller, and psychoanalysis as a means toward discovering depth and credibility. And while there is certainly no shortage of mediocre actors still willing to join James Lipton in the Actors Studio to opine about the challenges of starring in *Daredevil* and *Gigli,* increasingly such charades are no longer necessary. The real art in the contemporary entertainment industry is finding a way to force oneself into the game in the first place. This seems especially true in the music industry, where the disjunction between fame and talent seems most acute. To whit: an *American Idol* contestant enters the audition room and proves within seconds he has absolutely no talent, looks, charm, or charisma. Clearly about to be dismissed, he pleads earnestly with the panel, "Make me into a product, mold me into whatever you need to move records." Despite this demonstration of eager pliability, "mold-me" Idol does not pass on to the next round. The shock on his face reveals he truly believed his performance of insider knowledge would be the key to the kingdom of fame. Surely Simon, Paula, and Randy will respect that I, too, know this is all a charade, that with today's studio and promotional wizardry, even Helen Keller could be on *Top of the Pops.* And why wouldn't he think so? Ashlee Simpson's career continues to thrive despite repeated brushes with a disastrous real. Even before a calamitous appearance on *Saturday Night Live* when she was caught lip-synching to the wrong song, a "Stop Ashlee Petition" had been circulating for months on the Internet. "We, the undersigned, are disgusted with Ashlee Simpson's horrible singing and hereby ask her to stop," it reads. "Stop recording, touring, modeling and performing. We do not wish to see her again."[3] After the *SNL* debacle, Simpson delivered a stunningly terrible performance during the 2005 Orange Bowl and was roundly booed by a crowd of seventy-two thousand. Realizing that the entire franchise was in danger of slipping away, Simpson returned to *SNL* the next season to sing an acoustic ballad, not so much as musical entertainment, but as a freakish "proof-of-life" demonstration meant to foreground the absence of any electronic chicanery and thus vouch for her authenticity. Despite such attempts to repair her credibility, Ashlee still found herself targeted a few weeks later by a group of Toronto art students. Staging "Operation Boo," the students hoped to "take a stand against manufactured pop" by booing Simpson for a solid hour during a local record store appearance. Simpson no doubt laughed, or perhaps sang off-key, all the way to the bank.

Let Them Eat Hype

Perhaps there was a time when a wily band of Canadian art students might have prevented us from plunging ever deeper into the hyperreal paradoxes of meta-fame, maybe in the eras of David Cassidy or Tiffany or Debbie Gibson. For now, however, all such battles would appear to be lost—especially now that technicians at MTV have transformed a small coastal community in Southern California into a working laboratory for cultivating, nurturing, and harvesting the meta/meta-famous of the future. Having first performed their experiments in fame engineering in a series of *Real World* safe houses across the country, MTV has finally settled on *Laguna Beach* as ground zero in their project for slowly, inexorably rewriting Aaron Spelling's camp horseshit of the 1980s as the new social reality of teen California, and by cathode extension, the nation at large. And in this next brood of celebrity simulation, Paris Hilton may at last have some competition. MTV's reality series detailing the trials and tribulations of the town's rich, white, and photogenic high school students has recently propelled a pack of newly graduated meta-famers up the 405 to LA in search of acting gigs and recording contracts. As it turns out, in the backseat of Hilton's Bentley on the night Niarchos rammed into the delivery truck was *Laguna Beach's* Talan Torriero. While it may still be too early to pick America's next breakout asshole, Torriero certainly seems to have committed Hilton's playbook of notorious nonachievement to memory. The *New York Post* reports that shortly after the wreck Torriero demanded to work the press line at a trendy LA nightclub, but only after the stipulation that no one could ask him any questions about his vehicular mishap with Hilton and Niarchos the week before (because that is what the famous "do"—they make demands and stipulations before deigning to speak). "There were no takers," notes the reporter with laconic satisfaction (Johnson 2005: 6). But despite such sporadic resistance to his magnetic destiny, Torriero remains undaunted. "I'm doing an album, which is very exciting," he tells MTV news. "I'm supposed to be discreet about it, so I can't tell you what label I'm with, but it's a really big label push" (MTV 2005: n.p.). Can the former quarterback of Laguna Beach's football team actually sing? Who knows? But certainly, "rich and studly high-school jock" is right up there with "spoiled rich heiress" as a potential catalyst for another media empire of lust and loathing, helping to seal New Hollywood's new profile as an inescapable extension of everyone's worst high school nightmares.

When coupled with *Entourage, The OC,* and countless other sites of SoCal propaganda, meta/meta-fame would also appear to signal the final victory of Los Angeles over New York for the teenage and twenty-something imaginary. LA, which for years had to endure the missives of haughty New Yorkers (or worse, insufferably precious San Franciscans), has at long last, through its ongoing domination of the culture industries, recast itself as the new standard of youthful cool. In the process, what began twenty years ago as a caustic Gen-X skepticism for all institutions of culture and society has somehow morphed into an affable Gen-Y irony complacent with any and all modes of exploitative stupidity. If one could fast forward through the videotaped history of MTV, no doubt this transformation would unfold in the form of gritty Soho loft sets gradually collapsing to reveal the eternally sunny beach houses, movie premieres, and hillside mansions of the west coast. From its beginning, MTV was already clinging precariously to the last vestiges of an already wholly simulated countercultural authenticity, putting Huey Lewis videos in heavy rotation while the idealistic young VJs held out hope for a surprise visit from Lou Reed. No such confusion or schizophrenia exists today—MTV's transformation has been complete. Perhaps realizing across the postmodern eighties that its entire premise of "rock 'n' roll television" was fundamentally oxymoronic and ludicrous, the network gradually began to embrace the cynicism of its own compromises, and like the rest of the entertainment world, began promoting the hype industry itself as an art rather than as the traditional adversary to all that was holy and good. Today, there might be a few teenage throwbacks who still dream of moving to Greenwich Village to become a poet, a novelist, or an angry songwriter (and, yes, they would be suckers for thinking these vocations were still in demand). But, like Torriero, more and more seem comfortable with defining the path to self-actualization as a guaranteed rung on the ladder of the LA club scene, a pimped ride, and the beatific synergy of a "big label push"; in short, success now equals unlimited access to self, money, and sunshine. And, as fame becomes increasingly detached from talent, achievement, or even potential, we can look forward to a world where, more and more, only less and less talented people will be drawn to Hollywood—like cloned moths bonded by a gradually disintegrating genetic code attracted to an increasingly simulated flame.

As with his prescient divination of America's future obsession with terrorism and its gradual descent into mass obesity, Baudrillard also recognized the inevitability that California, like encephalitis, meningitis, and all other soporific diseases, would eventually tax the rest of the nation's ability to resist a cultural economy based wholly on the obscene performance of consumption, pleasure, idleness, and envy. "The sad thing about California is that all willed activity is derisory there," he observes. "Intellectual and social relations are mysteriously emptied of their content [. . .] beneath all its easygoing ways, it is a chivalric world, with eyes only for the stars, and a courtly world, in thrall to the seduction of business and the love affair with images" (1996: 41). A common, cheap, and archly French swipe at California dreaming, one might say. But, typically, Baudrillard goes beyond this bit of received stand-up comedy wisdom to get at the real heart of the matter, noting,

> What is hardest is that, in this idealized universe, it is not permissible to be bored. The need to preserve this paradisiacal reputation (much more than happiness itself) obviously makes life twice as difficult. There is an extraordinary pressure of collective responsibility. All new arrivals conform immediately; the solidarity is total. The Californians are committed to a job of advertising just as ascetic as the task of the Mormons with whom they share a geographical and mental space. They are a huge sect devoted to proving happiness, as others have dedicated themselves to the greater glory of God. (1996: 41)

Putting these comments back into the logic of stand-up comedy, a routine by HBO's comedian/pundit Bill Maher on 26 September 2003 illustrates Baudrillard's point—even as it eerily echoes the logic of Hilton's *Simple Life* persona. "You know, the rest of America feels about California the way the rest of the world feels about America," goes the set-up.

> They hate us because we do what we want. They think we're too blessed and too free, and it makes them nuts in the dreary hovels of Kabul and Tikrit and Lubbock, Texas[. . . .] Would anywhere else in America trade places with LA or San Francisco in a piss-soaked New York minute? You bet they would. Because I don't recall anyone ever writing a song called "I Wish They All Could Be Rhode Island Girls"!

As many have noted, humor always contains both a grain of truth and the sublimation of anger. In its unabashed region baiting, Maher's routine adds to the increasing burden placed on nonfamous non-Californians to perform as a miserable geographical Other, one that enables Los Angelinos stuck in traffic to fantasize about a bored (and preferably freezing) populace yearning for their perfect weather and the prestige that comes from living in proximity to the famous, meta-famous, and meta/meta-famous. Refusal to participate in this fantasy of a compulsory happiness stemming from the joys of a fame-based economy only elicits more confrontational hostility on the part of LA's cultural workers, usually in the form of yet another movie, sitcom, or reality series about what it's like to live in LA and somehow be connected to the entertainment industry. And if the endless staging of stars, convertibles, surfers, snowboarders, palm trees, and paparazzi should fail, there is always out-and-out name calling. "We have oranges, free oranges, everywhere," observes Maher. "What grows on the trees in Scranton, fucker?!"

As the most visible personifications of this peculiarly Californian aversion to the encroachment of occasional boredom, Hilton, Federline, Torriero, and the rest of the meta/meta-famous push this ritualized performance of happiness to ever more dizzying heights. Imagine, for a moment, the depth of commitment to "fun" required to go clubbing till three in the morning, wreck an expensive car, elude the police, travel to Vegas with a lemur in tow, buy $4,000 dollars in lingerie while trying to subdue said lemur, and then negotiate thousands of dollars in damages with hotel management after your boyfriend's antics get out of control— all in one week! Indeed, this performance of a "good time" seems so over the top, one suspects it could only be accomplished through some perfectly mixed eightball of uncut fame, narcissism, and mania.

As Hilton and her peers continue this "ascension to the limit," this testing of the "threshold of tolerance for the excess of obscenity," it would appear we are all doomed to live in the world of *Café Flesh*, an ambitious porno film from 1982. Written by its director, Stephen Sayadian, and subsequently legit screenwriter Jerry Stahl, the movie posits a postnuclear world where 99 percent of the world have become "sex negatives," capable of desire and yet unable to actually have sex. One of their few pleasures is to attend Café Flesh, where the last remaining sex positives engage in hardcore sexual performances for a masochistic audience (both in the Café's audience and the theater showing the film, a mise-en-abyme structure that makes this art-porno rather than simply porno-porno). In a riff on *Cabaret*, the entire proceedings are hosted by an obnoxious emcee, who taunts his audience by sneering, "I get off on your need." Scenes of hardcore pornography—the sex positives in the throes of ecstasy—are repeatedly intercut with the reactions of an envious, frustrated, impotent, and increasingly sweaty audience. If we replace or conflate sex with fame, as many already have, it is not difficult to see *Café Flesh* as an allegory about the growing rift between media-positives and media-negatives, fame-positives and fame-negatives. Hollywood used to be a factory that produced entertainment. Now, in the world of *Café Fame*, it would seem we exist wholly for the entertainment of Hollywood, an anonymous mass that must attend closely to their bipolar vacillations between privileged lethargy and frenzied enjoyment. What else could explain the unchecked narcissism of *The Simple Life*, Federline's "Y'all Ain't Ready," or anything linking the word "project" to any member of the *Laguna Beach* cast, other than their need to "get off on our need"? Perhaps this is why the public takes such great pleasure in puncturing the pretense of modesty in the celebrity class, their constant whining over a loss of privacy and the invasive threats presented by the public, paparazzi, and the occasional deranged stalker. It is rather like having to listen to sailors complain about getting wet. But in the end, maybe this is the only power left to the fame-negatives—to push the fame-positives into such absolute and complete obscenity that their powers and pleasures finally evaporate. Toward this end, the paparazzi should be encouraged and supported at every level, by federal law if necessary. All interferences and annoyances that can be hurled at the meta-famous should be attempted. Cut off their limousines in traffic. Put GPS tracers in their dry cleaning. Bug their homes for audio and video. Invite them to phantom charity events and photograph their confusion. Put their medical records and plastic surgery procedures on the Internet. Only if the meta/meta-famous become wholly visible 24/7 might they once again become invisible, or even better, irredeemably banal, a destiny Baudrillard argues to be the endpoint of all obscenity. "The obscene is what is uselessly visible—needlessly—with no desire involved and no effect achieved" (2003b: 44). What more could we hope for in describing our future in the world of the meta/meta-famous—a détente born of each party's mutual boredom.

Notes

1. After settling litigation about the tape, Hilton now donates her proceeds from its sale to charity.

2. Although it should be noted, Simpson's "stupidity" here instantly resulted in an offer for her to become the official spokesperson for *Chicken of the Sea* tuna. See Andy Dehnart, "Chicken of the Sea Wants Jessica to Be Its Spokesperson," 23 Oct. 2003, *Reality Blurred*, http://www.realityblurred.com/realitytv/archives/newlyweds_nick_and_jessica/2003_Oct_22_chicken_of_the_sea.

3. Bethany Decker, "The Stop Ashlee Simpson Petition," 2005, http://www.PetitionOnline.com/mod_perl/signed.cgi?StopAsh.

25

The Other Side of Fandom
Anti-Fans, Non-Fans, and the Hurts of History

Diane F. Alters

If a typical fan is someone who is immersed in a popular culture product, such as a television show, a movie, or even a book, and who might criticize the product from the perspective of one who wants only to make the product better, what about the viewer or reader who seems to offer nothing but active dislike? How might we understand the anti-fan who has plenty of opinions but dislikes a show so much that he or she seldom watches? And what about the non-fan who might watch only rarely but still finds the show or movie meaningful (Gray 2003: 73)?

This chapter suggests that we can learn much about a society by studying anti-fans and non-fans who are doing cultural work as they engage with, edit, or reject a variety of television programs, books, and other media in the context of the home. Using case studies based on ethnographic interviews of two sets of parents, this chapter argues that these particular anti-fans and non-fans created an ideal time-space nexus in their homes when they used media. Not only were they engaged in a process of identity formation, as Morley writes (Morley 2000) and as my colleagues and I have observed in other situations (Hoover, Clark, & Alters with Champ & Hood 2004), but they also engaged in "the indispensable dialogue with the past that accompanies any present" (Lipsitz 1990: 81) when they regarded mediated popular culture. The results recall Bahktin's chronotopic process of exchange (Bahktin 1981: 254), when history, the parents' experience, and cultural products were mingled and exchanged. In their dialogues with the past and their contemporary experiences, these parents created their own special chronotopes, or time-spaces, within the family home.[1] In the process, they linked their homes to the larger world through popular culture. Examining how they did so can help us understand the contradictory processes that define and maintain a culture.

In these case studies, I look at two sets of parents, the Walkers and the Farmers. They are anti-fans of some cultural products and non-fans of others, and in each case they worked in their views of history, contemporary times, their memories of television when they were children, and their roles as parents when they talked about the shows. To illustrate, I focus on their distinctly different views of the television show *Ellen*[2] and of a variety of children's cartoons. Their views of the text were emphatically social—that is, their views of U.S. society were bound up in what they said about television shows, movies, and books. They incorporated their views of contemporary U.S. society and history into the shows' chronotopes, creating ideal time-space nexuses, or domestic chronotopes, in their homes.

The work these two sets of parents undertook to evaluate popular media is cultural work.[3] Whether this work keeps the dominant culture going or exposes its cracks is an open question, to be answered over a longer span of time. But it's possible to look more narrowly at the parents' cultural work as examples of Raymond Williams's (1961, 1977) notion of a selective, interpretive process—for my purposes, a microprocess—specific to each family. This chapter suggests that the chronotopes of these two families are examples of two important but very different structures of feeling in contemporary U.S. society: a conservative, looking-to-the-past one that contains residual as well as dominant elements of the culture, and a more overtly contemporary structure of feeling that contains more dominant elements but in important ways distorts the past in terms of the present.

The ways the four parents constructed their chronotopes in this process seem very much related to Fredric Jameson's notion of "strategies of containment," or interpretive codes that deny contradictions and offer the illusion of narrative closure. A strategy of containment masks the "totality of history," including the "hurts," which are contradictions that would be unbearable without these strategies (1981: 52–53). Like Williams, Jameson conceives of people's readings of the past as "vitally dependent on our experience of the present" (1981: 11). Drawing from Jameson's concept, George Lipsitz observes that history contains unbearable contradictions that are graspable only indirectly, through popular culture (1990: xiii). Indeed, it was when they were asked to talk about popular culture prod-

ucts in the interviews that the Walkers and Farmers expressed their dissatisfaction with contemporary society and their interest in alternatives.

The setting—the family home—in which the parents did this cultural
work is significant. The parents saw their homes as places to control, to
make safe for their children. They wanted to keep out history that was
painful to them, and they did so by barring or altering certain media
products that they believed represented that history. Morley (2000: 3)
observes a constant attempt to police the family home, to keep it free of
alterity, as a way of defining who or what belongs in one's family—a
process of identity formation in modern life. Morley's concern, to explore
how home processes articulate with larger societal processes through television and other media, informed my own work in *Media, Home, and
Family* (Hoover, Clark, & Alters, with Champ & Hood 2004), which
describes a process of family identity formation that involves the way families engage with media. Beyond the question of identity formation as
families policed their homes, the problem of historical memory continually intruded in my ethnographic interviews. This chapter is an attempt to
explore the way these parents used the past to construct a safe place in
their homes free of painful memories. Constructing a safe place is something fans do, creating a kind of utopian space in popular culture, "a site
for constructing an alternative culture," as Henry Jenkins argues (1992:
282). The anti-fans and non-fans discussed in this chapter do something
quite similar. To create a safe place, a kind of utopia, they came up with a
time-space nexus, or chronotope, particular to them, a utopia of sorts that
they wanted their children—and themselves—to experience.

The Walkers

To situate the families socially: both are white, middle class in taste, by
choice somewhat precarious economically, and actively critical of U.S. culture, which they equated with television. The adults in both families
differed markedly in political attitudes, making all the more remarkable
the instances in which their critiques of various aspects of the culture are
similar.

The Walkers, who lived in a bungalow on a tree-lined street near the
center of a midsized Rocky Mountain city, were trying to figure out a way
to live in a culture they embraced and abhorred at the same time.[4] The
mother, Mara, and the father, George, preferred noncontemporary media

texts and sought to build a tradition for their family as an alternative to what they saw as mainstream culture. Indeed, they considered their work as media critics a part of their role as parents, to in effect keep alterity out of their home. The Walker parents are college-educated, and at the time of the interviews in the late 1990s, the parents of two boys, ten and seven, and three girls, four, three, and two months. George had a graduate degree. Mara was not in the paid-labor market; she kept house and home schooled the two oldest children and planned to do the same with the younger ones. George worked for a Christian organization. Both were evangelical Christians, an important, emerging mainstream segment of the U.S. population.

George and Mara looked to the 1950s as a time when things were more "moral," when "family" meant their middle-class family:[5] a salaried father (above $30,000 but below $70,000) and a stay-at-home mother. They looked to the past for much of popular culture, buying or borrowing children's books from the 1950s and early Disney movies or old cartoons. Over the previous decade, they had increasingly limited their children's television viewing, particularly after noting that their middle child was keenly interested in any screen display she encountered at the local mall. Eventually, the television was banished to the basement, behind the closed doors of an antique cabinet. No one in the family in a normal week watched more than three hours of television, Mara estimated. Still, the Walkers were conversant with many television programs, particularly children's, and a variety of movies and videos.

George was fascinated by contemporary media, having studied it as an undergraduate and graduate student. His background makes his yearning for the past all the more striking. Here, George and Mara are asked how they choose videos:

> Mara: Part of it is knowing which ones are what we would consider safe.
> George: And that even goes to books, Diane. If I see a book at the library book sale, and the title looks okay, and it was printed in 1950, I'll grab it. No questions asked. If it's printed in 1980, I'm not sure what kind of influences are going to be in there. I mean, I'm very cautious of our day, and the spin put on various things in our day.

George recalled a predictable, taken-for-granted atmosphere around television when he was a child that contrasted sharply with the attitude towards television that he and Mara sought to build in their home:

I'm on the tail end of the boomers [he was born in 1960] and so I grew up with the TV on. It was just *on*. I'd come home from school, I'd get some cereal, some Life cereal and sit down and watch whatever was on TV, for an hour and a half, two hours, till it was suppertime. I'm sure I didn't do that all the time. I'm sure it was not daily. But it was just a regular part of life.

Significantly, the Walkers' preference for entertainment texts from the 1950s was in part a conscious attempt to avoid all positive references to gays and lesbians. For example, they were upset that *Ellen*'s star, Ellen DeGeneres, appeared on *Sesame Street*. She intruded into a show they had assumed was "safe" because it had seemed to reflect their own very specific definition of family. Since her appearance, the Walkers had stopped watching *Sesame Street* regularly:

> George: She did a guest. It's sort of like, "I'm sorry. Now you are incorporating elements of the culture that aren't appropriate to this age." Whether or not I even agree with her. I mean, I don't see the need to do a guest star role for somebody that does a TV sitcom.
> Mara: Well, not that they discussed that issue on it.
> George: Well, I'm sure they didn't.
> Mara: They didn't.
> George: But it's indicative. That's not a good example, but it's indicative of the kind of things that have been incorporated into *Sesame Street*, and it's sort of like, there's better things to do with time.

DeGeneres's appearance was "at least an implicit endorsement here of who this person is, much like any media appearance," George added.

Clearly *Sesame Street* represented tension and contradiction for the Walkers, and their wariness of the show was connected to their position as anti-fans of *Ellen* and DeGeneres, who embodied a lifestyle they believed was immoral. They worked around the contradictions of contemporary media by watching old Disney classics, old cartoons, and videos of old movies that addressed families like theirs: nuclear, middle class, and heterosexual. They approved of these because they lacked positive references to gays and lesbians.

The Walkers' geographic location is also an important context and helps bring their individual narratives to the social level. They lived in a conservative city in Colorado whose voters in 1992 overwhelmingly supported a successful state ballot initiative that would have barred lesbians and gay men from certain civil-rights protections. The campaigns around the measure were bitter, and four years of legal challenges ended in 1996 when the U.S. Supreme Court supported a state supreme court decision declaring the measure unconstitutional (Wadsworth 1997). Seen in this context, the Walkers' choice of pre-*Ellen* entertainment was also a social decision. Since the early 1990s, gays and lesbians were often subjects of discussion and religious commentary, much of it heated and bitter. The Walkers' efforts to exclude what was disagreeable and painful to them were so thorough that George could also insist that Ellen DeGeneres's appearance on *Sesame Street* was a "nonissue for us because it's not a daily part of our lives." The children did not routinely watch *Sesame Street*—but they did not watch it because it was proscribed. The Walkers' choice of television shows—and the way they framed them for their children—were attempts to exclude alterity. They seemed to select a tradition—to localize Williams's term—and apply it to contemporary life despite the changes around them. The Walkers' chronotope, then, brought the 1950s into the present so that they could control the present in their home.

The Walkers' preference for noncontemporary television and books masked a hurt that was both painful and unbearable to the Walkers: the existence of homosexuality, a way of life their religious beliefs defined as immoral. Older cultural works were safe because they contained no representations that the Walkers recognized as referencing a family style that they fundamentally opposed. This family tried to control the present in terms of a particular moment in the past by policing the popular culture that came into their home. The Walkers' anti-fandom was an engagement with popular culture, as they actively chose residual elements in popular culture products and worked to keep their family within this residual culture, in a chronotope that reflected the way the Walker parents wanted their children to experience the world. Bakhtin describes this chronotopic process of exchange:

> The work and the world represented in it enter the real world and enrich it, and the real world enters the work and its world as part of the process of its creation, as well as part of its subsequent life, in a continual renewing of the work through the creative perception of listeners and readers. (Bahktin 1981: 254)

This way of engaging with popular culture was similar to the way another, very different family, the Farmers, dealt with popular culture. What follows is a look at the Farmers and the chronotope they constructed.

The Farmers

The Farmers, who lived in another small house in a contiguous neighbor-hood only a few miles from the Walkers, wrested very different meanings from the shows they watched and from their childhood television experi-ences.[6] They weren't fans of *Ellen,* having watched it only twice, but they did so out of a sense that watching would somehow help counter what they regarded as a virulent antigay atmosphere in their city. Rather, they were non-fans in the sense that a show that they watched rarely neverthe-less had meaning for them. The Farmer adults, Jane and Theo, identified with the small population of liberal Democrats in their conservative region. Unlike the Walkers, the Farmers weren't religious: Theo was an atheist, having pulled away in high school from his mainline Protestant church, and Jane had no formal religion. Like the Walkers, both were col-lege educated, and Theo had a graduate degree. Their annual income of about $20,000 was lower than the Walkers' and like the Walkers, they had little money for nonnecessities, though their tastes were middle class. They owned their house. Unlike the Walkers, they had a non-1950s family form: Theo's primary duties were at home, as he cleaned, cooked, shopped, and was the main caretaker for their daughters, eight and six. He sometimes did salaried work for short periods on contract, and when the girls were in school he worked on a novel he was writing. Jane worked in a low-paying job that dealt with public policy issues.

In effect, the Farmer adults regarded themselves as non-fans of televi-sion. "I don't really watch television," Jane said. Theo expressed surprise that most of his acquaintances had memorized television schedules; he did not know when most popular shows were on. However, both offered deft rundowns of scenes and characters in *Sesame Street* and *Power Rangers,* past favorites of their younger daughter. Their daily viewing, though lim-ited, was more than the Walkers reported.

Like the Walkers' disdain for all things Ellen, the Farmers worked hard to banish one particular kind of television programming: the news. Their critique of news was based on vivid television experiences in Jane's child-hood, described as she recalled a time when television schedules were important to her:

> Jane: Oh, I watched a *ton* of TV when I was a kid. Every night, what was on
> and what we were going to watch, every night. . . . I'd watch it by myself.

I'd come home after school and do a little homework, or watch, if I knew what was on, I would go on—We'd usually watch something right before dinner. Oh yeah, right before dinner we'd watch for half an hour. Mom knew. Dad was usually very regular about coming home, so she knew the shows were over. So that never to me was a conflict, but I don't know if she would tell you that. It didn't ever seem to me. We had to go and set the table, and we'd go up during the commercial, and she'd let us do that, set the table, come down. Never got us out of doing anything she wanted us to do. But it was definitely a pastime. Then we'd watch our shows in the evening, whatever they might be.

Diane: Do you remember a favorite show that you had?

Jane: Umm, not any more.

The regularity, the time spent, and the seamlessness with which Jane's watching fit with her family's routines were much more memorable than the shows she watched. In fact, her 1950s-style childhood nuclear family structure—which included a stay-at-home mother who had dinner on the table at a set time for a salaried father with regular daytime hours—worked well with the medium, as its purveyors intended.[7] Her own salaried mother/stay-at-home father family form was not designed for 1950s-style television. Instead, her children sometimes watched cartoons in the morning before school, and the closest television got to dinner was when Theo and their daughters rented movies and ordered pizza on the nights that Jane worked late.

The memory of unconflicted predictability around television took on a different character when Jane recalled watching news with her grandfather. It was through television news that Jane, who is white, first encountered images of American blacks, crime, and violence. She connected those three elements, but did not seem to draw such a negative portrait of white protesters of the Vietnam War. Born in 1958, she recalled "how mad everybody was. Remember Vietnam, the war, and the violence of all that. Especially in the early 60s, how awful that was."

Her sharpest memory was of watching the five o'clock news with her grandfather, who "ruled" when he visited. She would listen to him being "real racist about" televised rioting. Her recollection of television was not fondly nostalgic in the way that the Walkers' memories of old television shows were, but her interpretation of what she watched as a child had a bearing on her contemporary consideration of television. Later on, she came to believe that portrayals of African-Americans on television were false, and found her memories of her grandfather's racist commentary unsettling. News, she had concluded, was "too disturbing" for her daughters, who were not allowed to watch news shows. They were "too violent for kids," Theo said. "It's too disturbing for these guys," Jane added. "The mean-spiritedness of so much of it is so hard to understand." Jane's memories of watching television news reports were painful and affected the Farmers' decision to ban television news for their daughters, as they tried to contain this "hurt" of 1960s history.

Just as the Walkers tried to shield their children from bad influences on television, so too did the Farmers work to keep out a different kind of alterity. Besides their careful avoidance of news, the Farmers policed the content of children's cartoons. Unlike the Walkers, they found old cartoons far less safe and criticized them for the way they portrayed women and blacks. As Jane observed,

> The girls really like to watch old cartoons, like Cartoon Network. And they'll have old Tom and Jerry's and old, you name it, it's still on. And boy, do I notice the racism and sexism in those. Incredible! And I know that impacts them. And how women are treated. They're always sex symbols in those cartoons. They're always the weak person that's gotta be saved by the main character or the hero of the story, whatever character it is. And I notice that. Some of the action cartoons that they'll watch once in awhile, Captain Planet or something, usually have a pretty strong female character that's equal with men. They'll have their own special powers. But there generally is a couple of female characters in them, both villains and heroes. So I think there's a lot more of that. You would never have seen that. It would have been highly unusual, I think, to have seen that kind of character when we were a kid.

Indeed, it would have been highly unusual for Jane to have seen such female cartoon characters when she was a young child. Jane would have been well past early childhood when a woman cartoon superhero, Wonder Woman, was created, for example (Schneider, with Pullen 2001: 76). Thus when Jane cited televised cartoons as markers of social change, she noted changes set in motion after her own cartoon-watching years and in time for her children to see what she regarded as positive role models. The sexist cartoons were residual cultural products, and Jane and Theo worked to provide a different environment than the past that produced the sexist cartoons. They did this, for example, by joking about the sexist images and action in old cartoons:

Jane: We'll say things like, "Oh, that girl sure doesn't know what to do!" Or, "Oh, who'd want to be that lady in those high heels!" Or something like that. And talk a little. And they'll joke about it and say, "Yeah." And I get the sense that they separate it from themselves, being that character all of a sudden.

In this, the Farmers' chronotopes were in tune with the emerging-to-dominant critique of "traditional" sex roles, as their vision of the female superhero-as-role-model nicely dovetails with the networks' additions to cartoon fare. In these ways, the Farmers' reading of television reflected their political views, which were very different from the Walkers.'

The Walker and Farmer parents all described themselves as alert to content that was not "appropriate" for their children, and the term was so loaded with meaning that they had trouble defining "appropriate" in the abstract. They all agreed that sexual references were inappropriate for children, and that television programming contained too many references to sexual acts. The Farmers simply turned off the television when an image or story line seemed overtly sexual. The Walkers did the same. Both sets of parents also firmly believed that television was "too commercial," as George described it. All four adults described times they'd encouraged their children to be skeptical of television advertising. The Walkers taped Super Bowl broadcasts so they could skip over the commercials—thus effectively banishing sales pitches and sex at the same time. Jane Farmer told her children about a college friend of hers who had tossed a television out a window because commercials interrupted his hockey-game viewing. All, though, took for granted that television was "commercial" and felt their job as parents was to teach their children to think critically about the commercial aspects, but not necessarily to take collective action by, for example, lobbying for noncommercial television. With these constraints, all shared a definition of home—their particular and very different homes—as a place to keep out the "bad." Only at home, then, could they defend against the bad, and they went to extraordinary efforts to fashion time, space, and memory into chronotopes that allowed them to engage with popular culture and at the same time to interpret it in ways that seemed safe for their families.

These families' interpretations were their own constraints on history that made them uncomfortable, as they attempted to sidestep or avoid the history they abhorred. The Walkers did this by looking back to early television and books that contained no positive references to gays and lesbians, whose ways of living they regarded with religious disapproval. In contrast, the Farmers embraced some contemporary cultural products precisely because they cast a positive light on gays and lesbians, an impulse directly related to the political climate in their city. However, the Farmers, being non-fans of *Ellen*, did not talk extensively about the show but instead focused on such things as the positive portrayals of women they had seen in contemporary cartoons. Both sets of parents, then, attempted to avoid the "hurts" of history by constructing narratives that had better endings—the Walkers wanted a life free of obvious homosexuality, and the Farmers wanted a nonsexist world for their daughters. Both families tried to create these respective chronotopes within the boundaries of their home, even as their politics indicated a hope that they could eventually reproduce the terms of home in the culture at large.

Anti-fans and Non-fans and Their Relation to the Culture

Through their work as anti-fans and non-fans, these parents used popular culture products to think about the past and to define themselves in the present. The Walkers used their memories socially: if we keep popular culture from the 1950s around us, we can build a home environment that bars difference by employing the same constraints as some particular safe point in the past. The Farmers also had a particular, contemporary reading of old cartoons and were grateful for new, nonsexist ones they hoped would be a stronger influence on their daughters. This is also a social use of memory. However, Jane refused to let her daughters watch television news because her memories of watching news were so painful. In both families, one can see a tendency to distort the past in order to keep it in the present. As Lipsitz observed in another context, people use popular culture to discuss core contradictions in society that were indirectly reflected in popular culture (1990: xviii-xiv).

The Farmers embraced much about television that emerged from social changes in the 1960s and 1970s that brought more middle-class women into the workforce: characters and story lines questioning the female stay-at-home role in the family; presentation of new, nonsexist social relations and female superheroes in cartoons; and appreciation for emergent gay family forms as hinted at in *Ellen*. This marks them as anti-fans of the "old" in television entertainment and news, as the chronotope they constructed to deal with television distanced their children from news, which they banned, and old cartoons, which they interrupted with commentary.

In contrast, the Walkers embraced very little of contemporary television, and their anti-fan stance towards works that cast gays in a positive light emerged clearly in the way they engaged with *Ellen* and its main character. Indeed, as the gay family form began to be chronicled in *Ellen* and normalized elsewhere on television in *Sesame Street,* the Walkers tried to exorcise this social change from their household by creating their own, alternate tradition. Drawing on residual, 1950s-style cultural products, they constructed a chronotope very much rooted in the past. In doing this, they tapped into an already thriving alternative culture created within some segments of the vast Christian evangelical population, with various organizations offering alternative children's products (such as *Veggie Tales* and other children's shows sold on videos and, later, DVDs), advice about home schooling, and more overtly political efforts to limit civil rights of gays and lesbians.

It's striking that both the Farmers and the Walkers seemed to recognize as dominant the changes in family form and the decline of sexist images in cartoons. More significantly, both sets of parents seemed to feel they could have no effect on television itself, perhaps in part because of this dominance. Both families took for granted key things about U.S. television, including its aggressively commercial nature, for example. In the end, carefully constructing chronotopes within the family home was the only way they could deal with television.

Notes

1. I would like to thank Jonathan Gray for pointing out the connection between what these parents did and Bahktin's concept of chronotope, or time-space. Bahktin defined chronotope as "the instrinsic connectedness of temporal and spatial relationships that are artistically expressed in literature" (1981: 84).

2. *Ellen,* a situation comedy starring Ellen DeGeneres, ran from 1994 to 1998. In its fourth season the title character came out as a lesbian.

3. The notion that audience members do cultural work follows the work of Dan Schiller, who argues that audience members are doing labor within the second of two "moments" of cultural production that center on the media as sites of institutionalized cultural production and audience members as producers "who contribute to their own self-understanding" (1996: 194).

4. The Walkers were interviewed at their home over several weeks in 1999. Their names are pseudonyms, as are all names of interviewees discussed in this chapter. Most of the interviews cited here were conducted as part of the Media,

Symbolism, and the Lifecourse project at the University of Colorado at Boulder under a grant from the Lilly Endowment.

5. The nostalgic image of the "traditional" nuclear family is associated with the 1950s: father as breadwinner, mother at home with children in a middle-class, private, autonomous unit. Stephanie Coontz observes that this image was accurate, but only narrowly, as it was a "historical fluke" in the white middle class for a period in the 1950s. Most U.S. families before and since the 1950s have not fit this model, although it persists in popular culture (Coontz 1992: 28).

6. The Farmers were interviewed over several weeks in 1997. The two families did not know each other.

7. Indeed, as Lynn Spigel notes, television in the decades after World War II came to signify an ideal of family togetherness, expressed through advertising aimed at the middle-class, suburban, nuclear family (Spigel 1992: 44–45).

26

Afterword
The Future of Fandom

Henry Jenkins

By now, reading mass media coverage as symptomatic of the cultural status of fandom has become a central genre in fan studies. Witness the introduction to this collection, which explores some of the contradictions in the ways the mainstream media covers fans—patronizing Harry Potter fans as "Potterheads" even as they court Yankees fans in their sports section.

Now it's my turn to look at another signpost. *Newsweek*'s April 3, 2006, issue (Levy & Stone 2006: 45–53) has a cover story on "Putting the 'We' in Web," which describes the convergence of factors that is leading to the success of a range of significant new companies, including Flickr, MySpace, Drabble, YouTube, Craigslist, eBay, del.icio.us, and Facebook, among others. Each of these companies is reaching critical mass by "harnessing collective intelligence," supporting User-Generated Content, and creating a new "architecture of participation," to use three concepts much beloved by the ever-present industry guru Tim O'Reilly (2005).

Newsweek reduces the phenomenon of "social media" or "web 2.0" to the phrase, "it's not an audience, it's a community," arguing that such services transform the relationship between media producers and consumers. As they explain, "MySpace, Flickr, and all the other newcomers aren't places to go, but things to do, ways to express yourself, means to connect with others and extend your own horizons" (Levy & Stone 2006: 53). The article comments extensively on the way average consumers of brands and branded entertainment are playing a more active role in shaping the flow of media throughout our culture, are drawn together by shared passions and investment in specific media properties or platforms, and often create new context by appropriating, remixing, or modifying existing media content in clever and inventive ways.

Nowhere in the article do the authors ever use the term "fan."

Indeed, the whole discourse about "web 2.0" has been animated by a hunger to develop a new, more empowered, more socially connected, and more creative image of the consumer. Most of the key figures in the movement agree that the old-style consumer is dead, RIP. Here's cyber-columnist Clay Shirky on this point:

> The historic role of the consumer has been nothing more than a giant maw at the end of the mass media's long conveyer belt, the all-absorbing Yin to mass media's all-producing Yang. Mass media's role has been to package consumers and sell their attention to the advertisers, in bulk. The consumers' appointed role in this system gives them no way to communicate anything about themselves except their preference between Coke and Pepsi, Bounty and Brawny, Trix and Chex. They have no way to respond to the things they see on television or hear on the radio, and they have no access to any media on their own—media is something that is done to them, and consuming is how they register their response[. . . .] In the age of the internet, no one is a passive consumer anymore because everyone is a media outlet. (1999: n.p.)

Shirky, in effect, seems to be traversing the same terrain fan studies traveled several decades ago, reasserting the emergence of the active audience in response to the perceived passivity of mass media consumers. Of course, in this formulation, it is the technology that has liberated the consumer and not their own subcultural practices.

If everyone agrees that those people formerly known as consumers will gain a new role in this still-emerging digital culture, there's not much agreement about what to call that role. Some call such people "loyals," stressing the value of consumer commitment in an era of channel zapping; some are calling them "media-actives," suggesting that they are much more likely to demand the right to participate within the media franchise than previous generations; some are calling them "prosumers," suggesting that as consumers produce and circulate media, they are blurring the line between amateur and professional; some are calling them "inspirational consumers" or "connectors" or "influencers," suggesting that some people play a more active role than others in shaping media flows and creating new values.

Grant McCracken, the anthropologist and media consultant, calls such people multipliers:

> [T]he term multiplier may help marketers acknowledge more forthrightly that whether our work is a success is in fact out of our control. All we can do is to invite the multiplier to participate in the construction of the brand by putting it to work for their own purposes in their own world. When we called them "consumers" we could think of our creations as an end game and their responses as an end state. The term "multiplier" or something like it makes it clear that we depend on them to complete the work. (2005: n.p.)

When he's talking about consumers of manufactured products, management professor Eric Von Hippel (2005) talks about "lead users," that is, early adopters and early adapters of emerging technologies and services. Understand how these lead users retrofit your products to suit their needs and you understand important new directions for innovation. In a sense, fans can be seen as lead users of media content—consider for example the ways that the concept of the fan metatext (Jenkins 1992), linking together the back stories of series characters, prefigures our current era, when serialization has come to be the norm across all media properties.

Wired magazine editor Chris Anderson (2006) has offered a particular version of this argument about grassroots intermediaries creating value, what has come to be known as the "long tail." Anderson argues that investing in niche properties with small but committed consumer bases may make economic sense if you can lower costs of production and replace marketing costs by building a much stronger network with your desired consumers.

None of these commentators on the new economy are using the terms "fan," "fandom," or "fan culture," yet their models rest on the same social behaviors and emotional commitments that fan scholars have been researching over the past several decades. The new multipliers are simply a less geeky version of the fan—fans who don't wear rubber Spock ears, fans who didn't live in their parents' basement, fans who have got a life. In other words, they are fans that don't fit the stereotypes. These writers are predicting, and documenting, a world where what we are calling "fan culture" has a real economic and cultural impact; where fan tastes are ruling at the box office (witness all of the superhero and fantasy blockbusters of recent years); where fan tastes are dominating television (resulting in the kind of complexity that Steven Johnson celebrates in his new book, *Every-*

thing Bad Is Good for You [2005]); where fan practices are shaping the games industry (where today's modders quickly get recruited by the big companies). Indeed, many media analysts believe that these communities of prosumers, multipliers, loyals, influenciers, ahmm, *fans,* will play an even greater role in the future as people begin to explore the use of the video iPod as a distribution channel for media content and as people begin to talk about something fans have been promoting at least since the 1980s—subscription-based models for supporting the production and distribution of cult television series (Askwith 2005; Bowers 2006; Jenkins 2005b).

The commercial discourse represents only part of the picture. According to a 2005 study (Lenhardt & Madden 2005) conducted by the Pew Internet & American Life Project, more than half of all American teens— and 57 percent of teens who use the Internet—could be considered media creators. For the purpose of the study, a media creator was defined as someone who "created a blog or webpage, posted original artwork, photography, stories or videos online or remixed online content into their own new creations." Most have done two or more of these activities. Thirty-three percent of teens share what they create online with others. Nineteen percent remix content they found online (i.e. what we used to call poaching). Many of these young people are being drawn towards fan communities—not because of their passionate and affectionate relationship to media content but because those communities offer them the best network to get what they have made in front of a larger public. Educators are embracing these fan communities as sites of informal learning, as what James Gee (2004) is calling "affinity spaces."

A 2005 report on *The Future of Independent Media,* prepared by Andrew Blau (2005) for the Global Business Network, argued that this kind of grassroots creativity was an important engine of cultural transformation:

> The media landscape will be reshaped by the bottom-up energy of media created by amateurs and hobbyists as a matter of course. This bottom up energy will generate enormous creativity, but it will also tear apart some of the categories that organize the lives and work of media makers[. . . .] A new generation of media makers and viewers are [sic] emerging which could lead to a sea change in how media is made and consumed.

Blau's report celebrates a world where everyone has access to the means of creative expression and the networks supporting artistic distribution.

So, in a sense, my title is misleading. This isn't an essay about "the future of fandom." It's an essay that asserts that fandom represents the experimental prototype, the testing ground for the way media and culture industries are going to operate in the future. In the old days, the ideal consumer watched television, bought products, and didn't talk back. Today, the ideal consumer talks up the program and spreads word about the brand. The old ideal might have been the couch potato; the new ideal is almost certainly a fan.

I make a case for such a perspective in my new book, *Convergence Culture: Where Old and New Media Collide* (Jenkins 2006), which is in a loose sense a sequel to *Textual Poachers* (Jenkins 1992) in that it describes what has happened to participatory culture in the wake of a decade-plus of digital media, a world where it no longer makes sense to think of fans as "rogue readers" or "poachers," to use two oft-quoted formulations from that earlier book. Everyone's talking about consumers as active participants—we simply can't agree about the terms of our participation, which is why intellectual property is emerging as one of the key drivers of cultural and political policy at the present moment.

Again, let me say it, *fandom* is the future. I use the word "fandom" and not "fans" here for good reason. To me, it seems a little paradoxical that the rest of the people involved in this conversation are more and more focused on consumption as a social, networked, collaborative process ("harnessing collective intelligence," "the wisdom of crowds," and all of that), whereas so much of the recent work in fan studies has returned to a focus on the individual fan. Leave aside my concerns that a return to individual psychology runs the risk of reintroducing all of those pathological explanations that we fought so hard to dismantle. While sometimes a useful corrective to the tendency of earlier generations of fan scholars to focus on the more public and visible aspects of fan culture, this focus on the individual may throw out the baby with the bathwater. We now have tools for studying and concepts to talk about the social dimensions of fan culture, which is no longer the "weekend-only world" I described in *Textual Poachers* (Jenkins 1992), or even the kind of "just-in-time fandom" that Matt Hills (2002) wrote about—this kind of fandom is everywhere and all the time, a central part of the everyday lives of consumers operating within a networked society. Certainly, there are still people who only watch the show, but more and more of them are sneaking a peak at what they are saying about the show on *Television without Pity*, and once you are there, why not post a few comments. It's a slippery slope from there.

We should no longer be talking about fans as if they were somehow marginal to the ways the culture industries operate when these emerging forms of consumer power have been the number one topic of discussion at countless industry conferences over the past few years. We may want to think long and hard about what we feel about fans moving onto the center stage, but we should guard against our long-standing romance with our ghettoization. The old categories of resistance and cooptation seem quaint compared to the complex and uncharted terrain that we are now exploring. Increasingly, fan scholars have recognized that fan culture is born of a mixture of fascination and frustration, that appropriation involves both accepting certain core premises in the original work and reworking others to accommodate our own interests. We now need to accept that what we used to call cooptation also involves a complex set of negotiations during which the media industries have to change to accommodate the demands of consumers even as they seek to train consumers to behave in ways that are beneficial to their interests. Media companies act differently today because they have been shaped by the increased visibility of participatory culture: they are generating new kinds of content and forming new kinds of relationships with their consumers.

Media scholars have been understandably ambivalent about these shifts. There is a school of thought, for example, that links user-generated content with the downsizing of the creative economy, that sees these forms of commercially embraced grassroots expression primarily as a means of cutting costs by off-loading jobs onto consumers who now produce the content others are consuming and even create the networks through which that content is circulating. I certainly understand that perspective, especially when you consider that few of these media companies are passing the savings from this downsizing back to the consumer in terms of lower prices or fewer adverts. We should certainly avoid celebrating a process that commodifies fan cultural production and sells it back to us with a considerable markup. Yet, these same trends can also be understood in terms of making companies more responsive to their most committed consumers, as extending the influence that fans exert over the media they love, and fans as creating a context in which more people create and circulate media that more perfectly reflects their own world views. I can understand why we might now want to call this a democratization of culture—which is to read a social, cultural, and economic shift in overly political terms. But there is a new kind of cultural power emerging as fans bond together within larger knowledge communities, pool their information, shape each other's opinions, and develop a greater self-consciousness about their shared agendas and common interests. We might think of these new knowledge communities as collective bargaining units for consumers. These groups can be used for viral marketing or to rally support behind an endangered series, but they can also turn against brands or production companies that act in ways that damage the fans' shared investment in the property (Kozinets 1999).

I bring all of this up because of a tendency (even in the best of us) to see fan studies as a somewhat specialized, narrowly defined body of research that operates on the fringes of contemporary media studies. We still seem to feel a need to justify our topics, explain how and why we are spending so much time looking at these geeks. Think of it as a kind of colonial cringe—if popular culture is a bad object compared to literary studies, then fan research is a bad object compared to communications studies. Elsewhere, these same core concepts (appropriation, participation, emotional investment, collective intelligence, virtual community) are seen as central to discussions of economics, art, law, politics, education, even religion. Fans may not need to move out of their parents' basements, but fan scholars might need to get out of their offices a little more, talk to the political economist across the hall, the marketing professor one floor down, or the law professor on the other side of campus. Suddenly, after decades of brushing past each other on the way to the faculty meeting, these folks are talking about and thinking about the same things we are— they are just using a different language to talk about them. Maybe we should be paying some attention.

Why should fan scholars be having their own separate little conversation rather than playing a much more vivid and active role in the larger discussion about the present moment of media transition and transformation? Why are graduate students still having to explain why they want to do their dissertations on fan culture, and why are junior faculty worried that their interests may not earn them tenure? Why do we still allow ourselves to be browbeaten by the folks with the red pens who have always claimed the right to police our culture? We fail if we simply circle around the same theories and the same debates, if we introduce no new concepts and few new arguments to the stew.

In such a context, it is so exciting to see this collection bring together important fan scholars, old and new, and push them to think deeply about what's really at stake in their research. The essays here raise a whole new range of issues, theoretical models, and methodological approaches that might inform the study of fans and fandom. Perhaps most importantly, there has been a radical expansion of what we mean by fan culture—a movement to diversify the kinds of media content and fan activities we study (beyond the early focus on science fiction to include the full scope of the contemporary creative economy—sports, soap operas, the literary canon); a movement to expand the historical context of fan culture (to deal with fandom as a set of historically specific practices and cultural logics that have shifted profoundly over the past decade, let alone in the course of the past several centuries); and an expansion beyond American fans to understand fan culture as operating within a global context—and indeed, to understand fandom as a key driver opening Western markets to the circulation of Asian-made media products, for example. I am deeply excited by each of these moves to broaden the context and mission of fan studies and to thus complicate further our initial assumptions about what constitutes a fan.

And yet, at the end of the day, as fandom becomes such an elastic category, one starts to wonder—who isn't a fan? What doesn't constitute fan culture? Where does grassroots culture end and commercial culture begin? Where does niche media start to blend over into the mainstream? Or indeed, as some recent work in subculture studies suggests, might we have to face the reality that in an age where differences proliferate, where old gatekeepers wither, there may no longer be a "normal" way of consuming media. Maybe, as some subculture studies folks (Bennett & Kahn-Harris 2004) are arguing, there is no longer a centralized or dominant culture against which subcultures define themselves. Maybe there is no typical media consumer against which the cultural otherness of the fan can be located. Perhaps we are all fans or perhaps none of us is.

This would be consistent with the erasure of the term "fan" and the absence of the fan stereotype in recent media coverage like the *Newsweek* article (Levy & Stone 2006) with which this essay began. As fandom becomes part of the normal way that the creative industries operate, then fandom may cease to function as a meaningful category of cultural analysis.

Maybe in that sense, fandom has *no* future.

Bibliography

Aarseth, E 1997, *Cybertext: perspectives on ergodic literature,* John Hopkins University Press, Baltimore.

Abbas, A 1997, *Hong Kong: culture and the politics of disappearance,* Hong Kong University Press, Hong Kong.

Abercrombie, N & Longhurst, B 1998, *Audiences: a sociological theory of performance and imagination,* Sage, Thousand Oaks, CA.

Abercrombie, N, Hill, S, & Turner, BS 1980, *The dominant ideology thesis,* Allen & Unwin, Boston.

Aden, RC 1999, *Popular stories and promised lands: fan cultures and symbolic pilgrimages,* University of Alabama Press, Tuscaloosa.

Adorno, TW 1991, "The position of the narrator in the contemporary novel," in R Tiedemann (ed.), *Notes on literature,* Columbia University Press, New York.

Alasuutari, P 1999a, "Introduction: three phases of reception studies," in P Alasuutari (ed.), *Rethinking the media audience,* Sage, Thousand Oaks, CA.

Alasuutari, P (ed.) 1999b, *Rethinking the media audience: the new agenda,* Sage, Thousand Oaks, CA.

Algan, E 2003, "The problem of textuality in ethnographic audience research: lessons learned in Southeast Turkey," in PD Murphy & MM Kraidy (eds.), *Global media studies: ethnographic perspectives,* Routledge, New York.

Alters, DF 2003, "We hardly watch that rude, crude show: class and taste in *The Simpsons,*" in CA Stabile & MT Harrison (eds.), *Prime time animation: television animation and American culture,* Routledge, New York.

Althorp, W 1879, "Musicians and music lovers," *Atlantic Monthly* 43(256), 145–53.

American Historical Association 2005, *Statement on standards of professional conduct.* Retrieved December 14, 2005, from http://www.historians.org/pubs/Free/ProfessionalStandards.cfm.

Anderson, C 2006. *The long tale: why the future of business is selling less of more,* Hyperion, New York.

Andrejevic, M 2003, "Monitored mobility in the era of mass customization," *Space and Culture* 6(2), 132–50.

Ang, I 1985, *Watching Dallas: soap opera and the melodramatic imagination,* Routledge, New York.

Appadurai, A 1990, "Disjuncture and difference in the global economy," *Theory, Culture, and Society* 7, 295–310.

Armstrong, G 1998, *Football hooligans: knowing the score,* Berg, Oxford.

Arnold, A 1991, *Hindi filmi geet.* Ph.D. Dissertation, University of Illinois, Urbana-Champaign.

Askwith, I 2005, "TV you'll want to pay for: how $2 downloads can revive network television," *Slate,* 1 November. Retrieved April 2, 2006, from http://www.slate.com/id/2129003.

Asmodeus 1850, *The Jenny Lind mania in Boston; or, a sequel to Barnum's Parnassus,* publisher unknown, Boston.

Augé, M 1995 *Non-Places,* Verso, London.

Auslander, P 1999, *Liveness: performance in a mediatised culture,* Routledge, New York.

Babiniotis, G 1998, *Lexicon of modern Greek,* Center of Lexicology, Athens (in Greek).

Back, L, Crabbe, T, & Solomos, J 2001, *The changing face of football: racism, identity, and multiculture in the English game,* Berg, Oxford.

Bacon-Smith, C 1992, *Enterprising women: television fandom and the creation of popular myth,* University of Pennsylvania Press, Philadelphia.

Bailey, S 2005, *Media audiences and identity: self-construction in the fan experience,* Palgrave-Macmillan, New York.

Bakhtin, MM 1981, *The dialogic imagination,* trans. C Emerson & M Holquist, University of Texas Press, Austin.

Bale, J 1993, *Sport, space, and the city,* Routledge, New York.

Band, J & Schruers, M 2005, "*Dastar,* attribution, and plagiarism," *AIPLA Quarterly Journal* 33, 1–23.

Barker, M & Brooks, K 1998, *Knowing audiences:* Judge Dredd, *its friends, fans, and foes,* University of Luton Press, Luton, UK.

Barker, M, Arthurs, J & Harindranath, R 2001, *The* Crash *controversy: censorship and film reception,* Wallflower, New York.

Barthes, R 1972, *Mythologies,* Hill & Wang, New York.

Barthes, R 1977, *Image, music, text,* Fontana Press, London.

Barthes, R 2005, *The neutral,* Columbia University Press, New York.

Baudrillard, J 1990, *Fatal strategies,* Semiotext(e), New York.

Baudrillard, J 1996, *Cool memories II,* Duke University Press, Durham, NC.

Baudrillard, J 2003a, *Cool memories IV,* Verso, London.

Baudrillard, J 2003b, *Passwords,* Verso, London.

Bauman, Z 1998a, "Exit visas and entry tickets: the paradox of Jewish assimilation," *Telos* 77, 45–77.

Bauman, Z 1998b, *Globalization: the human consequences,* Polity, Cambridge, UK.

Baym, NK 2000, *Tune in, log on: soaps, fandom, and online community,* Sage, Thousand Oaks, CA.

BBC News 2005, "Bush's iPod reveals music tastes," 13 April. Retrieved January 31, 2006, from http://news.bbc.co.uk/1/hi/world/americas/4435639.stm.

Because AUs Make Us Happy n.d. Retrieved December 13, 2005, from http://strangeplaces.net/challenge/five.html.

Beekley, N 1849, diary, octavo vol. 1, American Antiquarian Society, Worcester, MA.

Benjamin, W 1968, "The work of art in the age of mechanical reproduction," in *Illuminations,* Schocken Books, New York.

Benjamin, W 1983, *Das Passagen-Werk,* R. Tiedemann (ed.), Suhrkamp, Frankfurt aM.

Bennett, A & Kahn-Harris, K 2004, *After subcultures: critical studies in contemporary youth culture,* Palgrave MacMillan, London.

Bennett, A & Peterson, RA 2004, *Music scenes: local, translocal, and virtual,* Vanderbilt University Press, Nashville, TN.

Bennett, S 1997, *Theatre audiences: a theory of production and reception,* Routledge, New York.

Bertrand, B 2004, "Yardtards and backyard BS." Retrieved November 20, 2005, from http://www.obsessedwithwrestling.com/columns/brianbertrand/03.html.

Bérubé, M (ed.) 2005, *The aesthetics of cultural studies,* Blackwell, Oxford.

Bielby, DD, Harrington, CL, & Bielby, W 1999, "Whose stories are they? Fan's engagement with soap opera narratives in three sites of fan activity," *Journal of Broadcasting and Electronic Media* 43(4), 35–51.

Bielby, DD, Moloney, M, & Harrington, CL n.d., "Where in the world is fan studies?" manuscript in preparation.

Bird, SE 1992, *For enquiring minds: a cultural study of supermarket tabloids,* University of Tennessee Press, Knoxville.

Bird, SE 2003, *The audience in everyday life: living in a media world,* Routledge, New York.

Bird, SE & Barber, J 2002, "Constructing a virtual ethnography," in M Angrosino (ed.), *Doing anthropology: projects for ethnographic data collection,* Waveland Press, Prospect Heights, IL.

Blau, A 2005, "The future of independent media," *Deeper News* 10(1). Retrieved April 2, 2006, from http://www.gbn.com/ArticleDisplayServlet.srv?aid=34045.

Bogiopoulos, N & Milakas D 2005, *A religion with no disbelievers: football,* Livanis Publications, Athens (in Greek).

Bourdieu, P 1984, *Distinction: a social critique of the judgment of taste,* Harvard University Press, Cambridge, MA.

Bourdieu, P 1993, *The field of cultural production,* Polity, Cambridge, UK.

Bourdieu, P 1998, *Pascalian meditations,* Stanford University Press, Stanford, CA.

Bourdieu, P 1999, "Structures, *habitus,* practices," in A Elliot (ed.), *Contemporary social theory,* Blackwell, New York.

Bowers, A 2006, "Reincarnating *The West Wing:* could the canceled NBC drama be reborn on iTunes?" *Slate,* January 24. Retrieved April 2, 2006, from http://www.slate.com/id/2134803/.

Brimson, D & Brimson, E 1996, *Everywhere we go,* Headline, London.

Brook, M n.d., *The fan fiction FAQ.* Retrieved December 13, 2005, from http://www.meljeanbrook.com/fanficread.php?file=fanficfaq.html&title=The%20Fan%20Fiction%20FAQ.

Brooker, W 2002, *Using the force: creativity, community, and* Star Wars *fans,* Continuum, New York.

Brooker, W 2004, "Living on *Dawson's Creek:* teen viewers, cultural convergence, and television overflow," in RC Allen & A Hill (eds.), *The television studies reader,* Routledge, New York.

Brooker, W 2005a, *Alice's adventures: Lewis Carroll in popular culture,* Continuum, New York.

Brooker, W (ed.) 2005b, *The* Blade Runner *experience: the legacy of a science fiction classic,* Wallflower, New York.

Brown, J 2001, "Personalize me, baby," *Salon,* April 6, 2005. Retrieved November 8, 2005, from http://www.salon.com/tech/feature/2001/04/06/personalization/print.html.

Brown, ME 1994, *Soap opera and women's talk: the pleasure of resistance,* Sage, Newbury Park, CA.

Bryant, WC II & Voss, TG (eds.) 1975, *Letters of William Cullen Bryant,* vol. 2, Fordham University Press, New York.

Bryce, J & Rutter, J 2001, "In the game—in the flow: presence in public computer gaming," poster presented at Computer Games and Digital Textualities, IT University of Copenhagen, March. Retrieved October 10, 2005, from http://www.digiplay.org.uk/Game.php.

Bryce, J & Rutter, J 2003, "Gender dynamics and the social and spatial organization of computer gaming," *Leisure Studies* 22, 1–15.

Bryce, J & Rutter, J 2006, "Digital games and the violence debate," in J Bryce and J Rutter (eds.) *Understanding digital games,* Sage, Thousand Oaks, CA.

Burkart, P & McCourt, T 2006, *Digital music wars: ownership and control of the celestial jukebox,* Rowman & Littlefield, Boulder, CO.

Burr, V 2005, "Scholar/'shippers and Spikeaholics: academic and fan identities at the Slayage Conference on *Buffy the Vampire Slayer,*" *European Journal of Cultural Studies* 8(3), 375–83.

Butsch, R 2000, *The making of American audiences: from stage to television, 1750–1990,* Cambridge University Press, Cambridge, UK.

Callahan, M 2005, "Potterheads: wizards of odd," *New York Post,* 15 November, 46–47.

Campbell v. Acuff-Rose Music, Inc., 510 US 569, 580 (1994).

Carr, D 2003, "For the press, a case that is an irresistible draw," *New York Times,* 5 June, C5.

Cavicchi, D 1998, *Tramps like us: music and meaning among Springsteen fans,* Oxford University, New York.

Cavicchi, D 2004, "Fans and fan clubs," in G Cross et al. (eds.), *Encyclopedia of recreation and leisure in America*, vol. 1, Scribner's, New York.

Chantraine, P 1964, *Dictionnaire etymologique de la langue Grecque*, Klincksick Editions, Paris.

Choi, Y 2000, "Han Suk-kyu stops official activity for recharging," *Daily Sports*, 15 January. Retrieved January 6, 2006, from http://enportssvc.joins.com.

Choicestream 2004, "eMusic licenses ChoiceStream's MyBestBets personalization platform to power groundbreaking 'Neighbors' and 'Top Fans' features." [Press Release] 22 September. Retrieved November 8, 2005, from http://www.choices-tream.com/pdf/cs_press_040922.pdf.

Chopra, A 2006, "Amitabh Bachchan has a cold," *New York Times*, 12 February. Retrieved March 1, 2006, from http://www.nytimes.com/2006/02/12/movie/12chop.html.

Ciecko, A 2002, "Ways to sink the *Titanic:* contemporary box-office successes in the Philippines, Thailand, and South Korea," *Tamkang Review* 13(2), 1–29.

Ciecko, A 2004, "Muscle, market value, telegenesis, cyberpresence: the new Asian movie star in the global economy of masculine images," in P Petro & T Oren (eds.), *Global currents: media and technology now,* Rutgers University Press, New Brunswick, NJ.

Cine 21 2002, "We met Han Suk-kyu who came back with a movie after three years," 2 May. Retrieved January 6, 2006, from http://www.cine21.co.kr.

Clapp, WE Jr. 1968 [1853], *A record of the Boston stage,* Benjamin Blom, New York.

Clark, D 2000, "New Web sites seek to shape public's taste in music," *Wall Street Journal,* 14 November, B1.

Click, MA forthcoming, *It's "a good thing": the commodification of femininity, affluence, and whiteness in the Martha Stewart phenomenon,* Ph.D. dissertation, University of Massachusetts, Amherst.

Coddington, A 1997, *One of the lads: women who follow football,* HarperCollins, London.

Consalvo, M 2003, "Cyber-slaying media fans: code, digital poaching, and corporate control of the Internet," *Journal of Communication Inquiry* 27(1), 67–86.

Coontz, S 1992, *The way we never were: American families and the nostalgia trap,* Basic Books, New York.

Cooper-Chen, A 1994, "Global games, entertainment, and leisure: women as TV spectators," in PJ Creedon (eds.), *Women, media, and sport,* Sage, London.

Corliss, R 2004, "In the mood for rapture" in *Time Asia Online.* Retrieved August 15, 2005, from http://www.time.com/time/asia/magazine/article/0,13673,501040531–641205,00.html.

Corner, J 1999, *Critical ideas in television studies,* Oxford University Press, Oxford.

Corner, J 2003, review of *The place of media power: pilgrims and witnesses of the media age, Media Culture & Society,* 25(3), 424–26.

Couldry, N 2000, *The place of media power: pilgrims and witnesses of the media age,* Routledge, New York.

Couldry, N 2003, "Passing ethnographies: rethinking the sites of agency and reflexivity in a mediated world," in PD Murphy & M Kraidy (eds.), *Global media studies: ethnographic perspectives,* Routledge, New York.

Couldry, N 2005, "The extended audience: scanning the horizon," in M Gillespie (ed.), *Media audiences,* Open University Press, Maidenhead, UK.

Craib, I 1998, *Experiencing identity,* Sage, London.

Crane, D 2002, "Culture and globalization: theoretical models and emerging trends," in D Crane, N Kawashima, & K Kawasaki (eds.), *Global culture: media, arts, policy, and globalization,* Routledge, New York.

Crane, G 1998, *Thucydides and the ancient simplicity: the limits of political realism,* University of California Press, Berkeley.

Crawford, G 2002, "Cultural tourists and cultural trends: commercialization and the coming of The Storm," *Culture, Sport, Society* 5(1), 21–38.

Crawford, G 2003, "The career of the sport supporter: the case of the Manchester Storm," *Sociology* 37(2), 219–37.

Crawford, G 2004, *Consuming sport: sport, fans, and culture,* Routledge, New York.

Crawford, G 2005a, "Digital gaming, sport, and gender," *Leisure Studies* 24(3), 259–70.

Crawford, G 2005b, "Sensible soccer: sport fandom and the rise of digital gaming," in JMA Bairner & A Tomlinson (eds.), *The bountiful game? Football identities and finances,* Meyer & Meyer Sport, Oxford.

Crawford, G 2006, "The cult of Champ Man: the culture and pleasures of Championship Manager/Football Manager gamers," *Information, Communication, and Society* 9(4), 496–514.

Crawford, G & Gosling, VK 2004, "The myth of the puck bunny: female fans and men's ice hockey," *Sociology* 38(3), 477–93.

Crawford, G & Gosling, VK 2005, "Toys of boy? The continued marginalization and participation of women as digital gamers," *Sociological Research Online* 10(1). Retrieved October 10, 2005, from http://www.socresonline.org.uk/10/1/crawford.html.

Csikszentmihalyi, M 2002, *Flow: the classic work on how to achieve happiness,* Rider, London.

Curtin, M 2003, "Media capital: towards the study of spatial flows," *International Journal of Cultural Studies* 6(2), 202–28.

Dahlgren, P 1995, *Television and the public sphere: citizenship, democracy, and the media,* Sage, Thousand Oaks, CA.

Dall, CH 1849–1851, journal, Caroline Healey Dall papers, Massachusetts Historical Society, Boston.

Dannen, F & Long, B 1997, *Hong Kong Babylon: an insider's guide to the Hollywood of the East,* Faber & Faber, London.

Darling-Wolf, F 2004, "Virtually multicultural: trans-Asian identity and gender in an international fan community of a Japanese star," in *New Media & Society* 6(4), 507–28.

Dastar Corp. v. Twentieth-Century Fox Film Corp., 539 US 23 (2003).

Davies, T 1992, "Why can't a woman be more like a fan?" in D Bull (ed.), *We'll support you evermore*, Gerald Duckworth, London.

Day, I 1990, *Sorting the men out from the boys: masculinity, a missing link in the sociology of sport*, Sheffield Hallam University Press, Sheffield, UK.

De Certeau, M 1984, *The practice of everyday life*, University of California Press, Berkeley.

De Saussure, F 1974, *Course in general linguistics*, trans. W Baskin, Collins, London.

De Zengotita, T 2005, *Mediated: how the media shape your world*, Bloomsbury, London.

Debord, G 1994, *Society of the spectacle*, trans. D Nicholson-Smith, Zone, New York.

Deem, R 1982, "Women, leisure, and inequality," *Leisure Studies* 1(1), 29–46.

Deem, R 1986, *All work and no play?* Open University Press, Milton Keynes, UK.

Dell, C 1998, "'Lookit that hunk of a man': subversive pleasures, female fandom, and professional wrestling" in C Harris & A Alexander (eds.), *Theorizing fandom: fans, subculture, and identity*, Hampton, Cresskill, NJ.

Desser, D 2003, "Consuming Asia: Chinese and Japanese popular culture and the American imaginary," in JKW Lau (ed.), *Multiple modernities: cinema and popular media in transcultural East Asia*, Temple University Press, Philadelphia.

Devine, F 2004, *Class practices: how parents help their children get good jobs*, Cambridge University Press, New York.

Devine, F et al. (eds.) 2004, *Rethinking class: cultures, identities, and lifestyles*, Palgrave, New York.

Dickey, S 1993, *Cinema and the urban poor in South India*, Cambridge University Press, Cambridge, UK.

Dictionary of American Slang 1967, Thomas Y Crowell, New York.

DiLullo, T 2003, "Tom Lenk," *Altzone.com*. Retrieved May 2, 2003, from http://www.buffy.nu.

Dizikes, J 1993, *Opera in America: a cultural history*, Yale University Press, New Haven, CT.

Doss, E 1992, *Elvis culture: fans, faith, and image*, University Press of Kansas, Lawrence.

Drake, A 1897, travel diary, Special Collections, mss. 315, Library of the School of Music, Yale University, New Haven, CT.

Drotner, K 2000, "Difference and diversity: trends in young Danes' media cultures," *Media, Culture, and Society* 22(2), 149–66.

Duncan, MC & Messner, MA 1998, "The media image of sport and gender," in LA Wenner (ed.), *MediaSport,* Routledge, New York.

Dunglison, R 1833, *New dictionary of medical science and literature,* C Bowen, Boston.

Dworkin, SL & Messner MA 2002, "Just do . . . what? Sport, bodies, gender," in S Scratton & A Flintoff (eds.), *Gender and sport: a reader,* Routledge, New York.

Eagleton, T 1996, *Literary theory: an introduction,* second edition, Basil Blackwell, Oxford.

Eco, U 1994, *The limits of interpretation,* Indiana University Press, Bloomington.

Ehrenreich, B, Hess, E, & Jacobs, G 1992, "Beatlemania: girls just want to have fun," in LA Lewis (ed), *The adoring audience: fan culture and popular media,* Routledge, New York.

Elias, N & Dunning, E (eds.) 1986, *Quest for excitement: sport and leisure in the civilizing process,* Basil Blackwell, Oxford.

Elliott, A 1999, *The mourning of John Lennon,* University of California Press, Berkeley.

ELSPA 2005, "Computer and video games: important facts at your fingertips." Retrieved November 4, 2005, from http://www.elspa.com/serv/factcards/Fact_Card_01.pdf.

ESA 2004, *Entertainment Software Association.* Retrieved October 10, 2005, from http://www.theesa.com.

Eskelinen, M & Tronstad, R 2003, "Video Games as Configurative Performances," in MJP Wolf & B Perron (eds.), *The video game theory reader,* Routledge, New York.

Eversmann, P 2003, "The experience of the theatrical event," in V Cremona et al. (eds.), *Theatrical events: borders, dynamics, frames,* Rodopi, Amsterdam.

FA 2003, "Background and Brief History," *The Football Association.* Retrieved November 22, 2005, from http://www.thefa.com/Womens/Reference-FAQ/Postings/2003/1.

Featherstone, M 1991, *Consumer culture and postmodernism,* Sage, Newbury Park, CA.

Fine, J & Friedman, W 2003, "Martha partners offer lukewarm support," *Advertising Age* 74(23), 1.

Fink, JS, Trail, GT, & Anderson, DF 2002, "Environmental factors associated with spectator attendance and sport consumption behaviour: gender and team differences in sport," *Marketing Quarterly* 11(1), 8–19.

Fish, S 1981, "Why no one's afraid of Wolfgang Iser," *Diacritics* 11(1), 2–13.

Fiske, J 1987, *Television culture,* Routledge, New York.

Fiske, J 1989, *Understanding popular culture,* Unwin Hyman, Boston.

Fiske, J 1992, "The cultural economy of fandom," in LA Lewis (ed.), *The adoring audience: fan culture and popular media,* Routledge, New York.

Foley, M 1999, *Have a nice day: a tale of blood and sweatsocks,* HarperCollins, New York.

Ford S 2006, *Fanning the flames: ten ways to embrace and cultivate fan communities*, white paper written for Convergence Culture Consortium, MIT.

Free, M & Hughson, J 2003, "Settling accounts with hooligans: gender blindness in football supporter subculture research," *Men and Masculinities* 6(2), 136–55.

Freedman, J 1983, "Will the Sheik use his blinding fireball? The ideology of professional wrestling," in FE Manning (ed.), *The celebration of society: perspectives on cultural performance*, Popular Press, Bowling Green, OH.

Friedman, EG & Squire, C 1998, *Morality USA*, University of Minnesota Press, Minneapolis.

Fromme, J 2003, "Computer games as a part of children's culture," *Game Studies* 3(1). Retrieved October 10, 2005, from http://www.gamestudies.org/0301/fromme.

Frontani, M 2002, "'Beatlepeople': Gramsci, the Beatles, and *Rolling Stone* magazine," *American Journalism* 12(3), 39–61.

Frow, J 1987, "Accounting for tastes: some problems in Bourdieu's sociology of culture," *Cultural Studies* 1(1), 59–73.

Frow, J 1995, *Cultural studies and cultural value*, Clarendon, Oxford.

Gallagher, B 1997, "Greta Garbo is sad: some historical reflections on the paradoxes of stardom in the American film industry, 1910–1960," *Images: A Journal of Popular Culture* 3. Retrieved November 8, 2005, from http://www.imagesjournal.com/issue03/infocus/stars9.htm.

Gansing, K 2003, "The myth of interactivity? interactive films as an imaginary genre," paper presented at MelbourneDAC2003 conference. Retrieved October 10, 2005, from http://hypertext.rmit.edu.au/dac/papers/Gansing.pdf.

Gee, JP 2004, *Situated language and learning: a critique of traditional schooling*, Routledge, New York.

Geraghty, C 2003, "Aesthetics and quality in popular television drama," *International Journal of Cultural Studies* 6(1), 25–45.

Giddens, A 1991, *Modernity and self-identity: self and society in the late modern age*, Polity, Cambridge, UK.

Gillmor, D 2003, "Moving toward participatory journalism," *Nieman Reports* 57(3), 79–80.

Giulianotti, R 1991, "Scotland's Tartan Army in Italy: the case for the carnivalesque," *Sociological Review* 39(3), 503–27.

Giulianotti, R 1995, "Participant observation and research into football hooliganism: reflections on the problems of entrée and everyday risks." *Sociology of Sport Journal* 12(1), 1–20.

Giulianotti, R 2002, "Supporters, followers, fans, and flaneurs: a taxonomy of spectator identities in football," *Journal of Sport and Social Issues* 26(1), 25–46.

Giulianotti, R 2005, *Sport: a critical sociology*, Polity, Cambridge, UK.

Glynn, K 2000, *Tabloid culture: trash taste, popular power, and the transformation of American television*, Duke University Press, Durham, NC.

Goffman, E 1968, *Stigma: notes on the management of spoilt identity*, Penguin, Harmondsworth, UK.

Goldberg, M 2000, "Mood radio," *San Francisco Bay Guardian*, 5 November. Retrieved November 8, 2005, from http://sfbg.com/noise/05/mood.html.

Goldman, A 2001, *The lives of John Lennon*, reprint, Review Press, Chicago.

Gorn, EJ & Goldstein, W 1993, *A brief history of American sports*, Hill and Wang, New York.

Gottlieb, A 2002, "Buffy's angels," *Oakland's Urbanview*, 25 September. Retrieved May 2, 2003, from http://www.metroactive.com/urbanview/9.25.02/buffy1–0239.html.

Gottlieb, J & Wald, G 1994, "Smells like teen spirit: riot grrrls, revolution, and women in independent rock," in A Ross & T Rose (eds.), *Microphone fiends: youth music and youth culture*, Routledge, New York.

Gottschalk, LM 1881, *Notes of a pianist*, JB Lippincott, Philadelphia.

Gouk, P 2004, "Raising spirits and restoring souls: early modern medical explanations for music's effects," in V Erlmann (ed.), *Hearing cultures: essays on sound, listening, and modernity*, Berg, London.

Gramophone 2006. January 26, 13.

Gran, J 1999, *Fan fiction and copyright*. Retrieved December 13, 2005, from http://www.alternateuniverses.com/judygran/copyright.html.

Gray, J 2003, "New audiences, new textualities: anti-fans and non-fans," *International Journal of Cultural Studies* 6(1), 64–81.

Gray, J 2005, "Anti-fandom and the moral text: Television without Pity and textual dislike," *American Behavioral Scientist* 48(7), 840–58.

Gray, J 2006, *Watching with* The Simpsons*: television, parody, and intertextuality*, Routledge, New York.

Gripsrud, J 1995, *The* Dynasty *years: Hollywood television and critical media studies*, Routledge, New York.

Gripsrud, J 1999, "'High culture' revisited," *Cultural Studies* 3(2), 194–207.

Grossberg, L 1984a, "Another boring day in paradise: rock and roll and the empowerment of everyday life," *Popular Music* 4, 225–58.

Grossberg, L 1984b, "I'd rather feel bad than not feel anything at all: rock and roll, pleasure, and power," *Enclitic* 8, 94–111.

Grove, L 2004, "We'll never have Paris again," *Daily News*, 23 December. Retrieved September 11, 2005, from http://www.dailynews.com/front/story/264804p-226754c.html.

Guernsey, L 2003, "Making intelligence a bit less artificial," *New York Times*, 1 May, G5.

Guttmann, A 1986, *Sports spectators*, Columbia University Press, New York.

Guttmann, A 1994, *Games and empire*, Columbia University Press, New York.

Gwenllian-Jones, S 2003, "Web wars: resistance, online fandom, and studio censorship," in M Jancovich & J Lyons (eds.), *Quality popular television: cult TV, the industry, and fans*, BFI, London.

Habermas, J 1989, *The structural transformation of the public sphere: an inquiry into a category of bourgeois society,* trans. Thomas Burger, Polity, Cambridge, UK.

Harrington, CL & Bielby, DD 1995, *Soap fans: pursuing pleasure and making meaning in everyday life,* Temple University Press, Philadelphia.

Harrington, CL & Bielby, DD 2005a, "Flow, home, and media pleasures," *Journal of Popular Culture* 38, 834–54.

Harrington, CL & Bielby, DD (eds.) 2005b, "New Directions in Fan Studies," *American Behavioral Scientist,* 48.7.

Harris, C 1998, "A sociology of television fandom," in C Harris & A Alexander (eds.), *Theorizing fandom: fans, subculture, and identity,* Hampton, Cresskill, NJ.

Harrison, T 1996, "Interview with Henry Jenkins," in T Harrison et al. (eds.), *Enterprise zones: critical positions on* Star Trek, Westview, Boulder, CO.

Hartley, J 1999, *The uses of television,* Routledge, New York.

Harvey, D 1990, *The condition of postmodernity: an inquiry into the origins of cultural change,* Basil Blackwell, Oxford.

Hayes, S 2002, "Theatre audiences as communities," *Salford Papers in Sociology* 32, Institute for Social Research, University of Salford, Salford, UK.

Hayward, J 1997, *Consuming pleasures: active audiences and serial fictions from Dickens to soap opera,* University Press of Kentucky, Lexington.

Haywood, T 1996, *A brief history of female football fans,* SNCCFR, University of Leicester. Retrieved November 22, 2005, from http://www.le.ac.uk/sociology/css/resources/factsheets/fs9.pdf.

Haywood, T & Williams, J 2002, *Women and football,* SNCCFR, University of Leicester. Retrieved November 22, 2005, from http://www.le.ac.uk/sociology/css/resources/factsheets/fs5.pdf.

Heidegger, M 1962 [1927], *Being and time,* Blackwell, Oxford.

Heo, M 2002, "Closing accounts of 2003 Korean film: a conversation between Jung Sung-Il, Kim So-young, and Heo Moon-young," *Cine 21,* 3 December. Retrieved January 6, 2005, from http://www.cine21.co.kr.

Hermes, J 1995, *Reading women's magazines: an analysis of everyday media use,* Polity, Cambridge, UK.

Higgins, C 2006, "Bach in demand: listeners hail Radio 3 festival a huge success," *Guardian,* 5 January. Retrieved January 6, 2005, from http://www.guardian.co.uk.

Hills, M 1999, *The dialectic of value: the sociology and psychoanalysis of cult media,* Ph.D. dissertation, University of Sussex, UK.

Hills, M 2002, *Fan cultures,* Routledge, New York.

Hills, M 2003, "*Star Wars* in fandom, film theory, and the museum: the cultural status of the cult blockbuster," in Julian Stringer (ed.), *Movie Blockbusters,* Routledge, New York.

Hills, M 2004, "*Dawson's Creek:* 'quality teen TV' and 'mainstream cult'?" in G Davis & K Dickinson (eds.), *Teen TV: genre, consumption, and identity,* BFI, London.

Hills, M 2005a, *The pleasures of horror,* Continuum, New York.

Hills, M 2005b, *How to do things with cultural theory,* Hodder Arnold, London.

Hills, M 2005c, "Ringing the changes: cult distinctions and cultural differences in US fans' readings of Japanese horror cinema," in J McRoy (ed.), *Japanese horror cinema,* Edinburgh University Press, Edinburgh.

Hills, M 2005d, "Who wants to be a fan of *Who Wants to Be a Millionaire?* Scholarly television criticism, 'popular aesthetics,' and academic tastes," in C Johnson & R Turnock (eds.), *ITV cultures: independent television over fifty years,* Open University Press, Maidenhead, UK.

Hinerman, S 1992, "'I'll be here with you': fans, fantasy, and the figure of Elvis," in LA Lewis (ed.), *The adoring audience: fan culture and popular media,* Routledge, New York.

Hobson, D 1982, Crossroads: *the drama of a soap opera,* Methuen, London.

Hofacre, S 1994, "The women's audience in professional indoor soccer," *Sports Marketing Quarterly* 3(2), 25–27.

Hoffman, W 1850, diary, BV Hoffman, William, New-York Historical Society, New York.

Holub, RC 1992, *Crossing borders: reception theory, poststructuralism, deconstruction,* University of Wisconsin Press, Madison.

Homer 1999 [ca. 700 B.C.], *The Iliad Books 1–12,* trans. AT Murray, Harvard University Press, Cambridge, MA.

Hong, F 2003, "Soccer: a world sport for women," *Soccer and Society* 4(2–3), 268–70.

Hoover, S, Clark, LS, & Alters, DF, with Champ, J & Hood, L 2004, *Media, home, and family,* Routledge, New York.

Horkheimer, M & Adorno, TW 1972 [1944], *Dialectic of enlightenment,* Seabury, New York.

Hu, K 2005, "The power of circulation: digital technologies and the online Chinese fans of Japanese TV drama," *Inter-Asia Cultural Studies* 6(2): 171–86.

Hughes, S 2003, "Pride of place," *Seminar* 525. Retrieved February 23, 2004, from http://www.india-seminar.com/2003/525.htm.

Hunt, L 2003, "Kung fu cult masters: stardom, performance, and 'authenticity' in Hong Kong martial arts films," in M Jancovich et al. (ed.), *Defining cult movies: the cultural politics of oppositional taste,* Manchester University Press, Manchester, UK.

Hunter, IQ & Kaye, H 1997, "Introduction," in D Cartmell et al. (eds.), *Trash aesthetics: popular culture and its audience,* Pluto, Chicago.

IDSA 2002, "Essential facts about the computer and video game industry." Retrieved October 10, 2005, from http://www.idsa.com/IDSABooklet.pdf.

In Y 2002, "Other Han Suk-kyu's film personas and their limits," *Pool* 13(1), 34–67.

Ingarden, R 1973, *The cognition of the literary work of art,* Northwestern University Press, Evanston, IL.

Interrogate the Internet 1995, "Contradictions in cyberspace: collective response," in R Shields (ed.), *Cultures of Internet: virtual spaces, real histories, living bodies,* Sage, Thousand Oaks, CA.

Iser, W 1971, "Indeterminacy and the reader's response in prose fiction," in JH Miller (ed.), *Aspects of narrative,* Columbia University Press, New York.

Iser, W 1978, *The act of reading: a theory of aesthetic response,* Johns Hopkins University Press, Baltimore, MD.

ISFE 2005, "Video gamers in Europe—2005." Retrieved November 4, 2005, from http://www.isfe-eu.org.

Jacobs, J 2001, "Issues of judgment and value in television studies," *International Journal of Cultural Studies* 4(4), 427–47.

Jameson, F 1981, *The political unconscious: narrative as a socially symbolic act,* Cornell University Press, Ithaca, NY.

Jancovich, M 2002, "Cult fictions: cult movies, subcultural capital, and the production of cultural distinction," *Cultural Studies* 16(2), 306–22.

Jancovich, M et al. (eds.) 2003, *Defining cult movies: the cultural politics of oppositional taste,* Manchester University Press, Manchester, UK.

Jancovich, M & Hunt, N 2004, "The mainstream, distinction and cult TV," in S Gwenllian-Jones & R Pearson (eds.), *Cult television,* University of Minnesota Press, Minneapolis.

Jansz, J & Martens, L 2005, "Gaming at a LAN event: the social context of playing video games," *New Media and Society* 7(3), 333–55.

Jauss, HR 1982, *Toward an aesthetic of reception,* University of Minnesota Press, Minneapolis.

Jenkins, H 1988, "*Star Trek* rerun, reread, rewritten: fan writing as textual poaching," *Critical Studies in Mass Communication* 5(2), 85–107.

Jenkins, H 1992, *Textual poachers: television fans and participatory culture,* Routledge, New York.

Jenkins, H 1997, "Never trust a snake! WWF Wrestling as masculine melodrama," in A Baker & T Boyd (eds.), *Out of bounds: sports, media, and the politics of identity,* Indiana University Press, Bloomington.

Jenkins, H 2000, "Digital land grab," *Technology Review* 103(2), 103–5.

Jenkins, H 2001, "*Intensities* interviews Henry Jenkins," *Intensities: The Journal of Cult Media* 2. Retrieved October 5, 2004, from http://www.cult-media.com/issue2/CMRjenk.htm.

Jenkins, H 2002, "Interactive Audiences?" in D Harries (ed.), *The new media book,* BFI, London.

Jenkins, H 2003, "Playing our song? digital renaissance," 2 July. Retrieved November 8, 2005, from http://www.mittechnologyreview.com/articles/03/07/wo_jenkins070203.asp.

Jenkins, H 2005a, "Games, the new lively art," in J Raessens & J Golstein (eds.), *Handbook of computer game studies,* MIT Press, Cambridge.

Jenkins, H 2005b, "I want my Geek TV!" *Flow* 3(1). Retrieved April 2, 2006, from http://jot.communication.utexas.edu/flow/?jot=view&id=936.

Jenkins, H 2006, *Convergence culture: where old and new media collide*, NYU Press, New York.

Jensen, J 1992, "Fandom as pathology: the consequences of characterization," in LA Lewis (ed.), *The adoring audience: fan culture and popular media*, Routledge, New York.

Jewkes, Y 2002, *Captive audience: media, masculinity, and power in prisons*, Willan, Portland, OR.

Jhally, S (dir.) 2003, *Wrestling with manhood: gender, race, and class in professional wrestling*, Media Education Foundation, Northampton, MA.

Johnson, R 2005, "Laguna boor," *New York Post*, 20 November, 6.

Johnson, S 2005, *Everything bad is good for you: how today's popular culture is actually making you smarter*, Riverhead, New York.

Jones, I & Lawrence, L 2000, "Identity and gender in sport and media fandom: an exploratory comparison of fans attending football matches and *Star Trek* conventions," in S Scraton & B Watson (eds.), *Sport, leisure identities, and gendered spaces*, LSA, Brighton, UK.

Jossie, F n.d., "Net perceptions hits the big time." Retrieved November 8, 2005, from http://www.interactive-pioneers.org/net_perceptions.html.

Juluri, V 2003a, "'Ask the West, will dinosaurs come back?' Indian audiences/global audience studies," in PD Murphy & MM Kraidy (eds.), *Global media studies: ethnographic perspectives*, Routledge, New York.

Juluri, V 2003b, *Becoming a global audience: longing and belonging in Indian music television*, Peter Lang, New York.

Kasson, JF 1990, *Rudeness and civility: manners in nineteenth-century America*, Hill & Wang, New York.

Kellner, D 1997, "Cultural studies vs. political economy: overcoming the divide," *Illuminations*. Retrieved September 1, 2005, from http://www.uta.edu/huma/illuminations/kell4.htm.

Kelly, W (ed.) 2004, *Fanning the flames: fans and consumer culture in contemporary Japan*, State University of New York Press, New York.

Kennedy, H 2002, "Lara Croft: feminist icon or cyberbimbo? On the limits of textual analysis," *Game Studies* 2(2). Retrieved November 2, 2005, from http://www.gamestudies.org/0202/kennedy.

Kerbel, M 2000, *If it bleeds, it leads: an anatomy of television news*, Westview, Boulder, CO.

Kerr, A et al. 2004, *New Media: New Media Pleasures?* STeM Working Paper: Final Research Report of a Pilot Research Project. Retrieved October 10, 2005, from http://www.comms.dcu.ie/kerra/source%20files/text/NMP_working%20paper%20final.pdf.

Kerr, A, Brereton, P & Kücklich, J 2005, "New Media—New Pleasures?" *International Journal of Cultural Studies* 8(3), 375–94.

Kim, HM 2004, "Feminization of the 2002 World Cup and women's fandom," *Inter-Asia Cultural Studies* 5(1), 42–51.

Kim, K 2004, *The remasculinization of Korean cinema,* Duke University Press, Durham, NC.

Kim, S 2002, "Net documentaries and blockbusters in South Korea," Documentary Box #20. Retrieved September 13, from http://www.city.yamagata.yamagata.jp/yidff/docbox/docbox2-e.html.

Kim, Y 2003, "Han Suk-kyu came back as double agent," *Cine 21,* 21 January. Retrieved January 6, 2006, from http://www.cine21.co.kr.

Kinder, M 1991, *Playing with power in movies, television, and video games: from Muppet Babies to Teenage Mutant Ninja Turtles,* University of California Press, Berkeley.

King v. Innovation Books, 976 F.2d 824 (2d Cir. 1992).

King, A 1998, *The end of the terraces,* Leicester University, Leicester, UK.

King, B & Borland, J 2003, *Dungeons and dreamers: the rise of computer game culture, from geek to chic,* McGraw-Hill, New York.

King, C 1993, "His truth goes marching on: Elvis Presley and the pilgrimage to Graceland," in JA Walter (ed.), *Pilgrimage in popular culture,* Palgrave Macmillan, London.

King, G & Krzywinska, T (eds.) 2002, *ScreenPlay: cinema/videogames/interfaces,* Wallflower Press, New York.

Kline, S, Dyver-Witherford, N, & De Peuter, G 2003, *Digital play: the interaction of technology, culture, and marketing,* McGill-Queen's University Press, London.

Kouwe, Z 2003, "Getting book suggestions online," *Wall Street Journal,* 29 July, D2.

Kozinets, RV 1999, "E-tribalized marketing? The strategic implications of virtual communities of consumption," *European Management Journal* 17(3), 252–64.

Kraidy, MM & Murphy, PD 2003, "Media ethnography: local, global, or translocal?" in PD Murphy & MM Kraidy (eds.), *Global media studies: ethnographic perspectives,* Routledge, New York.

Krishnan, M 1991, "Jhumri Tilaiya: abode of audio addicts," *Sunday Observer,* 26 January, 56.

Kuhn, A 2002, *An everyday magic: cinema and cultural memory,* IB Tauris, New York.

Kuhn, A 2005, "Thresholds: film as film and the aesthetic experience," *Screen* 46(4), 401–14.

Lady Macbeth 2004, *Plagiarism—please help stop its spread.* Retrieved December 13, 2005, from http://forum.mediaminer.org/index.php?t=msg&goto=620709&.

Lakoff, G & Johnson, M 1980, *Metaphors we live by,* University of Chicago Press, Chicago.

Lancaster, K 2001, *Interacting with* Babylon 5, University of Texas Press, Austin.

Lanza, J 1994, *Elevator music: a surreal history of Muzak, easy-listening, and other moodsong,* St. Martin's Press, New York.

Larbaleister, J 2002, "*Buffy*'s Mary Sue is Jonathan: *Buffy* acknowledges the fans," in R Wilcox & D Lavery (eds.), *Fighting the forces: what's at stake in* Buffy the Vampire Slayer, Rowman & Littlefield, Lanham, MD.

Lash, S 2000, "Risk culture," in B Adam, U Beck, & J Van Loon (eds.), *The risk society and beyond: critical issues for social theory,* Sage, London.

Laughey, D 2006, *Music and youth culture,* Edinburgh University Press, Edinburgh.

Lawrence, VB (ed.) 1988, *Strong on music: the New York music scene in the days of George Templeton Strong.* Volume 1, *Resonances, 1836–1849,* University of Chicago Press, Chicago.

Lee, D 2003, "Stars' audience mobility according to twelve producers," *Daily Chosun,* 2 November. Retrieved January 6, 2006, from http://www.chosun.com.

Lee, FLF 2005, "Spectacle and fandom: media discourse in two soccer events in Hong Kong," *Sociology of Sport Journal* 122, 194–213.

Lee, S 2003, "The theory of Han Suk-kyu." Retrieved January 6, 2006, from http://www.hansukkyu.org.

Lembo, R 2000, *Thinking through television,* Cambridge University Press, New York.

Lenhardt, A & Madden, M 2005, *Teen content creators and consumers.* Pew Internet & American Life Project. 2 November. Retrieved April 2, 2006, from http://www.pewinternet.org/PPF/r/166/report_display.asp.

Levine, L 1988, *Highbrow/lowbrow: the emergence of cultural hierarchy in America,* Harvard University Press, Cambridge, MA.

Levine, MP & Schneider, SJ 2003, "Feeling for Buffy: the girl next door," in JB South (ed.), Buffy the Vampire Slayer *and Philosophy,* Open Court, Chicago.

Levy, S & Stone, B 2006, "The new wisdom of the Web," *Newsweek,* 3 April, 2006, 46–53.

Lewis, J 1991, *The ideological octopus: an exploration of television and its audience,* Routledge, New York.

Lewis, LA (ed.) 1992, *The adoring audience: fan culture and popular media,* Routledge, New York.

Liang, L 2005, "Cinematic citizenship and the illegal city," *Inter-Asia Cultural Studies* 6(3), 366–85.

Liebes, T & Katz, E 1990, *The export of meaning: cross-cultural readings of* Dallas, Oxford University Press, New York.

Lincoln, B 1989, *Discourse and the construction of society: comparative studies of myth, ritual, and classification,* Oxford University Press, New York.

Lindloff, T & Taylor, B 2002, *Qualitative communication research methods,* Sage, Thousand Oaks, CA.

Lippmann, W 1922, *Public opinion,* Macmillan, New York.

Lipscomb, WP 2005, *The operational aesthetic in the performance of professional wrestling,* Ph.D. dissertation, Louisiana State University.

Lipsitz, G 1990, *Time passages: collective memory and American popular culture,* University of Minnesota Press, Minneapolis.

Lois & Clark *fanfic archive FAQ* n.d. Retrieved December 13, 2005, from http://www.lcfanfic.com/faq_archive.html#plagiarism.

London, S 2001, "How to know what the customer wants next," *Financial Times,* 13 July, 10.

Longhurst, B, Bagnall, G, & Savage, M 2001, "Ordinary consumption and personal identity: radio and the middle classes in the northwest of England," in A Warde & J Gronow (eds.), *Ordinary consumption,* Routledge, New York.

Longhurst, B, Bagnall, G, & Savage, M 2004, "Audiences, museums, and the English middle class," *Museum and Society* 2(2), 104–24.

Lowell, L 1880, diary, Lucy Lowell diaries, Massachusetts Historical Society, Boston.

Lowell, L 1884, diary, Lucy Lowell diaries, Massachusetts Historical Society, Boston.

Lowell, L 1886, diary, Lucy Lowell diaries, Massachusetts Historical Society, Boston.

Lowell, LBE 1845, diary, Lucy Lowell diaries, Massachusetts Historical Society, Boston.

Lunt, P & Livingstone, S 1996, "Rethinking the focus group in media and communications research," *Journal of Communication* 46(2), 79–98.

MacCabe, C 1981a, "Realism and the cinema: notes on some Brechtian theses," in T Bennett et al. (eds.), *Popular television and film,* BFI/Open University Press, London.

MacCabe, C 1981b, "*Days of Hope,* a response to Colin McArthur," in T Bennett et al. (eds.), *Popular television and film,* BFI/Open University Press, London.

MacDonald, A 1998, "Uncertain utopia: science fiction media fandom and computer mediated communication," in C Harris & A Alexander (eds.), *Theorizing fandom: fans, subculture, and identity,* Hampton, Cresskill, NJ.

Mactavish, A 2003, "Technological pleasure: the performance and narrative of technology in *Half-Life* and other high-tech computer games," in G King & T Krywinska (eds.), *Screenplay: cinema/videogames/interfaces,* Wallflower, New York.

Majumdar, N 2001, "The embodied voice: song sequences and stardom in popular Hindi cinema," in PR Wojcik & A Knight (eds.), *Soundtrack available: essays on film and popular music,* Duke University Press, Durham, NC.

Malcolm, D, Jones, I, & Waddington, I 2000, "The people's game? Football spectatorship and demographic change," in J Garland, D Malcolm, & M Rowe (eds.), *The future of football: challenges for the twenty-first century,* Frank Cass, London.

Mangan, JA 1986, *The games ethic and imperialism: aspects of the infusion of an ideal,* Viking, London.

Marcotte, A 2005, "The riot just couldn't be on MTV," *Pandagon,* June 24. Retrieved August 24, 2005, from http://www.pandagon.net/archives/2005/06/the_riot_just_c.html.

Marcus, GE 1998, *Ethnography through thick and thin,* Princeton University Press, Princeton, NJ.

Marcus, GE 2002, *The sentimental citizen: emotion in democratic politics,* Pennsylvania State University Press, University Park.

Marcus, GE, Neuman, WR, & MacKuen, M 2000, *Affective intelligence and political judgment,* University of Chicago Press, Chicago.

Marshall, PD 1997, *Celebrity and power,* University of Minnesota Press, Minneapolis.

Marshall, PD 2002, "The new intertextual commodity," in D Harries (ed.), *The new media book,* BFI, London.

Mattel, Inc. v. MCA Records, Inc., 296 F.3d 894 (9th Cir. 2002).

Mattel, Inc. v. Pitt, 229 F. Supp. 2d 315 (SDNY 2002).

Mattel, Inc. v. Walking Mountain Productions, 353 F.3d 792 (9th Cir. 2003).

McArthur, C 1981, "*Days of Hope,*" in T Bennett et al. (eds.), *Popular television and film,* BFI/Open University Press, London.

McBride, LB 2005, *Professional wrestling, embodied morality, and altered states of consciousness.* MA dissertation, University of South Florida, Tampa.

McConachie, B 1992, *Melodramatic formations: American theatre and society, 1820–1870,* University of Iowa Press, Iowa City.

McCourt, T 2005, "Collecting music in the digital realm," *Popular Music and Society* 28(2), 249–52.

McCracken, G 2005, "'Consumers' or 'multipliers': a new language for marketing?" *This blog sits at the intersection between anthropology and economics,* 10 November, 2005. Retrieved November 11, 2005, from http://www.cultureby.com/trilogy/2005/11/consumers_or_mu.html.

McKee, A 2001a, *Australian television: a genealogy of great moments,* Oxford University Press, Melbourne.

McKee, A 2001b, "Which is the best *Doctor Who* story? A case study in value judgments outside the academy," *Intensities* 1. Retrieved October 5, 2002, from http://www.cult-media.com/issue1/Amckee.htm.

McKee, A 2002, "Fandom," in T Miller (ed.), *Television studies,* BFI, London.

McKee, A 2003, "What is television for?" in M Jancovich & J Lyons (eds.), *Quality popular television,* BFI, London.

McKee, A 2005, *The public sphere: an introduction,* Cambridge University Press, Cambridge, UK.

McKinley, EG 1997, Beverly Hills, 90210: *television, gender, and identity,* University of Pennsylvania Press, Philadelphia.

McMahon, L 1998, "'While our souls together blend': narrating a romantic reader-ship in the early Republic," in PN Stearns & J Lewis (eds.), *An emotional history of the United States,* New York University Press, New York.

Meehan, ER 2000, "Leisure or labor? Fan ethnography and political economy," in I Hagen & J Wasko (eds.), *Consuming audiences? Production and reception in media research,* Hampton Press, Cresskill, NJ.

Mehta, M 2000, *Selections: cutting, classifying, and certifying in Bombay cinema,* Ph.D. dissertation, University of Minnesota, Minneapolis.

Michael, J 2000, *Anxious intellects: academic professionals, public intellectuals, and enlightenment values,* Duke University Press, Durham, NC.

Milikowski, M 2000, "Exploring a model of de-ethnicization: the case of Turkish television in the Netherlands," *European Journal of Communication* 15, 443–68.

Miller, T 2003, *Spyscreen: espionage on film and TV from the 1930s to the 1960s,* Oxford University Press, Oxford.

Miller, T 2004, "Trainspotting *The Avengers,*" in S Gwenllian-Jones & R Pearson (eds.), *Cult television,* University of Minnesota Press, Minneapolis.

Min, E, Joo, J, & Kwak, H 2003, *Korean film: history, resistance, and democratic imagination,* Praeger, Westport, CT.

Mondak, JJ 1989, "The politics of professional wrestling," *Journal of Popular Culture* 23(2), 139–49.

Moon, S 2001, "The production and subversion of hegemonic masculinity: recon-figuring gender hierarchy in contemporary South Korea," in L Kendall (ed.), *Under construction: the gendering of modernity, class, and consumption in the Republic of Korea,* University of Hawaii Press, Honolulu.

Moore, K & Rutter, J (eds.) 2004, *Proceedings of Mobile Entertainment: User-Cen-tred Perspectives,* CRIC, University of Manchester. Retrieved October 10, 2005, from http://les1.man.ac.uk/cric/Jason_Rutter/MEPro.htm.

Moran, J 1998, "Cultural studies and academic stardom," *International Journal of Cultural Studies* 1(1), 67–82.

Morgan, G 2004, *The real David Beckham: an intimate biography,* Metro Books, London.

Morinis, A 1992, *Sacred journeys,* Greenwood, Westport, CT.

Morley, D 1980, *The* Nationwide *Audience: Structure and Decoding,* BFI, London.

Morley, D 2000, *Home territories: media, mobility, and identity,* Routledge, New York.

Morton, GW & O'Brien, GM 1985, *Wrestling to rasslin': ancient sport to American spectacle,* Popular Press, Bowling Green, OH.

Mosco, V & Kaye, K 2000, "Questioning the concept of the audience," in I Hagen & J Wasko (eds.), *Consuming audiences? Production and reception in media research,* Hampton Press, Cresskill, NJ.

MTV 2005, "'Laguna Beach' star Talan Torriero prepping an album," MTV, 22 Sep-tember 2005. Retrieved October 8, 2005, from http://www.mtv.com/news/articles/1510199/20050922/story.jhtml.

Murphy, PD & Kraidy, MM 2003, "Towards an ethnographic approach to global media studies," in PD Murphy & MM Kraidy (eds.), *Global media studies: ethnographic perspectives*, Routledge, New York.

Murray, J 2001, *Hamlet on the holodeck: the future of narrative in cyberspace*, MIT Press, Cambridge.

Murray, J & Jenkins, H n.d., *Before the holodeck: translating* Star Trek *into digital media*. Retrieved February 22, 2006, from http://web.mit.edu/cms/People/henry3/holodeck.html.

Music Industry News Network 2001, "Savage Beast Technologies and Auditude join forces to offer complete solution for managing digital music," 1 November. Retrieved November 8, 2005, from http://mi2n.com/press.php3?press_nb=29246.

Naficy, H 1999, "The making of exile cultures: Iranian television in Los Angeles," in S During (ed.), *The cultural studies reader*, Routledge, New York.

Nam, S 2001, *I love beautiful boys*, Haenem, Seoul.

Napier, SJ 2001, *Anime: from* Akira *to* Princess Mononoke, Palgrave, New York.

Naughton, K 2002, "Martha's tabloid dish," *Newsweek*, 24 June, 36.

Naughton, K 2005, "Martha breaks out," *Newsweek*, 7 March, 36–44.

Negroponte, N & Maes, P 1996, "Electronic word of mouth," *Wired*, October. Retrieved November 8, 2005, from http://www.wired.com/wired/archive/4.10/negroponte_pr.html.

Nelson, LC 2000, *Measured excess: status, gender, and consumer nationalism in South Korea*, Columbia University Press, New York.

Newman, J 2004, *Videogames*, Routledge, New York.

Newman, N 2002, *Good music for a free people: The Germania Musical Society and transatlantic musical culture of the mid-nineteenth century*, Ph.D. dissertation, Brown University, Providence, RI.

Nicholas, KS n.d., Site Map. Retrieved October 27, 2004, from http://web.archive.org/web/20031014110731/members.aol.com/ksnicholas.

Nightingale, V 2003, "Improvising Elvis, Marilyn, and Mickey Mouse," in V Nightingale & K Ross (eds.), *Critical readings: media and audiences*, Open University Press, Maidenhead, UK.

O'Connell, P 2003, "What the made-for-TV Martha misses," *Business Week Online*, 19 May. Retrieved May 30, 2003, from http://www.businessweek.com/print/bwdaily/dnflash/may2003/nf20030519_7151.htm?chan=db.

O'Reilly, T 2005, "What is Web 2.0," *O'Reilly*, 9 August, 2005. Retrieved August 10, 2005, from http://www.oreillynet.com/pub/a/oreilly/tim/news/2005/09/30/what-is-web-20.html.

Osborne, P 2000, *Philosophy in cultural theory*, Routledge, New York.

Oxford English Dictionary 2005, online edition, Oxford University Press. Retrieved November 15, 2005, from http://0-dictionary.oed.com.library.

Palmer, D 2003, "The paradox of user control," paper presented to the Melbourne DAC 2003 conference, 19–25 May. Retrieved October 10, 2005, from http://hypertext.rmit.edu.au/dac/papers/Palmer.pdf.

Pandian, MSS 1992, *The image trap: MG Ramachandran in films and politics,* Sage, New Delhi.

Paquet, D 1997, *Korean film.* Retrieved January 6, 2006, from http://www.korean-film.org.

Park, E 2001, "Han Suk-kyu, Shin Hyeon-jun, Kim Hee-seon—overestimated actors and actresses," *Daily Hankook,* 4 November. Retrieved January 6, 2006, from http://www.hankooki.com.

Patterson, T 2000, "Doing well and doing good," Kennedy School of Government Working Paper no. 01–001. Retrieved December 20, 2005, from http://ssm.com/abstract=257395.

Pearce, L 1997, *Feminism and the politics of reading,* Arnold, London.

Pearson, R 1997, "It's always 1895: Sherlock Holmes in cyberspace," in D Cartmell et al. (eds.), *Trash aesthetics: popular culture and its audience,* Pluto, London.

Pearson, R 2002, "Shakespeare's country: the national poet, English identity, and the silent cinema," in A Higson (ed.), *Young and innocent? The cinema in Britain, 1896–1930,* University of Exeter Press, Exeter, UK.

Penguin 2005, "The Penguin Group: performance," *Pearson.* Retrieved September 30, 2005, from http://www.pearson.com/about/peng/perform.htm.

Penley, C 1997, *NASA/TREK: Popular science and sex in America*, Verso, London.

Peterson, RA & Anand, N 2004, "The production of culture perspective," *Annual Review of Sociology* 30, 311–33.

Peterson, RA and Kern, RM 1996, "Changing highbrow taste: from snob to omnivore," *American Sociological Review* 61, 900–907.

Philo, G & Miller, D 2001, "Cultural compliance," in G Philo & D Miller (eds.), *Market killing,* Pearson Education, Essex, UK.

Pinsdorf, MK 2002, "Greater dead heroes than live husbands: widows as image-makers," *Public Relations Review* 28, 283–99.

Postman, N & Powers, S 1992, *How to watch TV news,* Penguin, London.

Prasad, M 1998, *Ideology of the Hindi film: a historical construction,* Oxford University Press, New Delhi.

Preston, K 1993, *Opera on the road: traveling opera troupes in the United States, 1825–60,* University of Illinois Press, Urbana.

Prose, F 2002, *The lives of the muses: nine women and the artists they inspired,* HarperCollins, New York.

Putnam, RD 2000, *Bowling alone: collapse and revival of American community,* Simon & Schuster, New York.

Rabinowitz, P 1993, "'With our own dominant passions': Gottschalk, gender, and the power of listening," *Nineteenth-Century Music* 16, 242–52.

Radway, J 1984, *Reading the romance: women, patriarchy, and popular literature,* University of North Carolina Press, Chapel Hill.

Rajadhyaksha, A 2000, "Viewership and democracy in the cinema," in R Vasudevan (ed.), *Making meaning in Indian cinema,* Oxford University Press, New Delhi.

Redhead, S 1997, *Post-fandom and the millennial blues: the transformation of soccer culture,* Routledge, New York.

Rehak, B 2003, "Playing at being: psychoanalysis and the avatar," in MJP Wolf & B Perron (eds.), *The video game theory reader,* Routledge, New York.

Reidl, J, Konstan, J, & Voorman, E 2002, *Word of mouse: the marketing power of collaborative filtering,* Warner, New York.

Reilly, R 2001, "Kids are trying this at home!" *Sports Illustrated,* 12 February, 98.

Rhapsody 2005, "Help." Retrieved November 8, 2005, from http://home.real.com/product/help/rhapv3_ts/en/Rhapsody_Service.htm.

Ricœur, P 1996, "Die metapher und das hauptproblem der hermeneutik," in D Kimmich et al. (eds.), *Texte zur literaturtheorie der Gegenwart,* Philipp Reclam, Stuttgart.

Rinehart, R 1998, *Players all: performance in contemporary sport,* Indiana University Press, Bloomington.

Roberts, TJ 1990, *An aesthetics of junk fiction,* University of Georgia Press, Athens.

Robins, K 1995, *Into the image,* Routledge, New York.

Rodman, GB 1996, *Elvis after Elvis: the posthumous career of a living legend,* Routledge, New York.

Rose, A & Friedman, J 1994, "Television sport as mas(s)culine cult of distraction," *Screen* 34(1), 22–35.

Rowlings, C 1992, "You don't look the type: memories of being a young woman watching Bristol Rovers," in D Bull (ed.), *We'll support you evermore,* Gerald Duckworth, London.

Rutter, J 1998, "Wayne's World," in AA Berger (ed.), *The Postmodern Presence: Readings on Postmodernism in American Culture & Society,* AltaMira, Walnut Creek, CA.

Said, E 1979, *Orientalism,* Viking, London.

Sandvoss, C 2003, *A game of two halves: football, television, and globalization,* Routledge, New York.

Sandvoss, C 2005a, *Fans: the mirror of consumption,* Polity, Malden, MA.

Sandvoss, C 2005b, "One-dimensional fan: toward an aesthetic of fan texts," *American Behavioral Scientist* 48(7), 822–39.

Sandvoss, C forthcoming, "The end of meaning: the politics of transnational sport stardom," in C Sandvoss, A Bernstein, & M Real (eds.), *Bodies of discourse: sports stars, mass media, and the global public,* Hampton, Cresskill, NJ.

Savage, M 2000, *Class analysis and social transformation,* Open University Press, Philadelphia.

Savage, M, Bagnall, G, & Longhurst, B 2004, "Place, belonging, and identity: globalisation and the 'northern' middle class," in T Bennett & E Silva (eds.), *Cultures and the everyday*, Sociology Press, Durham, UK.

Savage, M, Bagnall, G, & Longhurst, B 2005, *Globalization and belonging*, Sage,
Thousand Oaks, CA.

Saxey E 2002, "Staking a claim: the series and its slash fan fiction," in R Kaveney
(ed.), *Reading the vampire slayer: the unofficial critical companion to* Buffy *and*
Angel, IB Tauris, London.

Schiller, D 1996, *Theorizing communication: a history*, Oxford University Press,
New York.

Schimmel, K, Harrington, CL, & Bielby, DD n.d., "Fandom: sport studies and fan
studies perspectives," manuscript in preparation.

Schneider, AR with Pullen, K 2001, *The gatekeeper: my thirty years as a TV censor*,
Syracuse University Press, Syracuse, NY.

Schott, GR & Horrel, KR 2000, "Girl gamers and their relationship with the gaming culture," *Convergence* 6, 36–53.

Sci-Fi Wire 2002, "Buffy getting darker," 15 January. Retrieved March 12, 2004, from
http://www.scifi.com/sfw/issue248/news.html.

Scodari, C 2003a, "Resistance reexamined: gender, fan practices, and science
fiction television," *Popular Communication* 1(2), 111–30.

Scodari, C 2003b, "Review of *Fan Cultures*," *Popular Communication* 1(3), 181–83.

Scodari, C 2004, *Serial monogamy: soap opera, lifespan, and the gendered politics of
fantasy*, Hampton Press, Cresskill, NJ.

Scodari, C 2005, "You're sixteen, you're dutiful, you're online: 'fangirls' and the
negotiation of age and/or gender subjectivities in TV newsgroups," in S Maz-
zarella (ed.), *Girl wide web: girls, the Internet, and the negotiation of identity*,
Peter Lang, New York.

Scodari, C & Felder, JL 2000, "Creating a pocket universe: 'shippers,' fan fiction,
and *The X-Files* online," *Communication Studies* 51, 238–57.

Sella, M 2002, "The remote controllers," *New York Times Magazine*, 20 October,
68.

Shaw, N 2003, "Cloning scapegoats: Martha Stewart does insider trading," *Social
Text 77* 21(4), 51–67.

Shaw, SM 1994, "Gender, leisure, and constraint: towards a framework for analysis
of women's leisure," *Journal of Leisure Research* 26, 8–22.

Shimpach, S 2005, "Working watching: the creative and cultural labor of the media
audience," *Social Semiotics* 15(3), 343–60.

Shirky, C 1999, "RIP the consumer, 1900–1999," *Shirky.com*. Retrieved April 2,
2006, from http://www.shirky.com/writings/consumer.html.

Sill, J 1840, diary, collection #600, vol. 2, The Historical Society of Pennsylvania,
Philadelphia.

Silverstone, R 1994, *Television and everyday life*, Routledge, New York.

Silverstone, R 2003, "Proper distance: towards an ethics of cyberspace," in G Listol, A Morrison, and T Rasmussen (eds.), *Digital media revisited,* MIT Press, Cambridge.

Sivathamby, K 1981, *Tamil film as a medium of political communication,* New Century Book House, Madras.

Sketches and business directory of Boston, 1860–1861 1861, Damrell & Moore and George Coolidge, Boston.

Smith, K 2005, "The inescapable Paris," *Vanity Fair* 542, October, 280–89 & 343.

Smith, L 2000, "We heard it through the Napster grapevine—all of it," *Los Angeles Times,* 10 September, 5.

Solowiej, L & Brunell, TL 2003, "The entrance of women to the U.S. Congress: the widow effect," *Political Research Quarterly* 56, 283–92.

Southworth, H 1850, diary, BV Southworth, Henry, New-York Historical Society, New York.

Souza, A 2002, "Wrestling the WWE." Retrieved November 5, 2005, from http://www.newenglandfilm.com/news/archives/o2august/wrestling.htm.

Spigel, L 1992, *Make room for TV: television and the family ideal in postwar America,* University of Chicago Press, Chicago.

Srinivas, SV 2000, "Devotion and defiance in fan activity," in R Vasudevan (ed.), *Making meaning in Indian cinema,* Oxford University Press, New Delhi.

Srinivas, SV 2003, "Film culture: politics and industry," *Seminar* 525. Retrieved August 18, 2004, from http://www.india-seminar.com/2003/525.htm.

Srinivas, SV forthcoming, "Hong Kong action film in the Indian B-circuit."

Stabile, C 2004, "Getting what she deserved: the news media, Martha Stewart, and masculine domination," *Feminist Media Studies* 4(3), 315–32.

Stacey, J 1994, *Stargazing: Hollywood cinema and female spectatorship,* Routledge, New York.

Staiger, J 1992, *Interpreting films: studies in the historical reception of American cinema,* Princeton University Press, Princeton, NJ.

Stallybrass, P & White, A 1986, *The politics and poetics of transgression,* Methuen, London.

Stark, SD 2003, *Meet the Beatles: a cultural history of the band that shook youth, gender, and the world,* HarperCollins, New York.

Stellin, S 2000, "E-commerce report," *New York Times,* 28 August, C8.

Sterne J 2003, *The audible past: culture origins of sound reproduction,* Duke University Press, Durham, NC.

Stierle, K 1996, "Werk und intertextualität," in D Kimmich et al. (eds.), *Texte zur literaturtheorie der Gegenwart,* Philipp Reclam, Stuttgart.

SunTrust Bank v. Houghton Mifflin Co., 268 F.3d 1257 (11th Cir. 2001).

Swalwell, M 2003, "Multi-player computer gaming: "Better than playing (PC games) with yourself," *Reconstruction: An Interdisciplinary Cultural Studies Community* 3(4). Retrieved November 22, 2005, from http://www.reconstruction.ws/034/swalwell.htm.

Taylor, R 1992, *Football and its fans*, Leicester University Press, Leicester, UK.

Theodoropoulou, P 1999, *Mapping out fanland*, MSc dissertation, LSE, University of London.

Thomas, L 2002, *Fans, feminisms, and "quality" media*, Routledge, New York.

Thompson, JB 1995, *The media and modernity: a social theory of the media*, Polity, Cambridge, UK.

Thorn, M 2004, "Girls and women getting out of hand: the pleasure and politics of Japan's amateur comics community," in W Kelly (ed.), *Fanning the flames: fans and consumer culture in contemporary Japan*, State University of New York Press, New York.

Thornton, S 1995, *Club cultures*, Polity, Cambridge, UK.

Thucydides 1920 [431 B.C.], *The history of the Peloponnesian War, vol. 2, books 3–4*, trans. CF Smith, Harvard University Press, Cambridge, MA.

Topel, F 2002, "Tom Lenk—Buffy baddie," *About.com*. Retrieved April 16, 2003, from http://actionadventure.about.com/library/weekly/2002/aa110402.htm.

Tsing, A 2005, *Friction: an ethnography of global connection*, Princeton University Press, Princeton, NJ.

Tufte, T 2000, "The popular forms of hope: about the force of fiction among TV audiences in Brazil," in I Hagen & J Wasko (eds.), *Consuming audiences: production and reception in media research*, Hampton Press, Cresskill, NJ.

Tulloch, J 1985, "Chekhov abroad: western criticism," in TW Clyman (ed.), *A Chekhov companion*, Greenwood, Westport, CT.

Tulloch, J 2000, *Watching television audiences: cultural theories and methods*, Hodder Arnold, London.

Tulloch, J 2004, *Shakespeare and Chekhov in production: theatrical events and their audiences*, University of Iowa, Iowa City.

Tulloch, J 2006, *One day in July: experiencing 7/7*, Little, Brown, London.

Tulloch, J & Jenkins, H 1995, *Science fiction audiences: watching* Dr. Who *and* Star Trek, Routledge, London.

Turkle, S 1995, *Life and the screen: identity in the age of the Internet*, Simon & Schuster, New York.

Turnbull, S 2005, "Moments of inspiration: performing Spike," *European Journal of Cultural Studies* 8(3), 367–73.

Turner, BS 2005, "Public intellectuals and British sociology since 1945," *Annual British Journal of Sociological Lecture*, London School of Economics, 11 October.

Turner, V 1969, *The ritual process: structure and anti-structure*, Aldine de Gruyter, New York.

Turner, V & Turner, E 1978, *Image and pilgrimage in Christian culture*, Columbia University Press, New York.

Tushnet, R 1997, "Legal fictions: copyright, fan fiction, and a new common law," *Loyola L.A. Entertainment Law Journal* 17, 651–86.

Twitchell, JB 1992, *Carnival culture: the trashing of taste in America,* Columbia University Press, New York.

Tyrnauer, M 2001, "Empire by Martha," *Vanity Fair* 493, September, 317–64.

Tyrnauer, M 2005, "The prisoner of Bedford," *Vanity Fair* 540, August, 110–18.

Urry, J 1990, *The tourist gaze,* Sage, Thousand Oaks, CA.

Van Dyke, H 1909, *The music lover,* Moffat, Yard & Company, New York.

Van Gennep, A 1960, *The rites of passage,* University of Chicago Press, Chicago.

Van Zoonen, L 1994, *Feminist media studies,* Sage, London.

Van Zoonen, L 2005, *Entertaining the citizen: when politics and popular culture converge,* Rowman & Littlefield, New York.

Vasudev, A 1978, *Liberty and license in Indian cinema.* Vikas, New Delhi.

Virdi, J 2003, *The cinematic ImagiNation: Indian popular films as social history,* Rutgers University Press, New Brunswick, NJ.

Vodička, FV 1975, *Struktur der Entwicklung,* Vogelkopf, München.

Von Hippel, E 2005, *Democratizing innovation,* MIT Press, Cambridge, MA.

Wadsworth, ND 1997, "Reconciliation politics: conservative evangelicals and the new race discourse," *Politics and Society* 25(3), 341–76.

Wallace, M & Halperin, I 2004, *Love and death: the murder of Kurt Cobain,* Atria, New York.

Wallis, RJ 2003, *Shamans and neo-shamans: ecstasy, alternative archaeologies, and contemporary pagans,* Routledge, New York.

Wann, DL & Thomas, JD 1994, "'Spectators' evaluations of rival and fellow fans," *Psychological Record* 44(3), 351–58.

Wearing, B 1998, *Leisure and feminist theory,* Sage, Thousand Oaks, CA.

Wellman, B 2002, "Designing the Internet for a networked society," *Communications of the ACM* 45(5), 96.

Whelehan, I 2000, *Over loaded: popular culture and the future of feminism,* The Women's Press, London.

Whitcomb, D 2005, "Paris Hilton 'only victim' of crash—spokesman," *Reuters,* 10 November. Retrieved November 11, 2005, from http://news.yahoo.com/s/nm/20051110/people_nm/hilton_dc.

White, C 2005, *The middle mind: why consumer culture is turning us into the living dead,* Penguin, London.

White, CB 1851, Caroline Barrett White papers, octavo vol. 3, American Antiquarian Society, Worcester, MA.

Whitman, W 1982 [1855], *Leaves of grass,* in J Kaplan (ed.), *Walt Whitman: Complete Poetry and Collected Prose,* Library of America, New York.

Wiener, J 1998, "Pop and avante-garde: the case of John and Yoko," *Popular Music and Society* 22(1), 1–16.

Williams, R 1961, *The long revolution,* Columbia University Press, New York.

Williams, R 1974, *Television: technology and cultural form,* Fontana, London.

Williams, R 1977, *Marxism and literature,* Oxford University Press, Oxford.

Williamson, M 2005, *The lure of the vampire: gender, fiction, and fandom from Bram Stoker to Buffy*, Wallflower, New York.

Willie, B 2004, "Boxcar Willie: the world's favorite hobo." Retrieved November 8, 2005, from http://www.boxcarwillie.com.

Wilson, P 2004, "Jamming *Big Brother*: webcasting, audience intervention, and narrative activism," in S Murray & L Ouellette (eds.), *Reality TV: remaking television culture*, NYU Press, New York.

Winnicott, DW 1974, *Playing and reality*, Penguin, Harmondsworth, UK.

Witchell, A 1994, "Y. Ono, optimist-pessimist, writes a musical," *New York Times*, 13 March, AE1–8.

Wolfe, AS & Haefner, M 1996, "Taste cultures, culture classes, affective alliances, and popular music reception: theory, methodology, and an application to a Beatles song," *Popular Music and Society* 20(4), 127–55.

Woo, HJ & Kim, Y 2003, "Modern gladiators: a content analysis of televised wrestling," *Mass Communication and Society* 6(4), 361–78.

Woodhouse, D 2001, *The postwar development of football for females in England: a cross-cultural and comparative study with Norway and the United States of America*, Ph.D. dissertation, University of Leicester, UK.

Woodhouse, D & Williams, J 1999, *Offside? The position of women in football*, South Street, Reading, UK.

Woodhouse, J 1991, *A national survey of female football fans*, Sir Norman Chester Centre for Football Research, University of Leicester, Leicester, UK.

Woodhouse, J & Williams J 1991, *Can play, will play? Women and football in Britain*, SNCCFR, University of Leicester, Leicester, UK.

Woodward, K 1997, "Concepts of identity and difference," in K Woodward (ed.), *Identity and difference*, Sage, London.

Wright, T, Boria, E, & Breidenbach, P 2002, "Creative player actions in FPS on-line video games: playing *Counter-Strike*," *Game Studies* 2(2). Retrieved November 4, 2005, from http://www.gamestudies.org/0202/wright.

Wright Wexman, V 1999, "The critic as consumer: film study in the university, *Vertigo*, and the film canon," in B Henderson & A Martin (eds.), *Film Quarterly: Forty Years—A Selection*, University of California Press, Berkeley.

Yahoo! 2005, "Yahoo! premieres Yahoo! Music Unlimited" [Press Release], 10 May. Retrieved November 8, 2005, from http://docs.yahoo.com/docs/pr/release1237.html.

Yano, C 2004, "Letters from the heart: negotiating fan-star relationships in Japanese popular music," in W Kelly (ed.), *Fanning the flames: fans and consumer culture in contemporary Japan*, State University of New York Press, New York.

Yates, SJ & Littleton, KL 2001, "Understanding computer game culture: a situated approach," in E Green & A Adams (eds.), *Virtual gender: technology, consumption, and identity*, Routledge, New York.

Yuletide FAQ 2005. Retrieved December 13, 2005, from http://www.yuletidetreasure.org/faq.shtml.

Cult of ~~the~~ Personality
Political Cartoons

About the Contributors

DIANE F. ALTERS is an editor at the *Denver Post*, covering education and religion. She is coauthor, with Stewart Hoover and Lynn Schofield Clark, of *Media, Home, and Family*.

GAYNOR BAGNALL is Senior Lecturer in the Sociology of Culture at the University of Salford, UK. He is coauthor, with Michael Savage and Brian Longhurst, of *Globalization and Belonging*.

DENISE D. BIELBY is Professor of Sociology and affiliate of the Center for Film, Television, and New Media at the University of California, Santa Barbara. She is coauthor, with C. Lee Harrington, of *Soap Fans: Pursuing Pleasure and Making Meaning in Everyday Life* and *Popular Culture: Production and Consumption*.

S. ELIZABETH BIRD is Professor and Chair of Anthropology at the University of South Florida. She is the author of *For Enquiring Minds: A Cultural Study of Supermarket Tabloids; The Audience in Everyday Life: Living in a Media World* (winner of Best Book Award, International Communication Association, 2004); and editor of *Dressing in Feathers: The Construction of the Indian in American Popular Culture*.

WILL BROOKER is Field Leader in Film Studies at Kingston University, London. He is author of several books, including *Batman Unmasked: Analyzing a Cultural Icon* and *Using the Force: Creativity, Community, and Star Wars Fans*, and editor of *The Audience Studies Reader* and *The Blade Runner Experience: The Legacy of a Science Fiction Classic*.

PATRICK BURKART is Assistant Professor of Telecommunications and Media Studies at Texas A & M University. He is coauthor, with Tom McCourt, of *Digital Music Wars: The Ownership and Control of the Celestial Jukebox*.

DANIEL CAVICCHI is Assistant Professor of American Studies at Rhode Island School of Design. He is author of *Tramps Like Us: Music and Meaning among Springsteen Fans* and coeditor of *My Music: Explorations of Music in Daily Life.*

BERTHA CHIN is a doctoral candidate at the School of Journalism, Media, and Cultural Studies at Cardiff University, Wales. Her thesis is tentatively titled *Exploring the Customs of Gifts and Governance in Online Fan Fiction,* and she has previously published in *Intensities: Journal of Cult Media.*

ANNE CIECKO is Associate Professor specializing in international cinema in the Department of Communication at the University of Massachusetts, Amherst. She is editor of *Contemporary Asian Cinema: Popular Culture in a Global Frame.*

MELISSA A. CLICK is a doctoral candidate at the University of Massachusetts, Amherst, and currently teaches at the University of Missouri, Columbia. Her thesis examines *Martha Stewart Living.*

NICK COULDRY is Professor of Media and Communications at Goldsmiths College, University of London, UK. He is author or editor of six books, including *Inside Culture: Re-imagining the Method of Cultural Studies; Media Rituals: A Critical Approach;* and *Listening beyond the Echoes: Media, Ethics, and Agency in an Uncertain World.*

GARRY CRAWFORD is Senior Lecturer in Sociology at the University of Salford, UK. He is author of *Consuming Sport: Sport, Fans, and Culture.*

VICTORIA K. GOSLING is Lecturer in Sociology in the Division of Politics and Sociology at Nottingham Trent University, UK. She has published in *Sociology* and *Sociological Research Online.*

JONATHAN GRAY is Assistant Professor of Communication and Media Studies at Fordham University. He is author of *Watching with* The Simpsons: *Television, Parody, and Intertextuality.*

C. LEE HARRINGTON is Professor of Sociology and Affiliate of the Women's Studies Program at Miami University. She is coauthor, with Denise Bielby, of *Soap Fans: Pursuing Pleasure and Making Meaning in Everyday Life* and *Popular Culture: Production and Consumption.*

MATT HILLS is Senior Lecturer in Media and Cultural Studies at Cardiff University, Wales. He is author of *Fan Cultures; The Pleasures of Horror;* and *How to Do Things with Cultural Theory.*

HENRY JENKINS is Director of Comparative Media Studies and the Deflorez Professor of Humanities at Massachusetts Institute of Technology. He is the author or editor of twelve books, including *Convergence Culture: Where Old and New Media Collide; Fans, Bloggers, and Gamers: Exploring Participatory Culture; Textual Poachers: Television Fans and Participatory Culture;* and *The Children's Culture Reader.*

DEREK JOHNSON is a doctoral candidate in Communication Arts at the University of Wisconsin, Madison. He has published in Ian Gordon, Mark Jancovich, and Matthew McAllister's collection, *Films and Comics.*

HUNJU LEE is a doctoral candidate in the Department of Communication at the University of Massachusetts, Amherst.

BRIAN LONGHURST is Professor of Sociology and Dean of the Faculty of Arts, Media, and Social Sciences at the University of Salford, UK. He is coauthor, with Nicholas Abercrombie, of *Audiences: A Sociological Theory of Performance and Imagination* and, with Michael Savage and Gaynor Bagnall, *Globalization and Belonging.*

LAWRENCE B. McBRIDE is a doctoral candidate at the University of North Carolina, Chapel Hill. He received his M.A. from the University of South Florida in 2005 for a thesis entitled *Professional Wrestling, Embodied Morality, and Altered States of Consciousness.*

TOM McCOURT is Assistant Professor of Communication and Media Studies at Fordham University. He is author of *Conflicting Communication Interests in America: The Case of National Public Radio* and coauthor, with Patrick Burkart, of *Digital Music Wars: The Ownership and Control of the Celestial Jukebox.*

ALAN McKEE is thirty-four, gym fit, cute, Scottish, and currently single. For a photo, email a.mckee@qut.edu.au.

ROBERTA PEARSON has been a *Star Trek* fan from her teens and a member of the Adventuresses of Sherlock Holmes (ASH) from her twenties. Her love of television is equalled only by Homer Simpson's. Despite this, she has managed to produce a few books and articles and to be appointed as the Director of the Institute of Film and Television Studies at the University of Nottingham.

ASWIN PUNATHAMBEKAR is a doctoral candidate in Communication Arts at the University of Wisconsin, Madison. He has published in *Biblio; International Journal of Cultural Studies;* and *Gazette: International Journal for Communication Studies,* and is currently coediting an anthology on Bollywood cinema and culture.

JASON RUTTER is Research Fellow at the ESRC Centre for Research on Innovation and Competition at the University of Manchester, UK. He is author, with Jo Bryce, of *Understanding Digital Games.*

CORNEL SANDVOSS is Lecturer and Subject Leader in Media and Cultural Studies, University of Surrey, UK. He is author of *Fans: The Mirror of Consumption* and *A Game of Two Halves: Football Fandom, Television, and Globalisation* and coeditor, with Alina Bernstein and Michael Real, of the forthcoming *Bodies of Discourse: Sports Stars, Mass Media, and the Global Public.*

MIKE SAVAGE is Professor of Sociology at the University of Manchester, UK, where he is Director of the ESRC Centre for Research on Socio-Cultural Change. His recent books include, with Gaynor Bagnall and Brian Longhurst, *Globalization and Belonging.*

CHRISTINE SCODARI is Professor of Communication and Women's Studies at Florida Atlantic University. Among her recent publications is *Serial Monogamy: Soap Opera, Lifespan, and the Gendered Politics of Fantasy.*

JEFFREY SCONCE is Associate Professor in the Screen Cultures program at Northwestern University. He is author of *Haunted Media: Electronic Presence from Telegraphy to Television* and editor of *Sleaze Artists: Cinema at the Margins of Taste, Style, and Politics.*

VIVI THEODOROPOULOU is a doctoral candidate at the London School of Economics and Political Science. Her work is included in *Broadcasting and Convergence: New Articulations of the Public Service Remit* and *The Digital Challenge: Media and Democracy.*

JOHN TULLOCH is Research Professor and Deputy Head of School (Research), School of Social Sciences and Law, Brunel University, UK. His recent books include *Trevor Griffiths; One Day in July: Experiencing 7/7; Shakespeare and Chekhov in Production and Reception: Theatrical Events and Their Audiences;* and, with Deborah Lupton, *Risk and Everyday Life.*

REBECCA TUSHNET is Associate Professor at Georgetown University Law Center. She has published in *The Yale Law Review, UCLA Law Review, Boston College Law Review,* and others.

Index